[illegible]

[illegible]

# DICTIONARY OF DAILY LIFE OF INDIANS OF THE AMERICAS

DICTIONARY OF

# DAILY LIFE OF INDIANS

OF THE AMERICAS

VOLUME ONE

AMERICAN INDIAN PUBLISHERS, INC.
177 F Riverside Avenue
Newport Beach, California

ISBN 403-09950-1

# INTRODUCTION

MEN FROM ASIA may have first penetrated North America between forty thousand and twenty thousand years ago, crossing the land bridge exposed by the lowered sea levels of the last glaciation. These first Americans began a tradition of independent biological and cultural evolution, the New World cultures, which along with those of the Old World have become the basis for the study of mankind.

The evolution of the New World cultures would end in 1492 with surety, with the intrusion of a cannon's blast upon the stillness of an October morning. But perhaps "end" is too strong a word: the cultural and physical evolution of 10 million or more American Indians continues today, now as an integral, rather than separate component in total human evolution.

American Indian cultures have been most seriously studied by the social science discipline, anthropology. Archaeologists, anthropologists who study past cultures, have provided literally tens of thousands of reports which form the basis for reconstructing cultures from the earliest times to the present. Ethnographers and culture historians are anthropologists who study living peoples working with written records, memories of times past, and, extensively, with ongoing cultural groups. Their research has also produced tens of thousands of reports on cultures from the Arctic to the tip of South America. Anthropological linguists, specializing in the structure and history of unwritten languages, have contributed analyses and classificatory data for representatives of all major New World language groups. This kind of data is another important source for inferences on temporal and spatial relationships.

Social science nowhere possesses as large a body of descriptive and analytical information on a world area of equivalent geographic size. On the one hand, anthropological research has provided an embarrassment of riches—data on the growth, development, and present condition of American Indian populations are so vast as to deny to any one person more than a fragmentary knowledge of the total. On the other hand, sadly, these vast data were collected at a time when anthropology, as a developing science, was in the descriptive-natural science phase of its growth—as most would agree it still is. Consequently, when the oft-studied Indians, meeting torment and destruction stemming from the kinds of culture contact situations they faced, sought assistance from their constant observers, few anthropologists had much to offer. Lacking general theories which permit decision-making on a scientific basis, most anthropologists responded as individuals and citizens. Consequently, only rarely in Latin America (as at Vicos, Peru, and occasionally in Brazil), and rarely in the United States, have anthropologists been in policy-making positions with respect to governmental actions taken toward the indigenous populations. For this reason, and not for lack of compassion nor for concern, most anthropologists have been ineffective in leading the search for a satisfactory life style for the contemporary descendants of America's earliest inhabitants.

## AMERICAN INDIAN CULTURE

### General Observations

Culture is the cumulative product of human

adaptation. Seen from this perspective, two significant facts, as pointed out by Betty Meggers, serve to introduce American Indian culture:—(1) cultural developments *in similar habitats*, whether in North or South America, show strong similarities, and (2) cultural development was far more rapid in some environments in North, Central, or South America than in others. The ultimate common origin for all populations, i.e. Asia, and the relative isolation of the Americas, are other considerations affecting the form of American Indian culture.

Meggers proposes six occupiable habitats in the Americas—forests, deserts, plains, the Pacific Coast, marginal zones, and the Arctic. With the exception of the Arctic, strikingly similar cultural groups developed in both North and South America where habitats were similar. For example, in forests, such as the tropical rain forest of the Amazon Basin or the Eastern Woodlands of North America, cultures tended first to develop a maximal efficiency in the use of wild resources, then, later, to adopt cultigens (cultivated plants whose wild ancestors are unknown) as a supplement. Population density in forests remains relatively low, and regular shifting of settlements is characteristic. Environmental limitations in forest areas, given the level of technology available, deterred the development of anything more than simple village-tribal organization.

Culture developed most rapidly in two regions of the central zone of the hemisphere where the environment was composed of two or more complementary habitats—desert and forest, coast and mountains, rivers and plains. The northern center in the Central Mexican highlands of Mesoamerica, and the southern center in the

Central Andean and coastal region of South America are collectively called Nuclear America. It was here that the cultivation of plants first occurred and where further supportive agricultural technology, such as irrigation, seed selection, and mass labor, contributed to the growth firstly of towns and cities, and later of states and empires. This nuclear center of the hemisphere began its rise to eminent position in the roster of world civilizations more than ten thousand years ago. Whether man in the New World learned to grow plants because of the simple co-existence in time and space of potential cultigens and suitable growing conditions, or because expanding populations required additional foods, horticulture, by about 2000 B.C., had become the most important basis of subsistence for residents of the growing villages and ceremonial centers.

More than fifty different plants were cultivated, most important of which were maize (or American corn), varieties of beans, squash, potatoes, manioc, sweet potatoes, gourds, tobacco, cottons, amaranths, and others. Native Americans had domesticated all the cultigens known to have been available to them (except the North American grape). The same is true of animals–dogs, turkeys, guinea pigs, llamas, and possibly parrots were domesticated; no other New World animals have been successfully domesticated since.

Cultural "energy" constantly "pulsed" from Nuclear America, penetrating, even if in a weakened form, all suitable habitats. Those lacking horticulture in A.D. 1500 were the inhabitants of the colder forests and woodlands (including most of what is now Canada); the grassy plains (including the pampas of South

America and the high plains east of the Rocky Mountains); and portions of the Pacific coast. Accompanying the diffusion of horticulture were various artifacts, such as types of pottery manufacture and styles, (although the making of pottery itself probably predates horticulture). Technology including simple metallurgy was also diffused, as also was architecture, which included temple mounds and other large ceremonial structures. Social ideas, which were associated with complex theologies, were also spread. Many of these cultural features can be found as far apart as northeastern Argentina, the Caribbean Islands, and, in what is now the United States, in Ohio, New York, and Wisconsin.

Thus, over a vast area of the hemisphere, the advanced level of complexity achieved in Nuclear America influenced the spread and development in subsistence base, technology, and associated social and religious aspects of culture. In a manner strikingly similar to the growth of civilization in the Near East and in Southeast Asia, the Western Hemisphere was well within the upper ranks of civilization developed on this planet five hundred years ago.

In marginal areas, where such influences were hardly felt, cultural forms in both North and South America followed a pattern thousands of years old, a form of adaptation fitting difficult environments and utilizing limited technology. Small social groups foraged the land of southern South America, northern Canada, the Arctic, the east Brazil Highlands, and most of western North America. The marginal pattern of life was a simple yearly recapitulation of varyingly successful harvesting and processing of wild plants and animals. Some marginals possessed pottery, others traded for or even cultivated a few agricultural products, and some increased their exploitative techniques with the development of efficient tool kits.

The success of the Inuit (Eskimo), for example, in the least hospitable habitat on earth, the Arctic, is a result of the development of social and cultural elements specifically adaptive to the subsistence in their icy habitat. An examination of Inuit housing, clothing, means of land and water transportation, and complex weaponry reveals details that are nothing short of ingenious devices adaptive to what is otherwise an unoccupiable zone.

The success of the Indians of the Northwest coast of North America is, in contrast, a result of the enriched faunal assemblage on both land and in the sea. The anadromous salmon (i.e. salmon ascending rivers from the sea at certain seasons in order to spawn), supplemented by schools of fish, shellfish, and sea and land mammals, were "harvested" by the Indians of this area. This bountiful subsistence base provided a life chance unequalled in the world for societies lacking domestic plants or animals, and some social and artistic forms developed analogous to those of complex horticultural societies.

The independence of the development of New World cultures is supported by considerable biological and archaeological data. The physical similarity–for example blood types, hair, and body build–of Amerinds to each other does not suggest recent immigration from any other quarter, excepting certain complexities in North West Canada. The archaeological record in the main reflects isolation, with few exceptions. The remarkable similarity in pottery styles in both the islands of Japan and along the coast of Ecuador approximately five thousand years ago, has led many experts to conclude that TransPacific voyages took place. Others have seen later oceanic trips from Southeast Asia to Central America, Phoenician contact with Brazil, African contact with Central America and the Antilles, and Vikings and Irish monks sailing across the North Atlantic in bullboats (shallow-draft boats made of bull skins).

The essential question is, how important an impact did these voyagers have? The domestication of plants and the beginning of village life had taken place before the earliest oceanic contacts have been postulated. Pottery may or may not have been present at the time in South America. And thus, the question remains open.

The preponderance of professional opinion, based on the evidence gathered by the mid-1970s, is that New World cultural development is due to parallel evolution, perhaps stimulated to some small degree by trans-oceanic contacts prior to Columbus.

## THE TRADITIONAL CULTURE OF THE NEW WORLD INHABITANTS

### Languages

All American Indian cultures possess fully developed, complex languages belonging to several major unrelated language stocks. There is not, nor was there ever, a single American "Indian" language. Rumors or reports of Indian groups that communicated by grunts or only hand signals are nonsense. Nor does there appear to exist any correlation between cultural complexity and the complexity of language structure. One would expect the dialect of Quechua spoken by the ruling class of Inca in Cuzco to possess a larger range of lexical (vocabulary) units than that of the culturally simpler Chiricahua Apaches but, given the necessity, Chiricahua nonetheless should prove adequate to express any thought, including those originating with culturally more complex people.

The number of languages in the New World depends upon the recognition of what constitutes separate languages. In many New World regions, contiguous social groups spoke totally unrelated languages or progressively divergent dialects of closely related languages. Thus, two hundred "languages" have been claimed for aboriginal California alone. Generally, however, anthropologists allow about two hundred languages in all of North America; approximately three hundred fifty in Central America; and nearly fifteen hundred in South America. These numbers underscore the degree of diversity characteristic of languages spoken by New World natives.

In terms of sound, Indian languages are not exceptional. Most of the consonant phonemes (basic units of speech in a given language) that are relied upon occur in Indo-European and other stocks as well. Grammatically, many Indian languages diverge sharply from common Indo-European patterns, but are well within world-wide language forms. In short, American Indian languages are diverse and complex and, if they contain few unique features, it will take hundreds of years to come to know their structure fully.

Research on American Indian language also stimulated a hypothesis regarding a possible relationship between language and culture. Language provides a frame through which to view reality and, because languages provide so many different kinds of frames, many different realities should be perceived by speakers of different languages. Thus cultures should co-vary with language as they adapt to differing perceptions of reality. This hypothesis has never been rejected, but research results to date have provided little substantial evidence to the point.

Genetic classification of languages is well developed and has proven a useful historical tool in the New World. The first systematizers of languages for North and South America proposed fifty and sixty stocks respectively. The numbers in each of these regions have been progressively reduced to seven and eight stocks in successive studies. Combined, these two classificatory schemes propose twelve stocks for the hemisphere as a whole, although many linguists believe these taxonomic reductions (i.e. reductions in the classificatory system) are based on inadequate data. Notwithstanding this criticism, Morris Swadesh suggested that all aboriginal New World languages could be included in six families, each representative of a separate wave of newcomers. Furthermore Swadesh, as well as some other linguists, has proposed tentative genetic relationships between some New World languages and such Old World stocks as Sino-Tibetan, Finno-Ugric, Malayo-Polynesian, and even Indo-Eruopean.

Linguistic research has led to the development of a tool for measuring the time since the separation of genetically related languages, based on the premise that the rate of lexical change occurs at regular and therefore measurable rates in related languages. Called "glottochronology," this technique permits inferences on the lengths of time separating the diverging members of single language stocks. Despite the flaws in the technique, the dates estimated often correspond with those derived by archaeological means.

## Social Organization and Social Institutions

The study of the social organization and social institutions of American Indians is a study of the interplay between ancient American general characteristics, regional variations brought about by varying habitats, history, accident, or other causes, and the influence of diffused items and complexes such as those from Nuclear America.

Some social-cultural characteristics of the most ancient Americans can be proposed on the basis of theoretical considerations, the known history of culture, as well as the nearly universal distribution of such traits among widely dispersed Marginal people at the time of European contact, or first study. Whether we speak of the Ona or Yahgan of southern South America, or the Pai Pai or Cree of North America, most or all of these ancient characteristics–characteristics first carried across Beringia (the land bridge between Asia and America which formerly crossed what is now the Bering Sea) thousands of years ago–may still be found.

The first migrants coming to the New World would have been in the form of small social groups numbering anywhere between twenty-five and two hundred persons. Their adaptation to a subsistence on wild plants and game is the economic context for their non-sedentary way of life and political independence. Such groups as these have come to be called "bands," and were internally organized around statuses determined largely by age, sex, and kinship factors. The family, nuclear or extended, was most likely the only formal kinship unit in bands; if extended, most commonly the form would have been patrilaterally (i.e. on the father's side). Leadership was probably vested in the most trusted individual, often an elder male. One of his main functions would be to serve as mediator between feuding members of his band or between his and neighboring bands. Socially, anthropologists would expect them to have practiced some form of familial exogamy (marriage outside the group), probably to have been polygynous (practiced forms of marriage in which a man had two or more wives at the same time), and perhaps to have preferred patri-local residence (centered around the residence of the husband's family). A low population density is estimated. Corporate descent groups, mans' societies, and other social complexities often associated with more recent Indians were probably not developed.

Bands continued to be found throughout the New World in the marginal zones and were scattered as enclaves among cultivators in the desert and forest regions. With the notable exception of the Inuit, they were possessors of simple technology, usually ancient in origin. In South America, some bands possessed loom weaving, pottery, rudiments of clothing, and other cultural items probably borrowed from their more complex neighbors. Nadene speakers (constituting a major language grouping, including Athapascan, Haida, and Tlingit) in North America, both Northern and Southern, possessed many characteristics borrowed from the Inuit on the one hand, and the Pueblo on the other. Thus, band people in contact with more complex cultures gradually acquired, environment permitting, more efficient subsistence means and became more tribe-like. This was one impact of the pervasive influences emanating from Nuclear America, and, later, must also have been a universal result of European penetration into the marginal areas of the New World.

Where collected food was exceptionally abundant, or where horticulture was practiced, social groups became larger, sedentism increased, and political alliances between societies became possible. Although statuses also derived largely from age, sex, and kinship factors, some positions, such as "chief," "sachem," or "ritual leader" came to be determined by society-wide approval. Such groups as these are given the formal designation as "tribes," and may cover wide areas and number thousands of members in dozens of residential locations.

Tribes occurred in zones contiguous to or in contact with Nuclear America, principally the forests and deserts, and in favored areas in the plains of North America, particularly in the well-watered valleys of the western tributaries of the Mississippi River.

Tribes often possessed unilineal corporate groups, most commonly patrilineal but also matrilineal, and many also practiced unilocal post-marital residence. Because of the increased population size, authoritarian leadership sometimes developed in New World tribes but, more often, tribes had leaders who functioned only in specific contexts, such as raiding or war, religious occasions, or as mediators. Occasionally, tribes possessed decision-making councils composed of respected individuals, most often male. Many tribes developed non-kinship sodalities, such as men's drinking societies, war clubs, shamans' organizations, ceremonial cults, and others. Standard tribal relations with other groups were ones characterized by trade and inter-marriage, but also suspicion and feud. Many tribes considered themselves at war with all with whom they did not have a formal peace. Because many tribes consisted of but one or two cooperating villages among dozens or hundreds of linguistically similar settlement groups, conflict and war on a small scale was a standard characteristic.

Unusual tribal forms developed in North America among Northwest Coast collectors, possibly around the Great Lakes where wild rice provided substantial storable food, and in portions of California, where the acorn served a similar purpose.

When groups of tribes amalgamate under central leadership, and adhere to one or more distributive residential centers with a large number of "sociocentric" statuses available either through achievement or ascription, tribes have formed into chiefdoms which, upon further development of governmental forms and expansion of boundaries, may become states, of which one type is the empire.

Chiefdoms tended to develop in habitats where a combination of natural resources and food production provided a large and dependable economic subsistence for good-sized populations. The only portion of North America north of Mexico to witness such developments were portions of the lower Mississippi River Valley and the Gulf Coast to the east of the delta. Here developed absolutist leadership, social classes if not castes, temple and burial mounds, extensive development of sumptuary goods (such as food, clothing, and furniture) and privileges, and multi-village political units. Other areas where similar cultures developed include many of the Caribbean Islands, Mesoamerica, and some northern and western coastal and highland regions of South America.

States developed only in Nuclear America, but here reached high levels of political, social and economic development. The ultimate development in the Andes was the empire. The factors leading to statehood are obscured by the passage of time, and there are no historic examples of the process to use as analogies. The archaeological evidence relating to the development of the state focuses on the material remains, such as monumental public architecture, or remains of highly developed trading systems. This and other kinds of evidence have led most authorities to infer that the roots of state development were set some three thousand years ago by the Olmec in Mesoamerica and the Chavín in the Andean Highlands. Their religious and artistic motifs spread widely, each ultimately coming to have influence upon the general area of the other.

In the early fifteenth century, the Inca, the Maya, and the Aztec were the ultimate holders of Nuclear America's flowering. Thousands of years of growth of skill and knowledge had produced social organization, technology, science, and ideology rarely bested to that time anywhere on earth.

**Cultural Characteristics**

Two broad generalizations can be made about the material, technological, and many other aspects of traditional American Indian culture. First, a survey covering the thousands of miles between the tip of South America and the frozen landscape of North America and comparing the characteristics of marginal peoples with those of Nuclear America reveal a very broad range of diversity across many levels of complexity. Secondly, although some features are basically similar to those found universally, the American Indian culture often contains categories and elements that give Amerind culture a distinctive and recognizable "flavor."

## 1. Habitations and Construction

Habitations ranged from the brush, bark, and dirt, lean-tos and wigwams of many band peoples, through tents and tipis, semi-subterranean pit houses, multiple family structures of wood or stone, huge stone or adobe apartment houses, and ultimately the massive mortared stone or cut stone structures of walled cities and ceremonial centers of Nuclear America. This area and nearby areas saw the emergence of city planning, vast irrigation projects, the building of bridges, and the establishment of guard and watch posts along paved highways hundreds of miles long. Europeans first seeing the centers of these developments believed New World cities to be superior to any of the Old World.

## 2. Technology

The earliest examples of woven basketry are found in the New World. Woven baskets appear nearly everywhere in the hemisphere, but especially fine examples are typical of western North America, both in the desert and in coastal regions. Both ceramics and woven textiles were widely distributed among all but people living in the marginal cultures; the creation and execution of unique forms and artistic motifs reached peaks of development in the Andes rarely matched elsewhere in the world. In Nuclear America, work in the softer metals, particularly gold, was remarkably skilled: silver, copper, platinum, and bronze were cast, soldered, hammered, and otherwise manipulated.

## 3. Weapons

Despite its relatively late appearance in the Americas, nearly all of the New World natives knew of and used the bow and arrow. (The inhabitants of many Caribbean Islands were an exception.) Bows ranged in type from the simple "self-bow," the only type found in South America, to the complex, recurved, sinew-backed bow of northern North America. The shape and size of bows and arrows varied greatly, and some groups produced a dozen or more types of arrow, depending upon their intended use. Spears and throwing sticks were widely distributed, as was the use of clubs of varying shapes. The bola (two or more stone balls attached to the ends of a cord and used for throwing at an animal to entangle it) was distributed from the Inuit to southern South America, although most groups between these points lacked it at the time the Europeans came. The blowgun was found in and around Nuclear America especially in the Amazon Basin, but also in southeastern North America. Other armaments of lesser importance were the poisoned darts and lances, slings, spear-throwers, javelins, harpoons, pellet-bows, and bronze and copper axes. Shields were widespread in use, and forms of armor were known to a few.

### 4. Clothing

Doubtless, the members of the majority of Amerind cultures went nude or nearly nude most of the time. When clothing was used, most commonly it took the form of genital coverings and some form of foot gear. Hides and skins, as well as woven fabrics, including the magnificent feathered cloths of Nuclear America, were made into draped tunics and capes rather than fitted garments. The most developed clothing were produced by the Inuit, closely followed by some contiguous Indian groups with their finely tailored hides and furs, waterproof seams and welts. Inuit goods are still imitated by those who must move through Arctic winters.

**5. Narcotics and Stimulants**

Tobacco, both wild and cultivated, was the most widespread stimulant, being either smoked, chewed with lime, snuffed into the nose, eaten, drunk, or licked wherever it was available. Corn beer and fruit wines were made by many cultivators, and were especially important in Nuclear America. Beers or wines were also made from the fruit of the mesquite tree, and from manioc, persimmons, plantains and bananas, honey, palm fruit and juice, sweet potatoes, algaroba, pineapples, and probably several dozen more vegetable sources. The juice of the agave and dasylirion (yucca) plants were made into *pulque* in northern Nuclear America. Because it is impossible for these beverages to reach high alcoholic potency, real drunkenness may have been rare. In America north of Mexico, the only potent halucinogenic used was datura (jimson weed), and possibly the fruit of *Sophora secundiflora*, commonly called the "mescal bean," although it is unrelated to the agave. Further to the south, however, peyote (*Lophophora williamsii*) was commonly used for religious purposes, as were various mushrooms.

In South America, maté (*Ilex paraguayensis*), with caffeine as the active agent, was a common drink, as was guarana, made from the vine *Paullinia*. *Erythroxylon coca* was commonly chewed in the Andes and in Central America. Plants of the genus *Banisteriopsis*, and datura were used in the Upper Amazon and Pacific Coast respectively, and perhaps a dozen or more hallucinogenic plants were less widely used. Use of hallucinogenics, especially in South America, was more common with horticulturalists than with people of the marginal cultures.

### 6. Myths and Legends

The ideological fabric of American Indian culture is, as are other cultures, made up of myths and legends, some being recognized as "true," while others are considered clearly fictional or supernatural. Universal themes in which the sun, moon, and stars combine with animals in creation myths, or legends having to do with ancestral people, are cast with American characters. Raven, coyote, spider, sloth, snake, jaguar, vulture, tapir, and other locally significant forms played trickster roles. Many legends, such as those of the Bungling Host, the Eye Juggler, the Flood, occur over wide areas. Certain themes, among which are those of cannibal monsters, forest demons, four brothers, twins, incest, salt, endo-cannibalism (cannibalism of members of one's own family or tribe), and transition from the mythical to "real" time, are common to both continents. Indian myths and legends usually cast people in inferior or weaker roles than those of the animals or supernaturals. Man as a privileged "guest" or as an equal in nature, rather than as a host or dominator, tended to encourage respect and awe toward natural phenomena.

## The Past POST-COLUMBIAN TRENDS

The most immediate result of European contact throughout the hemisphere, wherever it occurred, was a decline in numbers of the native population. American Indians had little or no resistance to many of urban Europe's epidemic diseases–measles, mumps, cholera, plague, small pox, and others. Whole populations were destroyed by rapidly-spreading diseases, while the original carriers scarcely contemplated this "Act of God." Secondary causes of population decline were: war, both between Europeans and Indians and among Indians alone; cultural disintegration and consequent malnutrition and starvation; spreading venereal diseases and resultant sterility;

and alcohol-related violence and ill health. Paradoxically, Indians who submitted and were reduced to living either in missions or on settlements became even more vulnerable to most of these causes of mortality.

Indians located along coasts and navigable waterways or near resources desired by the Europeans bore the first brunt of invasion and were quickly eliminated or absorbed. Wherever marginal, or low-level horticultural people came into direct contact with Europeans, they either submitted or were destroyed. For those who found some tenuous ground for co-operation with the invaders, a brief efflorescence became a possibility. For example, the constituent tribes of the Iroquois Confederacy during the seventeenth and eighteenth centuries found temporary power by acting together cooperatively as middlemen in the flow of furs and guns between Europeans and other tribes. The late eighteenth century witnessed the collapse of this economic role and its power, and consequently the confederation weakened. Few Indian groups found collaboration with Europeans to their long-term advantage; in the end, disease, alcohol, or political intrigue struck down even the so-called "friendlies."

The story was different among the people of the Nuclear area. Here, although millions and millions died by pox or sword, millions survived. Royalty and nobility, those who had provided political, scientific, and theological leadership to the peasants of the Inca, Maya, Aztec and other chiefdoms and states, were systematically eliminated by the Spaniards. They were replaced by new leaders, conquistadors, common soldiers, missionaries, and administrators appointed by the Spanish kings to establish Christianity and to introduce the material and social rudiments of Spanish culture. Individuals, groups, and even whole populations were uprooted and transported elsewhere in the colonies. Such people often lost their culture, becoming extensively acculturated. On the other hand, thousands of communities were relatively undisturbed as long as they paid tax or tribute, gave up overt native religion, and were so located as to escape either labor draft or land expropriation. Such communities maintained many traditional ways, but were now enriched by new iron tools, European crops such as wheat, and domestic animals such as the donkey and horse. Many such "folk" communities continue in existence at the present time.

Some of the most tragic pages of contact history were the least typical and often involved relatively small numbers of peoples. The inhabitants of the plains in both North and South America were the protagonists in one such tragedy. In both areas acquisition of the horse and gun led to an immediately increased effectiveness in hunting, a decrease in sedentism, and greater hostility between bands than had previously existed among the plains inhabitants. Inevitably, conflict developed between the plains people and the expanding, land-hungry Europeans. The same outcome occurred in both areas–the Indians were suppressed by the military.

In the United States, in Canada and in Brazil, and to a lesser degree in many other American nations, lands were set aside for Indians either as formal legal reservations or, as sometimes is the case in Mexico, on the traditional sufferance of local officialdom. Most Indians' lands were but a portion of their aboriginal needs, and often consisted of the least desirable land within their aboriginal range. Many groups were moved to reservations totally outside their native habitat and onto land unsuitable for aboriginal subsistence methods (or for that matter least desired by early farmers). Such people had little choice other than to change their lifestyle.

Some Indian societies managed to avoid either intense contact with Europeans or to compartmentalize the impact of such contacts. In the Amazon forest, many horticulturists have maintained their cultures nearly intact into the mid-twentieth century. Others, in the Canadian north woods, in the Mexican Sierra Madre, in south Chile, have survived culturally to a lesser degree by virtue of living in regions unsought by any number of non-Indians.

A few aboriginal band and tribal cultures have undergone intense acculturation (i.e. have engaged in cultural borrowing), yet have maintained an ongoing core of their ancient ways. Tarahumara, Navajo, some Araucanians, and some tribal Amazonians exemplify this type of post-contact change.

## THE PRESENT

### North America

All Inuit and Indians have undergone extensive acculturation, but perhaps only one-third to one-half of the known groups have totally disappeared since contact. Extensive intermarriage between Indians, whites, and blacks, has brought about greater physical variability among Indians than existed in pre-Columbian times. Also, since the beginning of the twentieth century, the number of Indians has increased so that one million or so Indians north of Mexico are at least as numerous as were their ancestors in A.D. 1500.

General and governmental attitudes toward Indians in the United States and Canada have been predominantly integrationist, although a growing tolerance of cultural pluralism is noticeable. All Indians are citizens with the full legal rights of citizens. Substantial prejudice, however, exists against Indians, especially in those areas where they are numerous. About half of the Indians in the United States live on or have rights to reservation land which is held in trust by the Bureau of Indian Affairs of the United States Department of the Interior. The Federal Department of Indian Affairs plays the same role in Canada. Most Indians resent governmental interference in their affairs, but few seek a total elimination of the Indian bureaus.

One hundred or so mutually unintelligible languages and dialects are still spoken, although nearly all Indians speak English or French as well. There is a growing tend toward migration from rural areas to the cities where most Indians join the urban poor. Some analysts have noted that the Indians have few problems not shared by the poor throughout many countries.

The degree of acculturation varies from group to group and from individual to individual. All Indians participate to some degree in the dominant economy, and most aspire to some or all of the luxuries and symbols of wealth their nations can provide. Many Indian societies possess factions that are conservative (usually the poorer and least powerful) and progressive (usually the best educated and most acculturated). Recently, a pan-Indian movement has developed, based principally among urban Indians. It offers hope that Indians, collectively, may come to exert political and economic influence as other ethnic and special interest groups have come to do before them. The Navajo, one hundred forty thousand in number, are by far the largest and, socio-culturally, the most successful of any of the relatively independent Indian societies in the New World.

**Latin America**

Any discussion of the situation of Indians in Latin America must deal with the question, who is an Indian? (This is also true to a lesser degree in North America.) "Indian" throughout Latin America is often used as a synonym for "poor" or "lower class." If the term Indian is confined to those still living under tribal conditions, then there are fewer than one million; if all who speak Indian languages are counted, then the number is probably more than 10 million with the greatest concentration in the Andean countries. Without doubt there are millions more today speaking Indian languages than there were at the time of first contact with the Europeans.

In Latin America, only tribal Indians are accorded any differential status by their states of residence, this being often very negative in nature. In some parts of Amazonia, Indians are still killed on sight. In Bolivia, for example, two-thirds of the total population of the nation is Indian and, in many rural areas, only Indians live. Thus, most rural development programs are *de facto* Indian programs.

In most nations throughout the hemisphere there is a growing concern with the perpetuation of Indian culture, fostered by Indians and non-Indians alike. This movement is most often led by educated Indians, but what is actually espoused is a kind of *indigenismo* (borrowing) rather than traditional American culture itself. Music, dances, painting and sculpture, handicrafts (especially jewelry), and other visible attributes of the native past are increasingly supported and encouraged. But maintenance of Indian religion, socio-political organization, and similar activities are not permitted. As a consumer market for native wares develops, marketing forces come into play. Artifacts and jewelry, once scarcely sold to a few collectors or tourists, have become important products entering the competitive marketplace of the world.

It is unlikely that few if any Indians formerly of band or tribal structure can survive this century with any substantial portion of their cultures intact. The simple need of states to develop monolingual populations results in the disappearance of native languages, which is perhaps the single most important retention if a culture is to survive. When this is combined with the expansion of road systems and schools, the acculturation of formerly isolated populations is virtually assured. One notable exception to this generality may prove to be the Navajo who, before the twentieth century is out, may become a state within the United States. In the Andean region, and elsewhere in Latin America, where millions of monolingual Indians are still to be found, growing world-wide humanism may bring about increased tolerance of ethnic pluralism as these nation states develop further. It is within reason to expect Bolivia, Ecuador, or Peru to continue to exhibit and perhaps to increase the role of the indigenous past in the cultural present.

## SIGNIFICANCE OF AMERICAN INDIAN CULTURES

Cultures developed by the native inhabitants of the Americas form a vital component in total cultures; only through examination of New and

Old World forms may students of cultural growth and development come to view the whole range of human genius. Because American Indians were possessed of the same intellectual endowments as other human populations, their achievements become another important segment in the study of culture itself. Through comparisons of Old and New World patterns perhaps it will become possible to specify with some exactitude the course of cultural evolution on this planet.

The most visible impact of New World cultures upon other areas of the globe was brought about by the diffusion of food plants, especially the potato and maize, followed closely by sweet potato, manioc, peanut (groundnut), and others. One or another of these crops became the bases for whole economies—for example the potato in Ireland. Tobacco, rubber, coca, the hammock, sisal fiber, the parka, and the canoe have had greater or lesser acceptance throughout the world. Several dozen more plants (tomato, chile pepper, squash, beans, avocado, pineapple, medicinals, etc.) and hundreds of lesser products (coiled baskets, syringes, kayaks, moccasins, tumplines, quill and bead decorative work, etc.) have enriched the cultures of the world. In the main, however, the flow of diffusion was in the other direction, from Europe and Asia to the Americas, and, from an overall view, the technology of Europe was influenced but not radically changed as a result of New World contact.

It is in the realm of political and military developments that the discovery of the New World had the greatest result. Wealth and power accumulated by the colonial nations brought to Europe as well as to North America a series of wars and territorial readjustments that are still unresolved. Spain, and then France and England, accumulated markets and raw materials that permitted primary economic growth. The economic power of England and France, first in North America, later in Africa and Asia, has resulted in continuous friction as other nations–Italy, Russia, China, and Japan–moved into world commerce. Thus, the discovery of the New World and the resulting exploitation has had a critical and continuing influence upon the course of world history.

It is also possible that sectors of the New World, especially those retaining extensive American Indian cultural survivals, may yet have greater significance in centuries to come. It has been frequently noted by anthropologists that many American Indians reflect substantially different attitudes toward one another and toward the world than is common to most Europeans. Indians tend to see nature as a partner with man, a partner to be respected and utilized with care; their perspective contrasts with those who see man as the center of creation having unrestricted rights over all he surveys–nature, land, and people. As the voice of America's Indian citizens comes to be heard more loudly, perhaps in positions of considerable political and economic power, their traditional ways may yet infiltrate the world of their conquerors and bring about a closer rapprochement than has heretofore been possible between members of the assimilating cultural traditions.

# A

**ABRADING TOOLS** were implements used to alter or shape objects through rubbing or wearing away. They were extensively used by the native peoples of the Americas in the manufacture of a wide variety of implements and ornaments. The tools were made from many different materials, including bone, deer-skin, gourds, bamboo, and sandstone. Even the human hand was at times used as an abrading tool.

**Major types**

Abrading tools may be divided into four categories: those used for grinding, sawing, drilling, or engraving.

**Grinding tools.** Of the many types of grinding tools, the most easily identifiable are grinding stones, whetstones, arrowshaft smoothers, and scrapers. Grinding stones, which are distinguished by their grooves, were used to sharpen tools, such as axes. They might be pieces of exposed rock used *in situ* or large stationary pieces of rock used on the ground or held in the lap. Many were sandstone. Whetstones, or handheld sharpening stones, were common among the Inuit (Eskimo), whose whetstone was often a slender tongue of nephrite, a type of jade. Arrowshaft smoothers have been found in many locations; they are stones, often sandstone, that have a groove shaped like a shaft along one surface. Scrapers were of many types and materials. One common type, the so-called thumbnail scraper, was a piece of stone small enough to be held between the fingers, with a steep cutting edge. This scraper was often used to work on animal skins. Although designed to cut, it was probably also used for abrasive purposes at certain stages in the skin-dressing process or to shape harder materials such as bone or stone. Other scrapers were made from bone, wood, fish tooth, and turtle shell.

Many grinding tools had no definite shape. Unshaped hand-held grinding stones were used to smooth stone tools that had been shaped by pecking (crumbling by repeated blows of a hammer-like instrument), as well as to shape a variety of miscellaneous implements such as fishnet weights, bone awls, and shell fishhooks. Grinding stones were also used to elaborate and smooth ornamental or artistic objects, such as the stone pipes common to tribes living in eastern North America and the wood, bone, ivory, and slate sculptures created by some Northwest Coast tribes. They also may have been used to help shape the stone used in building by Mesoamerican and Peruvian Indians. Grinding tools made from wood and bone were used by the Aztecs to polish opal, jade, and other precious stones; wood, gourd, bone, and shell grinding tools were used to polish pottery. Sometimes sand was used as a grinding tool. The Aztecs, for example, scoured the stones used in their lapidary work with special sands.

**Saws.** Saws were used to cut many materials, including metal, stone, and bone. Indians living in the Subarctic region used them to cut nephrite for adzes. Artisans living in Teotihuacán in central Mexico during the period AD 1-800 sawed plates of jade that were eventually reduced to a thickness of 1 mm. Any thin-bladed object might be used as a saw. Sandstone was an often-used material, and sandstone blades were frequently unshaped. The Inuits used thin pieces of shale to saw. Some saw blades were carefully shaped and their edges serrated. The Napa Indians in particular were expert at producing bone saw blades with serrated edges.

Saw blades might be harder or softer than the material to be sawed. When softer, an abrasive such as sand was added to the groove to assist the sawing action. The people of Teotihuacán, for example, probably used a hardwood saw aided by some kind of sand to cut their jade. Sometimes a thin strip of material, such as rawhide, was used in place of a blade. Sand was worked back and forth in the groove underneath the strip, or else it became imbedded in the strip, giving the Indian the equivalent of the modern-day rasp or file.

**Drills.** Drills were used throughout the Americas. The list of objects perforated by drill work is extensive. It includes leather skins, jade beads, stone tablets, shell columella, and other objects of bone, pottery, stone, and wood. Drills were also used to excavate stone vessels.

Drills consisted of a bit and a rotating apparatus. Bits were either solid or hollow. Solid bits, the most common type to be found in North America, were often made of stone or wood, although grass or bristles were sometimes used. Solid bits made of hard material were generally edged. Most had two edges; the pyramid-shaped bits produced by Indians of the Southwest and California, however, had three cutting edges, as did the jade bits used by the Inuits. Solid bits made of softer materials and most hollow bits were used in conjunction with an abrasive substance such as sand which was placed into the hole. Hollow bits, found often in mounds in Ohio and extensively in Mesoamerica, might be made of copper, bronze, bamboo, or bird bone. Extensive trial and error was needed to find an effective combination of bit and abrasive for the material being drilled.

Long drill bits, such as reeds or grasses, could be twirled between the fingers. Short stone bits were often manufactured with a base that expanded into a Y or a T shape. Such a bit could be held in the hand and turned. Short bits were also fastened onto shafts of

Smithsonian Institution, National Anthropological Archives

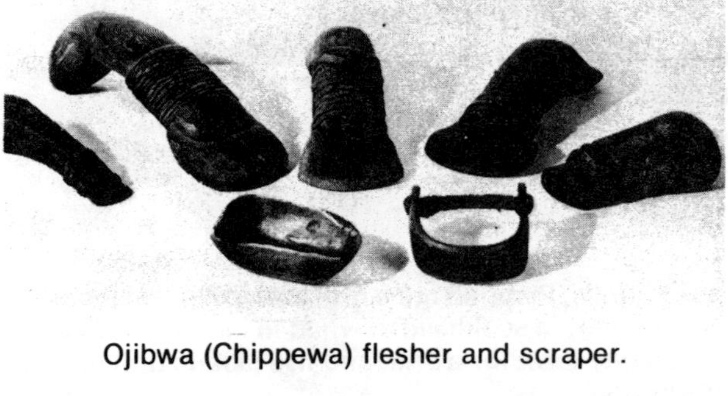

Ojibwa (Chippewa) flesher and scraper.

varying lengths. The shafts could then be twirled between the palms of the hands or between a hand and a thigh. Drills of this type were in use throughout North and Middle America and probably also had a wide distribution in South America. The bits were attached to the shafts in different ways. The tribes of the upper Xingú River basin in Brazil, for example, used wax and cotton thread to bind stone points onto shafts.

By the end of the 19th century, two mechanical innovations that increased the speed with which an object could be drilled were in use throughout North America. One was a strap wound around the drill shaft in various configurations and variously pulled or pumped to increase the rotational speed of the drill. The other was a drill cap or socket that was placed on top of the shaft and used to press the drill into the material being drilled. Modern-day anthropologists have not decided whether these innovations originated in Europe or in America. Evidence suggesting a

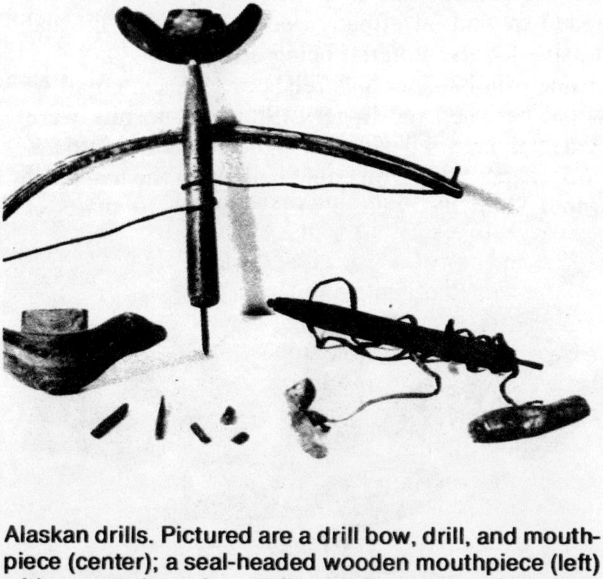

Alaskan drills. Pictured are a drill bow, drill, and mouthpiece (center); a seal-headed wooden mouthpiece (left) with a stone inset for a drill; and five jadeite drill points (foreground).

pre-Columbian origin is strongest for the strap drill used by the Inuits.

**Engravers.** Engraving was most often accomplished using sharp-pointed instruments. Tribes in the northern regions of North America, for example, used sharp bone points to engrave on bark. Other types of tools were also used. In Mexico, hollow drills held vertically or inclined at an angle were used by the Indians of Oaxaca to engrave stone, and the Indians of Teotihuacán may have engraved jade with a wood or stone abrader used in conjunction with sand. The materials upon which engravers worked varied widely. Pottery engraving was developed to a high art by the craftsmen of the Gulf states and by the Pueblo potters of the Southwest. Indians also engraved wood, horn, metal, and ivory.

### General characteristics

Abrading tools were in use at least as early as 10,000-9,000 BC. At this time, Indians living in the western plains of North America who were manufacturing Clovis Fluted projectile points used abrading tools to grind the fluting on these points near the base. The coming of Europeans to the Americas occasioned gradual changes: certain abrading tools — *e.g.*, the engraving points of the Northwest Coast tribes and the Inuit — were at least partially replaced by steel or iron points, and the replacement of pecked stone blades on tools such as axes reduced the need for grinding stones. European contact may also have taught Indians the use of such mechanical drilling apparatus as the pump and the bow. In the mid-20th century, traditional abrading tools were still in use in some areas. Tribes of the upper Xingú River basin in Brazil, for example, used a stone point attached to a shaft as a drill.

Although the process of abrasion was used in all regions of the Americas, the tools used to abrade differed from region to region. Some, such as the arrow-shaft smoother and the grooved grinding stone, were widely distributed. Others, such as the disk drill, were used only by certain tribes. The ingenuity of each tribe, the materials available to it for abrading tools, and the materials to be abraded all helped to determine the types of tools that were finally developed.

Modern attempts to test the effectiveness of traditional abrading tools have led to the conclusion that the traditional tools do work but that they must have taken considerable skill mixed with a large amount of trial and error to operate successfully. One investigator, for example, drilled a hole five inches deep in a piece of catlinite with a pump drill in three hours, but only after switching bits from one made of jasper, to one made of pine and assisted by wet sand, and finally to a bit made of ash assisted with dry sand.

**ACORN,** the decorative fruit of the oak tree, has remarkable, though generally neglected, value as a food source. Some European cultures have used it sparingly for human consumption and more extensively for fattening pigs. The American Indians, how-

Shretta, or Old Mary, a Klamath River Indian of California, leaching acorn meal to prepare it for soup *c.* 1900.

ever, have gone far beyond other cultures in its growth range (temperate and mountainous tropical zones) in exploiting the acorn, recognizing its many advantages, and learning to deal with its drawbacks.

The most obvious disadvantage of the acorn is the bitter taste resulting from the high content of tannin (tannic acid), which makes it not only unpalatable but also indigestible. Some acorns of the white oak (*Quercus alba*) can be eaten untreated; few acorns, however, have this ready-to-eat property. A second disadvantage is that an acorn diet can cause severe constipation. Nevertheless, the Indians recognized several advantages: ease of harvest, high fat and satisfactory protein content, remarkable versatility, and relative ease of storage.

The California Indians had the greatest knowledge of and dependence on acorns; of the more than 50 species of oak in the United States, 15 occur in California. Three of the most popular trees were the California live oak (*Q. agrifolia*), the California black oak (*Q. kelloggii*), and the California white oak (*Q. lobata*). Different tribes of California had quite distinct preferences in acorns, and there were laws concerning property rights to oak groves.

The Luiseño, a typical acorn-eating tribe of southern California, hulled and pulverized the nuts, then leached the meal with warm water and cooked it as a mush. The sand-basket technique of leaching was known in California from the southern Cahuilla to the Hupa of the Northwest Coast. Large baskets, filled with sand to contain the acorn meal, were placed in streams; this saved the labor of pouring water but presented the problem of the disastrous effect of sand on the teeth. To combat constipation, many Indians chewed the bark of the cascara bush (*Rhamnus purshiana*).

Several tribes stored the acorns in wicker sheds, sheltered from rain and vermin; the Wintun of northern California buried them in bogs.

The Indians of the Eastern Woodlands area generally favored the sweet, white oak acorns. The Potawatomi treated acorns in a lye solution made from hardwood ashes, then ground the dried nuts. The Ojibwa ate the fruits of the northern red oak (*Q. rubra*). The Menominee ground the fruit of the northern pin oak (*Q. ellipsoidalis*) into coffee and, after contact with the Europeans, used white oak acorns to make pies.

In other regions the acorn was less popular and abundant. Indians of the Southwest, such as the Tewa, used the nuts of the Gambel oak (*Q. gambelii*) and the Utah oak (*Q. utahensis*). The Navajo boiled acorns like beans. In the Southeast, the Choctaw used a leaching technique on the acorns of the water oak (*Q. aguatica*). The Klamath of the Plateau area established acorn camps during the harvest season.

Nonfood uses were common. The Luiseño used the acorns of the canyon live oak (*Q. chrysolepsis*) for gambling. The children of the Lacandon Indians of Mexico's Chiapas state used large acorns as spinning tops.

The Indians regarded the acorn as a bounty from above: it required no planting, cultivating, or difficult harvest. Several tribes founded oak societies to revere the tree. Although the acorn lore of California was rapidly vanishing in the 1970s, it was still seen by some as a possible help to forestall the dire threats of world food shortages.

**ADAPTATION, HUMAN.** Man, since his initial evolutionary development in the central latitudes of the Old World, has demonstrated a high degree of geographic mobility. As a result of his wanderings, he has encountered a number of new habitats. In many cases, such encounters have required adjustments in both his biology and his culture in order to ensure his survival. This experience has in part been responsible for much of the biogeographical variability that can be observed in the human species at the present time.

By the onset of the last glacial stage in North America, the Wisconsin (between 64,000 and 11,000 years ago), *Homo sapiens* (modern man) had successfully spread into temperate and possibly the Subarctic zones of the Old World. Still to be colonized at this time were the island groups of Oceania, the continent of Australia, and the New World. At some period, during either the maximal expansion of the Wisconsin Stage or its terminal phases, men crossed the Bering Land Bridge (Beringia) from Asia and entered the New World for the first time. After this initial invasion, it appears (from inferential archaeological evidence) that there were a series of migratory waves from Asia. The earliest migrations were probably dependent upon the periodic movement of glaciers over Beringia during the various substages of the Wisconsin.

**General aspects of adaptation**

Theoretically, there are two avenues that a population can take in adapting biologically to a new habitat. They are genetic adaptation (adaptive changes in gene frequency) and acclimatization (adaptive morphological and physiological changes in response to stress).

Genetic adaptation operates at the population level. It is the result of the temporal interaction between the genetic variability existing in the population when it enters a specific habitat and the selective stresses present in the habitat, mutation, gene flow, genetic drift (random changes in gene frequencies from generation to generation), breeding structure (mating patterns), and size of the population. Selection will set the general direction of evolution and the population will survive if it possesses and maintains sufficient genetic variability (*i.e.*, the necessary genes and genotypes) in the face of the selection pressures imposed upon it. For evolution to occur in small populations, those forces tending to promote genetic variability (mutation and gene flow) must override or balance the effects of genetic drift, which tends (along with directional selection) to reduce genetic variability.

Acclimatization, on the other hand, requires no genetic change in the population as a whole because it operates on the individual phenotype (biological character; the outward expression of genetic and environmental factors). Nevertheless, if genetic differences exist between individuals in their capability to acclimatize to stress and, as a result, the reproductive capacity is affected, this may lead over time to genetic changes in the population for those biological characters involved.

Acclimatizational processes in man may generally be regarded as either short-term or long-term. The first includes those phenotypic adjustments taking several seconds (*e.g.*, changes in heart rate during heat stress) to those requiring weeks or months (*e.g.*, tanning) to achieve. Because of the inherent physiological capability for change in those biological characters responsive to short-term acclimatization, many of the adjustments are reversible; *i.e.*, the phenotype can return to (or close to) its original state if the stress is alleviated. Long-term acclimatization, however, takes place in biological characters in which phenotypic adjustments are less rapid. Most of these processes are ontogenetic (*i.e.*, occurring during growth and development). In general, the resultant phenotypic adjustments display less reversibility, and most of the ontogenetic changes are completely irreversible if the stress is alleviated after the attainment of adulthood.

In order to discuss human biological adaptability and diversity in the native peoples of the Americas, it is necessary to examine some of the major environmental stresses encountered by human populations and the typology and etiology (origin) of the resultant adaptations. Six of these stresses which have been investigated in varying degrees are humid and dry heat, cold, differentials in ultraviolet radiation, nutritional (especially caloric) conditions, disease, and — for a small portion of mankind — hypoxia (the lowered oxygen content of the atmosphere in high-altitude habitats).

**Morphology and physiology**

There is some evidence that two general statements can be made in reference to the geographical distribution of body size and shape in warm-blooded species, including man. With some exceptions, the largest animals are found in the coldest parts of the geographical range (Bergman's rule), and the length of the extremities tend to be reduced in the coldest parts of the range (Allen's rule). Bergman's and Allen's rules appear to be different facets of the same biophysical phenomenon — that it is beneficial for a warm-blooded animal to have a reduced surface area-to-volume ratio (SA/V) in a cold climate and an increased SA/V in a hot climate. Since the amount of heat produced by metabolism is related to body size and mass, these rules are apparently associated with the need to reduce radiant heat loss from the body surface during cold stress and increase it during heat stress. Both rules have their bases in two physical laws which state that (1) when two bodies of dissimilar size have the same shape, the larger has a smaller SA/V, and (2) when two bodies of dissimilar shape have the same size, the more linear one has the larger SA/V.

Nutrition, disease, and hypoxia may also act, individually or collectively, to limit body size in some populations by affecting the metabolic process during growth and development. Nutritional stress does this by lowering the energy levels and/or dietary components necessary for the normal processes of anabolism (growth). Disease may operate to limit body size by increasing the metabolic requirements or, like hypoxia, by direct interference with anabolism, catabolism (energy release from carbohydrates, fats, and proteins), or growth-related endocrine function.

Skin color is another character that demonstrates geographical variability, tending to decrease from areas of high to low ultraviolet radiation (u-v). Skin pigmentation affects the amount of u-v reaching the lower levels of the epidermis, where ergosterol (an essential growth factor) is synthesized by the action of u-v. W. F. Loomis and other scientists believe that u-v has acted as a selective agent in causing genetic differences in skin color between geographically dispersed populations.

Finally, there are differences between geographic populations in their short-term physiological responses to heat and cold stress. These differences are more marked in the latter case and shall be briefly discussed below.

### Genetic polymorphisms

Genetic polymorphisms such as blood groups and other serological variants also show geographical variability. Since the expression of these characters is controlled completely by genetic factors, they are theoretically subject to direct environmental selection. This is in contrast to those biological characters that possess the ability to undergo phenotypic modification, thus allowing some amelioration of the selective action of the environmental stress being imposed.

**Table 1: The Frequencies (%) of Three Blood Group Polymorphisms Among American Indian Populations**

| | blood groups | | | | |
|---|---|---|---|---|---|
| areal population | A | B | O | Rh+ | M |
| Inuit | ¯25 | ¯2 | ¯73 | ¯100 | ▶60 |
| North America† | ◀15 | 0 | ▶85 | ¯100 | ▶70 |
| Central America | 0 | 0 | ¯100 | ¯100 | ▶90 |
| South America | 0 | 0 | ¯100 | ¯100 | ▶70 |

*Data taken from A.E. Mourant, *The Distribution of the Human Blood Groups* (1954) and A.E. Mourant, A.C. Kopec, and K. Domaniewska-Sobzcak, *The ABO Blood Groups* (1958). †The A blood group frequency is greater than 60% in Blood and Blackfoot Indians.

For many of the polymorphic systems, the interpopulation variability in phenotypic frequencies does not fit any apparent geographic pattern. Consequently, it is difficult to determine whether or not climatological factors are responsible. In some cases, associations with disease have been proposed. In one example of serological polymorphisms, a deleterious allele (genetic factor) is maintained in a given population because a physiological and, hence, reproductive advantage is conferred on the heterozygote in the face of an endemic disease (*e.g.*, sickle cell anemia and malaria). In another example, an individual is invaded by an organism "tagged" with an antigen-like structure which is homologous to that of one of the "self" antigens carried on the red blood cell. As a result, the immune system does not recognize the organism as "nonself," there is little or no antibody response, and the individual has a greater chance of acquiring the disease (*e.g.*, the higher incidence in some populations of smallpox among individuals of the A and AB blood types).

**Biological variability in Amerinds**

**The Inuit (Eskimo) and Aleut.** This group, which appears to be the most recently intrusive into the New World, at present inhabits both the Arctic and Subarctic fringes of North America and Greenland. Along with the Siberian Mongoloids and the Chukchi, Koryak, and Siberian Inuit, they form a close genetically-related population. The affinities of the Inuit and Aleut with these other groups is evident in the similarity of frequency of the blood groups ABO, MN, and Rh, and in their phenotypic characteristics of general body size, build, and facial structure.

The Inuit and Aleut are similar to the Asiatics and different from American Indians in possessing higher frequencies of blood group A, some blood group B (variable but small in frequency), and lower frequencies of the M allele (*see* Tables 1 and 2). It is noteworthy that among the Inuit there exist some geographical inconsistencies in blood group clines (graded series of morphological or physiological differences in related organisms). The central Arctic dwellers have lower frequencies of the $A_1$ variant, B allele, and $R_1$ variant (Rh system) in their blood than do those living in Alaska or Greenland.

Anthropometrically, the Inuit and Aleut may be described as being, on the average, small in stature with comparatively long trunks and short limbs, and as having a large cranium with variable cephalic index

**Table 2: Some Distinctive Genetic Features of the American Indian**

| | |
|---|---|
| ABO system | High frequency of O |
| MN system | High frequency of M |
| Rh system | Highest frequency of $R_2$; r and $R_0$ low or absent |
| Kell system | K may have been absent in pre-Columbian Indians |
| Duffy system | High frequency of $Fy_a$ |
| Diego system | High frequency of $Di_a$ |
| Lewis system | Almost all populations show Le(a-) only |
| Lutheran system | Almost all populations show Lu(a-) only |
| Hemoglobin types | Rare or absent |
| Color blindness | Low frequencies of defectives |

*Taken from J.V. Neel and F.M. Salzano, "A Prospectus for Genetic Studies on the American Indians," in P.T. Baker and J.S. Weiner, *The Biology of Human Adaptability* (1966).

(ratio of maximum breadth to maximum length), large, broad, and flat face, epicanthic folds, and a narrow nose with the nasal passage set well within the face (*see* Table 3). The smallest Inuit are found in northwestern Alaska and Greenland, while the cephalic index is lowest in Greenland and the central Arctic. Nasal index (ratio of breadth to length) values are fairly consistent throughout the Inuit-Aleut geographical range.

When placed under cold stress in the laboratory, the Inuit demonstrate more efficient mechanisms of thermoregulation (physiological adjustments which act to maintain internal body temperature) than do black and white Americans. This is seen in their heightened basal metabolic rates (BMR) and increased blood flow to the peripheries. This would function to allay frostbite or other tissue damage during cold stress (*see* Table 4).

**North American Indians.** Before the major advent of migrants of northern and western European stock into North America, the North American Indians were widely dispersed geographically. During this

**Table 3: The Means of Selected Anthropometric Parameters among Amerindian Populations***

| areal population | mean stature (CM) | mean cormic index (%) ‡ | mean cephalic index (%) | mean nasal index (%) |
|---|---|---|---|---|
| Inuit | 162.8 | 53.0 | 78.1 | 68.5 |
| North American Indians | | | | |
| Northwest Coast | 164.0 | — | 83.2 | 78.9 |
| Southwest | 168.9 | 52.8 | 81.3 | 79.5 |
| Plains | 167.5 | — | 81.4 | 72.0 |
| East | 171.5 | — | 80.0 | — |
| Central American Indians | 159.1 | 52.6‡ | 81.1 | 81.1 |
| South American Indians | | | | |
| Amazon Basin | 163.4 | 52.0§ | 80.1 | 81.4 |
| Tierra del Fuego// | 157.6 | — | 80.0 | 72.8 |
| Andes | 159.5 | 53.4 | 84.1 | 70.0 |

*All data except means for cormic index and that from Tierra del Fuego taken from A.J. Kelso, *Physical Anthropology* (1974) after R. Biassuti, *Le Razze e I Popoli della Terra* (1959); based on a small number of samples; means weighted by sample sizes. †Data (males) summarized from T.D. Stewart, *The People of America* (1973) and F.M. Salzano, *The Ongoing Evolution of Latin-American Populations* (1970); means weighted by sample sizes. ‡Maya Indians. §Arawak Indians. //Data taken from T.D. Stewart, *The People of America* (1973).

period, at least seven different habitats were exploited with a more variable economic base than that of the Arctic and Subarctic Inuit and Aleut, who were primarily hunters and fishermen. These habitats were the boreal steppe, the boreal forest, the temperate forest, the Great Plains region, the Great Basin, the desert areas of what is now the southwestern United States and northern Mexico, and the subtropical forest. It is highly probable that the great morphological variability demonstrated in this group — in both fossil and living populations — is a result of adaptation to the diverse econiches (lifeway /economic patterns) and habitats that existed.

It must be noted that, because of the fossil evidence, more can be said about morphological variability in pre-Columbian times and the representativeness of the modern anthropometric data than about the genetic polymorphisms. The latter could have been significantly altered over time by admixture and selection pressures provided by European-introduced diseases such as smallpox, which may have caused selection against the N as well as the A allele. If genetic polymorphism data are representative, then the North American Indians were probably similar to other pre-Columbian Amerind groups in not possessing the B allele. They would differ, however, from the Central Americans in their higher frequencies of N and differ from both in having higher frequencies of A (*see* Tables 1 and 2), particularly the $A_1$ variant, and lower frequencies of the Diego positive allele, $Di^a$.

The clines in body size and nasal index are fairly consistent in this group. The tallest people are found along a gradient that decreases from the eastern seaboard into the Plains. Thereafter there is a trend for a decrease in body size from a complex forming the Great Basin and southwestern (U.S.) desert into the Pacific coast and desert of northern Mexico (*see* Table 3). Nasal indices are variable and generally higher than those observed in the Inuit-Aleut population. The highest indices are to be found among groups in the warmest areas of North America, and the extremes in nasal narrowness and convexity occur among the Plains Indians. Cephalic indices are high throughout North America and larger on the average than those found in most Inuit-Aleut. There are few data on the physiological response to environmental stress in North American Indians, but one laboratory cold stress study of Arctic Indians has demonstrated that the typology of response to environmental stress in North American Indians, but one laboratory cold stress study of Arctic Indians has demonstrated that the typology of response is similar to that shown among the Inuit (*see* Table 4.).

**Middle American Indians.** At the time of the Spanish conquest this population occupied a small number of tropical and subtropical habitats that differed ecologically primarily as a result of altitude. For the most part, these populations were agricultural, although there were differences in their stages of cultural development. Biologically, this was a highly homogeneous population.

In their blood group frequencies the Middle Americans are quite similar to the Indians of North and South America. The essential differences are that they possess higher frequencies of $Di^a$ than the North American Indians and the highest frequencies of M found in the New World (*see* Table 1).

In stature and general body size these are the smallest of the various Amerind populations. Cormic and cephalic indices are comparable with other Amerind groups. On the average, nasal indices are high and similar to those values found among the Amazonian Indians of South America (*see* Table 3). There is some evidence that these peoples have higher basal metabolic rates (BMR) than do whites. This is noteworthy because there is a worldwide tendency for the BMR to decline with increases in mean annual temperatures.

**South American Indians.** This group is the most diverse culturally, ecologically, and biologically, of the major geographical Amerindian populations. In terms of technology and economic and social organization, they range from the most primitive hunters and gatherers to those of the high cultures of the Andes and Pacific coast. Their habitats include deserts; temperate, subtropical, and tropical forests (including montane and rain forest); savanna and plains; and high altitudes. Even the last mentioned habitat comprises a number of different zones; namely, the high altitude deserts, the *puna* region above 12,000 feet, and the portion of the *altiplano* (high plain) that lies between 9,000 and 12,000 feet above sea level and is suitable for agriculture.

On the basis of population size and geographical distribution, S. M. Garn recognizes three major divisions within the South American population. They may be termed the Amazonians, the Fuegians, and the Andeans.

In many respects the Amazonians bear a striking resemblance to the Indians of Middle America.

**Table 4: Physiological Differences Between Four Amerindian and an American White Population in Response to Total Body Cold Stress**

| | changes during chronic cold exposure in: | | |
|---|---|---|---|
| population | basal metabolic rate (BMR) | core temperature (Tc) | mean skin temperature (Ts) |
| American whites | Marked increase over initial precold stress levels | Decrease during cold stress † | Marked decrease ‡ |
| The Inuit and Arctic Indians | Initially slightly higher than whites; slight increase during cold stress | Decrease slightly greater than that in whites | Arctic Indians show a decrease greater than that in whites; the Inuit decrease not as marked as that in whites |
| Andean Indians (Quechua) | Initially similar to whites; similar increases | Decrease much greater than that in whites | Decrease similar to that in whites |
| Tierra del Fuegan Indians (Alacaluf) | Initially higher than whites; insignificant declines | Decrease similar to that in whites | Decrease similar to that in whites |

*Data (males) taken from H.T. Hammel, "Terrestrial Animals in Cold: Recent Studies of Man," in D.B. Dill, E.F. Adolph, and C.G. Wilbur, *Handbook of Physiology 4* (1964); based on tests from 3 to 8 hours in duration, temperatures variable. †The smaller decreases in whites compared to the Amerinds is probably due to the greater amount of subcutaneous fat in the whites. ‡On the average, the Amerinds maintain higher foot temperatures.

Primarily hunters and gatherers, the Amazonians, however, are taller, have flatter noses (although the nasal indices are similar) and broader faces, and are somewhat lighter in skin color than the Indians of Middle America (*see* Tables 1 and 3).

The Fuegians inhabit the cold and damp southernmost tip of South America. Traditionally, this group fished and dove for shellfish in the chilly waters around Tierra del Fuego. Because of their lifestyle and the fact that their material culture was limited, it is believed that they suffered some chronic cold stress. This may explain in part why, although short, they are somewhat heavy and have more fatty layers under the skin than the other Amerind groups. In general, their cephalic indices are similar to those of other South American populations. Their nose form, however, more closely approximates that of northern North American Indians (*see* Table 3).

Like the Inuit, the Fuegians have an average BMR greater than that of other Amerinds and whites. When exposed to cold stress they show a physiological response that is similar to that of whites, with the exception that there is little change in BMR (*see* Table 4).

More is known about the biology of the Andean population than of any other large Amerind group, and in a number of ways they present a different biological pattern than other Amerinds. In their blood group frequencies the Andeans are different from other South American Indians in possessing the A allele and in having higher frequencies of N.

Morphologically, the Andeans are short and thin, but they possess chest and lung volumes as large as those of much taller, low-altitude populations. They have larger hearts, greater circulatory blood volumes, and greater amounts of hemoglobin per body size, and they show greater peripheral vasodilation (*i.e.*, the caliber of the blood vessels in the muscles and other tissues is greater). All of these factors enhance the transport of oxygen from the air to the metabolizing tissue. As a result, the Andeans can perform work and survive at high altitudes where the oxygen is less than at sea level. The Andeans are also different in other morphological characters. Their cephalic indices are extremely high and, on the average, their cormic indices are even greater than those of the Inuit. Nasal indices are low and similar to those of the Inuit.

The Andeans also present a slightly different physiological response when exposed to cold stress. This is primarily due to the greater loss of heat from the body core (*see* Table 4). P. T. Baker and others believe that this is due to the smaller amount of fatty layers under the skin (which can act as insulation) possessed by the Andeans and to the increased blood flow to the peripheries. The latter may be a result of the primary action of hypoxia on increased peripheral vasodilation in this population.

**Conclusions**

Certain conclusions regarding the native peoples of the Americas can now be drawn in terms, first, of genetic polymorphisms and, then, of morphology and physiology.

**Genetic polymorphisms.** On the basis of blood groups, the Inuit-Aleut group which possesses the B but lacks the $Di^a$ allele, can be considered to be a separate genetic population from the American Indians.

Explanations as to why the American Indians, who are also an Asiatic-derived group, differ from the Inuit and Aleut and the Siberian Mongoloids are at best speculative. Four hypotheses that have been presented are of interest. (1) The ancestral Asiatic population was genetically dissimilar from modern Asiatics. (2) The migrants entering the New World were small in number and thus subject to Founder's Effect (in which migrants to a new location are not genetically representative of their original population) and/or genetic drift. (3) Differential selection pressures encountered in the New World resulted in changes in gene frequencies. (4) European-introduced diseases have caused rapid selective changes in gene frequencies in recent times. It is important to point out that these phenomena (along with the mating of individuals of different "races") might also account for some of the blood group differences that exist within and between the major geographical populations.

**Morphology and physiology.** As M. T. Newman, D. F. Roberts, and others note, there are some definite associations between certain morphological characters in the Amerind population and environment. One that has been mentioned previously is skin color. In general, Amerinds are not highly variable for this character, ranging with a few exceptions from light to dark brown. Differences that exist are probably the result more of tanning to u-v than of essential genetic differences between geographic populations.

In general, the Amerinds follow Bergman's rule. The smallest peoples inhabit the tropical and subtropical lowlands, and there is a tendency for size to increase with decreasing mean annual temperature. Some exceptions are the short, cold-stressed Andeans, Fuegians, and Inuit-Aleut. It is possible that limiting factors on the development of large body size are set for the Andeans (who are thinner than the Inuit and Fuegians) by hypoxia and for all three groups by the increased metabolic cost of thermoregulation and/or nutritional stress.

There are not adequate data to determine whether or not the Amerinds follow Allen's rule for general body shape. It is noteworthy, however, that the highest cormic indices are found in populations that undergo some chronic cold stress and that the lowest occur among the Middle American and Amazonian Indians.

There does not appear to be a definite association between head shape and climate in the Amerinds. Both the lowest (Inuit) and highest cephalic indices (Andeans) are found among cold-stressed populations.

A much clearer association is to be observed between nose shape and climate in the Amerinds. There are fairly regular clines from areas of high temperature and humidity to areas of lower ones. The apparent correlation appears to be with vapor pressure. The adaptive significance may lie in the fact that narrow noses tend to maintain moisture in the lungs and nasal epithelium during cold or hot-dry stress, and broad noses tend to augment its dissipation during hot-humid stress.

Although the above morphological-environmental associations are apparently the result of adaptive processes and are in part responsible for biological diversity within the Amerind population, the data are not adequate to infer either a genetic or acclimatizational etiology. The same may also be said of the variation in physiological responses noted for those Amerind populations living in cold habitats. At present many physiologists including K. L. Anderson are of the opinion that acclimatization is the major factor in creating physiological differentials. Further studies are required, however, to shed some light on the development of biological diversity within the Amerind population.

**ADHESIVES,** made by Indians of North and South America from animal, vegetable, and mineral substances, were used for a variety of purposes. Little is known concerning the history of their development, but adhesives are believed to have been used in Mesoamerica by about 300 BC, and the use of Indian-made adhesives continued into the 20th century in some areas.

**Adhesive-making techniques.** The Indian people used several techniques to make adhesives from animals. A widespread technique involved boiling selected animal parts until the otherwise insoluble protein collagen became soluble. Animal parts selected for this process by North American tribes apparently included bone joints (used by the Yokuts of California); glands from sturgeon (used by the Hupa of California); deer sinew and the tops of deer horns (used by Virginia Indians observed by the English settler Capt. John Smith in the early 17th century); and the skin from the heads of animals (used by various Plains Indian tribes). In South America, the technique was similar: the Aymara of Peru and Bolivia boiled strips of hide, and tribes living in the Gran Chaco region made glue from fish.

Other North American techniques utilized wax and egg albumen. The Inuits (Eskimos) obtained their adhesive albumen from a different source — blood. Wax was used as an adhesive by several South American tribes, including the Guató of the upper Paraguay River basin, the Northwestern and Central Ge of Brazil, the Sáliva of Venezuela, and the Guaná of Guyana and Venezuela.

Adhesives made from vegetable substances were manufactured by tribes from whatever materials were handy. Resin from coniferous trees was commonly used by North American tribes from the North to the Southwest. Gums and resins from other trees — *e.g.*, the mesquite and the greasewood — were also used. In Mesoamerica, the vegetable adhesive *tzacutli* is believed to have been made from the root of the orchid *Cranichis speciosa* early in the Christian Era. Flour or starch paste was used by Náhuatl-speaking peoples in central Mexico about 300 BC. In South America, resins and gums were used as adhesives by the Guató and the Guaná.

Mineral adhesives seem to have had a limited use in North America, with only bitumen being used by Indians of present-day southern Arizona and California. In Mesoamerica, where mortar was made from some type of mineral substance, possibly basaltic gravel or argillaceous lime, the use was extensive. Bitumen was also used.

**Uses.** The uses of adhesives were multifold. In North America, animal adhesives were used chiefly to make bows and arrows or, among the Plains Indian tribes, to cement pipestems to pipes. Vegetable adhesives were also used to set arrowheads onto shafts, and resins were in widespread use as waterproofing agents for canoes and baskets. Resins were also used for mending, joining, and inlaying a variety of materials. In Mesoamerica, *tzacutli* and flour or starch paste were apparently used in the construction of feather mosaics. In addition, *tzacutli* may have been used as the adhesive in making paper from the amate tree. The mineral adhesive bitumen was used in the construction of pearl, amber, and amethyst mosaics. In South America, vegetable adhesives were used by the Sáliva to glue arrowheads onto shafts. The

Guaná used a combined vegetable, beeswax, and powdered charcoal glue for the same purpose. They also used a variety of gums to glue feathers onto the body for ritual purposes.

Two unusual uses of adhesives, not yet fully verified in the mid-1970s, were to secure dental inlays in Teotihuacán (AD 100-600) and, more recently, to mend broken bones among the Sáliva.

Indians often combined several types of adhesives to increase their adhesive strength. The Yokuts mixed pitch with animal glue; the Inuits mixed blood with soot; and the Ge of Brazil mixed resin with chewed babassú seeds. The mixture used by the Guaná has already been mentioned.

**ADOBE** most commonly refers to a building material fashioned by the Pueblo Indians of the southwestern United States. Adobe bricks have been used by people in arid and semiarid regions of the world for thousands of years.

**General characteristics.** The word "adobe" derives from the Spanish word *adobar*, meaning "to daub" or "to plaster." Its evolution has been traced to earlier words in Arabic, Coptic, and Egyptian hieroglyphics meaning "brick."

In the English language, adobe possesses at least five different meanings, principally the building material made by the Pueblo Indians out of a mixture of clay, water, and grass or straw which is placed into wooden forms and later dried in the sun. Adobe may also mean the mortar used by the Pueblos as a bond to hold walls made out of adobe bricks or walls made out of stone and rubble. Sometimes the word refers to a watery mixture, used like plaster to cover walls of stone, adobe bricks, or reeds. Still again, adobe may mean the earth from which sun-dried bricks are made. Finally, it may refer to a house or other structure made of adobe brick.

Because adobe bricks are relatively easy to make, last a long time, and are good insulators, they have been used by people in arid and semiarid regions of the world for thousands of years. Sun-dried bricks appear at Ur in ancient Mesopotamia; they form the core of many Egyptian pyramids. They were similarly used in the Sun Pyramid at Teotihuacán in the Valley of Mexico about AD 100. At Copán, a Classic Maya site in Honduras, adobe was used as mortar. In the southwestern United States, particularly New Mexico and Arizona, and in northwestern Mexico, particularly the states of Chihuahua and Sonora, adobe appears in its various forms of plaster, mortar, and sun-dried bricks at many sites — *e.g.*, Keet Seel, Navajo National Monument, Arizona; Mesa Verde, Colorado; Pueblo Bonito, Chaco Canyon, New Mexico; and the pueblos of Zuñi, Acoma, Isleta, Taos, Pecos, and Zia.

**Pueblo adobe-making.** Pueblo villages attained a variety of styles and forms by AD 1100. In some cases, a village consisted of a cluster of one-story adobe and stone homes, arranged in a semicircle with adjoining walls. In other cases, like the stone-walled city of Pueblo Bonito, a village possessed several stories, contained 800 rooms, and had a population of as many as 1,200. By 1300 the big apartment complexes, like those at Pueblo Bonito and Mesa Verde, had been abandoned. Drought, attacks by Navajo and Apache nomads, internal dissension, and other factors have been offered as possible explanations.

One of the earliest descriptions of adobe-making was written by Castañeda, a Spanish soldier who accompanied the explorer Francisco Vázquez de Coronado in the 1540s. Describing what the Spaniards referred to as the province of Tiguex, which comprised 12 pueblos on both sides of the Rio Grande in present-day New Mexico, Castañeda wrote: "In general, these villagers all have the same habits and customs, although some have things in particular which the others have not. They are governed by the opinions of the elders. They all work together to build the villages, the women being engaged in making the mixture and the walls, while the men bring the wood and put it in place. They have no lime, but they make a mixture of ashes, coals, and dirt which is almost as good as mortar, for when the house is to have four stories, they do not make the walls more than half a yard thick. They gather a great pile of twigs of thyme and sedge grass and set it afire, and when it is half coals and ashes they throw a quantity of dirt and water on it and mix it all together. They make round balls of this, which they use instead of stones after they are dry, fixing them with the same mixture which comes to be like a stiff clay."

Although the Pueblo people of the Southwest did not possess a common language or a unified political system, they did share a common physical environment and they all were dependent upon corn-growing as the basis for their economy. In response to their needs for defense and shelter and because of the values placed upon the collective life, they all devised a similar architectural style. Their pueblos (Spanish for "villages") were characterized by many of the same features that had appeared by AD 1100: each village had one large communal building, varying in height from one to seven stories.

These buildings awed the Spanish in the 16th century and remain distinctive in appearance today. The overall visual effect is that of a stolid seriousness. There are no frills and few decorations. Ground floor rooms had no windows and no doors. Entrance to these rooms was made from above, by ladder. Inner and lower rooms were used primarily for storage. Outer rooms and roofs served as living and sleeping quarters. Additional stories rose above the first floor, in terrace fashion. The rooms in the upper stories contained small doorways and smaller windows. Such a building was an easy place to defend and a very difficult place to assault successfully, as Castañeda's chronicle reveals.

The walls of the pueblo were made of stone with courses of adobe as mortar. Where stone was not available in large quantities, it was used for the foundation, and adobe bricks as described by Castañeda formed the wall. Roofs began with a series of large logs called *vigas* which spanned the entire width of one room — as long as 14 feet. Subsequent layers of smal-

Cliff Palace, Mesa Verde, Colorado. Constructed primarily of adobe, it was inhabited more than seven centuries ago and is the largest known cliff-dwelling.

ler poles, reeds, and a final layer of mud formed the completed roof.

**Spanish influence.** The Spanish provincial capital at Santa Fe, established in the winter of 1609-10, reveals a blending of Pueblo and Spanish architectural forms and building methods. Thus, the Indian women who built the Governor's Palace between 1610 and 1614 made it out of adobe brick. The flat roof with projecting *vigas* was similar in appearance to the domestic architecture of the one-story Pueblo village. At the same time, Spanish features were also visible: windows and doors were framed with wood; a long portal (covered porch) graced the south side of the palace; the entire building was formed around a central, enclosed patio.

In the construction of the Governor's Palace the Spanish inaugurated a system whereby adobe bricks were mass produced prior to the time of their actual use. The former method of hand-shaped, irregularly formed adobe brick was no longer thought desirable, so wooden forms were introduced to manufacture the bricks. The adobe mixture was placed in wooden molds enclosed on four sides. After several days of drying they were removed, stacked on end, and slightly tipped to diminish wear in case of rain. The bricks made in this way usually required from two to four weeks to dry thoroughly.

Spanish technology further modified the appearance of adobe buildings. Their iron axes and adzes made it easier to cut and shape timber. The protruding *vigas* were cut down to a uniform length, and on the inside they were carefully trimmed and made rectangular in shape.

Spanish conquistadores and missionaries carried Pueblo architecture throughout the Southwest. Churches and missions, barracks and stables, prisons and shops were all made from adobe bricks and mortar. As the Christian population slowly increased, the Spanish increased the size of the churches. A wider nave required massive adobe walls in order to support the large cross beams of the roof.

The church of San Estevan at Acoma is but one example of the monumental scale celebrated by the Spanish. The main walls on either side of the nave were five feet and seven feet thick; the difference was intentional as the builders used the thicker wall as a fulcrum to hoist up the roof timbers, which were 40 feet long and 14 inches square.

Architectural historians do not seem to be in agreement about who were the builders of the adobe walled missions. Hugh Morrison states, in *Early American Architecture* (1952), "In general, women and children built the adobe walls, as they had in the pueblos; the men considered this beneath their dignity." In apparent contradiction, Carl W. Condit wrote in 1968 in reference to the church of San Estevan at Acoma that Indian women formed the adobe in molds into sun-dried bricks each weighing about 50 pounds, or about as large as one man could conveniently handle.

The merits of adobe construction accompanied the Spanish to California. Junípero Serra, a Spanish Franciscan missionary, and the Franciscans created a system of 21 missions along the 600 miles of El Camino Real between 1769 and 1823. Adobe, both sun-dried and kiln-burned bricks, was the basic building element.

**U.S. technology.** War and conquest in the 1840s once again brought new values and technology to the Southwest. The impact of the U.S. culture was most sharply felt after the arrival of the railroad in New Mexico in 1878. The cost of shipping lumber and brick from Kansas City and St. Louis was greatly reduced. No longer was it necessary to rely upon locally produced materials like adobe. Brick and frame houses and shops became common, and adobe seemed about to disappear.

**20th-century rebirth.** In the 20th century, however, there has been a rebirth of interest in adobe construction technique. The Great Depression (1929-39) caused the U.S. government to seek inexpensive housing methods. Others have become concerned about the conservation of energy and the wiser utilization of urban space.

In 1936-37 the Farm Security Administration, a branch of the U.S. Department of Agriculture, sought to help poor farmers and sharecroppers. It constructed a two-story adobe-walled dormitory for migrant laborers at Chandler, Arizona, a small town close to the Casa Grande National Monument. The adobe walls proved not only to be capable of sustaining the loads of the second floor and roof but also to be excellent thermal insulators.

The Pueblo concept of a multiple-level, terraced, contiguous dwelling was evident in an altogether different physical environment at the Montreal world's fair, Expo '67. Habitat '67 was 13 stories high, with 158 apartments. Reinforced concrete had supplanted adobe, but in form and function there were obvious similarities between it and Taos Pueblo.

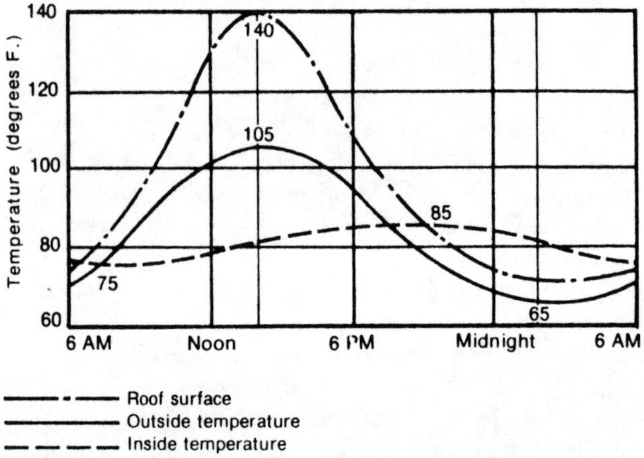


Thermal performance of adobe house. The high heat capacity of the thick adobe walls and mud roof acts to flatten out stressful thermal curve of the desert climate. From the book by James Marston Fitch, *American Building: The Historical Forces that Shaped it*, Vol. 1 (1972).

Recently, scientific studies by architects have confirmed what the Pueblo people have long known — adobe is an excellent insulator, providing maximum protection against summer heat as well as winter cold.

This fact, combined with the low cost of adobe construction and its relatively easy maintenance are all influences that may extend its use into the future. Examples of a continuing, vital Pueblo architectural style may be seen in the New Mexico State Art Museum, the National Park Service Headquarters at Santa Fe, and the Lovelace Clinic at the University of New Mexico.

DAVID J. O'NEILL

**ADOPTION** was practiced almost universally throughout the Americas. There were great variations in who might be adopted, for what purpose they were adopted, how they were adopted, and the status of the adopted person. Because ethnological descriptions often do not distinguish clearly between adopted people of low status, slaves, and serfs, it is difficult to define completely the variations in adoption practices.

**Adoptable persons.** Indians adopted both individuals and groups. In general, they might adopt people of other tribes or other races, either sex, and any age. Adoptions were not necessarily restricted to people from friendly tribes. The Iroquois of the northeastern United States, for example, commonly adopted warriors captured in battle. Whites and blacks were adopted by Indians. Although men and women were both frequently adopted, some tribes were less apt to adopt adult males than women and children while engaged in a war. For example, the Carib and apparently many other tribes of the Circum-Caribbean area tortured, killed, and ate male captives, rather than take them into the social structure.

Whole tribes, as well as individuals, might be adopted. The Iroquois were famous for this practice; at various times, they brought into their confederacy such tribes as the Erie, Saponi, and Tutelo. Adoption of the Tuscarora in the early 18th century was so important to the confederacy that its name eventually changed from the Five Nations to the Six Nations. It was not uncommon, when pressured by increasing white settlement, for small tribes to merge with each other or with larger tribes, although it is not always clear from records whether such arrangements were mere coexistence or involved adoption. Smaller groups, such as families, clans, and bands, could also be adopted.

**Circumstances leading to adoption.** The most common circumstance that led to adoption was war. Fighting resulted in dead or captured men, women, and children. The dead of the tribe were often replaced for magical or sentimental reasons with the captured. War also severely weakened tribes, who preferred adoption by a stronger people to dissolution. Such adoptions benefitted the stronger tribe as well by increasing its strength. Sometimes individuals left a weakened tribe to be adopted, even if the tribe itself was not. For example, Pueblo women reportedly fled to the Apache during the 17th-century wars with the Spanish.

Slavery in the southern United States also contributed toward adoption because many black slaves who escaped their white owners fled to the Indian tribes. Some were made slaves by the Indians, but others were adopted, a practice particularly frequent among the Seminole of Florida, who married many former slaves.

Finally, tribes throughout the Americas made specific raids to capture people for adoption, apparently for no other reason than to replenish their population.

**Purposes of adoption.** Indians practiced adoption for various reasons. A common, perhaps principal, purpose, was to replace members of a family who had died or been killed. Women often adopted new husbands or children for this purpose. In some tribes, at least, replacement of dead kin was important not only for personal reasons, but also for magical ones: adoption of a person similar to the deceased was believed to restore the magical unity of the clan or family broken by death.

Some tribes apparently adopted large groups of people to replace wartime casualties, or, since adoption sometimes involved the relocation or scattering of a conquered tribe, to assure continued control over the conquered tribe. When the Iroquois adopted the Tuscarora, they did so not only to strengthen their own power but also to give succor to a tribe severely threatened by white colonization. The Iroquois believed that the Tuscarora had formerly been a part of their people.

**Process of adoption.** It is not clear how adoption was accomplished in all tribes or to what extent the process differed. Almost certainly in those tribes in which adoption had magical or religious importance, as among the Fox of the midwestern United States, it was marked by special ceremony. There were ceremonies also among the Iroquois, who had special laws governing adoption. An Iroquois might honor a friend with adoption by giving him a temporary name in a naming ceremony, sometimes accompanied by a short string of shells. Permanent adoptions of individuals or groups had to be confirmed by the Iroquois chiefs. As reported in one source, the chiefs announced their approval by saying, "Now you of our nation, be informed that such a person, such a family, or such families have ceased forever to bear their birth nation's name and have buried it in the depths of the earth. Henceforth let no one of our nation ever mention the original name or nation of their birth. To do so will be to hasten the end of our peace." Individuals or groups requesting adoption were required to give a string of shells to their chosen clan as a pledge. For male war captives, an ordeal was provided that they might prove themselves worthy of adoption: they had to run the gauntlet between parallel lines of women and children with whips. Those that fell were killed.

**Status.** The status given an adopted person or group varied and sometimes changed over time. Among the Iroquois, a male captive who was adopted was immediately given the same privileges and responsibilities as the dead warrior he replaced. The Iroquois believed the adoption ceremony accomplished a sort of legal transmutation by which the adoptee's blood was figuratively changed to Iroquoian blood, thereby giving him the rights of citizenship. Female captives in many tribes were adopted fully when they married. Being of a different race did not necessarily preclude an adoptee from enjoying full rights of citizenship in a tribe. There are reported instances of both whites and blacks assuming high office in North American tribes.

Adopting tribes did have mechanisms to control the amount of status given their new members, however. In the case of individuals, the position into which he was adopted in the kinship group and the age assigned him upon adoption — for example, whether he was adopted as son, uncle, or husband — gave him a carefully defined status. In the case of adopted tribes, the same types of controls could be used. For example, the Iroquois originally adopted the Tuscarora as a nursling still swathed in the cradleboard, which greatly restricted that tribe's political role in the confederacy. Subsequent resolutions passed in the council gradually advanced the Tuscarora's status through the positions of boy, young man, and warrior, until finally they were awarded status equal to that of the original five nations.

There may have been other variations in status (*e.g.*, people who were given some rights but still remained servants), but ethnographic descriptions are vague on this distinction. One variation apparently unique to South American tribes was that of temporary adoption. Among the Tupinamba, who were a tropical forest tribe, male captives were kept for months or years, only to be inevitably eaten in an elaborate tribal ceremony. During the interim, however, the captive was given nearly every freedom except that of escape. He lived with a Tupinamba family, farmed his own land, and frequently married into the tribe.

How adoptees accepted their status undoubtedly also varied. It was not uncommon for whites adopted by Indians to refuse repatriation when it was offered. Some had to be forced to leave their new homes, while others left gladly. Adopted Indians were apparently often not welcome in their former tribe and therefore may have felt compelled to make the best of their adoption.

**Adoption of Indians by whites.** Indians were adopted by whites, but little has been written about their lives in white society. One source states that Indians adopted into white families could never be fully accepted as equals, although they might be treated kindly. Thus they were adopted and educated by whites only to become missionaries and be sent back to their own people, and not to be made full members of white society.

**Changes over time.** Little is known about how adoption practices changed over time. In North America, it has been reported that once Indians discovered they could ransom white captives for whiskey, powder, or guns, they were less likely to adopt them. This has not been proven, however, and Indians did continue to adopt whites during periods of white-Indian warfare.

Differences in adoption practices were linked to the location of the tribes and perhaps to the period in history in which adoption occurred. Male war captives were often adopted by North American tribes, but in northern Middle America during the Aztec reign they were sacrificed. In South America east of the Andes they were frequently killed and eaten, and west of the Andes the Inca of Peru returned them to their homes. Furthermore, although some subjugated tribes played important roles in the Inca Empire, it is not known if the Inca adopted these tribes in the manner practiced by the Iroquois. Although the practice of adopting individuals was common throughout the Americas, there apparently was little, if any, adoption of whole tribes east of the Andes.

**Contemporary practices.** In the 1970s, information about contemporary adoption practices was sketchy. Since warfare between South American tribes living east of the Andes was reported in the mid-20th century, it is probable that those adoption practices which traditionally stemmed from war still continued. In North America, some adoption practices had changed, others had not. Among the Nez

Percé and the Sioux, for example, relatives continued to adopt children informally, in the traditional way, but children were also sheltered and placed for adoption, sometimes outside the tribe, by government agencies. The Nez Percé apparently no longer practiced the honorary adoption of adults from other tribes. The Sioux, on the other hand, still adopted adults who had helped the tribe or its members. Adoption might be with or without a name-giving and a ritual that included singing, dancing, and giving of presents to friends, visitors, or the needy.

Col. William Holland Thomas (Wil-usdi'), in 1858. Adopted white son of the Cherokee chief Yonaguska, Col. Thomas (1805-93) succeeded to the chieftainship following Yonaguska's death in April 1839.

In the mid-20th century in the United States, government agencies and private organizations were placing Indian children for adoption in non-Indian families. By the mid-1970s, the Bureau of Indian Affairs and several organizations and adoption agencies opposed cross-racial adoptions. Although surveys by the Association on American Indian Affairs, Inc., showed that approximately 25-35 percent of all Indian children were separated from their families and placed in foster homes, adoptive homes, or institutions, there was still dispute over the extent of the practice. The charge that many Indian children were being adopted out of their tribe and thus losing their cultural heritage led to Senate hearings in 1974.

**ADULTERY,** while widespread in Indian societies, was condoned by only a few tribes, with traditional punishment varying in severity from ostracism to death. The enforcing agency also varied from the tribal government to the family or the individual.

**Punishment.** The severest punishment was death. The Aztecs of the Valley of Mexico were well-known for their rigid enforcement of laws against adultery. Adulterous men and women had their heads crushed between two stones; the women were strangled first. The law applied to all people, noble or common. In the nearby state of Texcoco, King Nezahualpilli (*c*. 1500) had his young wife and three of her lovers killed; another Texcoco king applied the death penalty against his sons.

Less severe punishments were more common. In some Teton Sioux tribes, the offended husband cut off his wife's nose and demanded payment from the guilty male. Among the Aymara of South America, an adulterous man suffered mild disapproval and was sometimes divorced; an adulterous wife was beaten and often divorced. Among the Maracapana of north central Venezuela at the time of the Spanish Conquest, an adulterous woman was returned to her father. In some southern California tribes, a hubsand had a choice: he could either kill his wife or trade her for the adulterer's wife. A Gallinomero man, however, had to buy the wife he had seduced.

Perhaps the most complicated punishment existed among the peoples of the Northwest Coast area of North America. Here social rank was of great importance. If a man of low rank committed adultery with a married woman of high rank, there was a prescribed ritual to be followed: (1) the woman's clan selected and killed two people from the man's clan; (2) the man's clan offered one of their own number, equal in rank to the woman, to be killed; (3) the offended husband was showered with gifts by the adulterous man's clan; and (4) the adulterous man often had to work off his debt to his own clan by becoming a slave to them.

Punishment for adultery among the Inuit (Eskimo) was flexible. An Inuit husband might often give his wife permission to sleep with another man, but he did this to seal a business transaction. If she committed adultery without his permission, he might feel constrained to kill her lover to clear his own honor, or he might simply have a song duel or a wrestling contest with the other man. An Inuit wife whose husband committed an adultery that offended her might divorce him by moving back to her own family; if they would protect her from his wrath, she was free.

The Amaní, who lived in the Cordillera Central region of present-day Colombia in the 1500s, devised a unique punishment. The male lover was killed; the female adulteress was imprisoned in a dark room in the building where her wedding had taken place until every man in the village who so desired had intercourse with her. Then she too was killed, and both bodies were left to rot in an open place near the village. At specified times, an elder would stand near the bodies and moralize to the populace about the evils of adultery.

In some tribes, such as the Winnebago, the punishment was social ostracism: the men jeered at an adulterous wife and made sexual jokes about her. In other tribes, a much smaller number, there was no stigma attached to adultery. Pueblo Indian tribes in the

Southwest seem not to have minded adultery, as long as it was discreet. Noblewomen of the Mbayá of northern Argentina could have their lovers over without complaint from their husbands. In western Brazil, a Nambicuara adulterer simply left the village for a few days to avoid the ire of the husband.

**Enforcement and assignment of guilt.** Enforcement of the penalities was handled by different agencies in different tribes. With the Aztecs, it was a government matter. With the Amaní, the whole village participated. Northwest Coast tribes left enforcement to the families. Among the Dakota and the Inuit, punishment usually remained an individual matter executed by the parties involved.

In the majority of tribes, both men and women suffered some punishment for their deed. Among the Tupinamba of Brazil, however, the male lover usually went unpunished to avoid a blood feud, while the female might be beaten, divorced, or even killed. On the other hand, the Hoopa of California, who put out the guilty man's eye for his crime, let the woman go (she was considered not responsible); and adulterers among the Indians in Honduras might have their earrings ripped forcibly out while their female counterparts went free.

There are few studies documenting how attitudes toward adultery have changed among the Indians. It is known that an Aymara man who formerly would have killed his adulterous wife, in the mid-20th century beat and divorced her. Harsher punishments have disappeared in the United States where federal laws supersede tribal law. Among the northern Inuit and some South American tribes whose contact with their federal government is limited, traditional punishments probably remain to a greater degree.

**ADZ** is a cutting tool that has a thin blade, usually arched, placed at right angles to a handle and is primarily used for woodworking, particularly shaping and trimming lumber. Adzes are found most extensively and with the greatest degree of specialization in the Arctic and Northwest Coast regions of North

America; they were also used in Middle and South America. Specimens have been found which may be 2,500 years old.

**Uses.** Uses of the adz were multifold. Several tribes used the adz to shape and shave a variety of wood products. Along the Northwest Coast, products included totem poles, house planks, and wooden boxes. Some Canadian tribes used the adz, in conjunction with charring, to hollow out canoes from tree trunks. In central Mexico, the Aztecs used the adz for decorative carving and, on the Gulf Coast in the Panuco River region, the Huastec probably used adzes to shape wood for their houses. In South America, the Tehuelche of Patagonia used small hand-adzes for woodworking. Adzes were also used to cut meat, dig roots, dress hides, and hoe.

**Blades and handles.** Adz blades varied widely in shape, size, and material. The larger blades, in profile, were typically either arched or flat on the side facing the handle and convex on the other side. Smaller blades might be straight with a narrow cutting edge or curved with a picklike point. Prior to European contact, most blades were made out of such nonmetallic materials as stone, hornbone, shell, and ivory. Exceptions were copper blades of the Old Copper Culture, located in Minnesota, Wisconsin, and upper Michigan, probably before AD 700; prehistoric copper blades found on the north Chilean coast; and pre-Columbian bronze adzes used by the Huastec.

Adz shafts were as varied as the blades. Most handles employed some type of elbow bend to which the blade was attached, thus giving it the proper cutting angle. Some handle shapes were characteristic of particular regions. Handles shaped like an inverted U come from the Puget Sound area and others that look like modern handsaw handles are found along the Northwest Coast from Alaska to the Olympic Peninsula. Handles were made from stone, wood, elkhorn, or bone, and some have leather knuckle guards.

Attachment of the blade to the handle was often done by lashing; another method of attachment was socketing.

**Historical notes.** Two of the earliest known uses of the adz apparently were during the La Florida Phase (500 BC-0) in the Sierra Madre region of northeast Mexico and by the Early Kachemak Bay culture (*c.* AD 100-500) of Cook Inlet, Alaska. The greatest change in adz technology occurred as a result of European contact, which brought iron and steel blades into high demand because of their strength and their ability to maintain a sharp edge. Handles were still made traditionally, however, after the Europeans came, and bone and shell blades continued to be used.

In the mid-1970s, the availability of sawed and planed lumber had cut adz use tremendously in the Northwest Coast region. It is not known how widespread adz use was in other areas of the Americas. The Mosetene (Chimane) of the eastern slopes of the Bolivian Andes were reported still to be using stone adzes hafted on a forked limb about 1920 and, in 1937-38, at least one tribe of Quechua in the Department of Cuzco, Peru, apparently was using an adz-hoe (*tacila*) with an iron blade.

**AGED, STATUS OF.** In Indian society, the aged were most commonly honored until the onset of senility or physical debility, after which their status dropped and they were neglected. Blameless suicide, abandonment, and mercy killing were all practiced by certain American tribes. The opposite extreme was also present: homage and diligent care until the moment of natural death. Although cultural guidelines existed in many tribes, the actual status of any one aged person depended also upon such unique circumstances as the personality and accomplishments of the old one, the relationships he or she had established with family or younger friends, and seasonal changes in food supplies. Since the arrival of the white man, the traditional status of the aged has changed somewhat.

### Definition of "aged"

There was no specific point at which an Indian was considered "aged" by his tribe. Many tribes had puberty rites for their young, but none had old age rites. The line between middle age and old age was blurred, with each aging person gradually accumulating the functions of the aged — such as chief, teacher, shaman, charwoman, firetender — at an individual pace. For example, as he became less able to do strenuous work, a Hopi leader would spend less time following his flock and more time tending his orchard, until finally he retired indoors to spend his time weaving or making sandals. A Maya woman acquired seniority and power in the household hierarchy of her extended family as older women relinquished their power or died. A Navajo medicine man slowly built his reputation and power as he memorized more chants and curing rituals. Menopause, a physical development associated with women at old age, was significant only in some tribes. A Papago woman past the state of menopause, for example, became eligible to develop curing or rainmaking powers.

In the 1970s, there was some dispute between Indians living in the United States and the U.S. federal government over the chronological beginning of old age. After Congress established 60 years as the minimum age for the elderly to receive food under a government-sponsored nutrition program, the chairman of the Seminole Tribe of Florida requested that the age be lowered from 60 to 50 years for the Seminole Indians. He based his request on statistics indicating that Indians died younger, on the average, than whites. (U.S. Public Health Service data from 1962-67 showed that the average age of death for Indians was 53, while for whites it was 68.) As of 1975, adequate research to determine if Indians developed the physical symptoms of aging (such as arteriosclerosis) at a younger age than whites had not yet been conducted.

### Traditional status

There have been few cross-cultural studies on the aged. The major, and perhaps only, study is *The Role of the Aged in Primitive Society* (1945) by Leo W.

Simmons. The following discussion is based on Simmons' organizational plan.

**Assurance of food.** As the aged became weaker, they were less able to get their own food. They either found someone to give them food, or they starved. Cases have been reported of the aged being neglected to the point of starvation or being abandoned when they could no longer feed themselves. One report, from the mid-19th century, described an emaciated old man, a Gosiute from the Great Basin in west-central Utah, who had been abandoned by his family near a spring with only a sagebrush windbreak and a rabbitskin robe. Abandonment was not practiced by all tribes. Among those who did, abandonment seems to have been more of a desperate action in time of famine than a general policy.

When food was available, it was shared in several ways, generally without discrimination based on sex. For example, an aged Creek Indian was guaranteed food from any family in his clan. Chiefs of the Omaha, a tribe of the central Plains, were expected to feed the aged. Among the Navajo, both relatives and strangers fed the old, who reputedly could bewitch those who refused them food. Some tribes, generally those that relied on collecting, hunting, or fishing, shared food in community ceremonies. For example, the Bellacoola of British Columbia held generous feasts at which the old could eat as much as they wished. In tribes with highly organized governments and legal codes, such as the Inca of Peru, food was stored and distributed to the aged by government decree. As an added bonus, the aged in many tribes could eat food that was taboo for the young. An aged Omaha could crack animal bones and feast on the marrow with impunity, but a youth attempting the same thing was warned that he courted sprained ankles and a soft heart in battle.

**Property rights.** If the aged controlled property, they stood a much better chance of being cared for and honored. Property could be used to secure services from unrelated people; it could be stored against the time when the aged person could no longer perform services for the community; and it could be used to buy food if community food stocks were low.

Property might consist either of possessions or of knowledge. Aged Aleutian hunters possessed a wealth of skillfully handcrafted weapons, tool kits, and bidarkas (one-man skin boats). Aged Papago men dressed skins and aged women plaited baskets, selling their products for corn and beans. Magic charms were in great demand among the Delaware: old women sold love charms, and old men designed and sold elaborate hunting charms for skins and food. Knowledge alone was often valuable. Aged Crow story-tellers were rewarded with a feast. Old Aleutian women held exclusive rights to the healing ritual called "to hold the belly," during which they massaged the stomach of the afflicted person so as to rearrange the distressed parts. Hopi and Navajo medicine men were paid well for performing their often elaborate curing ceremonies.

According to Simmons, the aged were less likely to control property in tribes that subsisted by collecting, hunting, or fishing than in tribes that herded or farmed. In addition, women were less likely to own property than men.

**Prestige.** The aged in a great many tribes were accorded special prestige, which might take many forms. The oldest member of a Kwakiutl family was addressed with special respect as *watsiti*. Aged Iroquois women reputedly had the power to stop a war if they disliked it, and aged men in many tribes were chiefs or held important positions in council. Among the Aztec, only those more than 70 years of age were allowed to get drunk publicly. Aged Omaha women could sit with their feet stretched out in public, and aged Pomo women could smoke and even take sweat-baths with the men.

The source of this prestige was twofold. First, the aged provided real services to the tribe. They might raise children, do chores, manufacture clothing and utensils, or tell stories and lead games through the long, dark winter nights. Aged Hopi men were often the organizers and leaders of complicated ceremonies that were the focus of Hopi social and religious life. Aged Point Barrow Inuit men were believed able to "talk up" an east wind that would drive the ice offshore and let the whales come in close. Second, earned prestige was often reinforced by parental teachings. Delaware parents praised any child who helped an older person, and they justified the seniority system, with a mixture of philosophy and practical considerations. The old, they explained to their children, should be honored because (1) they had accumulated valuable wisdom; (2) the Great Spirit had specially honored the old with a long life and to dishonor them might provoke the Spirit's anger; and (3) they would one day be old themselves and would want the same type of honor from their own children. So effective was this inculcation that early chroniclers report cases in which parties of younger Delaware allowed themselves to be led several miles out of their way rather than contradict an older guide.

Prestige was subject to limitations, however. Once an early elderly Indian became physically or mentally weak, he might be ridiculed or neglected. In general, women had more trouble acquiring prestige than men.

**General activities.** The aged were not confined to any one status by cultural guidelines. There was room for initiative, skill, and hard work to enhance their prestige and security. Notable areas of success were in entertainment and healing. Other more mundane but nonetheless appreciated activities included tending the fire while the family slept and chewing leather to produce softness. According to Simmons, herding and farming tribes offered more opportunities for the old to perform economically profitable chores. Hopi men, for example, might continue to work in their orchards until they were too feeble to leave the house.

**Political and civil functions.** The aged were naturally suited to wield authority in both family and tribe. To govern well required experience, wisdom, and perhaps a little added benevolence from the Great Spirit, all of which the old reputedly possessed. In addition, governing was an activity of the mind, not of the body. Political authority as chiefs, councillors, or judges was held by the aged in virtually all tribes, although such power was not necessarily restricted to the aged, for being old was seldom the only criterion for assuming power. For example, upward movement in the Council of Elders of the Chinantec of Oaxaca, Mexico, who directed social and religious activities for the community, depended on wealth and proven ability in addition to age. Only rarely were the aged guaranteed a place in government solely by virtue of their years but, if they had ability, the field of politics was open. In some tribes there was an added bonus. Among the Haida, for example, the rule was "once a chief, always a chief." A chief who became senile might be succeeded, but he retained the title of chief and some of the honor.

Although women seldom held political power, they joined men in control of younger tribal members through life cycle rites such as baptism and those marking puberty, marriage, and death. Thus, aged Arawak women touched biting ants held in a special plaited frame to a young girl's forehead, hands, and feet to assure that she would grow up strong and enduring. Yahgan men initiated young boys by confinement that included a three-day fast, ice water baths, lectures in child raising and tribal lore, and the burning of wooden splinters thrust into the arms.

**Use of knowledge, magic, and religion.** Storing knowledge was an important function of the aged. They were often too weak to contribute food to the tribe and so had both the time and the motivation to learn the old history, legends, or crafts and to use their knowledge to entertain or instruct. Aged Inca men were retained by rulers to memorize their history and put it to song. Ojibwa elders learned and repeated the ancient creation myths and explained what happened after death. Aged Hopi women perfected the intricacies of pottery and basketmaking, and Hopi men remembered the old land boundaries, hunting rituals, and initation rites. Aged Navajo men diagnosed diseases and put together complicated rituals involving sand painting, chants, dances, and offerings for cures.

The aged were often respected counselors. It was

believed that their nearness to death made them honest, and their accumulated wisdom gave them a unique perspective on the daily puzzles of life. Some knowledge, however, they guarded jealously and might part with only on their deathbed.

Aged shamans were common to all tribes. According to Simmons, men were more likely than women to become shamans. Shamans could effect other people or the spirits through the use of songs, herbs, dances, and charms. In some cases, they reportedly could transfer power by a laying on of hands, touching with spit, or transferring lice from their bodies to another. Navajo shamans allegedly could cure the impotence of old men by magical manipulation involving a large root, but the cure could be used only once a year and as a side effect made the user fat. Aged Polar Inuit women reputedly left their bodies on "soul flights" and visited the beyond to intercede for dying tribespeople. Herding or farming societies tended to have more highly organized religions. Among the Hopi, for example, aged men sometimes headed secret societies and organized the recurring kiva ceremonials.

**Functions of the family.** Various ways existed for the aged to strengthen their security through family ties. Aged Navajo women reportedly maintained economic control over their family by keeping ownership of the family herd. Their daughters lived nearby, and their sons-in-law were expected to follow their orders. Aged Yahgan men often married young girls; among the Onondaga, older women were sometimes preferred as spouses because of their experience. Aged Pomo instructed young relatives in hunting and initiated them with a ceremony that involved sweating over a sacred fire. Crow parents customarily gave their firstborn to the paternal grandparents when the child was about one year old.

**Reactions to death.** There were five paths open to the aged approaching death: they might be cared for, commit suicide, be neglected, be abandoned, or be killed. Customs differed widely. Suicide was discouraged in some tribes, such as the Southern Cheyenne (who believed that suicides were barred from a happy afterlife), and condoned in others, such as the Polar Inuit. Abandonment might carry no stigma or, as among the Omaha, be feared. (The Omaha tried to leave their old with a growing cornfield and simple necessities to placate the Great Spirit.) In some tribes, dying a violent death assured a better afterlife. Aged Inuits who requested death were thought to go immediately to the highest heaven near the Aurora Borealis so they might play football with a walrus head with their companions. Such ceremonies could be elaborate: an Ojibwa elder who requested death was treated to a dog feast that included prayers, chanting, dancing, and smoking before he was tomahawked in the head by his son. Simmons estimates that killing was more frequent in harsh environments, but even there the practice was not inevitable or necessarily frequent.

**Contemporary conditions**

By the 1970s, acculturation had partially changed the status and treatment of the old in many tribes.

**Factors producing loss of status.** Erosion in status, the most common effect, was due to several factors. First, the government of the country in which the tribe lived often disrupted the complex social and political authority of the aged by instituting its own system of authority. For example, elders of the highland Chiapas Maya formerly had nearly complete civil and political authority based on a rigid seniority system and the control of land inheritance. By the 1970s, however, the Mexican government had appointed younger men to positions of authority in government, granting sons land over which their fathers had no control, and settling in departmental courts Indian disputes formerly judged by aged family members.

Second, many young Indians could buy products that formerly only aged Indians had the skill or time to make. For example, in the Aleutian village of Nikolski, by 1954 the store bought dory was fast replacing the bidarka, a hand crafted skin boat that formerly was a valuable possession of an aged hunter.

Third, there had been heavy pressure, perhaps most

severe in the United States, on the Indian to conform to the white man's economy, culture, and government, and this had reduced in value much of the knowledge stored by the aged. It was a much more pressing need for a young Indian to learn how to make the money necessary to buy a dory, or a rifle and ammunition, or clothes than to learn to build a bidarka, flake an arrowhead, or dress skins. But the old, strangers to the white man's money economy, could not supply the young with that information. Neither could they guide the tribe successfully through the complex bureaucracy of the white man's government. As a result, younger educated Indians began to take positions of authority on tribal councils. Information the old could supply, such as tribal history and mythology, was frequently judged unimportant by the white man's school system.

Fourth, the economic pressure exerted by off-reservation job opportunities frequently split an extended family into scattered nuclear families. This made it more difficult for the entire family to contribute to the support of the aged and thereby increased the chance that they would be neglected.

Fifth, increased intermarriage had sometimes led to the disruption of family ties, although not always to the harm of the aged. For example, among the Nez Percé, many of whose aged were well off because of land inheritance, the trend was toward smaller extended families; intermarriage had led to increased intra-family competition, and thus the aged were less willing to take in relatives.

**Factors preserving status.** Erosion of status was by no means complete, however. In some tribes, the traditional status of the aged was preserved. Navajo aged still functioned as medicine men, and in fact received social security benefits from the U.S. government as self-employed doctors. Hopi aged still organized and led ceremonial dances and chants. Among the highland Chiapas Maya, although much of the belief in ancestral ghosts was gone, the aged were still honored as those who could speak to the ghosts. There was even some evidence that the importance of the aged was being re-established in areas where it had been temporarily lost because of the shock of adjusting to white culture.

Several tribes, including the Nez Percé and the White Mountain Apache, sponsored language programs to teach the young how to speak the traditional language fluently, a skill the aged still possessed. In addition, both Indian and white ethnologists showed increasing interest in capturing and preserving the oral history of the tribes, a project for which the old were indispensable. It would appear that although information stored by the old was no longer necessary for the physical survival of the tribe and individuals, it might have become essential to the psychological survival of the Indian in a white society. Furthermore, the trend toward tribal councils composed of younger, more educated men might disappear when all ages achieved a more uniform level of education.

**Indian aged outside the tribe**

Another vital question is that of how the aged fared among the whites in the countries in which they lived in the 1970s. In the United States, the only country for which information was available, Indian spokesmen believed that Indian aged were underprivileged when compared to white aged. For example, it was alleged that government programs designed specifically for the aged, such as nutritional programs that supplied food, gave out products that were appropriate for whites but not for Indians because the native people were unfamiliar with them. Indians were not able to take full advantage of available programs for several reasons, including transportation and language difficulties. Also, government aid remained largely inaccessible to aged Indians because they did not know it existed.

By 1975, scattered and uncoordinated efforts either to investigate or to act upon the Indian claims were in progress in the U.S. government. The Indian Health Service had begun a project to discover whether or not special programs designed for the Indian aged were needed. Two Indian organizations, the California

Rural Indian Health Board and the United Southeastern Tribes Intertribal Council, had contracted with the Indian Health Service to deliver health care, thus assuring its cultural acceptability. And, at least four low-budget projects brought needed services, such as in-home aid and transportation, to some Indian aged. There was, however, still no central information source established to monitor all programs affecting Indian aged. This was an improvement given primary importance by the Indian Advisory Council to the Senate Special Committee on Aging in 1971, but some government administrators considered it pointless because of the great regional variations in the programs offered.

SCOTT BECKETT

**AGRICULTURE.** One of the greatest accomplishments of the Indians of the Americas is their domestication of plants and their development of agriculture. In terms of modern world food production, any list of the dozen most used plants would include corn (maize), potatoes, beans, tobacco, and squashes — all of which are Indian domesticates. In terms of U.S. food production, corn, peanuts, and tobacco lead all the rest and again are Indian domesticates.

Perhaps as remarkable as the great modern use of Indian crops is the large number of plants (about 300) that the ancient Indians changed genetically from relatively unimportant wild plants to useful domesticates used in agriculture. These domesticates are man-made and as such are artifacts; the domestication of each plant is, in fact, an invention of a now very productive artifact. It might well be said that the greatest inventions of the Indians are in the field of agriculture. Many of these inventions were made in very ancient times — in fact, almost as early as the earliest domestications appeared in the Old World. Although archaeological knowledge of the origin and spread of the New World domesticates or cultivars is woefully inadequate, enough information has been accumulated to plot, at least in a preliminary way, the outline of some of their histories.

Further discussion requires the definition of the terms "domesticate" and "cultivar." A domesticate is a plant that has been consciously or unconsciously changed by man so that it is genetically unlike its wild ancestor. A cultivar may be defined as a plant changed consciously or unconsciously by man so that it grows or is planted in a new ecosystem or environment unlike that of its wild ancestor; although the plant may be changed morphologically, it usually has not been changed genetically. Often, it is difficult to distinguish one from the other with archaeological specimens, but the above classifications have considerable usefulness in understanding the process of plant domestication and ultimately of agriculture.

Definition of the terms "horticulture" and "agriculture" is also useful. Horticulture is an activity with emphasis on the planting of individual domesticates or cultivars in relatively limited plots or gardens (*hortus*, "garden" in Latin). Agriculture is an activity emphasizing the planting or sowing of relatively large numbers of a domesticate or cultivar in relatively large plots or fields (*ager*, "field" in Latin). Although ancient plant remains may yield dated information about domesticates or cultivars, they rarely reveal whether the inhabitants were practicing horticulture or agriculture.

## ORIGIN AND SPREAD OF NEW WORLD PLANTS

The origin and spread of Indian domesticates and cultivars during prehistoric times will be considered under two main heads, those of the Mesoamerican and Andean centers, with only brief mention being made of such sub-centers as the eastern part of the present-day United States and the South American lowlands.

### Mesoamerican domesticates and cultivars

In Mesoamerica, archaeological and botanical data have provided information on the origin and spread of three major kinds of crops — corn, four kinds of beans, and four kinds of cucurbits. Limited evidence is also available on the early domestication of the avocado, amaranth, agave, chili, prickly pear, sapote, and others, which represent a small proportion of the domesticates utilized in the region (*see* Table 1).

**Corn.** Of all the domesticated plants, corn was, and continues to be, the most important Indian food plant since prehistoric times. Although data on its origin and spread is far from complete, enough is available to permit tentative discussion. The pollen studies by William Sears and others on specimens from the Valley of Mexico seem to demonstrate that corn (*Zea mays*) was a native of highland Mexico during Pleistocene times. Studies of pollen from Oaxaca, Mexico, and corn studies in Tehuacán, Mexico, also indicate that corn (probably wild) was present in these regions between 8000 and 5000 BC, even though it seems not to have been much utilized as a food nor to have been planted.

The earliest known archaeological evidence of the actual use of corn as a food comes from Tehuacán and dates to about 5000 BC. Interpretations of these earliest cobs differ. Paul Mangelsdorf classifies all the earliest cobs as wild; Walton Galinat classifies only six or eight of these cobs having characteristics more like teosinte (a large animal grass sometimes considered the progenitor of corn) as wild; and the George Beadle group believes that none of these cobs are wild and that all of this earliest corn was derived from wild teosinte. So far, there is no archaeological or genetic evidence for the last hypothesis. More study is necessary, but both the Galinat and the Mangelsdorf interpretations seem to indicate that some wild corn was being utilized in Tehuacán by 5000 BC and both classify a few cobs, dated between 5000 and 4100 BC as Early Cultivated. Whether these are, in fact, cultivars or domesticates is difficult to determine exactly. The weight of genetic evidence, however, suggests the latter.

Certainly, by 3500 BC in the Tehuacán Valley, there were domesticates in the form of examples of the races Nal-tel and Chapalote and a group called Tripsacoid, which have been interpreted as crosses of teosinte with early corn. It might be added that cob examples of Nal-tel occur in Oaxaca at about the same time, while a few grains of pollen in Oaxaca and two pollen grains at Tlapacoya in the Valley of Mexico may indicate the use of corn by man in the early general period from 5000 to 4000 BC. To the north, Chapalote and Nal-tel seem to have arrived in Tamaulipas between 3000 and 2000 BC, while in Swallow Cave at Durango, Mexico, and possibly Dark Cave at Sonora, Mexico, some examples of Chapalote may be of this general time period. From Bat Cave in southern New Mexico, the earliest corn, roughly dating between 1500 and 500 BC, seems to be of this general Chapalote race.

Although evidence of corn from the Formative Stage of Mesoamerica during this general time period is very incomplete, there is a suggestion that both Nal-tel and Chapalote had spread over most of the area by this time. There is also some suggestion from San Marcos Cave in Tehuacán, as well as in the Tamaulipas caves, that the major development of the numerous corn races of Mexico occurred in this period or shortly thereafter. Although the genetic studies and breeding of corn at the Rockefeller Foundation have suggested how each one of the races evolved, there was little archaeological evidence available by the mid-1970s to date or document such developments.

There is evidence that new races of corn were entering the North American Southwest by the beginning of the Christian era or shortly thereafter, and that new races were evolving there. Exactly which varieties spread to the eastern region of what is now the United States is difficult to determine. There is some evidence, however, that a type of corn was being utilized, albeit in small amounts, in what is now Missouri, Kentucky, and other parts of the Midwest by the beginning of the first century AD, plus or minus 400 years. Archaeological evidence for the development of the various eastern races of corn, such as Northern Flints, is almost totally lacking, but some of it suggests that Northern Dents were diffusing down the Missouri River by AD 1000, while corn spread to the northeastern U.S. and southeastern Canada at about the same time. Some corn from the Alto Focus of eastern Texas (AD 700-1000) bears a resemblance to Nal-tel of northeastern Mexico and hints of another intrusion into the eastern U.S. that could have stimulated further developments. This matter, like all Eastern Woodland corn developments, needs considerably more study.

While study of the spread of corn north of its Mesoamerican center is woefully inadequate, knowledge of the southward diffusion is even more sparse. Pollen evidence from Chiapas, Mexico, and the Guatemala highlands suggests that corn did not arrive before 3500 BC. Rather incomplete pollen studies also suggest that corn did not appear in the Maya lowlands until about 2000 BC. A pollen profile from the Panama region and a few cobs from caves in the Ayacucho region of Peru suggest that corn arrived in these regions about 3000 BC. Although the number of adequately dated specimens from Ayacucho is small, there is a suggestion that the early cobs are of the Ayacucho race, which might be derived from Mexican Tripsacoid Chapalote races, and that these may have developed into the Confite and Morocho primitive races of Peru.

Further studies of Peruvian corn suggest that the multitude of Peruvian corn races developed out of Confite and/or Morocho. These early Peruvian races, however, did not arrive on the Peruvian coast or in northern Chile and Argentina until about 2000 to 1000 BC. There are also hints from Venezuela and Colombia, based upon the use of metates (stones used for grinding grain), that corn did not appear in the Tropical Lowlands until after that time period. All this South American data is woefully inadequate, however, and it will take considerable investigation to turn these speculations into hard archaeological "fact."

The spread of corn into the Old World after the time of Columbus is somewhat better documented. Two major early thrusts seem to have taken place in the 16th century — one into the Gold Coast region of Africa, perhaps from Brazil, and the other from western Mexico across the Pacific into the Philippines and China. During the 17th century, corn spread into most of the coastal regions of West Africa, as well as into the Congo River Basin, while in the following two centuries the plant became utilized across the continent to the east coast, Ethiopia, and the Nile Valley. Today it is a major African food staple. In Southeast Asia the spread was slightly slower. Although corn was an important source of food in coastal China and the islands of the southwest Pacific by the 1600s and 1700s, it did not spread inland into China or to Southeast Asia, India, or Australia until the 19th century. Corn never has become a major domesticate in Europe or the Near East, although it probably spread from the Caribbean into a few spots in these areas in the 16th century. During the 17th century it became utilized in a few regions of the Mediterranean, eastern Europe, and the Balkans, but not until the following century did it move mainly as cattle feed into the Near East, the rest of Europe, and the southern Russian and southwestern Siberian plains.

**Beans.** The second most common New World plant is the common bean, *Phaseolus vulgaris*. Botanists have suggested two possible wild ancestors for this plant, one in Guatemala and the other in South America. In the mid-1970s there was some slim evidence to indicate that they were domesticated independently and some suggestion of the time period of their domestication. In Mesoamerica, fully domesticated common beans occurred in southwest Tamaulipas in the Ocampo Phase (4000-2300 BC). In Tehuacán, a single pod was identified in a layer dated at 4200 to 4000 BC. It would seem that beans were domesticated in Mexico well before 4000 BC. They were probably not first domesticated in Tehuacán, Tamaulipas, or Oaxaca but in some region further south, because they do not appear in the southwestern U.S. until just before the first century AD in Tularosa Cave, New Mexico. A few Formative Period remains of beans suggest that their use was widespread in Mexico at least by 1000 BC.

When common beans arrived in the Eastern Woodlands is more difficult to determine. Some specimens from the Hopewellian Renner site in northwestern

**Table1: Cultivated and Domesticated Plants of Mesoamerica**

| common name | Latin name |
|---|---|
| **1. Cultivated for Edible Seeds** | |
| Amaranth | *Amaranthus cruentus* |
| Amaranth | *Amaranthus leucoarpus* |
| Apazote | *Chenopodium nuttalliae* |
| Bean, common | *Phaseolus vulgaris* |
| Bean, lima | *Phaseolus lunatus* |
| Bean, runner | *Phaseolus coccineus* |
| Bean, tepary | *Phaseolus acutifolius* |
| Bean, jack | *Canavalia ensiformis* |
| Chia | *Salvia hispanica* |
| Chia grande | *Hyptis suaveolens* |
| Maize | *Zea mays* |
| Panic grass | *Panicum sonorum* |
| Peanut | *Arachis hypogaea* |
| Sunflower | *Helianthus annuus* |
| **2. Cultivated for Edible Roots or Tubers** | |
| Coyolxóchitl | *Bomarea edulis* |
| Manioc | *Manihot dulcis* |
| Manioc* | *Manihot esculenta* |
| Potato* | *Solanum tuberosum* |
| Sweet potato* | *Ipomoea batatas* |
| Yam bean | *Pachyrrhizus erosus* |
| **3. Edible Fruits** | |
| Anona | *Annona purpurea* |
| Anona | *Annona glabra* |
| Bullock's-heart | *Annona reticulata* |
| Chayote | *Sechium edule* |
| Cherimoya* | *Annona cherimolia* |
| Llama | *Annona diversifolia* |
| Soursop | *Annona muricata* |
| Sweetsop | *Annona squamosa* |
| Avocado | *Persea americana* |
| Avocado | *Persea schiedeana* |
| Caujilote | *Parmentiera edulis* |
| Capulin cherry | *Prunus serotina* |
| Tejocote | *Crataegus pubescens* |
| Cashew* | *Anacardium occidentale* |
| Hog plum | *Spondias mombin* |
| Jocote | *Spondias purpurea* |
| Coconut* | *Cocos nicifera* |
| Elderberry | *Sambucus mexicana* |
| Guava | *Psidium guajava* |
| Guayabilla | *Psidium sartorianum* |
| Mamey colorado | *Calocarpum mammosum* |
| Sapote, green | *Calocarpum viride* |
| Sapote, yellow | *Pouteria campechiana* |
| Sapodilla | *Manikara zapotilla* |
| Squash, warty | *Cucurbita moschata* |

| common name | Latin name |
|---|---|
| Squash, summer | *Cucurbita pepo* |
| Squash, cashaw | *Cucurbita mixta* |
| Squash | *Cucurbita ficifolia* |
| Matasano | *Casimiroa sapota* |
| Sapote, white | *Casimiroa edulis* |
| Nance | *Byrsonima crassifolia* |
| Papaya | *Carica papaya* |
| Pineapple* | *Ananas comosus* |
| Pitahaya | *Hylocereus undatus* |
| Prickly pear | *Opuntia streptacantha* |
| Prickly pear | *Opuntia megacantha* |
| Prickly pear | *Opuntia ficus-indica* |
| Ramon | *Brosimum alicastrum* |
| Sapote, black | *Diospyros ebenaster* |
| **4. Pot Herbs and Other Vegetables** | |
| Chaya | *Cnidosculus chayamansa* |
| Chipilín | *Crotalaria longirostrata* |
| Pacaya | *Chamaedorea wendlandiana* |
| Tepejilote | *Chamaedorea tepejilote* |
| Tomato | *Lycopersicon esculentum* |
| Tomato, husk | *Physalis ixocarpa* |
| Yucca | *Yucca elephantipes* |
| **5. Condiments and Other Flavoring** | |
| Chili pepper | *Capsicum annuum* |
| Chili pepper | *Capsicum frutescens* |
| Vanilla | *Vanilla planifolia* |
| **6. Stimulants and Narcotics** | |
| Cacao | *Theobroma cacao* |
| Cacao | *Theobroma angustifolium* |
| Cacao | *Theobroma bicolor* |
| Maguey | *Agave atrovirens* |
| Maguey | *Agave latissima* |
| Maguey | *Agave mapisaga* |
| Maguey | *Nicotiana rustica* |
| Tobacco* | *Nicotiana tabacum* |
| **7. Fiber Plants** | |
| Cotton | *Gossypium hirsutum* |
| Henequen | *Agave fourcroydes* |
| Maguey | *Agave atrovirens* |
| Maguey | *Agave tequilana* |
| Sisal | *Agave sisalana* |
| **8. Dye Plants** | |
| Achiote* | *Bixa orellana* |
| Indigo | *Indigofera suffruticosa* |
| **9. Cultivated for Its Resin** | |
| Copal | *Protium copal* |
| **10. Cultivated as Hosts for Wax and Cochineal Insects** | |
| Piñoncillo | *Jatropha curcas* |
| Cochineal cactus | *Nopalea cochenillifera* |

| common name | Latin name |
|---|---|
| **11. Cultivated Fruits Used as Utensils** | |
| Bottle gourd | *Lagenaria siceraria* |
| Calabash | *Crescentia cujete* |
| **12. Cultivated Plants Used for Living Fences or Construction** | |
| Dahlia | *Dahlia lehmannii* |
| Pitayo | *Pachycereus emarginatus* |
| Yucca | *Yucca elephantipes* |
| Piñoncillo | *Jatropha curcas* |
| **13. Ornamental Plants** | |
| Cypress | *Taxodium mucronatum* |
| Dahlia | *Dahlia coccinea* |
| Dahlia | *Dahlia excelsa* |
| Dahlia | *Dahlia lehmannii* |
| Dahlia | *Dahlia pinnata* |
| Marigold | *Tagetes erecta* |
| Marigold | *Tagetes patula* |
| Tiger flower | *Tigridia pavonia* |
| Tuberose | *Polianthes tuberosa* |

**Probably not native to Mesoamerica.*

Missouri that might be dated at just after the beginning of the Christian era have been tentatively identified as *Phaseolus vulgaris*. Remains of beans in more easterly Hopewellian sites of this time period, however, are lacking. More reliable evidence of the use of beans in the Midwest comes from the Mississippian site, roughly after AD 700. They do not appear in the Northeast until Owasco times (*c.* AD 1000), but they do seem to have spread down the Missouri into the Plains area just slightly earlier.

The above-mentioned common beans are all elongate varieties and seem to have had a separate domestication and different spread from the more rounded varieties of South America. The earliest of the South American group found so far comes from levels of Guitarrero Cave of the Callejón de Huaylas in highland Peru, dated between 6000 and 5000 BC. Some beans from Ayacucho, slightly farther south in the Peruvian Andes, have been dated at 4000-3000 BC. The spread of beans from these earlier centers to other parts of South America is not well documented, but they do not appear to have arrived on the Peruvian coast until between 2000 and 1000 BC. When they spread through the western Andes and into the tropical lowlands, as well as northern Chile and Argentina, is even less well known, although some experts surmise that the movement occurred in the last two millenia before the European discovery of America.

The spread of beans into the Old World after that time is not quite as well documented as is the spread of corn and seems to be slightly different. Again, there appears to have been an early thrust across the Pacific from western Mexico in the 16th century, but documentation of the spread of this plant is made difficult because of the linguistic confusion of terms for Old World and New World beans. The other major thrust was out of the New World gulf area to the Mediterranean parts of Europe, Africa, and the Near East during the 16th and 17th centuries and later on to the Near East as well as Europe, the latter being somewhat limited by climatic restrictions.

Three other species of beans were grown in Mexico, but knowledge of their origin and spread is less well documented archaeologically. Wild runner beans (*Phaseolus coccineus*) have been found in early archaeological contexts in both Tamaulipas (1700-1500 BC) and Oaxaca (8000-7000 BC), but domesticated runner beans did not appear until the Late Formative in Tehuacán (300 BC). Their occurrence in northern Mexico and the southwestern U.S. in the third to fifth centuries AD suggests a slow spread northward, while modern distribution studies suggest they may have been domesticated south of Tehuacán in or before Formative times. Knowledge of the origin and spread of tepary beans (*Phaseolus acutifolius*) is equally limited, but a large number of seeds did occur in a cave in the Tehuacán Valley in a stratum that dates to about 3000 BC. Other dated specimens come mainly from the southwestern U.S. and are only about 1,000 years old. Not only was the spread of these two bean types limited to the New World, but neither one has been used to any significant degree in the Old World.

The final member of the bean family — lima beans (*Phaseolus lunatus*) — is used to some extent in the

Old World and was an important group in both Mesoamerica and the Andean area. Knowledge of its origin and spread, however, is not complete. In Mexico, the earliest lima beans — a small variety often called sieva beans — did not occur in Tehuacán, Tamaulipas, or Yucatán much before AD 1000, and they are only slightly more recent in the southwestern U.S. This domestication seems to have been independent of that in the Andean area, where some domesticated large varieties of lima beans occur in the Callejón de Huaylas between 5000 and 4000 BC. These seem to have spread to coastal regions by 2500 BC and the rest of the area at still later dates.

**Cucurbits.** The other major group of domesticates in Mesoamerica were the cucurbits — the pumpkin (*Cucurbita pepo*), warty squash (*Cucurbita moschata*), cashaw squash (*Cucurbita mixta*), and the gourd (*Lagenaria siceraria*). *Cucurbita mixta,* on the basis of peduncle specimens, was definitely domesticated in Tehuacán by 3000 BC, and domesticated seeds of the plant possibly occurred there as early as 5500 BC. Probably, it had diffused through most of Mexico by the beginning of the Christian era and was in Tamaulipas a few centuries later. It does not seem to have arrived in the U.S. Southwest until about AD 1000.

Pumpkins seem to have had a longer history and a wider distribution, but the place of their origin is unknown. Archaeologically, pumpkin seeds occur very early in Mesoamerica, between 7000 and 5500 BC in Tamaulipas, before 8000 BC in Oaxaca, and possibly at 5200 BC in Tehuacán. The earliest specimens that were definitely domesticated are the six peduncles from Tamaulipas dated between 2300 and 1900 BC. Pumpkins appear in the Southwest in preceramic levels at Bat Cave and Tularosa Cave at about 1000-500 BC; by that time they were probably widespread in Mesoamerica and were present in the midwestern U.S. Their spread down the Missouri River into the Great Plains, as well as into the Northeast Woodlands, may not have occurred until AD 1000.

The history of warty squash (*Cucurbita moschata*)

is even less clear. A possible early peduncle occurred in Tehuacán by about 3300 BC, and many specimens dating from 4000 to 2500 BC have been found in coastal Peru. Whether these were independent inventions or whether both diffused out from a single unknown center is difficult to determine. Warty squash appeared in Tamaulipas by 1500 BC and may have spread all over Mesoamerica by that time. There is some evidence that it arrived in the Southwest by the first century AD, but when or if it arrived in the southeastern U.S. is unknown. Archaeologists are also ignorant of the spread of warty squash to other parts of South America.

Even more confusing is the problem of the origin and spread of the gourd. It is found in very early (before 7000 BC) contexts in highland Peru and Mesoamerica, but botanists report that closely related wild species are native to Africa. Further, the origin and spread of New World cucurbits in the Old World is almost totally unknown.

**Other plants.** Although other domesticates or cultivars have been found in archaeological contexts in Mesoamerica, little information about their histories is available. Locally utilized Mesoamerican fruits such as black sapotes (*Diospyros digyna*), white sapotes (*Casimiroa edulis*), and chupandilla (*Cyrtocarpa procera*) occur in Tehuacán at about 4000 BC, while coyol (*Acrocomia mexicana*), ciruela (*Spondius mombin*), and tree gourds (*Crescentia cujete*) were found in layers that date just before the beginning of the Christian era. Pollen profiles in Oaxaca and the Valley of Mexico, as well as seeds from Tamaulipas and Tehuacán, hint that amaranthus may have been planted well before 5000 BC. Archaeological remains of plants later utilized to some extent in the Old World have also been found; they include the avocado (*Persea americana*), chili (*Capsicum annuum*), agave, and prickly pear (*Opuntia*), all possibly domesticated by 6000 BC. Jitomate, or ground cherry, in Tehuacán and chocolate (possibly cacao) in the Maya region may have been planted before the first century AD. From very late prehistoric levels in Tamaulipas, there is some rather poorly documented evidence that tobacco and indigo blue were being utilized. Guava and peanuts dated at just before the Christian era and cotton dated at about 2500 BC — all of which may have been originally domesticated in the Andean center — were uncovered in sites in the Tehuacán Valley. Also, deposits in Tamaulipas dated between AD 100 and 900 have yielded sunflower seeds, a crop that became important in the European economy during the 20th century.

### Eastern Woodlands domesticates and cultivars

Sunflowers (*Helianthus annuum*) may have spread into Mesoamerica from the U.S. Southwest, for they occur in deposits in Bat Cave dated at about 1000 BC. There are hints that this plant may have been originally domesticated in the midwestern U.S. This points to the possibility of a secondary area of plant domestication in North America, specifically in the Midwest. Re-analysis of older, poorly excavated caves in Kentucky and Arkansas, and recent excavations in central

**Table 2: Cultivated and Domesticated Plants of the Eastern U.S.**

| common name | Latin name |
|---|---|
| **1. Cultivated for the Edible Seeds** | |
| Beans, common | *Phaseolus vulgaris* |
| Corn | *Zea mays* |
| Canary grass | *Phalaris* sp. |
| Knotweed | *Polygonum* |
| Lamb's quarter | *Chenopodium* sp. |
| Pigweed | *Amaranthus* sp. |
| Sunflower | *Helianthus annuum* |
| Ragweed | *Ambrosia trifida* |
| **2. Edible Fruits** | |
| Marshelder | *Iva* sp. |
| Pumpkin | *Cucurbita pepo* |
| Squash, warty | *Cucurbita moschata* |
| **3. Fruits Used as Containers** | |
| Gourd | *Lagenaria siceraria* |
| **4. Narcotics** | |
| Tobacco | *Nicotiana* sp. |

Illinois, give increasing evidence that a number of local cultivars or domesticates — such as marshelder (*Iva* sp.), lamb's quarter (*Chenopodium* sp.), pigweed (*Amaranthus* sp.), knotweed (*Polygonum* sp.), canary grass (*Phalaris* sp.), and giant ragweed (*Ambrosia trifida*) were being planted between 1000 and 150 BC. With the exception of the sunflower, none of these seems to have spread out of the Eastern Woodlands, nor did they affect European economies.

### Andean domesticates and cultivars

The list of the Andean domesticates and cultivars is every bit as impressive as that of the Mesoamerican centers. Many more archaeologically preserved plant remains have been found in Peru than in Mesoamerica, most of them from the dry Peruvian Pacific coast. Few of them appear to have been originally domesticated in the coastal area, and samples from the crucial highland, montane, or selva regions are sadly lacking. The origin and spread of important Andean crops such as corn, common beans, lima beans, and gourds have already been discussed to some extent in the section on Mesoamerica, thus the discussion of Andean cultivars and domesticates will be relatively brief.

**The potato.** Of the various domesticates of the Andes, one that is very important in modern world economy is the potato (*Solanum tuberosum*). While its origin and prehistoric spread is not well documented, its diffusion after European contact has been well plotted. The potato appears to have spread out from South America to northern Italy in the 16th century and through France and Germany to the British Isles in the following century. Then, in the 18th century, the potato spread to eastern North America, Mexico, and the Caribbean, as well as to most of Europe and a few islands in the southeastern Pacific. In the 19th century the potato spread through most of Asia and Africa, the United States, and the southeastern coastal region of South America.

Botanists suggest that the potato was domesticated in highland southern Peru near the modern Bolivian border. This hypothesis is confirmed by fragments in human feces found in association with hoes and majanas in the Chihua Phase (4000-3000 BC) in Ayacucho. The presence of hoes in many of the latest preceramic manifestations (3000-1700 BC) in the highlands of central Peru suggest that the use of potatoes was widespread at that time, while actual specimens of potatoes appear in the Peruvian coast in Chavinoid times (1000-500 BC). Perhaps this was the period during which this domesticate spread throughout the Andean area.

**The sweet potato.** Another Andean root crop that has become a widespread world crop is the sweet potato (*Ipomoea batatas*). Some botanists, on the basis of the distribution of wild relatives of the sweet potato, suggest that it may have been twice domesticated — in the islands of the southwestern Pacific and in the lowland areas of Peru. The occurrence, however, of sweet potatoes in archaeological contexts dated about 1000 BC from the coast of Peru and the lack of definite evidence of archaeological sweet potatoes in the South Pacific may indicate a diffusion from Peru across the Pacific in either prehistoric or early historic times. Be that as it may, the sweet potato became widespread in Southeast Asia, India, and China by the 17th century. It may also have spread out of the Andean area in late prehistoric times or the 16th century into Brazil, Venezuela, Colombia, Central America, and, perhaps, the Antilles. The sweet potato seems to have crossed the Atlantic in the 16th century via two routes: one into the Gold Coast of Africa and then, during the next two centuries, into most of South Africa; the other into the western Mediterranean area and then into North Africa, the Near East, and southern Europe by the 19th century.

**Coca, lucuma, and quinoa.** The other three Andean crops for which some archaeological distributional evidence is available are coca (*Erythroxylon coca*), lucuma (*Lucuma bifera*), and quinoa (*Chenopodium quinoa*), none of which became important in Old World subsistence systems. Although wild relatives of lucuma and coca exist in the lowlands of eastern Peru, the earliest remains uncovered by the mid-1970s occurred in Ayacucho between 4000 and 3000 BC. These plants did not occur in the central Peruvian coast until 2100 to 1750 BC. Quinoa occurred in highland Ayacucho between 5500 and 4200 BC, while pollen profiles suggest that it appeared just as early in the Junin area. Specimens from coastal Peru, Chile, and highland Argentina suggest that this plant had spread throughout the Andean area by 1000 BC.

**Other plants.** Numerous other plant remains occur in archaeological contexts in Peru, but knowledge of their origin and spread is limited. A listing of some of them, however, indicates the relative antiquity of plant domestication and cultivation in this nuclear area. Achiote (*Bixa orellana*) and *Cucurbita crescentia,* both lowland plants, occurred in the highlands by about 5000 BC, while achira (*Canna edulis*) and pacae (*Inga feuillei*) occurred in the Peruvian highlands and on the coast by 2000 BC. Canavalia beans (*Canavalia plagiosperma*), cotton (*Gossypium barbadense*), guava (*Psidium guajava*), peppers (*Capsicum frutescents*), and galactia occurred on the coast by 2500 to 2000 BC, while peanuts (*Arachis hypogaea*) appeared only slightly later. Further, between 1500 BC and the beginning of the Christian era, pepino (*Solanum muricatum*), avocado (*Persea americana*), and two kinds of squashes (*Cucurbita moschata* and *C. ficifolia*) occurred on the coast, to be followed by jicama (*Ipomoea jicama*), another squash (*Cucurbita maxima*), higarroba (*Prosopis juliflora*), caigua (*Cyclanthera pedata*), cherimoya (*Annona cherimolia*), ciruela de fraile (*Bunchosia armeniaca*), guanábana or soursop (*Annona muricata*), granadilla (*Passiflora*), pineapple (*Ananas comosus*), coconut (*Cocos nucifera*), tumbo (*Passiflora mollissima*), tuna (*Cactus*), anu (*Tropaeoliem tuberosum*), canihua (*C. pallidicaule*), lupine (*Lupinus mutabilis*), oca (*Oxalis tuberosa*), and ullucu (*Ullucus tuberosus*) in the period from AD 1 to 1000.

| common name | Latin name |
|---|---|
| **1. Cultivated for Edible Seeds** | |
| Bean, common | *Phaseolus vulgaris* |
| Bean, lima | *Phaseolus lunatus* |
| Bean, jack | *Canavalia ensiformis* |
| Cacao | *Theobroma cacao* |
| Castor bean and oil | *Ricinus communis* |
| Corn | *Zea mays* |
| Inga | *Inga feuillei* |
| Peanut | *Arachis hypogaea* |
| **2. Cultivated for Edible Roots** | |
| Arracacha | *Arracacia xanththarrhiza* |
| Arrowroot | *Maranta arundinacea* |
| Cacabo | *Xanthosoma* sp. |
| Cassava, sweet | *Manihot utilissima* |
| Cassava, bitter | *Manihot esculenta* |
| Hualusa | *Colocasia esculenta* |
| Potato, sweet | *Ipomoea batatus* |
| Yam | *Dioscorea* sp. |
| Xantia | *Xanthosoma sagittifolium* |
| **3. Edible Fruits** | |
| Avocado | *Persea americana* |
| Caimito | *Chrysophyllum cainito* |
| Frutus de lobl | *Solanum lycocarpum* |
| Guava | *Psidium guajava* |
| Lumuma | *Lucuma obovata* |
| Mamona | *Ricinus communis* |
| Papaya | *Carica papaya* |
| Pepion | *Solanum muricatum* |
| Pineapple | *Ananas comosus* |
| Plantin | *Musa paradisiaca* |
| Sapilla | *Cucurbita maxima* |
| Surinum cherry | *Eugenia unifora* |
| Squash, warty | *Cucurbita moschata* |
| **4. Condiments** | |
| Aji | *Capsicum* sp. |
| **5. Stimulants and Narcotics** | |
| Barbasco | *Lonchocarpus nicou* |
| Coca | *Erythroxylon coca* |
| Fish poison | *Clebadium vargasii* |
| Nissolia | *Nissolia* sp. |
| Tephrosia | *Tephrosia toxicaria* |
| Tobacco | *Nicotina tabacum* |
| **6. Fiber Plants** | |
| Agave | *Agave* sp. |
| Bacaiava palm | *Acrocomia* sp. |
| Cotton | *Gossypium barbadense* |
| Cotton | *Gossypium hirsutum* |
| Pupunha palm | *Guilielma gasipaes* |
| Razor grass | *Scleria* sp. |

| common name | Latin name |
|---|---|
| **7. Dye Plants** | |
| Achiote | *Bixa orellana* |
| Genipa | *Genipa americana* |
| **8. Cultivated for Resin** | |
| Mangabeira | *Hancornia speciosa* |
| **9. Cultivated Fruits Used as Ute** | |
| Gourd | *Lageneria siceraria* |
| Tree gourd | *Crescentia cujete* |
| **10. Plants Used for Tools or Construction** | |
| Chonta palm | *Guilielma gasipaes* |
| Reeds | *Arundo conax* |
| Uba cane | *Gynerium sagittatum* |
| **11. Plants Used for Beads** | |
| Rhammid | *Rhammidium* sp. |
| Jobi | *Coix lacryma* |

### South American Tropical Lowlands domesticates and cultivars

Little concrete archaeological evidence exists to determine the domestication and cultivation of plants in the South American Tropical Lowlands. Cassava (manioc; *Manihot esculenta*), which intruded onto the Peruvian coast at about 1000 BC, is thought to be basic to the Tropical Lowland subsistence system. Although there is good documentation for its historic spread from Brazil into Africa in the 17th century and then across the southern part of that continent to the Indian Ocean and the islands of Southeast Asia, its origin and prehistoric spread is relatively unknown. Griddles, usually connected with the preparation of cassava, occurring in Colombia and Venezuela by 1000 BC and perhaps as early as 2000 BC, may be taken as evidence that cassava was originally domesticated in the northern Tropical Lowlands. Exactly when that domestication took place is difficult to determine. Root crops such as sweet potatoes, achira, achiote, and peanuts, as well as other plants with wild relatives in the Lowlands such as the avocado, papaya, *Cucurbita crescentia*, pineapple, coca, and jack beans grew in the Andean sequence as early as, or earlier than, cassava and could be the original basis for the tropical subsistence pattern. Also, there is the possibility that all these Lowlands domesticates were grafted onto an earlier intrusive highland complex composed of corn, peppers, lima beans, and common beans, all of which are important elements of the Tropical Lowlands system.

The archaeological histories of other plants that are part of the Tropical Lowlands complex are totally unknown. This group includes annona or cherimoya (*Annona squamosa* and *A. reticulata*), arrowroot (*Maranta arundinacea*), jicama (*Pachyrrhizus* sp.), taro (*Xanthosoma sagittifolium*), mamey (*Mammea americana*), papaya (*Carioca papaya*), peach palm (*Guilielma utilis*), and store apple (*Chrysephyllum cainilo*).

**Table 4: Cultivated or Domesticated Plants of the Tropical Forest**

| common name | Latin name |
|---|---|
| **1. Cultivated for Edible Seeds** | |
| Bean, common | *Phaseolus vulgaris* |
| Bean, lima | *Phaseolus lunatus* |
| Bean, jack | *Canavalia ensiformis* |
| Cacao | *Theobroma cacao* |
| Castor bean and oil | *Ricinus communis* |
| Corn | *Zea mays* |
| Inga | *Inga feuillei* |
| Peanut | *Arachis hypogaea* |
| **2. Cultivated for Edible Roots** | |
| Arracacha | *Arracacia xanththarrhiza* |
| Arrowroot | *Maranta arundinacea* |
| Cacabo | *Xanthosoma* sp. |
| Cassava, sweet | *Manihot utilissima* |
| Cassava, bitter | *Manihot esculenta* |
| Hualusa | *Colocasia esculenta* |
| Potato, sweet | *Ipomoea batatus* |
| Yam | *Dioscorea* sp. |
| Xantia | *Xanthosoma sagittifolium* |

| common name | Latin name |
|---|---|
| **3. Edible Fruits** | |
| Avocado | *Persea americana* |
| Caimito | *Chrysophyllum cainito* |
| Frutus de lobl | *Solanum lycocarpum* |
| Guava | *Psidium guajava* |
| Lumuma | *Lucuma obovata* |
| Mamona | *Ricinus communis* |
| Papaya | *Carica papaya* |
| Pepion | *Solanum muricatum* |
| Pineapple | *Ananas comosus* |
| Plantin | *Musa paradisiaca* |
| Sapilla | *Cucurbita maxima* |
| Surinum cherry | *Eugenia unifora* |
| Squash, warty | *Cucurbita moschata* |
| **4. Condiments** | |
| Aji | *Capsicum* sp. |
| **5. Stimulants and Narcotics** | |
| Barbasco | *Lonchocarpus nicou* |
| Coca | *Erythroxylon coca* |
| Fish poison | *Clebadium vargasii* |
| Nissolia | *Nissolia* sp. |
| Tephrosia | *Tephrosia toxicaria* |
| Tobacco | *Nicotina tabacum* |
| **6. Fiber Plants** | |
| Agave | *Agave* sp. |
| Bacaiava palm | *Acrocomia* sp. |
| Cotton | *Gossypium barbadense* |
| Cotton | *Gossypium hirsutum* |
| Pupunha palm | *Guilielma gasipaes* |
| Razor grass | *Scleria* sp. |
| **7. Dye Plants** | |
| Achiote | *Bixa orellana* |
| Genipa | *Genipa americana* |
| **8. Cultivated for Resin** | |
| Mangabeira | *Hancornia speciosa* |
| **9. Cultivated Fruits Used as Ute** | |
| Gourd | *Lageneria siceraria* |
| Tree gourd | *Crescentia cujete* |
| **10. Plants Used for Tools or Construction** | |
| Chonta palm | *Guilielma gasipaes* |
| Reeds | *Arundo conax* |
| Uba cane | *Gynerium sagittatum* |
| **11. Plants Used for Beads** | |
| Rhammid | *Rhammidium* sp. |
| Jobi | *Coix lacryma* |

## INDIAN AGRICULTURAL PRACTICES

The preceding section examined the origin and spread of plants in terms of archaeological investigations. A discussion of horticultural and agricultural techniques among American Indians, however, is presented in terms of major New World culture areas at the time of European conquest.

### Northeast Woodlands agriculture

An agricultural system based upon corn, beans, and squash and greatly supplemented by hunting and food collecting diffused into the Northeast Woodlands of the present-day United States and Canada. Fields were cleared in the woodlands by the slash-and-burn technique, usually undertaken by men wielding axes and adzes. Planting and harvesting were undertaken by women, except in a few tribes of Maine. Agricultural implements consisted of the pointed stick, wooden spade-like tools, and bone, stone, or shell hoes. In spite of the use of fertilizers such as fish and ash, new fields situated away from waterways had to be prepared every three or four years. Exchange of agricultural produce was mainly on a barter basis and operated along kinship lines.

Ceremonies connected with agriculture were relatively simple, with a few planting (green corn) and harvesting rituals. Inadequate archaeological information suggests that these practices developed out of an earlier well-defined horticultural system involving a few domesticates in present-day New York by Owascoid times (roughly AD 1000). Further, it appears that this caused the population to increase greatly. Much investigation is needed to test this hypothesis.

### Eastern Woodlands agriculture

Closely related to Northeast practices were those found in that part of the Eastern Woodlands culture area that is now the midwestern U.S., where agricultural developments are slightly better documented. Cultivated and domesticated plants from both local and outside developments were being utilized between 1000 BC and AD 700, but whether the cultivation was of the level of agriculture or of horticulture (mainly in river bottoms or elsewhere) is unknown. There seems to be more secure evidence that agriculture was practiced by the Mississippian Period (roughly after AD 900). It was probably of a slash-and-burn type and more intensive along major waterways such as the Missouri, Mississippi, Illinois, Wabash, and Ohio rivers. Although there is no evidence of the use of fertilizers, the harvesting and planting practices, agricultural tools, division of labor, exchange systems, and ceremonial aspects seem to have been similar to those of the Northeast. Whether agriculture caused populations to increase, or whether growing populations in an earlier horticulture period brought about the use of agriculture, is difficult to determine.

### Prairies and Great Plains agriculture

Probably derived from this Midwestern development, as well as from the southwestern Woodlands, is the agriculture of the Prairies and Great Plains. Much of it seems confined to the Missouri River and its tributaries; definite evidence for such practices is dated after AD 1000. This intrusion of the corn-beans-squash complex seems to have augmented greatly the local populations. Growing practices were more of a flood plain nature rather than of the slash-and-burn type, although the latter may also have occurred. Whether it was preceded by a horticultural stage using imported or local domesticates is unknown. Planting and harvesting practices, agricultural tools (with the exception of bone or wood rakes and hoes made from buffalo scapula), the division of labor, exchange systems, and ceremonies appear to have been similar to those in the Northeast and Eastern Woodlands.

### Southeast agriculture

If these three areas were considered as a single region of similar agricultural practices with only minor local variations, the Southeast culture area might be classified into the same general category. Including the southeastern U.S., Louisiana, Arkansas, eastern

Texas, and Oklahoma, this area gives limited and provocative evidence of horticulture or agriculture with domesticates or cultivars preceding an intensive river bottom agricultural period after about AD 700. Planting and harvesting activities, the division of labor, and simple agricultural tools are similar to those previously mentioned. Settlement pattern studies, however, indicate that populations greatly increased after the utilization of intensive river bottom agriculture. Also, exchange systems and ceremonial practices connected with agriculture seem, on the basis of ethnographic findings, much more complex than those of the previous areas. Whether this was because of the connections between the Southeast, perhaps up the Red and Arkansas rivers, and the Southwest or because of late influence from Mesoamerica, once facetiously referred to by archaeologists as resulting in the Buzzard Cult of the Southeast, has yet to be explained.

**Southwest agriculture**

Although the U.S. Southwest, or the Oasis area, was a "middle man" in the diffusion of basic domesticates for agriculture to the Eastern Woodlands, its subsistence system was relatively unique. There are hints from Cochise and the San Pedro Phase of southern Arizona, as well as from the preceramic remains in Tularosa, Cordova, and Bat caves, that some sort of early horticultural system using the domesticated trinity of Mesoamerica plus the sunflower from the Eastern Woodlands led to sedentary village-pithouse culture patterns in this area.

Agriculture — arising both from internal developments and further influence from Mesoamerica — began in the Southwest at about the beginning of the Christian era. Although it showed considerable variations in time and space, some features gave the culture area coherence. Tools were mainly the digging stick (sometimes forked), a sword-like weeding stick, and a wooden rake-like tool. Except for the eastern peripheries and relative intrusions from the Plains, planting and harvesting were done by men. Further, a series of planting and harvesting ceremonies with lineage relationships had Mesoamerican overtones, as did the patterns of distribution of food products, which may be classified as kinship, socio-ceremonial, and even folk market exchange systems.

Because of considerable ecological variations in this harsh, dry environment, as well as varying distances from the Mesoamerican center, Southwest subsistence practices show some range. Subsistence agriculture, based upon seasonal rainfall in a number of micro-environments, occurred about 1,000 years earlier (about the first century AD) in the southern part of the zone than it did in the north. Flood plain agriculture and irrigation had a somewhat similar temporal and spatial distribution, although irrigation was never of major importance or practiced on a large scale in the northern part of this culture area. While populations seemed to have increased under agriculture, there is little evidence of major economic, social, and political changes concomitant with irrigation. Considerably more research is necessary before the implications and resultant social processes involved in the great Oasis area of North America are understood.

**Mesoamerican agriculture**

The Southwest culture area was closely connected with Mesoamerican agricultural developments, which were much more complex and less easy to fathom. Evidence of the development of various systems of agriculture from horticulture and food collecting in the highland Tehuacán Valley of Mexico is, however, available.

The waning of the Pleistocene (about 7500 BC) with its drastic diminution of the animal biomass coincided at Tehuacán with the development of numerous subsistence options and the acquisition of considerable eco-knowledge. The above conditions brought a shift from the Ajuereado culture system, characterized by nomadic microbands of hunters, to the El Riego culture system, characterized by micro-macrobands, seasonal migration, and varying subsistence options practiced each season in specialized micro-environs.

Hunting predominated in the dry winter season, seed-collecting in the spring, fruit-collecting in the fall. During the two millenia (7000-5000 BC) in which the El Riego culture flourished, the seed-collecting activities of spring and summer led to the selection of certain productive genetic sorts of corn, mixta squash, and amaranth (domesticates). The fall-fruiting wild avocado (a cultivar) was removed from its natural habitat outside the valley to watered areas within the valley.

This supplementation of food-gathering with domesticates and cultivars — together with the possible planting of them and resultant increasing population — led to the new culture of Coxcatlan (5000-3500 BC), which has been described as a seasonal macro-microband type with horticulture. Not only were the local domesticates of corn, mixta squash, and amaranth being planted in "gardens" but imports such as the gourd, moschata squash, chili, and common beans were added to the *barranca* system of horticulture. Planted in well-watered gardens in a system known as hydro-horticulture were the avocado, a local cultivar called chupandilla, and other imports such as black and white sapotes.

The increasing amounts of imports and the improvement in the corn crop by selection and hybridization gradually led to the development of the Abejas culture (3500-2300 BC). This cultural system had a community pattern of central-based bands. Some *barranca* agriculture (*i.e.*, the planting of domesticates, mainly improved corn, in fields along river or stream flats during the rainy season) was practiced. This ever-expanding new means of food production not only yielded increasing food surpluses but led to a sedentary village way of life such as that of the two following cultural phases — Purron (2300-1500 BC) and Ajalpan (1500-900 BC). While the same agricultural and horticultural systems with more rigorous corn hybrids continued relatively unchanged, the population seemed to have increased greatly during late Ajalpan times, when new exchange systems both of the market and socio-ceremonial variety occurred.

These factors brought about the Santa Maria culture phase (900-150 BC), including a nuclear village settlement pattern and irrigation agriculture. This new subsistence system, which yielded two or three crops a year instead of one, was coupled with further cultural exchanges to produce the Palo Blanco culture (150 BC-AD 700). Palo Blanco, with a population that was more than six times as great as that of the previous phase, included large towns and sacred cities, a new urban-like market system, more intensive irrigation agriculture that included some new plants, and the use of orchard culture (the growing of groves of fruit trees), slash-and-burn agriculture, and, perhaps in northern Puebla, *chinampa* (floating garden) agriculture or horticulture.

The final phase of Tehuacán — the Venta Salada culture (AD 700-1530) — saw no new subsistence system, but irrigation agriculture was intensified. There is some evidence to suggest that ceremonialism connected with agriculture greatly increased and that new "state" controlled systems of exchange (often involving foodstuffs) such as taxes, tribute, imports, and exports emerged. Whether this development of agriculture was typical of highland Mexico remains to be seen, for there is much highland environmental variation. It is doubtful that these developments pertained to the lowlands, where slash-and-burn and flood-plain agriculture predominated in historic times. In spite of the wide variation of subsistence systems in Mesoamerica, however, there are a number of features that were widespread. Everywhere men cleared, planted, and harvested, and cultivation tools were simple (mainly the planting stick). Further, complex systems and ceremonialism were usually associated with agriculture.

### The Circum-Caribbean area

These agricultural features stand out in marked contrast to those of the Circum-Caribbean area. Both root (cassava) and seed (corn) crops were grown by the slash-and-burn method, although there have been occasional reports of irrigation. Both sexes were involved with agriculture, the men usually clearing the fields, the women planting, and both harvesting the crop. Ceremonies and exchange systems connected with agriculture were relatively simple.

### Tropical Forest and Marginal activities

Closely related to Circum-Caribbean agriculture was that of the Tropical Forest tribes. Again, some seed crops such as corn, beans, and squash were grown, but root crops of cassava and yams predominated. A number of fruits and hallucinogenic plants were also utilized. The division of labor sometimes included both sexes in agriculture, as in the Circum-Caribbean, but there seems to have been a tendency for men to do most of the work where agriculture was most intensive. Women take over these duties among the few tribes where agriculture or horticulture was not as important. Again, exchange systems of foodstuffs and ceremonies connected with agriculture were not complex, although ceremonies concerned with drugs were both sophisticated and numerous.

Related to the Tropical Forest tribes as well as to the Andean complex, somewhat depending upon geographical location, are the so-called Marginal tribes of South America. From many standpoints these peoples should not be considered as part of another agricultural group since most of them practiced horticulture rather than agriculture. Both men and women seemed to have been involved with these activities, and there is little mention in the meager ethnographic documents of agricultural tools, ceremonies, or exchange systems.

### South American agriculture

The Andean center of South American agriculture is radically different from its surrounding or secondary centers. Although much more documentation is needed, the outlines of the history of agriculture for two small regions of Peru — the central coast near Lima and the Ayacucho Valley of the south-central highlands — are known.

**The Ayacucho Valley.** Following the end of the Pleistocene and the extinction of the megafauna about 9000 BC, there was a gradual shift during the Puente (9000-7200 BC) and Jaywa (7200-5700 BC) phases from a subsistence pattern of hunting to one that included seasonally scheduled food-collecting. By Piki Phase times (5700-4300 BC), wet season collecting activities were supplemented by the use of domesticates such as gourds, squash, and perhaps quinoa, as well as of tamed guinea pigs. The following Chihua Phase saw horticulture of these plants and of intrusive ones such as potatoes, common beans, coca, lucuma, and corn, and the pastoring of domesticated guinea pigs as supplementary to the scheduled seasonal collecting subsistence system. There is also evidence from nearby Junin that the llama and alpaca may have been domesticated and that herding of the llama, alpaca, and guanaco were undertaken.

The adoption of this herding complex and other factors in the following Cachi Phase (3000-1750 BC) brought about a fundamental change in the Ayacucho economy. It would appear that there evolved a vertical economy in which the subsistence pattern based on potato growing and camelid herding in the higher elevations became integrated with an agricultural and/or horticultural subsistence pattern at lower elevations through a redistribution system, perhaps along kinship lines. This practice of acquiring a whole economy by the mechanism of a redistribution system became a fundamental theme in all later Andean subsistence patterns.

In the following Formative Stage (*c.* 1750-400 BC), the redistribution system seems to have had a more religious or ceremonial emphasis, and to have been relatively confined to local areas. At this time, new plants, terracing, and small-scale irrigation supplemented the agricultural practices of the lower elevations, while new plants and alpaca and llama herding were added to the subsistence pattern of the higher areas. During the period from 400 BC to about AD 600, the redistribution system acquired a more secular (political) emphasis and a regional as well as a local level. Storage systems, irrigation, and terracing became complex. The Classic Period (*c.* AD 600-1100) saw the rise of the Huari (Wari) Empire under which the redistribution system took on an imperialistic nature of areal or international scope, as it did in the following Postclassic Inca period. Probably many of the complex administrative, economic, and ceremonial aspects of the Inca subsistence pattern developed at this time.

**The Peruvian central coast.** Here again, with the waning of the Pleistocene, new subsistence options such as plant-collecting, shell-collecting, and fishing were developed. Although the archaeological evidence is meager, it seems that these developments led in Arenal and Luz times (7500-5500 BC) to some sort of scheduled subsistence pattern of shell- and plant-collecting on the coast during the dry season, and hunting, trapping, and plant-collecting in the *loma* during the wet season. The growth of more successful food-gathering techniques on the coast and of a series of strategic sites that could be exploited from a base led to the rise of sedentary hamlets or base camps by Canario times (5500-4200 BC). Throughout the following Encanto Phase (4200-2500 BC), increasing sedentarism and population occurred together with the acquisition of a few domesticates such as gourds, squashes, and canavalia beans. In the final preceramic period (2500-1750 BC), further increases in population and acquisition of more domesticates — including cotton, achira, pacae, guava, galactia, pepper, corn, lima beans, lucuma, sweet potatoes, and peanuts — produced a shift from supplemental horticulture to agricultural village life. This development was tied to a successful maritime economy, and perhaps even camelid herding, by a well organized redistribution system. In this horizontal economy, coastal marine products flowed into mid-river, agriculture-based redistribution centers and then were sent to up-river and highland communities, while upland products such as meat, potatoes, and up-river seasonal agricultural products came into the mid-river centers, which in turn redistributed them, as well as their own products, to down-river and coastal communities. Irrigation seems to have followed this period. Later developments on the coast paralleled highland development, although imperialistic redistribution states never developed on the coast. Chimú, Ica, and Nazca, however, may have been steps in that direction.

**General characteristics of Andean agriculture.** Within central Peru, there were considerable variations in agricultural developments and practices, and for the whole Andean area from central Chile to Colombia such deviations from a single pattern were even greater. Nevertheless, certain general themes did occur. Together with camelid herding, root and seed crops were grown in different environments and integrated into a single subsistence complex. The Peruvian center had a wider variety of domesticates, and Colombia to the north produced less root crops and practiced little or no herding. Also, the peoples of the central region used fertilizers and practiced crop rotation, both of which are little mentioned for the northern and southern peripheries. Irrigation seems to have been utilized to some extent everywhere. Agricultural tools — the hoe, shovel, and some sort of clod breaker — occur throughout the area, although the clod breakers of the central area had distinctive doughnut-shaped stone weights. In addition, a complex foot plow was used. In terms of the division of labor, both men and women worked the fields together, except in some parts of Colombia where only men undertook such practices. State control of the division of labor and the redistribution of agricultural products was complex in the area of the Inca Empire, but simpler redistribution systems seem to have existed elsewhere. Ceremonies connected with agriculture were practiced throughout the region, but they were more complex and more rigidly controlled in the central area.

## THEORIES OF AGRICULTURAL DEVELOPMENT

The general overall relationship between population growth and agricultural development is often regarded as a fundamental condition resulting in cultural change. It appears that whereas the initial domestication of plants and horticulture or agriculture lead to greatly increased populations, population pressures, and cultural change, the converse is also true. For both Ayacucho and Tehuacán, and perhaps the Southwest, the gradual accumulation of more and more domesticates (*i.e.*, horticulture) led to sedentary life, agriculture, greatly increased populations, and then profound changes in culture. On the Peruvian coast and perhaps in the Eastern Woodlands, however, a successful food-collecting pattern led to sedentary life and greatly increased population. The people then acquired more domesticates until they became agriculturalists, which in turn led to further population increases. After this initial stage of village agriculture, the general increase in population led not only to a variety of cultural changes but also to the development of new agricultural techniques. In the Andean, Mesoamerican, Southwestern, and perhaps the Circum-Caribbean areas, one of those new agricultural practices was irrigation. The results in terms of population, however, were not similar. In Mesoamerica and the Andean area, populations seem to have increased greatly, causing great culture changes, after irrigation, while in the Southwest and perhaps the Circum-Caribbean there was no evidence of significant population increase.

At this stage of New World archaeological investigation, no all-encompassing generalizations can be made about the relationship of population and agriculture. One fact, however, is clear. Agriculture is the key variable to an understanding of the phenomena connected with population growth and population as a factor of culture change in all societies.

It is perhaps ironic that modern civilization — which is so dependent upon agriculture, much of which resulted from the remarkable effort of the Indian — has reciprocated those generous donors with disease, liquor, gunpowder, and attempted cultural annihilation.

Richard S. MacNeish

**ALABASTER,** an ornamental mineral known as onyx marble or Mexican onyx, has been used for centuries by the Indian peoples, especially in Mesoamerica, for decorative and religious purposes. Composed of translucent calcite and aragonite, it is really neither onyx nor marble. It is not to be confused with modern alabaster, which is an aggregate of gypsum (calcium sulfate).

**Usage in North America.** Alabaster was used by the North American Indians as far back as 2,000 years ago, especially by the tribes located in what are now the northeastern U.S. states, Georgia, the Mississippi Valley, the Rocky Mountain region of Colorado, and California.

Wyandotte Cave in Crawford County, Indiana, was actually an aboriginal alabaster mine. It was dissolved naturally out of the bedded limestones of the geological time span known as the Mississippian Period. The alabaster was quarried mainly from the surface. Deer antlers were used as picks to unearth the alabaster. Inside the cave, the Indians broke off the stalactites, which were composed of alabaster and limestone.

In the southwestern U.S., the Pueblo Indians mixed powdered alabaster with gypsum and water and used it as a whitewash on their homes. They also expertly carved the mineral into religious fetishes, which were used in their ceremonies. In later years, the selenite form of alabaster was and still is, to some extent, used for windows by the Southwest tribes. It has the unique property of being easily separated into thin sheets akin to window glass.

The Plains Indians roasted large blocks of gypsum alabaster into a powder that was used to clean and whiten dressed skins. It was also used to whiten the gummed tips of feathers used in decorative work.

**Usage in Mesoamerica.** Probably the most frequent usage of the Mexican onyx alabaster was by the Indian peoples of Mexico and Central America. The Indians of the Teotihuacán dynasty of 500 BC were great stone cutters and stone carvers. With only crude stone tools, they carved exquisite figurines and vases out of alabaster. The Mixtecs of Central America took

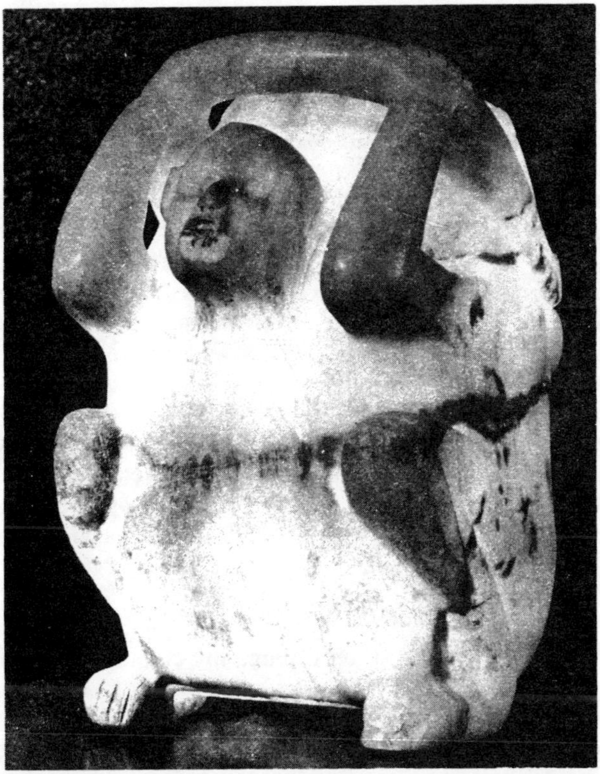

Alabaster effigy jar from Mexico. Dating from the Post-classic Period, the jar represents a monkey holding its tail over its head. Height 31.5 cm.

great delight in *tecali*, as they called alabaster. They carved beautiful bowls and vases, which were decorated with three-dimensional effigies of monkeys, turkeys, and rabbits. The vases were typically pear-shaped.

The Aztecs of the Valley of Mexico also used alabaster, which they carved into the shapes of their deities. The Mayas of Chichén Itzá carved alabaster vases and animals. Some fabulous specimens have been found in the Sacred Cenote, where the Mayas made sacrifices and offerings to their water god.

Alabaster was not used by the Indians of South America.

**ALCOHOLIC BEVERAGES.** The term "alcohol" when used in reference to alcoholic consumption by Native Americans of all tribes is an exceedingly value-laden and emotion-evoking one. It is historically wedded to the image of the drunken native, murdering and marauding on the western frontiers. It is equally associated with the image of the "drunken Indian," still widely prevalent today. This stereotype is operative not only in urban areas, where North American Indians are often seen as transitory nomads, but is found in any area where natives of any tribal affiliation reside. To many people, fear of drunken, lewd, and licentious natives living in the vast sociological unknowns of reserves and reservations is a predominant theme in Indian-white relationships. Generally speaking, those images that are operative in associating Indians with alcohol are, in varying degrees, negative ones.

**General considerations**

Because of this stereotyping, any consideration of the use of alcoholic beverages within the framework of indigenous societies, whether past or present, is necessarily a delicate matter. The task of presenting data about native consumption of alcoholic beverages is often rendered more difficult because of the assumptions underlying the various scientific and pseudo-scientific attempts that have been made to deal with the subject. In addition, alcohol production and consumption, as well as resultant degrees of behavior modification, among the many tribal societies of Native America have been at various levels. Thus, while some tribes have traditionally been isolated from alcohol, others made their own alcoholic beverages in pre-Columbian times, some used alcohol only under certain circumstances, and some actively engaged in bizarre, or at least altered, behavior in consequence of its use. Finally, fragmentary observations, postulates, theories, and conjectures about Native Americans abound in the literature dealing with the nature, function, and use of alcohol.

In view of the many assumptions and subjective

statements about the utilization of alcohol, its use in the aboriginal world needs clarification. It becomes necessary to place in perspective the historical and socio-cultural milieu in order to obtain a satisfactory rationale for its use and/or misuse. More saliently, such a background needs to be appraised to facilitate understanding of this controversial issue.

The production of alcoholic beverages is evidently tied to such variables as the availability of resources. Each tribe's use of alcohol was dependent upon such related factors as raw materials, knowledge of brewing techniques, and patterns of consumption. More significantly, several "given" factors operative in the socio-cultural levels of the different tribes have to be taken into account. Thus, it is commonly assumed that certain cereal grains used in the distilling of inebriating beverages were strictly limited to those tribes who were horticulturalists. There were, however, many tribes who were semi-horticulturalists, if not fully developed horticulturalists, who were not manufacturers of alcoholic spirits. On the other hand, there are evidences that some tribes brewed intoxicants from vegetal materials that they had gathered. Caution must therefore be exercised in evaluating historical and ethnological data relating to the use of alcohol.

Before European contact, the New World was not entirely without alcohol. Alcoholic drinks were widely used in South America, throughout the Circum-Caribbean region, and in Mesoamerica. The Indians of what is now the United States and Canada, however, with the exception of those in the Southwest, had no alcoholic beverages before the European contact. Why the use of alcohol did not spread farther northwards from Mexico remains a puzzling question to which an answer has not yet been found. The circumstance is the more paradoxical because most of the North American Indian tribes had both wild and cultivated plants that they could have used for fermentation.

### Regional variations

Aboriginally, the consumption of alcohol roughly correlated to areas of intensive agriculture in South and Central America and Mexico where corn (maize) was grown. In the tropical rain forests, some tribes used the staple manioc (tapioca).

**In Mesoamerica.** In Mexico, alcoholic beverages were primarily developed from maize. Other sources were wild plums, pineapple, and sarsaparilla roots, as well as the sahuaro and pitahaya cacti, and pods from the mesquite tree. (After the Conquest, brandy and tequila constituted a further refinement of distilled liquors.) In northeastern Mexico, however, the wild plants agave (maguey) and *Dasylirion* (sotol) were the raw materials used. That these wild plants were a staple food over a large part of Mesoamerica has been postulated by the U.S. anthropologist Harold Driver. As with most diffusional postulates, it is difficult to establish what technique of manufacture was employed in each of the areas where the plants were known. Mesquite and screwbeans (tornillo) were, however, fermented by adding water to the dried cakes of flour made from them. In discussing the manufacture of agave wine (pulque, or neutle), Driver notes that the principal nutritional element of the sap of the agave plant is sucrose sugar. When fermented, the alcoholic content varies from three to four percent. It also contains quantities of vitamins B and C.

Other raw materials used in Mesoamerica include fermented honey (*balche*) which was especially popular among the Mayan speakers who kept stingless bees. Chacs, the rain god of the Yucatán Mayas, was offered a beer made from bark.

In precontact Mexico, excessive drinking seems to have occurred as a part of some religious ceremonies. "Pulque ceremonies" seem to have been common. Alcohol-induced dreams seem to have been associated with supernatural power and were seen as a means of dealing with daily life situations. Public inebriation was punishable by death among the Aztec nobility, among the priesthood, and among students in the *telpuchcalli* (house of youth). For a commoner, the normal penalty was whipping for the first offense and death for the second offense. If found drunk, Aztec youths were beaten to death or strangled with a rope in a public place. On ceremonial occasions, however, old people were allowed to drink together without punishment. In rituals of human sacrifice among the Aztec, alcohol and drugs were often given to the victim as well as to the priests in preparation for the ordeal.

**In South America.** In areas of South America where maize was cultivated, a corn beer known as *chicha* was consumed. Among the Inca, *chicha* was used in connection with sacrifices during festivals.

In most of South America, according to the U.S. anthropologist John Murra, maize was grown primarily for beer-making or for ceremonial purposes. In describing rites and crops in the Inca state, Murra quotes an Andean writer named Poma, who says of the Chinchaysuya (northern and coastal Peruvians) that, "although small in stature, [they] are brave, as they are fed on maize and drink maize beer, which gives strength." Poma further noted a harvest festival in the Peruvian highlands where "the villagers drank and ate and sang and for three nights kept vigil over Mama Zara, Mother Maize, a shrine erected in every house by wrapping the best cobs in the family's best blankets."

In Inca society, the vestal virgins (*acllacuna*) brewed the sacramental *chicha* which was poured in libation to the greater glory of the Sun (Inca).

In Colombia, when warfare occurred between the highland Muisca and the slope-dwelling Panche, drinking bouts preceded or followed combat. These bouts apparently functioned as a means to ensure social cohesion and to allow the assertion of personal rank.

Also with respect to South America, Driver notes that the Achagua of eastern Colombia and Venezuela manufactured *chicha* in a wooden trough. Their drinking parties involved the painting of their bodies, assembling in the men's clubhouses, and singing to the accompaniment of musical instruments.

Among the Sirionó who inhabit the forests of eastern Bolivia, wild honey was fermented into beer. A man invited his male relatives and friends for a drinking party, while his wife invited her women kin for a separate party. Only elderly men and women were allowed to drink together. An audience gathered as the men grew more intoxicated, after which wrestling bouts were begun which continued until the participants collapsed in an alcoholic state. Interestingly enough, the deepest drinker, the best hunter, and the most generous of nature were those who possessed the qualifications sought for in chieftainship. Every two years a beer party was held in which all members of the hunting band participated as a renewal rite.

In present-day highland communities from Mexico to Bolivia, fiestas are held, in connection with which large expenditures on food and drink are made. One anthropological authority has analyzed the fiesta system as constituting one of the traditional mechanisms for exercising external control over indigenous communities. Exploitation by church and civil authorities is implicit in the allegation that, in contemporary Andean life, men rarely volunteer to carry a *cargo* ("burden"). Usually, a man is chosen against his will and persuaded to accept the task when drunk.

**In North America.** Various theories of the North American Indians' use of alcohol have emerged since the time of contact. European explorers, trappers, traders, military men, sailors, and government agents apparently presented a frontier model for the native's drunken conduct. The presentation aspect of liquor possibly fit into the native etiquette of gift-giving, but it soon became a ritual aspect of trading, and finally liquor seemed to be the item of trade itself.

Early accounts, such as the *Jesuit Relations,* the 17th-century chronicles of that religious order's work among the Indians, and the accounts by Quaker missionaries, particularly among the Iroquois groups, relate horror stories concerning the drunken actions of

North American natives taken under the influence of alcoholic stimulants. The Code of Handsome Lake, a syncretic religion founded by a Seneca prophet, was a response to cultural deprivation and pressures exerted by a dominant society. The new belief system that it represented constituted an adaptive mechanism to a state of social disorganization resulting from the excessive use of alcohol. Also known as the Longhouse religion of the Iroquois, the religion persists to the present day. Adherence to the beliefs of the Native American Church, which has a strict proscription against the use of alcohol, is another instance of a native reaction to the destructive effects of the intrusive liquid.

It is a well-known fact that the early traders and trappers who entered the alcohol-free areas of North America were well-stocked with this liquid incentive in order to facilitate the expansion of their influence and the establishment of their control in native areas. Along with such trade goods as cloth, knives, and beads, alcoholic beverages of various concoctions and varying degrees of dilution formed one of the elements used in the initial bargaining for furs, foods, women, and land. Diffusional aspects were therefore directly tied in with the fanning out of these agents of change in the indigenous societies. Patterns of liquor consumption and expected behavior after imbibing were apparently elements of the drinking role suggested as models for the aboriginal groups.

Despite the many early accounts of a historical nature dealing with white and Indian relationships, it is almost impossible to place in a coherent frame the trading patterns among the native peoples. It is entirely possible that in the intertribal contacts there was little trafficking in liquor. The consumption patterns and the drunken orgies described would suggest that the indigenous peoples tended to consume, rather than to barter with other natives. There is, of course, no question but that the newly introduced "fire water" produced adverse and tragic effects on individuals as well as on native societies. Drunken orgies and vicious behavior took their toll on native groups throughout the early interaction period in North America. As one contemporary writer has stated: "The Indian soon learned that one could literally get away with murder if one was drunk or pretended to be."

The debilitating effects of alcohol were general for most tribes and, in consequence, attempts were made to control its sale and use. Tribesmen pleaded with colonial governments to prevent rum traders from entering their areas. Yet, ironically, many natives seemed eager to experience the altered states resulting from alcoholic consumption. Many writers correlate this with the importance of dreaming, vision-questing, and other indigenous states associated with aboriginal lifeways. Wilbur R. Jacobs, in *Dispossessing the American Indian* (1972), delineates the pattern of trade in the following terms: ". . . the trader could easily induce his warriors to have a free 'dram' of rum before the business of barter began. This was the fatal step for the Indian. One dram called for another, and before long the tribesmen were thoroughly drunk. The trader could then literally steal the skins and furs, slipping off into the night with his prize." Some traders who wished to maintain contact with native groups, did not, however, employ such tactics.

Profitable trade in furs, women, and in many cases land defied effective controls. There are instances in which treaties were enacted while the principal headmen were swayed by liquor. Jacobs, for example, indicates that the traders "duped intoxicated tribesmen into selling large tracts of land."

In 1832 a federal law was passed that prohibited the sale of alcohol to Indians. This was scarcely a deterrent for bootleggers, however, who made lucrative profits through illegal sales. The effect, however, was to encourage Indians to consume all the spirits before they could be apprehended by the law officers, thus reinforcing the pattern of quick consumption. Old patterns of sharing also did much to facilitate immediate use. The cultural discourtesy implicit in insulting a kin or friend by refusing offerings of alcohol was yet another factor that helped to establish the syndrome referred to as "Indian drinking."

**Contemporary attempts to deal with the problems of alcohol**

In August 1953, U.S. Public Law 277 removed the prohibition against the sale of liquor to natives outside reservations. It also allowed tribal governments to opt for either the sale or the restriction of sale of liquor on reservations. In 1975 there were approximately 55 tribal groups that permitted the sale of intoxicants on reservations. Earlier, in 1963, Canada had enacted similar legislation which permitted tribal governments to permit or exclude alcohol in reserves.

In the mid-1970s it was safe to say that drunkenness was widespread in Native American life. This apparently reflected drastic changes in native societies, which accompanied the demolishing of endemic social control mechanisms and the imposition of new cultural values and controls. It also reflected the feeling of powerlessness among native groups, and the subordinate position held by native enclaves in the socio-economic and educational systems of the dominant society.

Many native groups have established committees on alcoholism on reservations, have sponsored research projects and workshops, and have organized national groups to meet this social problem. This is in addition to the fact that Indian alcoholism has been the focus of many sociological and anthropological studies.

Much of the research has been explained in cultural terms. For example, one contemporary authority has claimed that groups in the western Arctic area of Canada drink as a substitute for following shamanistic patterns of behavior. Another authority attributes Teton Sioux drinking to individual concern for prestige and power at a time when traditional culture is being undermined. More recently, the same authority, Gerald Mohatt, in *The Drinking Man* (1971), has indicated that "boredom, lack of job opportunities, inferior education, prejudice, and the language barrier began to accentuate the old motivation for drinking — to overcome feelings of powerlessness and lack of respect resulting from all these barriers." Yet another authority, Nancy Oestreich Lurie, has presented an interesting idea by stressing the purposefulness of drinking among Indians to confirm the stereotype of "the drunken Indian." Essentially, she sees drunkenness as a form of social protest.

Whatever the reasons, Indian encounters with crime and subsequent arrests are highly correlated with alcohol ingestion. This is true in both rural and urban areas. Countless studies present statistics for each group.

Dysfunctional and destructive drinking patterns tend to be perpetuated as normative in various societies. Since the use of alcoholic beverages is customary in most human societies, Native Americans can possibly develop new approaches to alcohol consumption and to its negative effects upon most of their lifeways. Because of their powerless position, however, it is non-Indian authorities, rather than the Indians themselves, upon whom the onus rests for undertaking the review of the external system of arrest, trial, incarceration, parole, re-arrest, and rehabilitation of natives that is so evidently needed if new directions are to be developed.

BEATRICE MEDICINE

**ALPACA** (*Lama pacos*) is, along with its larger relative the llama, one of the domesticated members of the lamoid group of the camel (*Camelidae*) family of hooved mammals; it shares with its wild relatives, the vicuña and guanaco, certain peculiarities distinguishing it from the llama. All four are associated with the Indians of the Andean region of South America; the Incas in particular prized the alpaca for its fine and abundant wool. Whether this gentlest and wooliest of the lamoids was in some long-past era bred from the guanaco or the vicuña is undetermined.

Early European commentators noted the strong attachment of the alpaca to its Indian master, a loyalty emphasized by its quiet, stubborn refusal to be transplanted from the Andean highlands, especially the Lake Titicaca region of Peru and Bolivia, and the sparse, marshy grasses that are the alpaca's preferred diet. Its name is usually attributed to the Aymara Indians, although some think its source is the Quechua word *paco* ("russet") combined with the Spanish *el* ("the"). In fact, the alpaca's modern range closely approximates the Aymara's historic territories (its range has apparently shrunk from earlier eras).

Alpaca stand about four feet high and five feet long; they may live for 15 years. Their lush wool creates a heavy appearance, though they are rather slight; a grown male yields about 40 pounds of meat. Two species are usually designated: the "common" (*L. huacayo*) alpaca and the *L. suri*, which gives more and finer wool. Their fleece is usually pure black or brown; the rare white wool was much prized by the Incas, who restricted alpaca wool's use to the nobility and segregated the animals by color to prevent multicolored animals.

The alpaca is easily managed by the Indian shepherds; the Aymara play a flute to summon their flocks and use a simple sling to deal with strays. Alpacas willingly accept the companionship of llamas. Though like all cameloids they chew a cud, they apparently do not have the unpleasant habit, familiar in both llamas and camels, of spitting profusely on an antagonist when aroused. The Incas and others used alpacas for sacrifice, not only in religious ceremonies but also in diplomacy. The Colla Indians may have worshipped the alpaca as their chief deity prior to their defeat by the third Inca emperor Lloque Yupanqui (*c.* 1200). Other secondary uses included rendering the meat into the dry "jerky" called *charqui*; using the dung as a fuel (since alpaca territory is both cold and treeless); and — though not commercially — making blankets of the hide. The alpaca was virtually never made a beast of burden.

The process of gathering alpaca wool remains much the same as it was under the Incas. Traditionally, an alpaca is sheared every two years. The Indians crowd a herd into a corral and hack away at the wool with a sharp instrument (modern sheep shears are undesirable). The yield may be as much as 12 pounds from a *suri*. Arequipa in southern Peru is the processing site for an extensive export trade.

The alpaca's existence was threatened by an ill-advised importation of Spanish sheep. Unlike its Inca masters, however, it withstood that challenge and remains one of the Indians' most valuable links with their illustrious ancestors.

**AMBER** is a fossil tree resin that has frequently been used as a gem by the native American, primarily in the area that is now Alaska.

**General characteristics.** Amber, most commonly, is a product of the prehistoric pine tree *Thuja occidentalis*, which flourished 60,000,000 to 40,000,000 years ago. It has been found in many parts of the world, although today it has become a rarity, being found mainly on the Baltic coast, where deposits of glauconitic sands, or "blue earth," have yielded large quantities of the substance. Generally, amber is found in only weakly compacted sediments because compression and heat build-up would destroy it. Amber varies in color, but it is usually a light yellow to brownish gold. A milky-white opaque variety is known as bone amber.

Amber beads from Alaska. Obtained from the Point Barrow Inuit, these appeared in the *Bureau of American Ethnology Annual Report*, 1892.

**Regional usage.** The gem was used by the Indian peoples of both North and South America for thousands of years, although the predominant users were the native peoples of the far North. The natives of the Aleutian Islands relied heavily on river gravels and marine benches for their supply. They devised an ingenious, highly successful method of mining. They spread a walrus skin between two boats at the bottom of a steep bank containing the amber and loosened the earth and gravel so that it fell into the skin. The amber was then sorted out by the natives and used both as an ornament and as a religious object.

The Koniaga Indians of Kodiak Island, Alaska, placed amber on the graves of the wealthy. They valued amber highly for its rarity, and it has remained for them an expensive article of commerce. The Koniaga made distinctive ear ornaments and pendants out of the deep-yellow fragments.

Other Alaskan Indians and the Inuits (Eskimos) were avid traders of amber. Their supply was traced to Asia as a source. Although rare now, amber is still being found in coal bed outcrops in the Aleutians. A place called Amber Bay attests to its former abundance in this area.

Prehistoric usage is attributed to the Mound-building cultures of present-day Ohio; traces of amber have been found in their graves although it was seemingly not a common artifact. In Mesoamerica, the Aztecs seem to have been the major users of amber, using it primarily as an ornament. Amber was used by the Mayas as a mosaic stone set in plaques, such as the one discovered at Chichén Itzá in Yucatán, Mexico. Its chief use by the Incas of South America was in the making of jewelry, especially necklaces.

Almost no amber was being utilized by the Indian peoples in the mid-1970s because of its extreme rarity.

**AMULET** is a natural or man-made object believed to have special magico-religious powers of providing protection against various dangers or of bringing good fortune or strength. Amulets were commonly used by

Indians to ensure good hunts, to ward off disease, and to impart strength.

The words "charm" and "talisman" are often used as synonyms for amulet, although charm may instead refer to the magical formula that may be sung or recited to confer magical efficacy on the amulet, and talisman sometimes means an object that has the power not merely to bring luck or safeguard against danger but to work wonders. An amulet may also be distinguished from a fetish (*q.v.*), which is generally a focus for specific rites, such as prayers and offerings, although this distinction, too, may be difficult to apply.

**General characteristics**

Amulets are usually worn or carried on the person (as necklaces, pendants, anklets, bracelets, or attachments to clothing), but they may also be kept in places where their effects are desired (as in a field or a building). Natural amulets are often objects of unusual rarity, shape, or color, with unusual features or abnormalities; they may include stones, gems, metals, teeth and claws of animals, feathers, bones, plants, wood, or human hair. Man-made amulets are often representations of natural or of sacred or lucky objects, objects of a material considered to have magical powers, or objects incribed or engraved with charms, signs, symbols, or figures; they may include small models of animals, humans, or other objects, cloth, stone implements (*e.g.*, arrowheads), strings or threads, rings, or beads. These man-made amulets may be set apart from ordinary objects by being manufactured at a particular time or by a particular process, which is often a magical rite during which a charm is recited to confer the power desired. A similar rite may be performed when the amulet is first put in place or when its effectiveness is sought for a specific event or purpose.

The purposes of amulets include curing disease, promoting fertility, imparting strength, ensuring success in various ventures, protecting generally, and protecting specifically against witchcraft, supernatural beings, accidents, and illness. Amulets are often used by particularly vulnerable people, such as children, the sick, and women in childbirth, and by people whose occupations are particularly dangerous or dependent on luck, such as hunters, warriors, and gamblers.

Amulets are thought to derive their power from their connection with natural and supernatural forces. They may be based on a belief in sympathetic or imitative magic — *e.g.*, the Mocoví people of the Chaco region in South America tied deer hooves to their ankles and wrists to acquire the swiftness of the deer, and the Haida Indians of the Northwest Coast of North America believed that stones shaped like seals would help seal hunters catch their prey — or on a belief in a magical efficacy inhering in an object.

**Regional variations**

Amulets are still used throughout the world, although such use is discouraged by Christian churches. The following survey illustrates some important types of amulets used by Americans Indians, but it is by no means an exhaustive listing. Furthermore, since the complete magico-religious systems to which the amulets belong cannot be discussed in detail here, the meanings and functions of the amulets can only be briefly sketched.

**North America.** Among the Inuits (Eskimos), the use of amulets strongly reflected belief in imitative and sympathetic magic. Hudson Bay Inuits, for example, sewed amulets to their clothing to avert disease and to bring them luck and desired qualities. The tip of a caribou tail or the hair of a successful hunter was sewn onto a coat to ensure good luck in caribou hunting. Strips of caribou skin around a girl's wrists were thought to make her skillful in cutting and sewing skins. Bear teeth attached to a boy's shirt made him fearless of bears, and seal teeth ensured success in seal hunting. Insects attached to clothing were believed to prolong life. A piece of flint sewn on the sleeve imparted strength to the hands and arms. Oil drippings from lamps were considered valuable amulets against supernatural enemies and as hunting charms. For good luck in whaling, Alaskan Inuits of Point Barrow wore flaked flint representations of whales suspended around their necks on strings or on their jackets. Some implements of ancient Alaskans have been preserved as amulets.

Among the Eastern Indians, amulets were often associated with what the Algonquian-speaking peoples called *manitou* and the Dakota called *wakan*; *i.e.*, a sacred power inhering in an object and felt as an expression of spirit. The Huron, for example, often regarded objects that seemed unusual in some ways as possessing supernatural qualities, and they kept them for good luck. A stone found in the entrails of an animal that was particularly difficult to kill would be worn as an amulet. Dreams revealed the specific sphere in which the amulet was useful. Many amulets were revealed in or associated with visions. A Montagnais hunting amulet in the form of a decorated pack strap was worn on the trail by a hunter who had had a vision about getting game. The strap was generally kept in secret so that it did not lose its power. Various observances, such as smoking tobacco and dancing, were associated with its use.

Among the Plains Indians, amulets were often associated with war activities. Buffalo-hide shields carried into battle were thought to owe their effectiveness to the medicine objects attached to them, such as a buckskin bag of charms, or to the designs painted on them, rather than to their physical properties. Among the Dakota, for example, animals that were hard to kill, such as lizards, turtles, and spiders, were often represented because they were believed to confer this property on the wearer. Amulets were also used for purposes other than war. Amulets made of umbilical cords were common. Dakota and Assiniboine navel amulets were often in the form of turtles, which were believed to preside over women's diseases. Typical hunting amulets were the Blackfoot buffalo rocks, which were small stones found on the prairie that helped to assure success in buffalo hunts.

Among the people of the MacKenzie River Basin in

northwestern Canada, amulets were important for the everyday concerns of hunting and fishing. Dogrib Indians carried antler points, a piece of birch, or a deer bone while hunting to attract their prey. The bird bills and feet and the jackfish toes and claws attached to Ojibwa (Chippewa) fishing nets were considered essential for success. The Shoshoni of the Plateau region hung powdered spruce needles in a buckskin bag around a baby's neck to prevent illness. Spruce needles were also part of a popular love charm. The Haida of the Northwest Coast had an amulet for acquiring riches that required the theft of clippings from valuable items as an essential part of it.

In the Southwest, Apache warriors commonly used small buckskin bags attached to their belts and filled with a yellow powder (usually a certain pollen) for a variety of ceremonial purposes. Sacred cords, made by shamans and decorated with various beads, shells, or pieces of wood, were believed to protect warriors from bullets, to help cure the sick, to aid crops, and to identify thieves. Zuñi amulets were often natural concretions or strangely eroded rocks, and many were associated with elaborate ceremonial observances and with Zuñi mythology.

**Middle America.** Amulets were important in everyday life in ancient Mexico. When they walked about at night, pregnant women carried small pebbles, ashes from their fireplaces, or some incense to prevent the child from crying constantly; prospective fathers carried small stones or tobacco to protect the child from heart disease. Modern descendents of the Aztecs hang pouches of bitumen around the necks or wrists of children to prevent disease and injury. Modern Maya Indians use amulets for protection against the evil eye and for curing. Among the Cuna Indians of Panama, a sick person gives some glass beads to a medicine man to wear for protection against the illness while he is trying to cure the patient.

**South America.** Inca men of Peru carried amulets in the form of animals, maize, or potatoes in a small coca bag. Modern Quechua Indians of Peru use stones as amulets for food, cattle, sheep, llamas, and sorcerers. Diviners determine whether a stone has magical properties and, if so, for what purpose. Chaco Indians of the central plains of South America regard red headbands or red shirts as protection against the supernatural. Hunting amulets may take the form of a wax image, a bag made of a rhea's neck and containing diverse parts of plants and animals, a pouch worn around the neck and containing medicinal plants, or deer hooves attached to wrists and ankles for speed. Itinerant Aymara shamans from Bolivia travel widely, trading in amulets, herbs, and medicines. Stone, clay, bone, metal, and bezoar stones removed from the stomachs of llamas and vicuñas are worn on the person as amulets or stored in coca bags. They are thought to protect children from evil spirits and to ward off disease and witchcraft. Small stone figures representing men and women are tied together for love charms. Amulets in the shape of a human hand give luck in weaving and protect against fatigue. Certain amulets in the form of a human, a fish, or a phallus are smeared with the blood of sacrificial animals and serve as family guardians. Other animal-shaped amulets are used in fertility rites for livestock.

JOAN REIBSTEIN

**ANCHOR STONES,** slabs of rock used as anchors, were common in both North and South America wherever Indians used boats. In construction, they varied from rough, unworked boulders to carefully shaped cubes, spheres, and doughnuts. Some were naturally grooved; others had artificial holes or grooves cut in them to hold a rope without slipping.

It is not known where and when anchor stones originated. Since native peoples throughout the world used them, and since bark, skin, balsa, and dugout boats were common many millenia before the Christian era, they may well have been brought to the Americas by Asian immigrants who predated the American Indian. Furthermore, no data exists concerning how anchor stones changed over time, but it is plausible to assume that, as stone-working techniques improved in the Americas, more time was spent shaping stones and there was less of a tendency to use only natural boulders.

Anchor stones have been found throughout the Americas. Locations include the Northwest Coast, the northern California coast, along the Illinois River in present-day Illinois, along the Susquehanna River in Pennsylvania, near the Delawa : River in New York, and in the Titicaca Basin of Bolivia and Peru. The shape, size, material, and workmanship of the stones vary widely at each location. For example, I'linois stones varied from a 25-pound unworked river rock to a 34½-pound sandstone sphere that was pains-'akingly pecked into shape from a cube and then grooved. Anchor stones generally weighed between 15 and 50 pounds. Apparently, each boatsman judged his anchor requirements by the weight of his boat and the swiftness of the water he boated in, then picked a suitably sized rock and shaped it to his particular aesthetic and functional needs.

At the end of the 19th century, anchor stones were popular among both Indians and whites. Fishermen all along the eastern seaboard used them as cheap, easy-to-replace anchors. With the greater availability of metal anchors, however, use of anchor stones became less common, although the Aymara Indians in Peru and Bolivia were still using them in the 1970s.

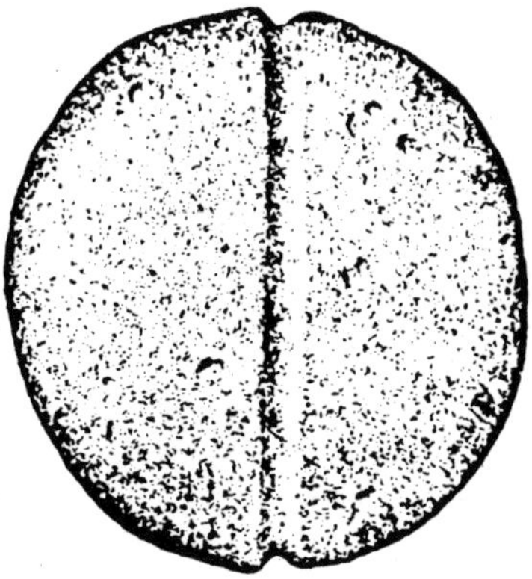

Anchor stone from the Illinois River Basin.

**ANKLET,** generally defined as a bracelet for the ankle, is a bracelet that among Indian peoples may be worn anywhere between the knee and the foot. Anklets are worn in all parts of the Americas and are made from a variety of materials, including leather, fur, feathers, teeth, seeds, human hair, and shells. Indians began wearing anklets in prehistoric times and continue today.

**Styles and uses.** There is no typical anklet. Style and material vary from tribe to tribe. In general, tribes use those materials most available to them. Plains Indians of the United States use leather, fur, and metal bells. The Bóroro of Bolivia plait cotton bands. The Mbayá of Argentina make their anklets from human hair, and the Ona of Tierra del Fuego use braided sinew or plaited grass. At times, however, the desire for anklets made from exotic materials has stimulated trade: before European contact, both the Indians of what is today inland Georgia and the Aztecs of the Valley of Mexico traded with Indians on the Gulf Coast for shells to make anklets.

Ornamentation is a use for anklets common to all parts of the Americas. Other uses vary regionally. North American Indians use them as rhythmic noisemakers during dances. This use is much less frequent in South America. Among South American tribes. Purí and Coroado young women wrap bark strips below their knees and around their ankles to slenderize their joints; the Carajá of central Brazil crochet cotton bands around their children's ankles to assure them healthy growth; the Mataco shamans of the Gran Chaco region wear deer-hoof anklets while dancing to frighten away the disease demons from sick patients. During the 17th century, Carib women of the West Indies wore anklets made of basketry to make their ankles swell attractively and to distinguish them from captive women.

The frequency with which anklets are worn varies by climate. Tribes in cooler areas normally wear anklets only for dances and ceremonial occasions. Where warmer climates prevail and fewer clothes are worn, anklets often become a permanent part of the costume.

**Historical notes.** It is not known when Indians began wearing anklets. One of the earliest known uses — 900 BC — is among Indians in the Guatemalan highlands, who wore stone, shell, jade, and rope anklets. The Aztec had mosaic anklets set with precious stones, as well as copper, stone, and bone anklets when the Spanish conquistador Hernán Cortés conquered them in 1521. Anklets were also in use in the Caribbean region and South America when the first European arrived in the early 16th century.

In remote areas, anklets are used today much as they were in the past. Where contact with whites has been extensive, some changes have resulted. Artificial materials, most commonly metal bells and glass beads, have been added to the natural materials used to construct anklets. Adoption of dress styles of the white culture has, in warm areas, lessened the frequency with which anklets are worn. The general adoption of white medical practices has largely eliminated the use of anklets by medicine men in rituals, although North American tribes still use anklets extensively during ceremonies and dances.

**ANVILS** were used by Indian peoples of the Americas to work metal and stone. Usually comprised of stone, they ranged in size from natural masses of rock used in place at quarries to small portable stones. Occasionally, an anvil of specific shape was utilized for a specialized purpose. For example, a sharp-edged anvil may have been used in notching an arrowhead.

**AQUEDUCT** refers to a man-made conduit or artificial channel for conveying water. A number of different designs were employed by the Indian peoples, usually to serve one of two functions — to convey water either for drinking or for irrigation. Some aqueducts did both. In at least one instance, an aqueduct was built to divert a stream for architectural reasons. Aqueducts described in available sources

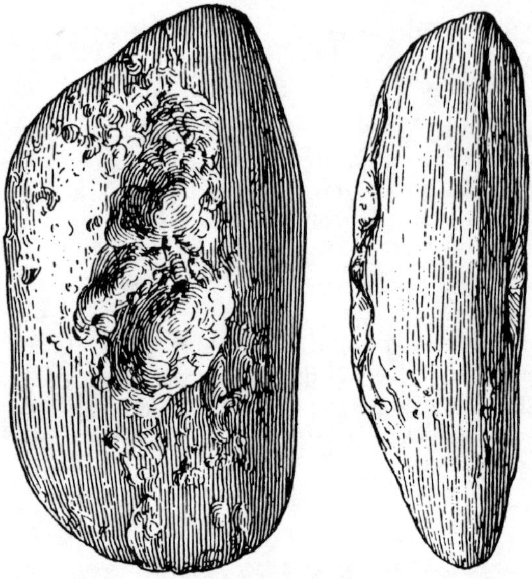

Limestone anvil from the Argentine coast, top and side view. Taken from *Bureau of American Ethnology Bulletin 52* (1912).

were built in prehistoric or historic times by Indians in four areas — southwestern United States, central Mesoamerica, northern Colombia, and Peru.

**Regional variations.** In the southwestern United States, the most extensive aqueducts were completed by the Hohokam peoples in southern Arizona between, it is generally believed, the first century AD and 1400. The Hohokam aqueducts were canals dug through earth or in some places volcanic rock to depths of up to 25 feet (8 meters). Some are an estimated 10 miles (16 kilometers) long. A typical aqueduct was 7 feet (2 meters) deep by 4 feet (1.2 meters) wide at the base, expanding to 30 feet (9 meters) wide at the top. Sides and bottom were tamped and plastered with clay to minimize seepage. The Hohokam dug their aqueducts in the Gila and Salt river valleys, and one source estimates that 300 miles (483 kilometers) of aqueducts exist in the Salt River

Valley alone. Other aqueducts were dug by inhabitants of Peñasco Blanco in the Chaco Canyon area of northwestern New Mexico; these were lined with slabs of stone and clay.

In central Mesoamerica, archaeological remains of aqueducts exist in several areas. At San Lorenzo in the present Mexican state of Veracruz, there are stone aqueducts built by the Olmec between 1150 and 900 BC. At Palenque, a Maya site in the present Mexican state of Chiapas that was occupied between AD 300 and 900, there are remains of an underground vaulted aqueduct, apparently built to divert a stream beneath a ceremonial structure.

In the Valley of Mexico, several famous aqueduct systems were built by the Aztecs and nearby peoples. Between 1431 and 1472, Nezahualcóyotl, ruler of Texcoco, built a complex aqueduct system believed to have watered his pleasure gardens. It included two elevated aqueducts 22 meters above the ground, a main ditch aqueduct dug partly through bedrock and partly lined with masonry, and a system of secondary ditch aqueducts for the actual irrigation. The Aztecs living in Tenochtitlán, their island capital, built two famous aqueducts, primarily to bring drinking water to the city. The first, constructed during the reign of Moctezuma I (1440-68), brought water from the spring at Chapultepec, an estimated distance of three miles (5 kilometers). Hernán Cortés, the Spanish conquistador, described this aqueduct as being built of stone and mortar and consisting of two channels, each as wide as a man's body. Only one channel at a time was filled with water; the other was left dry so it could be cleaned. Where the aqueduct crossed a canal, the water passed through a hollow bridge. The second aqueduct was added a few years later, during the reign of Ahuítzotl (1486-1503), to supplement the supply of drinking water to Tenochtitlían's rapidly increasing population. It brought water from Coyoacán, possibly along the Ixtapalapa causeway.

In Zempoala, which is believed to have reached its height around 1519, the Totonac built an extensive underground masonry aqueduct system that drained excess water not used for drinking into nearby irrigation canals.

In South America, the most extensive archaeological remains of aqueducts are found in the Peruvian culture area. Here, apparently before AD 1000, on the north Peruvian coast near Ascope, the Mochica built a massive earthwork wall with a channel cut in the top to bring water through the Chicama Valley. The wall is about 4,500 feet (1,400 meters) long. In the Moche Valley, also on the north coast, where Chan Chan, capital of the Chimú Kingdom (*c*. 1000-1471) was located, the Indians built an extensive aqueduct system to bring water from the Río Moche, miles away in the mountains. The main canal was a stone-lined channel atop a stone and earth embankment that in some places was 60 feet (18 meters) high. At Machu Picchu, high in the mountains near Cuzco, aqueducts were used by the Inca between 1476 and 1534.

Other aqueducts in South America have been found in northern Colombia near the Cauca River. They were built by the Aburrá, probably before the 15th century.

**General characteristics.** Distribution of water from main aqueducts was accomplished through the use of public fountains, secondary aqueducts, and water sellers. According to some sources, the Aztecs of Tenochtitlán employed all three: a public fountain in the center of the city, small ducts that brought water directly to the houses of the rich, and water sellers who bought their water from government tax collectors at special outlets in the main aqueduct and then took it by boat to other sections of the city. Archaeological evidence in Zempoala indicates that the temple complex and the more imposing residences there benefitted from a well-developed secondary aqueduct system: underground ducts brought water into house or compound cisterns, from which it was later led off to irrigation canals.

Sometimes religious ceremonies were held to mark the opening of an important aqueduct. At Tenochtitlán, for example, a contemporary source reported that Ahuítzotl offered birds, flowers, and incense to the first water that arrived in the aqueduct constructed during his reign, and later, when the water flow contributed to flooding, he had high officials' hearts thrown into the aqueduct in an effort to obtain relief from the problem.

Aqueducts were an impressive engineering achievement of prehistoric and historic Indians. Although in some areas they were used by people that were purely agrarian, such as the Hohokam, in other areas they contributed to the growth of urban centers, such as Tenochtitlán, by making water available for drinking and high yield agriculture. Some of the aqueducts, such as those constructed by the Hohokam and the Mochica, were being used in the mid-20th century by both Indian and white populations.

**ARMOR.** The type of armor used by American Indians differed greatly from that of other world cultures, largely because the Indians did not generally practice metalwork. Hence, the most effective form of European body armor, the suit of mail, had no equivalent in the Americas. The Indian peoples, however, almost universally used several other materials to protect their warriors.

It is essential to distinguish two major categories: body armor, resembling clothing; and parrying armor, or shields. For most Indians of Subarctic North America, the shield was the only form of armor, while the Inuit (Eskimo) of the Arctic and many South American tribes did not have the shield, but developed unique forms of body armor.

The origins and early development of American Indian armor are uncertain because of the lack of written records and the relative scarcity of actual specimens. The effects of the arrival of white men have been better documented. Although the introduction of firearms elsewhere prefigured an end to defensive armor, the Indians modified and in many cases preserved their armor. Moreover, with the "inheritance" of horses from the Spanish, they developed new forms of protection.

**North America.** The Inuit, who in so many respects seem a stepping-stone from Asian culture, shared with the Chukchi across the Bering Strait in Siberia a form of plate armor traceable to Japan and not found elsewhere in the Americas. The Aleut used the Inuit mode of handiwork in lashing the armor, but they applied it to a wooden rod-type of armor, used not only by such nearby Indians as the Northwest Coast Sitka and the Plateau region Klamath but also by tribes as distant as the Iroquois and those of Virginia.

The Northwest Coast Indians had a remarkably sophisticated array of body armor. Typical was the skin armor of the Tsimshian, made of animal hide. Twined wooden slats or rods were used by tribes from the Sitka in Alaska to the Hupa in California; a specimen construed as a greave (armor for the lower leg) has been found. With the arrival of the white man, the Tlingit attached iron plates to buckskin neckpieces for chest protection. The Tlingit and Haida made heavy wooden helmets with visors.

Neighbors of the Northwest Coast Indians shared some characteristic armor: the Shasta of the California culture area used the rod-and-slat types, while the Shoshoni of the Great Basin glued antelope skins together to protect their horses and themselves.

The skin type of armor, especially the leather or hide shirt, was widespread, although its use dwindled with the advent of firearms. In 1609 the Mohawk suffered severe losses before the French explorer Samuel de Champlain and his Algonquin allies, who were armed with matchlocks; thereafter, the Mohawk abandoned their leather coats and evidentally took up guns themselves. Other members of the Iroquois Confederacy, such as the Onondaga and the Seneca, allegedly used rod-type armor, as did the Indians of Virginia. The scanty reports of body armor in the southeastern United States indicate both leather and wood construction.

Leather had a great effectiveness against arrows, which were used in the open regions of the Plains and Southwest. Such tribes as the Comanche fashioned leather armor for their horses, and the Navajo, on mastering the horse, adopted an extremely heavy leather shirt too cumbersome for men on foot.

The shield was the characteristic defensive equipment of North America, and the Plains Indian was its master. Shields were invariably circular in shape, ranging in size from 12 to 26 inches in diameter. Larger, more elaborately constructed shields were used for ceremonial purposes. The most effective material was hide from the thick hump on a buffalo's neck, hardened with glue from the hooves. One or two thongs of rawhide or similar material served as a handle. Such a shield was slung over the left arm or shoulder, leaving the warrior's hands free for his bow and arrow. A valued shield, traditionally made by the medicine man, was handed down through generations.

The Southwestern Indians were second only to the Plains tribes in shield craftsmanship. Because they fought more on foot, their shields were generally larger and heavier. The Mohave and others used horsehide or deerskin. The Pima evidently attached wooden handles to hide shields, while such tribes as the Navajo made entire shields of corded or slatted wood. Before the Spanish period, the Pueblo Indians reportedly turned their genius for basketry to shield construction.

In the Eastern Woodlands and Southeastern regions, where fighting was normally hand-to-hand in dense woods, shields were rare. The Mohawk and some of their allies carried shields of netted cedar wood while on march. Indians of Virginia used shields made from bark, and Carolina Indians employed bark and cane in shield construction.

**Mesoamerica.** In Mesoamerica, cotton-padded suits were used as body armor. There are no surviving specimens, but much information has been gathered from the codices (picture-writing manuscripts) left by the advanced civilizations. Among the Toltecs, Aztecs, and others, only the nobility and higher ranks wore full armor. The "common" soldiers wore armor of henequen, yucca fiber, or other plant materials.

along with quilted caps. A Maya warrior's armor was light if he used a throwing-stick (atlatl) and heavy if he threw a spear. Wooden helmets, many quite elaborately designed, often protected the head and face. The thick, quilt-like armor was virtually impenetrable to arrows, but it was also extremely awkward. One of the reasons for the defeat in 1525 of the Pipil Indians of El Salvador at the hands of the Spanish under Pedro de Alvarado was the awkwardness of their armor.

Other types of body armor were found in the Mesoamerican region, though not in great abundance. The Tarascan Indians of Michoacán state, Mexico, are credited with wooden helmets, body pieces, and greaves, all plated with copper and gold. The Mosquito Indians of Honduras wore animal (probably ocelot) skins for defense, as did other tribes of the Panamanian Isthmus.

There are several splendid specimens of what are probably ceremonial shields of the classical Mexican cultures. War shields, however, are well-documented in the codices and early Spanish records. The Aztec war shields were usually round and of modest size. The Nahua word *otlachimalli* ("cane-shield") indicates that the material was solid bamboo-cane strips, woven with thick thread; they were so effective that the Spanish adopted them.

The shields of the Maya were of two main types, a small round one worn over the back and a larger, flexible shield carried by two thongs; the latter was used only by warriors of high status. The Maya and other peoples of Mexico often used turtle shells for their shields. On the Isthmus, shields made from the hide of the tapir were used by the Bribri and the Tirribí of Costa Rica.

**South America.** Armor seems to have been less common among the Indians of South America. Shields were particularly rare, being restricted mainly to the coastal regions of the northern half of the continent.

The Incas probably adopted their body armor of metal-reinforced cotton-padded tunics, wooden or quilted helmets, and occasional animal skins from

Mexico. A truly remarkable innovation, however, was an enormous single sheet of sturdy cloth used to protect up to 100 warriors.

Beyond the Andean civilizations, body armor was most common in the Gran Chaco region. The Abipón of Argentina used the hide of tapirs, lined with "tiger" (possibly ocelot) skin. Such tribes as the Mocoví of Brazil, the Toba of Argentina, and the Mbayá of Paraguay, used jaguar skins. In other regions, the Araucanians, originally of Chile and later of the Argentine pampas, used such materials as sealskin and cowhide. The Tehuelche of Patagonia and the Atacameño of Chile are credited with cloth or leather tunics and helmets.

Shields found in South America varied widely in size, shape, and material. In the Cauca Valley of Co-

*Courtesy of Barbara A. Leitch*

Peruvian Indians, one with helmet and other with shield, in 17th-century French engraving.

lombia, the Quimbaya allegedly fashioned shields from human hair, while the Arma used gold. Tapir skin was used by Indians of the Orinoco and upper Amazon, such as the Jurí and the Tupinamba. The Tehuelche and the Araucanians made shields of various types of hide. Wooden shields occurred among several tribes, including the Carib of Guyana, the Jívaro of Ecuador, the Desana of the northwestern Amazon, and the Warrau of Venezuela. Shields made of basketry were found among the Omagua of western Brazil and Peru and the Achagua of the upper Orinoco.

**Significance of Indian armor.** Except for its almost universal use, the most striking aspect of American Indian armor was its endurance in the face of firearms. Many tribes clung to their armor long after its practicality had diminished or disappeared. The armor no doubt also served religious and social purposes, as its elaborate decoration suggests. In the Inca and Maya civilizations armor became a mark of rank, though originally the different types of armor served a practical end. The warbonnet of the Plains Indian, for another example, had perhaps once served a defensive purpose but, long before the coming of the white man, became a symbolic property. Still other tribes adapted their armor to meet the new challenge. Only with the victory of the white man in the 20th century did such development end.

JAMES R. CRAWFORD

**ARROWHEAD,** the striking end of an arrow, was made by Indians throughout North America for use in hunting and in war. They were also an important part of Indian weaponry in Middle and South America, although less is known about their distribution. Some tribes used arrowheads for ceremonial purposes. They vary considerably in size, shape, and material; many are ingeniously suited for a particular use, such as stunning birds so they may be captured alive. The manufacture of arrowheads decreased significantly after the introduction of firearms to the Americas, although they are still an important weapon among some South American tribes. Classification of arrowheads has helped archaeologists chart cultural development of, and cross-cultural influence among, Indian tribes.

**Composition.** Arrowheads were made from a great many different materials. The Polar band of Inuit

William Curtis Farabee, The Central Arawaks (1918)

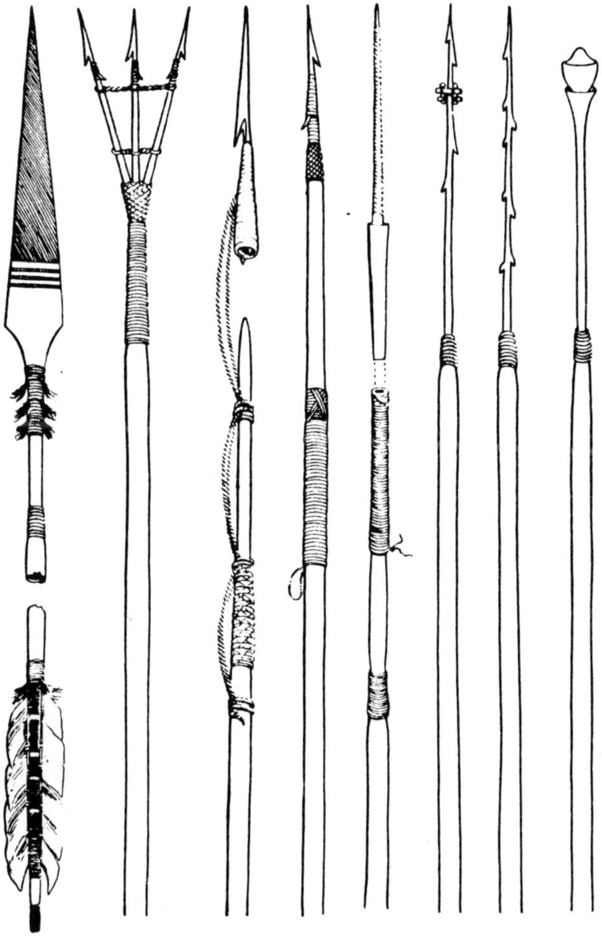

Arrowhead types used by the Central Arawak tribes of South America. Included are a three-pronged leister point and a detachable harpoon head tied to a shaft.

(Eskimo), for example, reportedly discovered and used meteoric iron for arrowheads; other tribes burned wrecked European ships to recover iron bolts and nails. Indians in the southern and eastern areas of the United States used wild turkey-cock spurs; some tribes in eastern Brazil used stingray spikes. Other materials used in North America included flint, jasper, agate, quartz, shell, bone, ivory, and horn. Some materials were more commonly used in certain regions of the continent; *e.g.*, obsidian predominated west of the Rockies and copper was preferred in the Lake Superior region and along the Coppermine River in the central Arctic. Flint and obsidian were commonly used in Mesoamerica. In South America, stone was apparently the most commonly used material in the western and southern regions, with wood, bone, and bamboo being preferred in the tropical regions.

**Hunting and war uses.** Arrowheads designed for hunting by the Inuit and by South American tribes in the tropical forest regions of the Orinoco, Amazon, and Paraguay river basins differed according to the type of game to be shot. For hunting bear in the Arctic, the Inuit used long, nearly parallel-sided flint arrowheads. For deer and smaller game, the points were pencil-shaped and edged with notches to induce rankling and bleeding. The Inuit hunted fish with three-pronged, barbed arrowheads (leister arrowheads) made of horn, bone, or ivory. Barbed harpoon heads, recoverable by a lanyard, were also used for fishing. To hunt birds, the Inuit used arrowheads with a broad, sometimes Y-shaped striking surface.

Arrowheads used by the South American tribes for hunting were equally diverse. Large game was hunted with lanceolate bamboo points that had long cutting edges — 20-70 cm in length. The edges were sometimes barbed or serrated. Large and small game was hunted with wooden pencil-shaped points, some tipped with a single splinter of bone tied so that its sharpened rear formed a barb. Fish were hunted with leister points or harpoon heads. The leister points, with two to seven prongs, were also used to hunt large birds. A harpoon head was generally detachable from the shaft, which doubled as a float and was attached to the head with a lanyard. When harpoon heads were used to hunt large game, the detached shaft dragged behind the animal and hindered its escape. Birds were hunted with blunt-tipped arrows, the heads of which were round or conical pieces of wood; other arrowheads were made from lumps of wax or short sticks, tied in an X shape.

Arrowheads used to kill people were equally specialized. In North America, for example, when large stone arrowheads proved ineffective against the chain mail shirts of the Spanish, the Indians of the Southeast reportedly began shooting untipped cane arrows that splintered when they hit the mail and sent sharp slivers between the links. The Apache of the Southwest used detachable points that were harder to remove from a wound. Some tribes used poisoned arrowheads. The Salish of western Canada, for example, used rattlesnake venom as a poison.

Evidence of the killing power of arrowheads occasionally occurs in graves: two skeletons discovered in central California had arrowheads imbedded in their spinal columns.

**Ceremonial uses.** In addition to hunting and war, arrowheads were sometimes used for ceremonial purposes. An obsidian arrowhead was found in the hand of an Indian body in a grave near Oakley, California. Apache mothers reportedly tied arrowheads to their baby's clothing as magical protection from harm.

**Manufacturing techniques.** Three techniques commonly used to make arrowheads were percussion, pressure flaking, and grinding. Percussion and flaking were used to shape stone arrowheads. During the Owasco Period (*c*. AD 1000-1300) in present-day New York, for example, artifacts found suggest that rough shaping was done by hitting a slender, cylindrical antler tool (indirect percussion). Finer shaping was done by applying pressure with a bone tool (pressure flaking). Grinding could be used to sharpen both mineral and nonmineral heads. Among some tribes living in California, a limited number of craftsmen made all the arrowheads, but among the tribes living in the

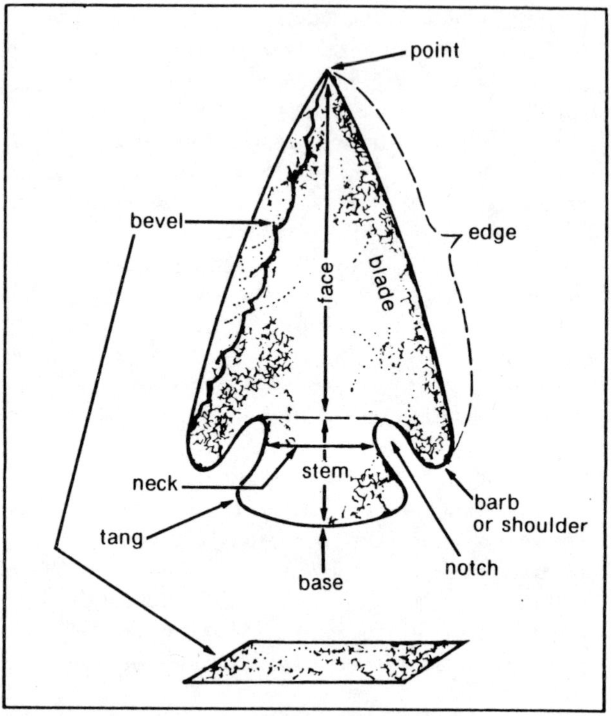


Diagram illustrating different parts of an arrowhead. Certain shapes of arrowheads sometimes characterized a particular region, culture, or time period.

Great Basin and Plateau regions of the United States, there was less specialization.

Arrowheads were attached to their shafts by various combinations of lashing, gluing, socketing, and notching. In one method, reported for tribes in the southern United States, the arrowhead was inserted into the split end of a cane shaft, and the juncture was then wrapped with moistened deer sinew or strips of buckskin and glued. As the wrapping dried, it tightened. Some tribes in the tropical forest regions of South America used resin, wax, and a binding of peccary hair to attach the head. Many stone points were manufactured with accentuated stems or notches so they might be lashed more securely. Some points were attached directly to the shaft, others first to a foreshaft which was then bound to the shaft or inserted into it. One type of South American point made from a sharpened monkey humerus had a socket in its base into which the shaft was inserted.

**Classification.** A comprehensive typology that classified arrowheads found in North America by shape was formulated by Thomas Wilson of the U.S. National Museum and published in the annual report of the Smithsonian Institution for 1897. Wilson divided arrowheads into four divisions: leaf-shaped, triangular, stemmed, and peculiar. The divisions are further subdivided into classes.

Arrowheads found in North America have also been classified by region. Obsidian points with bifurcated stems, for example, are found mostly in the southern portion of the intermountain plateau west of the Rockies. One classification of arrowheads by locale is that of Robert E. Bell, published in *Special Bulletin No. 1* of the Oklahoma Anthropological Society.

In the mid-1970s, there were no continent-wide classificaton systems available for arrowheads found in either Middle or South America. There were, however, typologies for arrowheads in specific regions, such as the Valley of Mexico and the Tropical Forest region of South America. According to *The Handbook of South American Indians* (1947), edited by Julian H. Steward, the only classification of stone arrowheads in South America is a 1929 map showing the areas where they have been found.

A chronological classification found in a particular region can give scientists insight into how the culture or cultures in that region changed over time. It can also help resolve questions of cross-cultural influence, such as the impact of migration, war, or trade. For example, the Mississippian culture, spread over the southeastern and mid-continental sections of the United States from *c.* AD 700 to the time of European contact, was characterized in part by cultural traits that had arisen earlier in Mesoarmerica. Archaeologists believe these similarities may indicate cultural diffusion from Mesoamerica to the Mississippian culture region. As evidence in support of this theory, a similar type of small-stemmed projectile point was used in both regions; it appeared first at Teotihuacán in central Mexico between AD 100 and AD 600 and in the Mississippian culture area about AD 700 to AD 900.

Often arrowheads, the heads of spears and atlatl darts, and knife blades cannot be positively distinguished unless the shafts or weapons are found together with the points. Size is sometimes used to separate arrowheads from spear and dart heads, but there is no general agreement on the maximum size for arrowheads, estimates ranging from 2½ to 4 inches.

**Distribution.** Information detailing the distribution of arrowheads is incomplete. Present data indicate that they became widespread in North America sometime after AD 500 and were in nearly universal use by the 16th century. The situation in Middle and South America is less well known. At the time of the Spanish Conquest in 1519, the atlatl and dart, rather than the bow and arrow, were the principal weapons of the Aztecs.

When the whites came to the Americas, the manufacture of arrowheads changed. North American Indians began to use iron extensively, either preshaped or as a raw material, and some made arrowheads from glass.

Indians in North America largely gave up the manufacture of arrowheads and adopted firearms as weapons after the rapid-firing breech-loading rifle had been perfected and ammunition was readily available. In the mid-1970s, a few North American Indian craftsmen still made arrowheads. In the tropical forest regions of the Orinoco, Amazon, and Paraguay river basins of South America, arrowheads made from traditional materials — wood, bone, bamboo, and stingray spikes — were still in widespread use in the mid-1940s.

SCOTT BECKETT

**ASSIMILATION** is defined as the appropriation and transformation or incorporation into the substance of the assimilator, or the absorption of one group or population into the cultural tradition of another group or population. This process is distinguishable from acculturation, in which intercultural borrowing is marked by the continuous transmission of traits and elements between diverse peoples, resulting in new and blended patterns. Acculturation also refers to the resultant modifications occurring in a culture through direct and prolonged contact with a more advanced society.

Assimilation is the descriptive term used for one of the processes that Native Americans underwent during much of their history of contact with European populations in the New World. The alternatives to assimilation were not many — annihilation or accommodation to some digestible version of European culture. Geographic isolation protected only a few groups of limited numbers.

**Theoretical considerations.** When examining the process of assimilation in the Western Hemisphere, the problems of description at first appear enormous. The anthropologist Elman Service, however, provided a model that is useful for understanding the differential responses to European contact by Native Americans in Latin America. He suggests that the types of contact made between Europeans and different Indian groups, and the resultant degree of assimilation, were determined by the social and political systems of the particular Indian societies. The three basic patterns of contact were reflected in the 20th century in three physical and cultural types of Latin American populations. These were almost pure European, as in Costa Rica, coastal Brazil, and parts of the Antilles; mestizo, as in Paraguay, interior central Chile, lowland Peru, interior Central America, and parts of Venezuela and Colombia; and pure Indian, as in the highlands of Peru, Bolivia, Ecuador, Mexico, and Guatemala.

Service argues that varying colonial policies and institutions were responses to the diversity of cultural patterns possessed by the Native American communities themselves. He assumes a singularity in Spanish and Portuguese means and goals with respect to the exploitation of their American colonies — *i.e.*, the use of captive labor for mining, agriculture, and other forms of tribute. Means to these goals changed to meet contrasting native reactions, which depended upon the level of sociopolitical complexity of the particular indigenous community. Viewing the history of contact with millions of densely settled people in the Mesoamerican and Andean highlands, other scholars have suggested that the easiest adjustments were made when the Europeans and Indians were the most culturally similar, and that the Indians were most likely to survive as a people when the adjustment was the least difficult. Service described the process of contact as basically that of state institution with state institution, having a direct effect on only a few Indian communities at first.

**South America.** This construction would explain the survival of great masses of highland Native American descendants of the great Andean cultures, whose intensive agricultural lives were interrupted only by the replacement of officials in the controlling hierarchy.

In the lowlands, where once intensive native economies based on essentially the same technology as the highland communities flourished, are Latin America's mestizo populations. Swift mestization and assimilation were facilitated by the lack of stable sociopolitical institutions to bar the physical and cultural onslaught of the Europeans. The natives had something to gain, and little to lose, in flight from European colonists. There was space to hide, and capture meant personal, not community, slavery. No sociopolitical system was formidable enough to offer either long-term resistance or a structure whose leadership could be supplanted by the Europeans.

Assimilation did not actually occur in what Service calls "Euro-America." There, marginal groups with the simplest sociocultural development met extermination or expulsion, with those surviving individuals risking capture and enslavement. In many tropical areas, enslavement was equated with mestization, the most efficient method of assimilation. Service maintains that in this area assimilation did not occur because nearly all the Indians escaped or were killed. Lack of cultural buffers left them powerless in the face of European political institutions.

**Colonial Spanish North America.** Service's model can also be applied to southwestern North America. The nomadic band organizations of the Navajo, Ute, and Apache were so structured as to allow the Indians to retreat from the Spaniards. The Rio Grande Pueblo peoples, however, with their stable agricultural communities and greater sociopolitical complexity, offered the invaders the opportunity for direct, immediate control and acculturation. Only the Zuñi and Hopi evaded absorption to any extent because of their geographical isolation.

Roman Catholic diocese records for the Rio Grande territory indicate rapid mestization among captured nomadic tribes in the first two centuries of Spanish hegemony in the area, in accord with Service's hypothesis. Yet, the Pueblo communities were indirectly dealt with for tribute and services, leaving them largely unaltered and subject to "very slow" acculturation as described by Service's Indo-America typology.

Assimilation of Native Americans in California under the Spanish duplicated in many respects the Roman Catholic mission experiences in Latin America. Village groups were rounded up and placed on the missions, where the priests imposed Spanish culture upon native institutions, adding Roman Catholicism and European customs as a cultural overlay. Death from disease and social pathology, however, brought about the failure of this endeavor. The missions failed and the deculturated survivors drifted off into the general population, with some rancherias and communities being re-established. in all probability, California in the 20th century contained more assimilated Native Americans than any other of the United States. The reclamation of Alcatraz Island in

1969 by Native Americans was attempted by many who knew only that they were "Indian" in their genetic history, but had been culturally disinherited by the upheaval of California's European invasion. In addition, many other young Native Americans participated who were two and three generations removed from their tribal backgrounds and who came from other parts of the country. Many of them also lacked a clear idea of their cultural origins but, perhaps in contrast to their parents and grandparents, sought to repair the lost strands of their heritage.

**Colonial French North America.** The French conquest of North America in many respects resembled that of the Spanish elsewhere. Although plantations and captive labor were not feasible, the exploitation of the fur trade bore a similar impact upon native groups in Canada and the northeastern United States. The French could not assert control over groups whose society was based on the extended family and the band. Instead, decimated by disease and warfare, band groups dissolved and single members adjusted themselves into the invading system. The French and, later, British and American fur trade systems relied in large part upon this phenomenon. The Iroquois, however, with their complex set of sociopolitical institutions, maintained their autonomy for some 150 years in the face of French and British military and political pressures.

**Colonial British North America.** For most of the Atlantic seaboard, the fur trade passed by swiftly or not at all. English colonists, who had been farmers in Europe, sought to transplant their lifestyle to North America. Their conflict with the native horticulturalists resembled an interspecies competition — in which one variety survives at the expense of the other — reflecting Service's model for lowland Latin America. Mestization proceeded quickly, but disease and warfare ran apace. Ultimately, New England's native population proved unadaptable to slavery, a topic much discussed in historical literature. Along the Atlantic coastline, those colonial agriculturalists who required slaves had to look to Africa for them since, like Latin American lowland populations, the natives simply faded into the interior or died out, leaving inadequate numbers to perform the needed toil.

The conquest experience of the Canadian natives ran the range from complete annihilation (as with the Beothuk) to reservations, squatter communities, and the thousands of deculturated "mixed-bloods" known as the Métis. With the exception of some British Columbian chiefdoms and the Canadian Iroquois, there were no complex native sociopolitical structures with which the Europeans needed to contend. Assimilation progressed far more slowly in the central provinces and northern territories than on either coast, as might be suspected. The remoteness of some Athapascan and Cree groups make even contemporary contact minimal.

**The United States.** East of the Mississippi, most native populations were dissolved by means of disease, outright military action, murder, migration, or the panorama of social pathologies sometimes called "the expectable residue of conquest." Genetic assimilation was probably of high proportion throughout the region; only some geographical cul-de-sacs allowed remnant natives space in which to survive. The isolated groups were rarely composed of a single tribe, a major exception being the Cherokee of Tennessee and North Carolina. For the most part, the cul-de-sacs were and are still to be found either along political borderlines — as in the areas of the Lumbee, Catawaba, Haliwa, and Croatan — or in prohibitive geographical settings — as in the areas of the Miccosukee, Houma, and Malecite. Because of the genetic mix of many of these refugee populations, some are not identified as Native Americans, or "Indians." It can probably be demonstrated that there is as much (or as little) "Indian" genetic in-put among the Carolina Lumbee as among the Appalachian Melungeon, but the former have received federal "Indian" status, while the latter are federally invisible.

In the late 1700s and 1800s, Thomas Jefferson was one of the few who espoused removal for Native

Navajo Indians from New Mexico as they arrived (above) at Carlisle School *c.* 1880 and (below) six months after their arrival. Founder of the school, Capt. Richard H. Pratt, is at rear of upper photo.

Americans, to "protect" them from the lacerations of cultural contact. Andrew Jackson made it a policy not to protect, but to relieve, the natives of their lands east of the Mississippi River. Thousands of people from hundreds of tribes were peaceably or militarily coerced into abandoning their homes for new ones in Indian Territory (present-day Oklahoma and Kansas). Thousands died and hundreds escaped along the way to become genetically and culturally absorbed by white families, especially in Arkansas, Tennessee, and Missouri. Those who completed the journey were first placed on reservations and then, through the loss of land during the allotment period of the 1870s and 1910, became reservationless and often landless members of the states of Oklahoma and Kansas. Only a few reservations continue to exist in these two states.

A great deal of assimilation has occurred in Oklahoma and Kansas, although some clusters of relatively unmixed natives still exist, as in the eastern Oklahoma Cherokee area and west around Anadarko in the Kiowa Apache and Comanche region. It is said that to become governor of Oklahoma, one must have "Indian blood" to get the vote.

Warfare and the massacre of the bison herds seal the fate of other Western tribes. They were either removed to Indian Territory or shut up on reservations. The remoteness of the reservations and the general racist hostility of the whites has kept cultural and genetic assimilation to a minimum. On some of these reservations, such as the Pine Ridge Reservation, deep political hostilities exist between families and individuals based on their "full-blood" or "mixed-blood" status. There is an implication that the degree of native "blood" correlates with the degree of white cultural assimilation. But culture does not necessarily reflect genetic makeup, nor is the reverse true. A "full-blood" may have been born and raised in New York City without knowing a single element of native culture, and a genetic Japanese may be raised as a Navajo and be a Navajo, despite biological ancestry. In other words, blood quantum does not strictly translate into culture quantum.

Depopulation came soon to the Northwest Coast tribes, due largely to diseases brought by sailors. Yet some village groups managed to avoid decimation through the benefit of geographical isolation. The degree of white native miscegenation seems less easy to gauge in this area than others. For lack of adequate studies of genetic admixture, phenotypic—often very impressionistic — judgments are made with a poor understanding of the native substrata, which may have contained traits that approximated white range, such as skin color and hairiness.

**The Arctic.** The Canadian and Alaskan Inuit (Eskimo) suffered the throes of European influence sporadically over a long time period. Apparently, their isolation ended by the late 20th century. Assimilation into Canadian and U.S. culture will be a slow process, however, because of geographic isolation. Over the centuries, Russian settlers filtered through the Aleutian Island chain, mating with and acculturating the Aleut. Many Aleuts now bear the surnames and physical features of Russians. Yet cultural assimilation is not noticeably "Russian" in content as much as it is American, reflecting the U.S. purchase of Alaska from Russia and increasing U.S. contact after World War II.

**Future prospects.** It is believed that some 16,000,000 citizens of the United States can claim some Native American genetic admixture. New England in particular can be regarded as a site of large-scale miscegenation during the 17th and 18th centuries. Whole bands of Native Americans were genetically "swallowed up" wherever disease and military action took a minimal toll. This situation occurred along the entire seaboard, as well as in the northern regions of Vermont, New Hampshire, and Maine. For centuries in the New World, assimilation of the natives has stood as public policy, while private norms have abhorred miscegenation. Obviously, ideals are not necessarily norms.

In the United States in the late 20th century, a new

attitude toward Native Americans arose among non-Indians and Indians themselves. A new respect and self-respect was building. Formerly "assimilated" Native Americans began to re-identify with their heritage, and thousands of Americans began to claim some native ancestry in ever-increasing numbers. In the changing climate of acceptance, this emphasis upon identification could only aid in the development of a healthy, strong, pluralistic world.

SHIRLEY HILL WITT

**ATHLETICS** are vital elements in Native American life, both past and present. They are interwoven with the many dimensions of individual cultures, the economy, social and political organization, as well as ritual life. In this context, "athletics" is used to refer to those sport phenomena which involve physical exertion and competition between individuals or groups. Included in this definition are such activities as competitive racing, jumping, swimming, fighting, throwing, and shooting (e.g., bow-and-arrow), as well as ball and other skill games.

While many of these activities were probably common in the pre-Columbian Americas, archeological data on athletic behavior are limited. However, there is evidence of stone ball courts in Middle America, in parts of the American Southwest, and in the northern sector of South America. Archeologists have also uncovered many "chunkey yards" in the American Southeast. These are specially prepared playing fields on which men competed at a type of hoop-and-pole game in which contestants attempted to strike a rolling stone with a pole. Graphic and pictorial representations of athletic activities have been uncovered in several areas of nuclear Middle America, and many items labeled as "gaming devices" by archeologists have been discovered in prehistoric sites throughout the Native New World. For example, both stone and clay balls have been found in many locations, while perhaps the most unusual find was a miniature racket uncovered in a Peruvian child's grave with a definite pre-Columbian date.

From an archeological perspective, it is safe to suggest that native inhabitants of the pre-historic Americas were athletically active. However, only in certain areas of Middle America can one decipher, with any degree of detail, the nature and extent of these sport activities.

Nevertheless, if one combines pre-historic data with that collected by historians and ethnographers, it is possible to draw a composite picture of the athletic diversity of traditional Native American life.

The most commonly known and popular of sport activities engaged in by the original inhabitants of the New World continents can be grouped into three major areas: (1) stress and endurance competition (e.g., running, tumbling, acrobatics, wrestling and boxing), (2) games of skill (e.g., archery, snow skate, hoop-and-pole, chunkey, and ring toss, (3) ball games (e.g., hip ball, hand ball, double ball, foot ball, and racket or stick ball).

**Stress and endurance competition**

Running games were widespread throughout the New World, but the most famous runners were the *Tarahumara* of Northern Mexico whose name for themselves *(rarámuri)* actually means "runners." Capable of running great distances, they were noted for their stamina. Recently, physiologists have studied the *Tarahumara* and have suggested that the group illustrates the human body's great capacity for stress. It is no accident, they say, that these Native Mexicans have no incidents of cardiovascular ailment.

Another popular sport, relay racing, has been known in certain parts of South America. Among the Northwestern and Central *Gê* of Eastern Brazil, for example, tribesmen raced while carrying large tree trunks that weighed as much as 200 pounds each.

On the other hand, ball racing was found primarily in the North American West and in Northern Mexico. The *Bannock* played a game in which they would kick inflated beef bladders over long distances in competitive groups. The *Tarahumara* men still play a kickball game called *rarajípari,* in which a light wooden ball is kicked along a course that may be as many as twelve miles in length. Running back and forth along the course, they have been known to play at this game for as many as 48 consecutive hours.

Tumbling and acrobatics, athletic forms requiring both strength and coordination, were highly developed in nuclear Middle America, but not in other areas of the New World. There are many drawings and carvings that attest to the importance of these activities in the civilizations of pre-historic Mexico.

Team wrestling and boxing, on the other hand, were common in certain parts of Native South America. In fact, different wrestling holds were highly stylized and unique to particular groups among the many tribes competing in the sport. For example, the *Tapirapé* specialized in neck holds. Team wrestling often pitted one kin group against another as among the *Aymara* where competing units represented opposing moities.

**Skill games**

Among the many skill games, those utilizing the bow-and-arrow were probably the most common. Archery competition has been found in most areas where the bow was employed. It was viewed as a pleasurable pastime as well as good training for both the hunt and warfare.

Snow snake, another skill game, was an athletic contest in which the combatants threw javelins or smaller darts for distance, either along snow or ice or through the air. The *Chippewa* of Wisconsin, for example, carved very elaborate devices called *shoshiman* (slipping sticks) that they would bend at one end, much like an ice-skate runner. Then they would prepare a course on the ice and compete with each other, gliding their sticks at great speed along the pre-determined route.

The hoop-and-pole game was wide spread in Middle and North America, but is seldom encountered in the literature on Native South America. In this event, contestants threw spears or shot arrows at a small hoop or ring that was rolled along the ground. Points were accumulated either by striking the object or by causing the spear or arrow to come to rest adjacent to the hoop at the completion of its roll.

One athletic event closely related to the hoop-and-pole contest, was chunkey. Found primarily in the North American Southeast, this game was played by rolling a large wheel-like object, called a chunkey stone, down the middle of a prepared course. Two contestants ran beside the rolling stone at some small distance and hurled large poles at the moving target. Points were scored in the fashion typical of hoop-and-pole games.

Ring toss games were also popular in many areas of the Native Americas. These events generally involved throwing large rings or hoops and catching them on sticks or arrows held in the hand. Related to these, were the games in which objects (e.g., pebbles, balls) were thrown or pitched toward a line or hole. For many years, the Mississippi *Choctaws* have played a game they call *rings,* in which participants toss large metal washers toward a specially prepared hole in the ground.

**Ball games**

The most significant athletic contests engaged in by Native Americans were the ball games. The ball itself was ubiquitous in the pre-Columbian New World, but varied in material, shape, size, and construction. Balls were made of leaves, rags, cornhusks, hide, hair, wood, stone, and clay, as well as rubber. The development of rubber ball games took place in those areas of Northern South America and Mexico where rubber-bearing flora occurred naturally. Probably as a result of experimentation with the extraction and treatment of latex, the rubber ball evolved. Then, as a major trade item it soon was present in most of the major settlement areas from Northern Mexico south to Northern Brazil and Peru, at a date well in advance of European contact.

Of the many types of ball games in the prehistoric Native American world, the most visible, was the formal hip-ball game. Archeological evidence for this game, specifically, the sunken, stone-slab lined courts, had been found in the area from present-day southern Arizona into northern South America. The game was played on these classic stone courts which were specially constructed for this large-scale sporting event. The object of this two-team event was to keep the rubber ball in the air by hitting it with the thighs or buttocks—the use of hands, feet, or head was prohibited—and knock it over the wall at the opponent's end of the court. If either team was able to put the ball through the stone ring at the side of the court, it was an automatic win. However, that happened only infrequently.

The game was often played between native towns, and the competition was fierce and bruising, often fatal to individual combatants. The rubber ball itself was hard and heavy and capable of inflicting physical damage. For this reason, many groups (e.g., *Aztecs)* wore protective equipment, such as aprons, when they played.

A type of ball game that may pre-date the formal hip-ball contest is an event called the "circle game." Centered largely in northern South America, this "domestic sport" was played by men and women alike and entailed little or no competition. Standing in a circle, a group of persons simply attempted to keep a ball aloft by hitting it with hands or feet. An example of such a sport is the South American *pillma* game, in which players form a ring and attempt to keep the ball in the air by throwing and catching the ball from below their waists.

A type of football was also common in Native South America and parts of North America. Using a ball made of stone, buckskin, corn husks, or rags, two teams competed by kicking the sphere back and forth between two goals. Points were scored by striking the ball against the goal of the opponent.

A variety of handball games were also part of the athletic repetoire of many Native Americans. Opposing teams composed of either men or women threw a ball made of rags or cornhusks up and down a field and attempted to score by hitting the opponent's goal post with the ball. One type of handball played by the *Nishinam* of California was a boy's game in which three participants used a wooden ball, tossing it between three bases or corners. The object of the game was to exchange bases with another player without being hit by the third player, who would attempt to hit the runners with the ball while they were off base. Points were scored with each successful throw.

Another type of ball game found only in midwestern and eastern Native North America is double ball. The double ball itself is constructed by attaching two rubber, wooden, or clay balls with a short leather thong. Two teams of combatants sling and catch the gaming device with small, hand-held sticks. Points are scored by moving the ball across an opponent's base line at either end of the field.

Many ball games using a bat or a stick were native to the New World. For example, a type of hockey was played among the *Araucanian* peoples of South America, in which balls of wood, rope, or stone were hit along the ground, using a club with a handle at one end and a specially carved striking surface or face at the other.

Another important ball game was shinny. A North American phenomenon, it was primarily a woman's event, although it was played by the men on occasion. In this contest, competing teams hit a ball toward the goal of their opponents with short sticks. The *Navajos* played shinny with a bag-shaped ball and used either wooden posts or blankets for goals which one had to strike with the ball in order to score.

Racket games are known in parts of South and Middle America, but are most common in North America, particularly in the East and Southeast. Using one or two rackets made of sticks curved at one end to form a loop across which was woven a net of sinew, players caught, threw, and moved the small deer-hide ball (about the size of a golf ball) from one end of the field to the other. A player was only allowed to touch the ball with his stick, and points were scored by striking, crossing, or penetrating the opponent's goal. The formal racket game, which often pitted town against town and on occasion, tribe against tribe, is the parent game of modern lacrosse.

There is good evidence to support the notion that the racket games, as well as shinny and hockey, are related to the wide-spread descendants of a ball-and-stick game that was ancestral as well to the competitive rubber-ball game. Hitting the ball with a stick or racket may thus predate propulsion by hips and feet in a competitive game situation.

Notable among the racket game players of Native America are the *Choctaws* of the North American Southeast. Traditionally, *toli* or stickball, as the *Choctaws* refer to the contest, was played in a formal match between representative teams ot two communities. Often the game was scheduled by town elders as a deliberate ploy to avoid other more violent forms of conflict, including war, that might be threatening to erupt. The two teams would meet on the scheduled day,

Chocktaw ball players with lacrosse sticks, from a lithograph by George Catlin, 1836.

and amidst much ritual, feasting, and celebration, play would continue until one team was able to amass a previously agreed upon number of points, an accomplishment that might take as many as three or four days. There was no limit to the number of players a team was allowed to field, as long as their opponent could match that total. Also there were no boundaries, left or right, only goal posts at the two ends of the field, and these might be at any imaginable distance from each other, depending on the layout of the playing grounds and the size of the teams. It was not unusual for a formal *Choctaw* stickball match to engage three or four hundred players on a playing field several hundred yards in length.

Like most Native America athletic events, the formal racket game was characterized by total community involvement and extensive gambling. Among the *Choctaws,* for example, huge scaffolds would be built at opposite ends of the playing field on which persons from the two competing communities would place items to be bet on the outcome of the game. There were no odds; everyone wagered on their own representative team, and the winners took all. Often the spoils were extensive: money, food, tools, clothes, animals, and other forms of private property. Sometimes players even wagered their own services or those of their wives and children.

Ritual activity was also an important dimension of Native American athletic events. In fact, Culin* suggests that many of these games were only secondarily play in nature.

> *Back of each game is found a ceremony in which the game was a significant part. The ceremony has commonly disappeared; the game survives as amusement, but often with traditions and observances which serve to connect it with its original purpose.*

Ritual was certainly an important element of the formal *Choctaw* stickball match. Medicine men, sorcerers, rainmakers, and drummers from both competing communities were all involved, utilizing their respective skills to affect the game's final outcome. "Fixing" players' legs and arms, putting spells on opposition, enlisting the support of the Sun and its power, and leading preparatory dances and signs, the ritualists were a dominant force in the events of the game. In many ways, the formal racket ball match was as much a contest between ceremonial practioners as between players.

In addition to these economic and ritual functions, athletic events in Native American life also served as physical exercise, training for hunting and warfare, entertainment, and instruments of socialization. Furthermore, sporting competition was a mechanism for the definition of social and political boundaries, for the facilitation of community interaction, and for the creation of settings in which basic cultural values were expressed.

**Athletics and change**

During the past 100 years, modern Western sports have begun to replace traditional ones in many Native American communities. Baseball, soccer, and basketball have had the widest acceptance, but other activities like football, hockey, and softball have also become popular in some areas. Introduced by government agencies, missionaries, educators, and other outsiders, these phenomena have been seen by many as effective acculturative devices, mechanisms by which the Native American adoption of European values would be both provoked and facilitated. However, recent research has suggested that in the adoption process, modern Western sports function more as cultural maintenance systems than as facilitators of acculturation. For example, basketball was introduced among the Ramah *Navajos* in Western New Mexico in the 1930s and '40s by members of the local, Anglo-Mormon population. Yet, as late as 1970, the *Navajos* were playing a type of basketball that was radically different from that engaged in by their white-Mormon neighbors. Their style of play, strategies, sense of purpose, managing techniques, competitiveness, and overall perception of the game are so unique that the label "Navajo basketball" is justified. In this case, it is quite clear that basketball has been of little culture-change significance. The Navajos have

> *...simply borrowed a new form of play and molded its essentials to fit ongoing needs and values. In this sense, basketball is providing recreational and entertainment opportunities for members of the Navajo community without forcefully subjecting them to the Wall Street ethic of White America.**

**Contemporary Native American athletics**

Despite the tendency to structure play in a way that conforms to local tradition, Natives of both the American continents have usually taken modern sports very seriously and have often produced outstanding teams and individual athletes. Soccer teams in Latin America, hockey and lacrosse teams in Canada, baseball and basketball teams in North America, and outstanding track teams in many areas are just a few of the expressions of Native American participation and excellence in contemporary athletic activities.

Also, there are many special organizations and events that serve to focalize Native American athletic interests. For example, the National Indian Activities Association, organized in 1973, sponsors annual basketball and boxing tournaments as well as rodeos for its membership. Other important Native American athletic events include the World Eskimo-Indian Olympics, the

---

* Blanchard, Kendall A. 1974. *Basketball and the Culture-Change Process: The Rimrock Navajo Case.* Council on Anthropology and Education Quarterly 5 (4): 8-13.

U.S. All-Indian Golf Tournament, several major rodeos, and baseball, basketball, bowling, and softball tournaments.

Many American Indian athletes have competed successfully in college, Olympic, and professional sports. The most famous Native American athlete is Jim Thorpe, the *Potawatomi-Sac* and *Fox,* who amazed the sport world by winning both the Pentathalon and the decathalon in the 1912 Olympics and went on to establish himself as one of the greatest players of the early years of professional football.

The American Indian Athlete Hall of Fame includes many other outstanding performers, including: Frank Hudson (*Laguna* Pueblo), Ed Rogers (*Chippewa*), Gus Welch (*Chippewa*), Walter Johnson (*Paiute*), Jim Wolf (*Kiowa*), Albert Hawley *(Gros Venture* and *Assiniboine*), John Levi (*Arapahoe*), and Bemus Pierce (*Seneca*) in football; Charles A. "Chief" Bender *(Chippewa),* Allen P. Reynolds *(Creek),* in baseball; Chief Jay Strongbow *(Cherokee),* boxing; Angelita Rosal *(Sioux),* table tennis; Jesse Remick *(Choctaw*), basketball; and Ellison Brown *(Narragansett*), track and field; as well as many others.

Native American athletes of recent reknown include Rod Curl, golf; "Wahoo" McDaniel, football and wrestling; Jim Nielson, hockey; Sonny Sixkiller and Roman Gabriel, football.

KENDALL BLANCHARD

**AWL** is a small pointed tool used universally by the Indians of the Americas. It was made of bone, ivory, shell, wood, thorns, stone, or copper, and iron and steel after their introduction. Awls were sometimes hafted, and some were carved and otherwise ornamented. They were often carried on the person and kept in ornamented cases or sheaths of cane, bone, wood, metal, or hide.

The awl was used from the time of the earliest inhabitants of North America and is common archaeologically. One of its major uses was for making holes and manipulating thread in the sewing and lacing of hide and bark for clothing, boats, containers, and sewn coverings of dwellings. For these purposes it served in part instead of the eyed needle which was extremely rare among the prehistoric Indians north of Mexico, except among the Eskimos. Another major use of the awl was as an aid in the various tying and weaving techniques of basketry construction and ornamentation. Awls were used also in pottery-making and woodworking and were one of the Indian's most common and versatile tools in the tasks of daily life.

**AX** is a chopping tool with a grooved stone head in contrast to the ungrooved celt. Grooved stone axes were common in aboriginal America and had a wide range of forms. Ax heads were made from diorite, syenite, granite, or other hard rock, but some were made from softer stone such as sandstone or slate, and some rare specimens were of copper. The blade was usually formed by pecking and grinding a stone into a thick wedge shape with rounded corners. Normally one groove was made completely or partially around the head, perpendicular to the long axis, although some grooves were oblique. Multiple-grooved ax heads were common in the Pueblo area. The wooden handle was attached by a withe or strips of rawhide lashed around the head in the groove. Some axes were made with one or more parallel flutings or shallow grooves that ran the long way of the ax, possibly for ornamentation. Size varied greatly from an ounce to over thirty pounds; with the normal range from about one to six pounds. The extreme sizes were probably for ceremonial use.

Axes were used primarily for chopping and quarrying, but also were used in war and hunting and for ceremonial purposes. The chopping of wood was probably often accomplished in conjunction with charring. Stone axes were widely distributed wherever suitable stone was available, but were rare in British Columbia, Alaska, Florida, and the Pacific States. After European contact the stone ax was quickly replaced by the iron ax.

# B

**BAGS AND POUCHES.** The greatest body of knowledge about the Indians of the Americas comes from the firsthand observations of white men from Columbus to the present time. This span of barely 300 years, unfortunately, represents a minute percentage of the 40,000 or more years that we now know men have lived in these lands.

It is not surprising therefore that knowledge of such normally perishable utilitarian artifacts as bags and pouches in pre-Columbian times is dismally meager. Pottery and stone arrowheads, for example, are far less vulnerable to deterioration or destruction by the elements than are hemp, cloth, twine, or leather bags, as archeologists' reports confirm.

It should be added that there seems to be no avid interest in Indian bags and pouches among archeologists to compare with that for pottery and textiles. References to bags and pouches tend to appear in inventories of gravesite and midden findings, and often receive only casual references elsewhere.

If school children are lucky enough to learn of any Indian artifacts besides bows, arrows, moccasins and pottery, they may have learned that the Plains Indians devised a pouch called a parflèche, usually made from buffalo hides stretched taut on a frame to cure and shape. Named by French explorers, its meaning is still unclear; but one conjecture, with linguistic logic, suggests that parflèche means "protect from (deflect) arrow"—much like the French *parasol* (protect from sun) or *parapluie* ("umbrella," protect from rain). White men saw the parflèche used like a saddle bag; but if it were to "protect from arrow" it would have been worn on the body. If, as some theorize, it was made to contain arrows, it was not shaped, for economy of space, like the traditional cylindrical quiver, although deep enough to contain arrows.

As both a saddle bag and storage bag, it was used to hold the dried buffalo meat called pemmican, as well as other foods. The flat surface of the parflèche provided an ideal medium for painted designs, rarely absent on Plains Indians artifacts.

In 1899, pioneer archeologist Richard Wetherill discovered a Basket Maker mummy, dating back to the early part of the Christian era, in a cliff cave at Grand Gulch, Utah. Among the items buried with the mummy was a prehistoric bag, woven from yucca fiber, and far older than the relatively sophisticated parflèche seen by white men in the 1700s.

Believed to be thousands of years old, prairie dog skin bags have been found in Oklahoma, still containing ears of corn. From the later Basket Maker period, skin bags have been found with shelled corn. Similar bags, with the dogs' heads at the opening, held, as H.M. Worthington notes, "oddly shaped stones or other objects thought to have some ceremonial significance."

Apocynum fiber was used for twined bags. Some of them were decorated by dyeing threads; others, by painting, both inside and out. Cornmeal and what was possibly dried fruit have been found in such bags. Often, large bags were split to serve as wrappings for corpses, especially children's. The largest found are about two feet deep. Still other bags found in Basket Maker sites were made of cedar bast, but what they once held is not known.

In the 2nd century AD, Pueblo Indians were using buckskin bags to accommodate their bows and to make quivers for arrows. At that time, skin bags were also used to hold seed corn.

John Upton Terrell, who combs the most reliable sources of Indian data, painstakingly compiled a list of nearly 250 artifacts and commodities traded among prehistoric North American Indian tribes. His list includes: medicine pouches, pin pouches, scent pouches, clothing bags, paint pouches, ceremonial medicine bags and tobacco pouches, skin and fur bags, and parflèches.

In the 1300s or 1400s, the Aztecs of Mexico not only wove bags to contain cacao beans, cochineal dye, and cotton, but also used drawings of such bags to record numerical information. A bag of cacao beans, for example, signified the number 8,000; 20 was indicated by a bag of the dye; 400, by a bale—virtually a bag—of cotton.

Equally unique were the remarkable Aztec feather and cloth woven bags which survived into the 1800s. Evidently solely for decorative rather than utilitarian purposes, bright-colored feathers were tied into the fabric during weaving.

In Peru, the Moche Valley Indians used pouches to carry beans bearing inscriptions, still undecoded, which may have been a form of writing. Early Peruvian Indians, from roughly 500 to 300 BC, are known to have had fabric bags with straps.

The chewing of coca, generally permitted only to the Inca nobility, led to the use of pouches to transport the coca. The pouch or *chuspa* was usually worn between cloak and tunic. Among possibly the oldest bags in all the Americas were those made of wide-mesh cotton twining by Peruvian Indians who lived in Huaca Prieta in the 2nd and 3rd millenia BC.

OSCAR E. NORBECK
ROLAND E. BURDICK

**BAKING STONES** is a name applied to a numerous class of prehistoric stone relics found principally on inhabited sites in California. They are flattish, often rudely rectangular or somewhat oval plates, sometimes convex beneath and slightly concave above, and rare specimens have obscure rims. Usually they are made of soapstone, and often show traces of use over fire. They rarely exceed a foot in length, are somewhat less in width, and perhaps an inch in average thinkness. The characteristic feature of these plates is a roughly made perforation at the middle of one end, giving the appearance of a huge pendant ornament. This perforation served, no doubt, to aid in handling the plate while hot. Some of these objects may have been boiling stones to be heated in the fire and suspended in a pot or basket of water for cooking purposes. This utensil passes imperceptibly into certain ladle-like forms, and these again into dippers, cups, bowls, and globular ollas in turn, the whole group forming part of the culinary outfit. A remarkable ladle-like object of gray diorite was obtained from the gravels 16 feet below the surface in Placerco, California. It is superior in make to other kindred objects. The baking stones of the Pueblo Indians, employed in making wafer bread, are smooth, oblong slabs set over the fireplace.

**BALL GAMES.** Games of dexterity in which balls were mainipulated, volleyed, or thrown by use of rackets, sticks, the hands or other parts of the body were widespread among the aboriginal people of the Americas. Ball games were common in all geographical regions from the Arctic Circle to Tierra del Fuego.

With few exceptions, the games were played by men, women, and young adults, and there were usually sexual distinctions in participation. Although some games appear to have been played simply for amusement, most were usually played during specific times or in association with specific ceremonial or religious activities such as fertility, regeneration, or first fruits ceremonies or initiation rites. Games were also played to cure illness, produce rain, or ensure crops. However, by the time details of most games were recorded, much of the ceremonialism and ritual had disappeared. No longer part of a ceremony, games were often played simply for amusement, yet maintained certain observances and rites that suggest the purpose they originally served: taboos regarding food and sexual activities, anointment and fumigation of objects used in the games, and pre-game dances. In a majority of games, the ball, often a symbol of the sun, earth, or moon, was considered sacred and could not be touched with the hands. In some cases, however, especially in South America, ceremonial significance was retained.

Games of the North American Indians have been grouped into the following categories according to the mode of play: racket ball, shinny, double ball, ball race, football, hand-and-foot ball, tossed ball, juggling, and hot ball.

Racket ball, played by most tribes of the eastern United States and Canada, was the most popular game of the great Algonquian and Iroquoian tribes of northeastern United States (e.g. Delawares, Passamoquoddy, Penobscot, Onondaga, Seneca), southeastern Canada (e.g. Nipissing, Caughnawaga), and the Great Lakes region of both countries (e.g. Chippewa, Menominee, Miami, Huron, Mohawk). It was also the national game of the great Muskhogean tribes of southeastern United States (Chickasaw, Choctaw, Creek, Seminole) as well as of the Iroquoian Cherokee. The game was also popular among the Algonquian and Souian tribes of the north-central region and Great Plains of the United States (e.g. Cheyenne, Sauk and Fox, Iowa, Oto, Winnebago, Santee, Yankton). Farther west, it was less popular but was played by the Assiniboin and Chinook of northwestern United States, the Salish tribes of British Columbia, and several California tribes (e.g. Pomo, Yokuts, and Nishinam).

In the game's most common form, each player carried a single racket of wood with a sinew or hide net for catching, carrying, and throwing the ball, which was usually stuffed deerskin but sometimes wood (Caughnawaga, Huron, Peoria, Chippewa, Santee, Winnebago, Pomo). The great tribes of the Southeast used two rackets and the Tepehuan and Tarahumare of Chihuahua, sticks with spoon-like ends. The goals were usually two poles (sometimes one) set at each end of a playing field that was usually several hundred yards long. Racket ball was a contest of tribal and sometimes intertribal teams with reported numbers ranging from a few to hundreds. Players tried to catch the ball and carry or throw it toward the opponent's goal, while the opposing team tried to prevent scoring, capture the ball, and score. Among some of the tribes of southeastern United States, the game was considered a substitute for war. In most instances it was a man's game, but women sometimes played (Huron, Peoria, Shawnee, Missisauga, Passamaquoddy, Choctaw). A specialized kind of racket ball, played in the Southeast, had only one tall goal post in the center of the field. Among the Creeks, an animal skull or a wooden image was placed atop the pole, and the ball was thrown at it with a racket. Apparently related to a game formerly played among the Timucua of Florida, this game survived among the Creeks, Cherokees, and Chickasaws until the 20th century.

Although shinny was apparently universally played by the tribes of continental United States, this team sport has been reported with more frequency among the tribes of the central region, the Great Plains, the Rocky Mountains, the Pacific northwest, California, the desert Southwest, and northern Mexico (Opata and Zuaque of Sonora, Tarahumare). Also reported as far north as the Western Eskimo, it employed a ball commonly of buckskin (eastern and plains regions), wood (Pacific coast, Southwest, northern Mexico), or whalebone (Makah). The players usually carried a single bat or stick, curved or sometimes flattened on the striking end, to drive the ball toward the goals, which were usually two posts at each end of the field. However, two blankets on the ground (Crows), a single pole (Menominee, Shuswap, Omaha), and a line on the ground (Makah, Navaho, Eskimo) have been reported. The ball might be kicked as well as batted. Shinny was a woman's game in most tribes, but it was played only by men in some tribes and by both sexes in others.

Double ball, reported throughout eastern United States and Canada, the Great Plains, northwestern region, California, Southwest, and northern Mexico, employed two balls or other objects connected by a thong. They were usually buckskin, but some tribes used connected billets (Hupa, Klamath, Chippewa, Papago, Tarahumare, Achomawi, Shasta) or balls of plaited leather (Pima, Papago). Each player carried a curved stick, usually plain but sometimes forked (Shoshoni, Paiute), to throw the balls by the thong toward the goal or home base, which was usually a goal line but sometimes poles at the ends of the field (Chippewa) or two piles of earth (Omaha, Zuñi). The field varied from a few hundred yards to a mile long. Except for some tribes in northern California (e.g. Hupa, Nishinam), the game was exclusively for women.

The ball race was apparently confined to the tribes of the Southwest, California, and northern Mexico, the only exception being the Bannock in Idaho. Two contesting players or teams kicked or tossed a ball or similar object around a predesignated course. Balls were stone (Pima, Mono, Tewa, Maricopa), wood (Papago, Pima, Mojave, Yuma, Tarahumare, Tepehuan, Zuaque, Cocopa of Sonora), hard gum (Papago), or stuffed buckskin (Wasama, Mono). Billets (Navaho, Keres, Tewa, Zuñi), an inflated bladder covered with sinew net (Bannock), and a cube of pitch and horsehair (Hopi) were also reported. The Tarahumare allegedly took their name from the ball race. Tarahumare and Zuaque women played the game but used sticks to drive the ball.

Football has been reported in all sections of the continent north of Mexico, but seems to have been most popular among the Eskimo. Balls of deerskin (Micmac, Eskimo, Nishinam, Mono, Paiute) or stone (Chukchansi) and two poles or sticks (Micmac, Paiute, Topinagugim, Nishinam, Mono) or lines (Winnebago, Eskimo, Chukchansi) as goals have been reported. Football was a team sport played variously by men, men against women, or men, women, and children together. The object was to kick the ball across the line or between the poles. Some Eskimo groups also used whips to drive the ball. Among the Creeks and Chickasaws, men could only kick the ball, but women could use their hands and feet.

Hand-and-foot ball was a woman's game in which a large buckskin or bladder ball was dropped or struck down by hand and kicked back. Usually, one woman played at a time, and the object was to kick the ball up and catch it (Arapaho and Cheyenne) or to keep it in the air by kicking (Mandan, Comanche, Winnebago). The Western Eskimo played a game in which two or four women bounced and kicked a ball to each other.

Under the name of *tossed ball* have been listed specialized games which violated the general rule that the ball was not to be touched with the hands: volley ball keep-it-up (Tlinglet, Choctaw, Natchez, Blackfeet, Abnaki, Niska, Central Eskimo), keep-away (Nishinam, Ntlakyapamuk, Miami, Kwakiutl, Western Eskimo), and toss-and-catch (Assiniboine, Hidatsa, Choctaw, Montagnais).

Foot-cast ball was apparently peculiar to the Chuckcansi and Apache of California, who tossed a heavy stone ball with the top of the foot. Juggling balls of stone or clay, though probably more widespread, have been reported among the Central Eskimo, Nascapee of Labrador, Achomawi, Bannock, Shoshoni, Ute, and Zuñi. Hot ball was peculiar to the Chukchansi and Mono. As a training exercise, young boys tried to retrieve a heated stone ball thrown into the darkness.

To these North American games should be added *ulé,* a rubber-ball game similar to the classical game of Mesoamerica, played until the 18th century by the Tepehuan and Tarahumare. On a designated court or field, players crouched on hands and feet, caught the ball on their shoulders, hips, and knees, balanced it, and tossed it until it went out of the playing field, was missed, or hit another part of the body. Leather devices on hips and buttoks protected players from the hard ball. Discovery of about thirty formal ball courts in Hohokam sites in Arizona suggests that the game may have been played in southwestern United States.

## MESOAMERICA

Popular ball games in Mesoamerica have been classified into three categories according to the mode of propelling the ball: handball, stick ball, and hip ball. Leaf or cornhusk balls have been reported in volleying and, sometimes, hockey games, and hide and hair balls have been reported for throwing and catching. Handball games have been reported among the Nahua of central Mexico, the Zapotec of Oaxaca, the Mixtec of Guerrero, and the Tarascans of Michoacan. Gloves, which suggest use of the hands, have also been reported in relation to ball games. Balls of wood, rubber, stone, and clay have been reported for juggling. Various stick ball games have been reported. Racket games similar to that of North America were played as far south as the Cahita of northern Sinaloa and southern Sonora. Hockey games similar to that of South America and shinny of North America have been reported among the Cahita, Tarascans, and Acaxee of western

Durango. Among the Tarascans, hockey was played between two players or teams and sometimes with two balls or at night with a ball of maguey roots which burned slowly as the game progressed. Games using bats were reported among the Tarascans and the Guasave of Sinaloa.

Hip ball, or the *tlachtli*, played throughout Mesoamerica, was related to the formal ball courts that, according to the Spanish conquerers, were a part of the architecture of every Aztec city. These rectangular structures had stone walls along the sides, often containing elaborate relief sculpture. At mid-court a stone ring was set into each wall. Perhaps the oldest court is at Xochicalco. Others are at Cobá, Piedras Negras in Guatamala, Copán in Honduras (the most southerly Classic Mayan site), Tula (Postclassic Toltec), El Tajín (Classic Vera Cruz), Tikal, Xumal, and Etzná (Maya), Monte Alban (Zapotec), Yagul (Mixtec), and Tenochtitlan (Aztec). Perhaps the best known courts are at Chichén Itzá in Yucatan where there are seven known courts, the largest with a 480 x 120 feet playing field, high stone walls in which the rings are set twenty feet above the field. Little is known about the court game which the Spanish believed was a religious activity or ritual as well as a sport for the Aztec upper classes. In Classical times, players apparently kept a hard natural-rubber ball in play and drove it into their opponents' half of the court by use of the buttocks, thighs, or knees, and in Postclassic times they apparently used their hips, knees, or elbows to drive it through one of the stone rings on the court walls. The players wore leather or wooden girdles, knee-caps, and leather aprons to protect themselves. Researchers have tended to give the game a cosmic interpretation, the court representing the sky, the ball the sun, and the rings the sunrise and sunset or, possibly, the equinoxes. The *tlachtli* was widespread from the Preclassic period until conquest, and courts have been

Scene from the Codex Magliabecchi of two men playing ball.

found as far away as Puerto Rico and Arizona. In Postclassic times it was played as far north as the Guasave. During the early colonial period, it was played among the Otomi of central Mexico, the Nahua, Tarascans, Zapotec, Quiche of Guatamala, Huastec of Tamaulipas and San Luis Potosi, Cahita, Acaxee, and others. Although the game died out in central Mexico early in that period, it apparently survived until the 20th century in remote parts of Sinaloa and Vera Cruz and perhaps among the Quiche.

## SOUTH AMERICA

In South America, games of ball are found throughout the continent and may be classified according to the mode of play: games in which balls are thrown or volleyed toward a goal or are kept in the air, *pillma*, hockey, and football. Juggling had been reported but rarely. Unless otherwise indicated, these games have been reported during the present century.

Games in which balls of rubber, maize leaves, or other materials were volleyed or thrown were common throughout South America. Rubber-ball games were common among tribes in regions where natural rubber was accessible. Usually team games played between youths or men of different moieties, villages, or tribes, they were sometimes festival games as among the Witotoan tribes of the Para-Paraná and upper Caquetá River in Columbia, and they were usually attended by complex ceremonialism. In most games, rules proscribed the use of hands or feet in keeping a hard, natural-rubber ball off the ground and in driving it toward a goal at either end of a playing field. Players from tribes on the right bank of the Guaporé River, the Chiquito of eastern Bolivia, and the Chané of the eastern slopes of the Bolivian Andes kept the ball in play by butting it with their heads, the Araono of the Madiera headwaters used their stomachs, and the Muenane of the upper Caquetá used their knees. A minority of tribes allowed the use of hands or feet or both (Macushi of southern British Guiana, Sherente of eastern Brazil), knees, hands, and feet (Witoto), and, with somewhat different rules, head and feet (Mojo of the Madiera headwaters). The Apinayé of eastern Brazil and the earlier Otomac of the Orinoco also had games in which a rubber ball was struck with a bat. The mode of play and the protective devices such as leg-guards of the Mojo and bark belts with which the Araono protected their stomachs suggest a relationship of the popular rubber-ball game and the court games of Mesoamerica. However, there is an absence of ball courts with stone walls on the South American continent. Maize-leaf balls are common throughout the Andes regions and the Amazonian, Orinocoan, Guianan, eastern Bolivian, eastern Brazilian, and Chacoan areas. Both men and women played games in which a maize-leaf ball was usually thrown or volleyed with the palm of the hand. Yahgan men and women of the mountainous islands of Cape Horn used the palms of their hands to keep in the air a ball of seal gut stuffed with feathers and grass. The Ona of Tierra del Fuego played a similar game.

A specialized volleying game was the *pillma*, in which players stood in a circle and a rush ball was thrown from beneath the thigh and was volleyed by hand and kept in the air. *Pillma* was peculiar to the Araucanians of middle Chile and the Patagonian and Pampean peoples, such as the Tehuelche and Puelche. At the time of European contact, it was the second most important sport of the Mapuche-Huilliche.

Hockey, the national sport of the tribes of the Chacoan area, the Araucanians, and the related Patagonian and Pampean peoples, was mainly confined to those areas. The ball was usually wood but might be plaited rope (Mbayá-Caduveo) and sometimes stone. The sticks were usually curved at one end, but the Chiriguano and Chamacoco of the Chacoan area used rackets, painted their bodies, and wore decorated hair nets. A rough game which frequently resulted in injuries, hockey was considered by these peoples as a substitute for war. Among the Araucanians, men, women, and children played. In former times, it was the most important game of the Mapuche-Huilliche, who

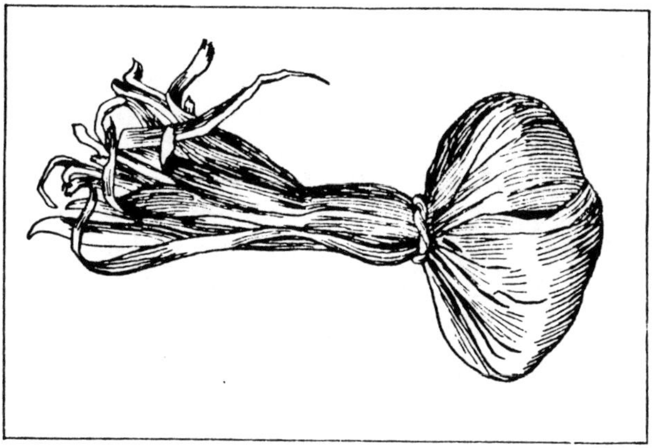

Maize-leaf ball, Taulipang, Macushi

played to the accompaniment of flutes and drums before huge crowds of spectators.

Football was reported as a woman's game among the Pampean peoples such as the Puelche.

It is not unusual for the same game to be described in strikingly similar details concerning rules, objects of the game, or modes of scoring among peoples of different geographical regions and different linguistic stocks. The hockey game of South America and of northern Mexico differs little from the shinny played by tribes of the Great Plains. The rubber-ball game of South America is strikingly similar to that of Middle America. And the double ball game is similar throughout North America. Differences in the objects used in the game appear to vary according to ecological conditions rather than to linguistic stock. Yet most games are of such antiquity and the evidence is so slight that borrowing has rarely been demonstrated.

DANIEL F. LITTLEFIELD, JR.

**BARK** has been an important raw material throughout the American forests and even in some only partly wooded areas. The broad classes of bark usage all have counterparts in other parts of the world, but some specific uses and particular species of trees used are unique to the New World.

Bark for artifacts is left as is or separated into layers. Slabs of the heavier barks are house coverings, floors, bedding, objects to be carved, and other items. Thinner, more pliable bark, or inner bark, is used for containers, canoes and other purposes. *Bast*, i.e. inner bark, is pounded with grooved mallets, in single or multiple layers, to form thin, pliable *bark cloth*. The bast layers are sometimes soaked and overlapped, so that very large cloths are produced. Bark cloth does not have very good shear (tear) resistance but is otherwise satisfactory and can be used like any light cloth; its use is retricted to warm climates. Paper-thin bark cloth is also a writing or painting surface.

The inner and middle layers are sources of strips, strands or coarse fibers which are used as sewing thread, cordage and ligatures, tied into netting, or woven into basketry, hammocks and some fabrics. Fibers and strips are shredded or torn out, sometimes after presoaking, while larger strips are generally sliced from the bark.

Many barks contain such substances as dyes, flavorings, drugs, arrow poisons and other agents. These are used in pulverized form or the substances are extracted. Tanning with bark or its extracts was unknown in most of the pre-Columbian New World except for Mesoamerica and possibly Central America and the Andean region. Many native Mesoamericans today tan with oak or mahogany bark.

Miscellaneous uses include cork and caulking, bedding and lining containers, and carrying fire on smoldering pieces.

There is in the Americas no parallel to the important Polynesian practice of cultivating paper mulberry trees for the making of bark cloth. Some *Strychnos* spp. vines whose bark is used for arrow poisons are occasionally cultivated in northeastern South America, as are some *balche* trees for flavoring among the Maya, but these are sporadic practices. The bark of trees cultivated for other purposes has uses but systematic cropping for bark cannot be said to exist.

Certain specific uses of bark parallel those of other parts of the world, but one should not accept these instances as *a priori* evidence of transoceanic diffusion. Many are obvious uses and ubiquitous in forested regions, e.g. house coverings, bedding and bast cordage. Even bark canoes, although technologically rather sophisticated, are made of unreshaped bark, are found in widely scattered areas of Africa, Asia,

Australia and the Americas, and thus seem best explained by independent invention. Psychotropic bark decoctions are prepared in West Africa and opposite areas of South America, but the species used are different and psychotropic drugs from all sources have a fairly continuous world distribution. There is a better case for the diffusion of bark cloth, which is made throughout much of the tropics but is especially important in the Pacific and occurs mostly in western parts of the Americas. But an hypothesis of bark cloth diffusion is hard to test archeologically because of the material's poor preservation in the humid areas in whcih it is mostly found.

Bark was a common house covering in North America through the Subarctic to the Great Lakes and the Northeast, and sporadic use is reported southward into Mesoamerica. The Iroquois formed the sides and roofs of their longhouses almost entirely of overlapped bark slabs over a pole framework. Moose and caribou hides were preferred for Subarctic tipis but the thin outer bark of the paper birch *(Betula papyrifera)* was often substituted.

Birch bark containers and canoes were also common in these northern regions. The bark was folded into seamless, rectangular vessels used for holding solids and liquids. Sizes ranged up to two or three gallons and some were employed for stone boiling or even direct boiling at some distance from the fire. These containers were common from central New England to southwestern Alaska. Bark canoes were not found in coastal Alaska but otherwise had much the same distribution. The Iroquois, who lacked paper birch trees of sufficient size, fashioned their canoes from elm or hickory bark, and some similar canoes were of secondary importance to the Cherokee. The eastern Algonquian-speaking peoples fashioned the largest and most sophisticated birch bark canoes, and Algonquians brought these into New England. Probably the Newfoundland Beothuk made the most use of birch bark: in houses, oceangoing canoes, containers and trays of all descriptions, lining for storage pits, and shrouds for the dead. Overall, there is reason to consider birch bark artifacts to be of primary origin in the Algonquian Subarctic.

Bast fiber clothing was known in North America. In the Southeast, mulberry bast strands were roughly interwoven with nettles and other materials to form women's skirts. Shredded cedar bast was gathered into shirts and skirts in the Plateau and the southern and central Northwest Coast, and into women's aprons and hip cloths in parts of California.

Bast strips and strands were used for basketry in most forested areas and even in parts of the Southwest, although grasses, splints and other materials were more important. Other uses included tying together house members (Southeast, Northeast), and tying to form fish nets (western Alaskan Eskimo, Northeast) and bird nooses (Iroquois).

Dark colors were widely extracted from bark. even in some arid western areas, and were employed to stain basketry and sometimes textiles. In California, a red dye was obtained from alder bark. The Creek soaked hides with oak bark but apparently only long enough to stain them, not to produce tanning.

Substances extracted from bark in Mesoamerica include tanning agents and brown, black and red (Maya) dyes. Most Maya also flavor fermented sugarcane juice or diluted honey with the bark of the balché tree. The Northern Tepehuan add *Quercus crassifolia* bark as a "catalyst" to fermenting maize mash. Bark extracts were of some importance in the Aztec pharmacopeia and remain a common ingredient in herbal medicine.

Bark cloth is common today among the Lacandon Maya and was probably once in general use in the tropiçal Mesoamerican lowlands. In the pre-Columbian central Mexican civilizations, paintings and ideographs were made on bark cloth, a practice which survives among the Otomi in "witchcraft". Bast is also used in the lowlands for basketry, cordage, nets and hammocks.

Bark cloth is found in parts of lowland Central America and along the west coasts of Colombia and Ecuador (Chocó, Cayapa) and was likely once continuously distributed southward from Mesoamerica. It is also prepared from the Orinoco-Amazon borderlands southward to the Chaco and is of premier importance in northern and eastern Bolivia and along some tributaries of the upper Amazon. Articles made in these latter areas include tunics, breech cloths, aprons, skirts, shirts, masks, and mosquito nets.

Bast fibers are woven into shirts by the Sirionó and formerly into blankets in the Chilean archipelago. Bast fiber basketry is common in the Amazonian lowlands, not only for conventional baskets but also for manioc pulp squeezers and hammocks, but other coarse fibers are also in general use for these purposes. Bast cordage is widespread in the tropical lowlands; a frequent use is binding house members.

Native South Americans extract from bark an impressive variety of substances, including red, black (eastern lowlands), yellow and blue (Mapuche) textile dyes. *Strychnos* spp. and some *Ficus* spp. supply active ingredients for arrow poisons, including curare, in most of the eastern lowlands. The list of drugs includes several that have been adopted in Western medicine: curare, *Cascara* laxatives, and quinine and other *Cinchona* alkaloids, although the latter are probably post-Columbian and not necessarily an Indian discovery. Two psychotropic drugs are decocted: *epéna* from *Virola* spp. (Orinocò-Rio

Negro region) and *latua* from *Latua pubiflora* (Mapuche).

Bark canoes and containers have been made along the northeastern littoral and in the Chilean archipelago, but these were seamed and had to be sewn with bast threads or animal sinews and caulked. In both of these regions pieces of bast were also put to an array of miscellaneous uses, including such items as climbing straps, cigar wrappers and bandages.

Bark is readily replaced by trade and industrial materials for most artifacts. Bark in canoes and containers was out of use by early in this century everywhere except along the Brazil-Guianas border. As bedding or house covering, it survives mainly among isolated, impoverished peoples, and bast fibers mostly survive in remote tropical forests. Bark cloth is meeting increased competition from cotton textiles even among the remote Lacandon and eastern Bolivians. Bark dyes are scarce today, but extracted drugs survive quite well in local herbals.

DANIEL E. VASEY

**BASKETRY** has been one of the most predominate crafts of American Indian cultures, as well as the oldest. Containers woven from grasses and strips of plants—often flexible in shape—were utilized throughout the hemisphere, particularly in the American Southwest and East. Understandably, the Plains Indians relied more upon containers made from hide, Northwest Coast Indians generally used wooden containers, and the containers used by Indians in most parts of Canada were made from bark, an abundant resource. Basketry was a highly developed art, principally in those areas of the United States where baskets were the most commonly used form of container and where they were indispensible in the daily life of the tribe. Baskets were used in cooking; for gathering, carrying, and storing food; for transporting water; and in ceremonies. Basketry hats were worn by both men and women in the Northwest Coast to shield them from the rain, and by women throughout the United States who used the woven caps to protect their heads when supporting large loads.

An Indian woman on the Agua Caliente Reservation making a basket.

Basketry is a craft generally assigned to women, and the majority of the baskets as well as the bags and mats used in everyday life are created by women. Certain exceptions can be found, however; baskets used solely by men, such as in fishing, were woven by men. Since the advent of white settlers, Indian men usually made many of the baskets which were created for trade purposes. Basketry was rarely a full-time job for the artisan; only recently have individual women gained acclaim as basket weavers.

Baskets were crafted in a wide variety of sizes and forms, depending on which materials and method were used by the basketmaker. The three major forms of basketmaking are coiling, twining, and plaiting; these methods have been traced to their roots in prehistoric North America and Meso-America, which are reflected in the development of basketry in traditional Indian cultures.

Coiling, twining (also called *wicker*), and plaiting are individual processes which utilize the two components of basket weaving (the warp and weft) in different ways. As a result, a basket made by coiling, a basket made by twining, and a basket made by plaiting the organic elements each has a unique appearance. In some cases baskets have been created which incorporate more than one of these processes.

Coiling and twining are most common among the basket-making Indians who live in the Western part of North America, while plaiting is the dominant method used by dwellers of the Eastern segment. The nomadic lifestyle inherent in the hunting cultures inhabiting the central part of North America precluded a strong usage of basketry. In the desert, where pottery was fairly unknown, the baskets (frequently bottle-shaped) used for carrying water were water-proofed with an exterior coat of pitch. Baskets used in cooking, particularly boiling, were tightly woven from very fine stems and roots so that upon contact with boiling water the basket would expand and become a virtually watertight container. These aspects of basketry were not necessary in the East, as pottery was widely used there for carrying water and in cooking.

Most coiled baskets were woven extremely tight, as the wefts (flexible element) were sewn vertically around the horizontal warp (foundation element). Basketry made by twining could vary, since the process was more flexible. These baskets could be tight or loose: the warp is vertical in twining, and pairs of the warp are connected by horizontal weft elements, also in pairs, which are twisted between them. Because of the flexibility, most materials were transported or stored in twined baskets in the West. Dishes and plaques were also woven in this style.

In the East, where pottery vessels were widely used to transport water and for cooking, coiled and twined basketry did not develop to such and extent, and the waterproofing processes found in the West were unnecessary in the East. Plaiting was traditionally the predominant form of basketry, as it produces a loosely woven container. In plaiting, both the warp and weft elements are woven with no distinction made as to comparative size, shape, or vertical as opposed to horizontal importance. Plaiting is a fast, uncomplicated process. Plaited basketry has also survived among the tribes of some Indians of the Southwest, such as the Hopi and Jemez, and historically was also made by the Pima and Papago. The materials used in plaiting were coarse flat strips, often cut uniformly, as opposed to the thinner round stems and roots used in coiling and twining. The sources of the materials varied depending on the region, so that plaited baskets have been found which were woven from strips of cane, wood (hickory or oak) and even rawhide.

Bags and mats were woven from basketry techniques throughout areas where basketry

Haida basketry hat.

skills were developed, but it is in the manufacture of containers where the richness and sophistication of North American Indian basketry are most dramatically seen, especially in the integration of design elements and functional manufacture. As in all American Indian crafts, the finely attuned aesthetic system flourished: decorative patterns were organically related to the careful design and subsequent usage of the objects created.

Basketry became the most significant craft of Indian artisans in California, and the basketry of this area was more highly developed than anywhere else in North America. Each tribe showed a distinctive usage of color, pattern, form, and overall style. In California the basketry was generally coiled and twined; the rounded or spherical surfaces are covered with geometric shapes and stylized human figures, often in red against a light or dark background. The Pomo of central California exhibit the height of basketry development in that area—the very finely crafted coiling and twining skills combined with the colorful geometric patterns to create a style of basketry which shows the precision and inventiveness of the craft.

Northwest Coast basketry, mostly straight-sided containers, was uniformly covered with rows of repeating geometric design patterns. Basketmakers of the East were careful artisans whose colorful vegetable dyed baskets were heavily decorated. The designs were generally geometric and also included abstracted animal representations. The Chitimacha in the Southeast incorporated a plethora of decorative patterns into their basketry, which was woven through the 1930s. Today, however, very little basketry is being created. Perhaps the most prolific manufacture of basketry is taking place in the American Southwest. The Hopi, Apache, Pima, and Papago tribes still practice the old basketry skills and the recent commercial interest in Indian crafts has encouraged the basketmakers to continue their manufacture with some 20th century variations in materials and motivations. For example, the Papago, whose coiled baskets were traditionally made of willow, now utilize yucca.

Recently containers have been woven in the non-traditional shapes of humans and animals and miniature baskets have been developed to conform to white traders' demands. The Hopi coiled basketry which is still used today in plaques, jars, and bowls is alive with the colorful red, black, and yellow designs. Sometimes geometric, sometimes representative of life forms, the patterns created in Hopi basketry are marvelously vibrant. Hopi basketry has undergone a development from coarse coiling to a finer treatment of this technique; and in fact, contemporary Hopi basketry has not degenerated in quality, but has matured since the beginning of the century.

Throughout the North American Indian cultures, the status of basketry as a craft has altered considerably. In areas where basketry continues to be made for use in daily life as utensils and in a ceremonial context, the skills of the basket weaver have grown concurrently and there has been an increased development in basketry design. Where commercialism and trading with non-Indian cultures introduced new materials and utensils and have eliminated traditional ceremonial needs of the Indians, the traditional skills of basketmakers have degenerated. The commercial demands of collectors, traders, and Indian craft guilds upon the basketmakers has also altered the quality and quantity of the baskets produced. The oldest extant craft has changed considerably in the many thousands of years of its existence in North America.

## SOUTH AMERICA*

### Basketry fibers

The most available and obviously the most adaptable of South American basketry materials come from various palms. Many objects can be plaited from fresh leaves, but for finer work palm splints are prepared.

**Palm leaves.**—Among courser objects are floor mats braided from long slender leaves of burití palm *(Carajá)*, sleeping mats made of spathes of palms *(Yuracare)*, thick mats made of palm stems to serve as rafts *(Paressí)*, and interlaced palm leaves set as weirs across streams *(Guarayú)*. The most widespread of baskets made of freshcut palm leaves are the temporary carrying baskets of various forms. Temporary hammocks are made in a few minutes by interlacing the tips of the buriti leaflets *(Bacäiri)*. Rough fire fans are constructed of a green leaf by plaiting its elements to the desired shape *(Mojo* and others). Most of the fire fans, however, are woven of ribbons split from palm leaflets *(Bacäiri* and others). Some of the most striking patterns in twill technique are found in the palm-splint fans of tribes in the northwest Amazon area, upper Xingú region, eastern Bolivia, and Mato Grosso. The patterning depends largely upon the uniform size of prepared materials.

The fan-leaf palm used in some areas *(Cayapó)* has its petiole stripped from it. This can be made to yield ribbons from one-eighth to one-half inch in width by from 3 to 12 feet in length. Strands from the pimpler palms *(Astrocaryum tucuma)* are septa pulled away singly and split. Prepared material of these types shrinks considerably and basket makers work with it in the morning while the air is still damp. Manioc sqeezers, sieves, and trays are plaited of splints stripped from the midrib of long leaves of the cokerite palm *(Maximiliana regia)*, or of splints from other palms (Guiana Indians, Northwest Amazon tribes). Other basketry types made of palm-fiber splints are baskets for supplies and storage *(Chiquito, Cayapó, Sirionó*, tribes of eastern Brazil), funnel-shaped fish traps *(Wapishana*, etc.), mats for "blankets" over finer grass "sheets" *(Canella)*, and the fine mats patterned in twill technique *(Mosetene, Guató, Yaruro*,

---

*This section is taken from volume 5 of the *Handbook of South American Indians*.

*Apinayé, Cayapó).* Palm-leaf splints make the sails on the craft manned by the Guiana Indians, *Arawak*, and *Carib*.

Palm fiber of finest quality is required by the *Cayapa* for trinket baskets. This is stripped from the under side of the palm leaf blade and is often dyed. The *Yaruro* make hunters' pouches from narrow strips into which the cortex of the palm has been divided. The *Tapirapé* make both their flexible and rigid forms of buritî fiber. Telescoping palm-leaf baskets are made either by sewing even-width strips of palm leaves or by folding them to make "plaited" boxes. Both types are in use on the Caiarí-Vaupés and Aiarí Rivers for storing feathers, beads, and other small possessions. Similar forms are made by the *Macushí, Wapishana, Warrau*, and others.

Palm "straw" is prepared for *Motilones* and *Quechua* hats and for feathered crows of the *Yamamadí* and *Botocudo*. That which comes from trees *(Carludovica palmata)* growing at 5,000 feet elevation is considered best quality by Patuso hat makers of Colombia. The bushy palm growing in Jamaica furnishes excellent straw for hat making. Just before the spathe expands, it is cut off, and the narrow outer blades are divided legthwise into ribbons of widths depending upon the quality of the hats to be woven. After boiling in water and drying in the sun, the strips become round compact straws.

**Leaf and grass fibers.**—Grass has limited uses among basket and mat makers. That growing on table lands in *Quechua* and *Aymara* territory and on the banks of Rio Chaparé is used for hats. The *Carajá* make a kind of netted cap of grass; the *Mojo* use arrow grass *(Gynerium sagittatum)* for some baskets. A few mats are fine enough in texture to require grass in their making *(Motilones, Mosetene, Canella)*. the *Mosetene* plait arrow grass; the *Canella* make bed "sheets" of either babarsie or anaja and use them with their buritípalm "blankets."

Pima basket designs.

In coiled basketry, grass is used by the *Aymara,* who sew a spiralling bundle to the splint foundation with a fine grass braid. Its most noteworthy use is among southern tribes. The Fuegian or half-hitch coil is done over three or four stems of grass placed together as the foundation element. The same coarse native grass is employed for all coiled work of the region. Each round stem is flattened and made more pliable by chewing it. Braided grass or thongs make handles on Fuegian baskets.

Peruvian natives of the puna and those near Piura weave Panama hats of paja toquilla straw; for second-quality hats they use paja or macora, which grows wild. Both must be collected at the right stage of growth and when weather and temperature are favorable. It may take months to collect material for a choice hat.

Leaves, other than palm leaves, are less common basketry materials. The *Carib* of the West Indies plait baskets from latania leaves split into ribbons and scraped clean with mussel shells; the *Taino* wove some baskets from biheo leaves and maguey fiber. Eastern Peruvian tribes make leaf pockets for small possessions and hang them up in the rafters.

**Rushes and reeds.**—The rush (totora) is valuable to the *Aymara* and *Quechua,* who live in the regions of Lake Titicaca and the Coast. It grows from 6 to 8 feet high, and is used for walls, roofs, mattresses, balsas, and sails. The *Lengua, Chamacoco,* and other Chaco tribes make huts of rush mats; other Chaco Indians occasionally plait sleeping or sitting mats. The *Mojo* lash together bundles of reeds for rafts.

The process of preparing and splitting the canelike stem (itiriti, a species of *Ischnosiphon)* is employed by Guiana Indians. Stems of this reed are about 10 feet long; the diameter yields 8 or 12 strands. Baskets of diverse uses, such as manioc squeezers, sifters, and crab carrying baskets, are made of itiriti. When the material is split very fine, the basket walls appear like cloth. Smaller basketry objects are woven of split stems *(Carajá)*; fine reed bakets are twined with cotton thread *(Mojo)*; small reeds are held together by twining elements to form a straining mat (*Huanyam*, *Bauré*). A thin bundle of rush or straw is the foundation material in *Páez* and *Moguex* hats. Some of the crudely woven *Yahgan* baskets for taking fish are made with reeds; so are some of the fine coiled baskets of the *Yahgan* and *Ona* which have reeds for the foundation. Some of the finest reedwork is in the narrow feather-decorated fillets worn by *Cayapó* maidens, and the *Arawak* men's telescoping trinket or shoulder baskets of split reed (maranta).

**Cane and bark.**—The slender, flexible, woody stem of bamboo and rattan has special qualities to recommend it: form, body, usually a surface gloss, and ability to take dyes well. Most distinctive cane basketry shows geometric designs in contrasting dark and light elements; the outer green skin left on bamboo gives surface pattern. Cane-woven objects have varied uses: manioc squeezers are made of rattan (Purús River Indians); flat sieves of bamboo strips *(Tupí-Cawahíb)*; and beeswax-lined containers for liquids and burden baskets of bamboo splints *(Caingang)*. Also of bamboo strips or cane are double-walled baskets of the hinged-cover type, which the *Jívaro* pattern with geometric motifs; long baskets for holding communal treasures *(Tucano)*; and cylindrical baskets with open, hexagonal weaves *(Nambicuara)*. The effective cover basketry on *Carajá* and *Cayapó* weapons is black and white cane work. The *Páez* and *Moguex*, *Chocó*, *Cuna*, and *Tule* also twill with cane strips.

Manioc squeezers of the *Bora* are made of palm-bark splints, cut into narrow strips. *Cashinawa* women make trinket baskets of embauba bark. Small and large baskets of rough splints are made in open weaves by the

*Talamanca;* the *Araucanian* baskets are woven of the inner bark of certain trees, especially the ṅyocha *(Greigia landbechii).*

**Roots, vines, withes.**—Vines and "aerial roots" of the sort which hang from trees are extremely useful for basket materials and for twines and ropes. The *Cayapa* obtain aerial roots by pulling on them. Usually they come free at their base and measure from 75 to 100 feet in length. Baskets which must be durable and stand strain, as well as some finer *Cayapa* baskets, are woven of the roots. In some baskets *(Cuna)* the wrap element consists of the whole root; in others, the material is split into long thin ribbons, made uniform in size and smoothed.

Pliant stems of creepers come in many sizes and lengths. "Bush rope" (a *Carludovica)* is one of the materials plaited by the *Carib* and *Arawak* for sturdy packbaskets. Vine fibers are also used by Purús River Indians for strong containers. The *Carajá* weave mats of climbing vines (sipos). The hollow cylinder belts *(Patamona, Macushí)* are of vine fibers.

The *Jacaré* make carrying baskets of willow shoots, the *Mosquito* and *Sumo* plait withes, and the *Yahgan* make crude dip nets of split twigs. Probably many other tribes employ these rougher materials for durable baskets. Indians on the Orinoco and Rio Negro make cone-shaped fish creels of long flexible ozier twigs.

## Basketry techniques

**Wicker and checker.**—These two basketry weaves are the simplest forms of two-element interlacing. Wicker weave is accomplished by carrying each active element (the weft) over and under each successive passive element (the warp), a procedure frequently referred to by the formula "over-one under-one." Neither the term "wicker" nor the principle of interlacing changes when for any reason the warp consists of two or more smaller elements which are never separated. In checkerwork single elements are often broader than in wicker or a unit of two or more active elements passes over and under units consisting of an equal number of passive elements. The appearance of the weaving is similar to that of a checkerboard whether the emphasis be on the vertical-horizontal or on the diagonal as in much of the mat work.

The list of tribes producing basketry by either wicker or checker or both weaving forms is a long one. The following are representative: Many Central American districts; the Isthmus of Panama; the Caribbean Islands; *Cayapa* (who use no other techniques for tightly woven burden baskets, bottle-shaped bait baskets, globular carrying baskets, etc.); *Aymara* (wicker trays); *Araucanians;* Indians of Jamaica; hat makers of Colombia, Ecuador, Northern and Southern Peru; Guiana tribes: *Carib* and *Arawak* (manioc squeezers, cone-shaped fish traps—woven with spiraling weft by the *Wapishana*—knapsacks, foundations for feather headdresses), *Tucano* (baskets for suspension); upper Xingú River tribes *(Bacaïri* knapsacks); eastern Bolivia includes the *Yamiaca* and *Atsahuaca* (wickerwork), *Yuracare*, *Guató* (baskets, mats, and fire fans in checker weave), *Mojo,Churapa* (Panama hats), *Mojo, Huanyam, Guarayo* (traps of wickerwork with spiraling weft), and *Chiriquano* (common forms of basketry); *Bororo* (palm-leaf baskets in checker weave); Chaco (many types of basketry); and *Abipón* (baskets in which babies are carried).

**Twills.**—Twill are recognized by lines of short or long steps diagonally crossing the surface of a fabric. Each step is formed by passing the weft over at least two warps; diagonals are formed by the regular progression of the weft element one to the right (or left) on each successive movement around the basket or across the mat. Stiff materials, such as cane, produce effective twills, and basket makers rely upon the comination of texture and technique for striking patterns.

Twilling is very old; it appears in the Peruvian workbaskets with lids so frequently found in women's graves on the Coast. There is also evidence of both coiled and twilled basketry in the markings on pots found in *Diaguita* territory.

Twilling is widely distributed; in some districts it is a dominant technique. The *Cayapa* and others usually weave the "even" twills, the two-and-two and three-and-three twills. In these the weft steps or overfloats across two or three warps and under the same number. Noteworthy *Cayapa* examples are their telescoping baskets, mats, and fans. The *Páez* and *Moguex* make a few twilled baskets; but among Guiana and northeastern Amazon tribes, where varieties of weaves and techniques are familiar, the even twills are dominant. Twilled basketry from the northwest Amazon area is similar; among *Witotoan* tribes twills predominate. Even twilling is specifically mentioned for the *Yaruro* and *Boro*. *Gê* tribes weave twilled trinket baskets; the *Canella* make twilled mats. The *Cayapó* make twilled arm bands, cover-basketry for weapon handles, carrying baskets, and sleeping mats. Chaco basketry is primarily twilled and wickerwoven. Other occurrences of twilling are the southeastern Panamanian tribes, *Motilones*, *Bacäiri*, *Paressí*, *Itonama*, *Guató*. *Chiriguano*, *Guaraní*, *Bororo*, *Tapirapé*, *Carajá*, and *Cainguá*.

**Basketry decorations.**— All tribes do not decorate basketry. The *Pamore* weave plain mats, and *Chiriguano* and *Chané* seldom ornament theirs. The *Cayapa* weave undecorated, simply decorated, and intricately patterned basketry. A larger number of tribes show considerable interest in patterns, and these, whether used as free-standing units or in continuous borders, are usually developed out of the twill weaves. Palm materials make twilling with clearly defined patterns. Panama and Guiana Indians, those of the western Amazon (especially the *Jívaro),* and the *Caraja* and *Cayapó* make the most of twill techniques. The work of these peoples shows an interest in variety, for, although twilling is a simple technique, it does present difficulties whenever modifications of length, order, or direction of the overfloats are attempted. Intricate designs are evidences of mainpulative skills and recognition of possiblities. The *Yaruro* consciously vary their baskets by changing the weave type. This is also characteristic procedure among primitive cloth weavers.

Design motifs are strongly geometric in woven basketry; there is no evidence that curvilinear motifs were regularly attempted through employment of very narrow weaving materials. Few names appear to be given to basketry motifs, but almost all are based on steps, diamonds, zigzags, triangles, and hollow squares.

Combinations of surface and structural decorations are conspicuous for their rarity: the *Tapirapé* smear the finished basket with black genipa, and design motifs of negative-pattern type are developed by scraping away the color; the *Canella* paint simple geometric designs in yellow on their twilled baskets. Covered baskets made by the *Waiwai* and in use among the *Wapishana* have long cotton strings tied in knots for a decorative effect; feathers are in favor among these and other Guiana tribes. The *Huarpe* decorate sections of their twined baskets with tufts of rose, violet, red, and green wool yarns incorporated during the weaving. Rings and crosses are the motifs.

**Twining.**—Twined basketry of the simple two-strand type has one set of rigid warp elements and the weft elements working in pairs. The warps are wrapped by twisting the weft strands a half turn on each other between each two single warps or groups of warps,

Twining is weakly developed technique in South America although a few items are reported from widely separated areas: among *Carajá* twining and twilling are dominant techniques. Close twining has an old history among the *Huarpe*, whose baskets were famous in the 17th century; even today the *Huarpe* make a covered bowl-shaped workbasket with a thick coil at the top. *Cayuvava* twined baskets show certain adaptations of the technique. The *Mojo* lidded reed baskets have twining elements of cotton threads.

Spaced twining is adapted to several uses: it is the technique in mats for straining manioc flour *(Huanyam, Baure, Bacäiri, Carajá); for small honey strainers (Chorití, Ashluslay)*; for funnel-shaped fish traps *(Wapishana);* and for carrying baskets (Northwest Amazon tribes). Small mats of "roll-up" type are made by the Guiana Indians; large mats suitable for roof and wall covers are constructed of rushes held together with twining wefts *(Mbayá, Pilagá, Toba).* One of the most unusual forms of mat work, the *Aymara* sail, is also twined.

**Open weaves.**—Techniques used for many carrying baskets and knapsacks in order to keep them light in weight are called lattice-type, hexagonal weave, open weave and three-element work. The characteristic feature of the hexagonal weave is the passage of weaving elements in three directions: horizontally, obliquely upward to right, and obliquely upward to left.

**Coiled basketry.**—Basketry depending for its form on a coil of fibers sewn in place as it spirals from bottom to top is characteristic of tribes in the far south and on the west coast: the *Ona, Yahgan, Alacaluf*, and *Araucanians*. The technique is reported from the *Chocó* and *Cuna*, but it is seldom used, and from the *Pancarurú*, *Apinayé*, and *Mataco*. The latter group may have acquired it from Mestizo neighbors. The

*Quechua* and *Aymara* also make coiled baskets. Unlike standard methods, the *Aymara* form their bowl-shaped containers over a foundation made of a series of radiating splints to the interior surface of which the coils are sewn. Some coiled baskets have come from excavations on the Peruvian coast and in the *Atacameño* area.

The greatest development in coiling is among tribes of Tierra del Fuego and up the Chile coast. The sewing technique employed is the half-hitch done over a foundation, a type call Fuegian or half-hitch coil. Work is begun in the usual manner with foundation materials of grass stems shaped to form a small disk. At the turning point from bottom to side, the disk is suspended bottom up by a cord from a support. From this point on to the finishing coil, the weaver's two hands are free to sew and coil. The only essential tool is a small wooden or bone awl for piercing.

The *Yahgan* have four types of coiled work: the first two are based on half-hitches over a foundation, the third is a half-hitch without foundation, and the fourth is a wrapped or knotted half-hitch employed in constructing dip nets. Open-mesh, coiled baskets made by these people vary in size, shape, and use. Two baskets have round bottoms, one of them a bucket-shape, about 7 or 8 inches in diameter. Both kinds have handles of thong or plaited grasses. These are typical *Yahgan* baskets, and, as the *Southern Ona* names for theirs are similar to the *Yahgan* names, it is probable that the former were borrowers. An "ordinary large mesh basket" attached to the end of a harpoon handle becomes a dip net.

### Basketry colors

Many ordinary baskets are woven in natural colors, but there are three general methods of bringing contrasting colors into the patterning: (1) By using elements whose colored surface and reverse sides differ. *Chocó, Tule*, and *Cayapa* weavers manipulated elements to produce mats or baskets with all light or all dark surfaces, or combination of dark and light; (2) By using elements of different natural color. Guiana and *Arawak* weavers choose contrasting warps and wefts; the *Caingang* leave the outer green skin on bamboo splints. By turning the individual elements, the basket exterior shows alternate bands of green and white; (3) By dyeing one series of weaving elements. Black is most often mentioned *(Chocó, Tule,* northwestern Amazonian tribes, *Wapishana,* Purús River Indians, upper Xingú tribes, *Southern Gê, Guaraní).* The *Wapishana* scrape and bleach some strips for stronger contrast with black-dyed elements.

Red dye is made from achiote by the *Cayapa and the Rio Negro and Central American tribes. The Cayapa* stain their hoja blanca with red by rubbing achiote, the coloring matter, on the stem. Colored strips are occasionally used for geometric designs in trinket baskets and fans.

Basket materials gathered in the fall by Fuegian tribes are red from the first frosts; the color fades in a few weeks. The *Chocó* employ cauto, the pigment of *Genipa americana,* for jet black dye; the *Northwestern Gê* make yellow paint for surface decorations.

## Division of labor

In the Guiana area both men and women make baskets, but some objects usually made by women in one district may be made by men in another. Also, craftsmen of both sexes may weave in the same tribe (southeastern Panama tribes).

Among northwest Amazon tribes women are the chief basket makers, but men help and occasionally weave by themselves. In Jamaica straw hats are the workmanship of women and girls, but when outdoor work fails or the weather is bad, men take a hand. Among northern and southern Peruvian tribes both men and women plait hats. Women are the chief or the only basket and mat makers among *Jívaro, Cayapa, Yaruro, Motilones, Huanyam, Bororo,* and Yahgan.

In most Indian tribes basketry is plaited by men. More tribes in which basketry is a masculine craft and mentioned, but in some of them women weave small containers for personal belongings *(Macushí, Cashinawa),* or make provisional burden baskets *(Apinayé),* or baskets of special shapes, such as the *Sherente* oval basket. It may be assumed that wherever provisional burden baskets are constructed men know how to plait them from various palm leaves. Hat making and the making of basketry frames for feather headdresses appear to be

Carrying basket from Straits of Magellan. Coiled in half-hitch or buttonhole stitch.

predominantly in masculine hands among *Jívaro,* Rio Negro tribes, *Chiquito,* Rio Chapre tribes, and *Chané.* Basketry is specifically referred to as one of man's tasks for *Island Carib, Arawak, Carib, Acawai, Warrau, Wapishana, Tariana,* Rio Xingú-Madeira tribes, *Nambicuara, Guató, Chimane,* and *Northwestern* and *Central Gê.* Men excel as basket makers among British Guiana tribes; in some they always weave the cassava squeezers and fire fans. *Macushí* men make their own fine shoulder baskets for small possessions; *Caingang* men make waxlined containers for liquids as they are needed.

## Basketry lacking

Basket weaving is unknown or not practiced in some South American areas. The *Camacan* do not weave, nor do tribes on the upper Xingú or in the Chaco, except those marginal tribes *(Caduveo)* in contact with basket-making neighbors. Basketry is unknown to the *Tehuelche, Puelche,* and *Chono.* Some of these peoples live in regions lacking suitable fibers for basketry; some use netted objects in place of baskets. A few tribes plait only provisional palm-leaf baskets *(Sirionó),* or make headdresses requiring slight knowledge of techniques *(Botocudo),* or use basic manipulations only in traps and fishing gear.

Abundant basketry material from Peruvian sites is retrievable. Museum collections are small as yet, and no intensive studies have been made. Ancient basket makers appear to have been satisfied with expertly woven and sewn objects made for use. Most decoration consists of simple geometric units in one or two colors. Native styles and tastes were expressed not in basketry but in cloth through extraordinary combinations of techniques and colors.

There is no mention of *Chibcha* basketry; but the few mixed descendents of the ancient *Haurpe* still weave beautiful baskets, thus confirming historical references to their craftsmanship.

## Household basketry

**Carrying baskets.**—Baskets for packing in loads of fruits, heavy roots, and firewood, and for transporting utensils and household goods are in common use among many South American tribes. Some baskets are provisional contrivances (*Tupi-Cawahíb* rucksack) made by ingeniously knotting two green palm leaves together. As soon as the leaves become dry, the burden basket is worthless. Such rough containers may be strong enough for carrying large objects or an animal. *Cayapa* temporary baskets are pouch-shaped; northwest Amazon tribes find many uses for a deep square basket reinforced with two foundation rods. The whole thing is constructed in 5 minutes and discarded at the end of the trip. Sturdy baskets of this general type made by braiding together the leaflets of a single palm leaf are reported from northeast Amazon tribes and the *Bacaïri, Mojo, Chamane,* etc. who do not construct temporary pack baskets include the *Chorotí, Ashluslay, Toba, Papiete, Mataco, Quechua,* and *Aymara.*

Most burden baskets are woven with concern for durability. Two main types are constructed: large bowl-shaped or cylindrical baskets with tumplines and baskets with frames, the "knapsacks". The first type, widely distributed, is used by both sexes.

Shapes, sizes, materials, and construction techniques vary from one tribe to another. Some cylindrical baskets flare outward (*Cayapa*); some are straight-sided (*Jívaro*); West Indian *Carib* make large pyramidal shapes; one *Jacaré* form is square. Manioc carrying baskets of northwest Amazonian tribes measure approximately 20 inches each way. Characteristic features are the square bases, straight walls, circular rims, and checker or twined weaves. Many large baskets are loosely woven in checker or open hexagonal weave to lighten weight *(Arawak, Warrau, Tucano, Cashinawa, Omagua, Cocoma, Paressi, Mojo, Chapacurans). Coroado* carrying baskets are about 30 inches long, the depth also of the *Jívaró* basket. A narrow basket used by *Northern Cayapó* for transporting crops is only 10 inches high; they have also a bowl-shaped type with tumpline; *Araucanian* carrying baskets are similar. Simple baskets for transporting toods are mentioned for the *Cuna, Witoto, Chiquito, Chimane, Aweicoma, Shokleng,* and *Carajá. Abipón* mothers carry babies in wicker baskets on their shoulders when they travel; the *Tule* make an oblong burden basket designed to carry a bar of prepared cacao.

Totally different in construction from all these is the coiled bucket-shaped carrying basket with plaited handle which is standard equipment for the *Alacaluf* canoe.

No one term adequately describes the "knapsack" carrying baskets with wooden frames. Some are slipper-shaped. They are usually longer and more strongly built than the ordinary packing basket. The rectangular form is characterized by open top and outer side. Reinforcement consists of a frame of rods with the two side members projecting below the basketry to serve as legs. The contents of the loaded basket are kept in place by cords lacing across the open side. Mats and covers woven to size and shape give added protection. The knapsack is supported on the carrier's back by a tumpline. It is the principal carrying device in the Guiana area; and is also in use among upper Xingú tribes in Belize and Guatemala. The *Bacäiri* knapsack has a framework of wicker hoops, an elliptical one at the bottom, longer ones lashed together forming back and two sides. Each oval opening is filled in with interlacing bark strips.

Of undoubted post-Columbian origin are large pannier market baskets suspended across the backs of donkeys (Jamaica).

**Food-storage baskets.**—Every tribe must have storage containers for provisions. Guiana Indians make special baskets for farina. They are small truncated cones lined with leaves, according to accepted methods, in order to prevent flour from sifting through. More leaves covering the top are firmly held with interlaced splints. Openwork wicker baskets with rounded bottoms, frequently mounted on legs, are used in the same area for storing foodstuffs. Large containers in open hexagonal weave for lightness are much in evidence among northwest Amazon tribes. The *Nambicuara* make low square palm-leaf baskets for manioc and maize flours; the *Sirionó*, who weave only simple basket types, make palm-leaf containers for their harvests; and the *Carajá* make a square basket especially for tobacco. The *Tapirapé* storage baskets for manioc or corn flour have a squarish base and narrow round top. Storage baskets are frequently hung up under the eaves or from the house rafters: an ordinary cylindrical basket *(Cayapó)* has a woven handle for this purpose. Food utensils and calabashes are stored by *Mosquito* and *Sumo* in round withe baskets.

Several tribes make small watertight containers for liquids *(Aweicoma, Shokleng, Caingang, Guayakí)*. The general method is to coat the weaving elements with wax or to apply a coat to the finished basket. *Caingang* workmanship is carefully done. Shapes are similar but sizes differ from receptacles holding a cup of water or honey to others holding a gallon.

*Alacaluf* rush storage baskets are coiled or sewn.

**Cassava squeezers and sieves.**—Manioc roots in being transformed to flour are peeled, grated, and squeezed to express the poisonous juice; the substance remaining is dried, pounded, and sifted. Most of the equipment is basketry. Cassava presses and sieves are essentials in the household equipment of some tribes from the upper Rio Negro across to the Guianas and south to the *Chiriguano*. All descriptions of presses are similar in basic details. The cylindrical form is closely twill-woven of fine splints; the tube measures from 5 to 8 feet by 5 to 7 inches in diameter *(Wapishana, Wiawai, Macushí*, etc.*)*, to 7 to 10 feet by about 6 inches in diameter *(Bora*, etc.*)*. The extended weaving at both ends of the tube forms loops. The top loop, so constructed as to leave an opening at one side, permits suspending the press from a support; the bottom loop, beyond the closed end, permits passage through it of a lever or bar. Application of pressure sometimes by one or two women sitting on the bar, elongates the compactly filled cylinder, reduces its diameter and expresses the juice.

Among northwest Amazon tribes the cassava press is a long mat of plaited bark fiber about 10 inches wide, which is wound spirally around the mass of grated manioc and twisted. Vaupés River Indians spread grated manioc over a tray supported from a tripod and force out the juice by hand pressure.

Sifters, in use among many tribes, remove hard particles from lumpy dry manioc meal. Forms are generally square with low rims raised by tying on small sticks. These extend beyond the corners and support the sieve on the woman's lap. She steadies the frame by bracing her outstreched feet against the distal end. Finely woven disks and square sieves are reported from tribes on the upper Xingú, *Bacäiri* and *Tupí Cawahíb*. The *Chiriguano, Chané*, etc., use round basketry sifters for corn. They are also reported for the *Mojo, Huanyam, Bauré, Paressí, Chapacurans*, and *Guayakí*.

*Yuracare* strainers are bowl-shaped. The *Carib* have basket strainers for drinks; *Chorotí* and *Ashluslay* have special small strainers for honey.

**Tray types.**—Trays are shallow basketry forms with rims, and are frequently so closely woven that they can be used to hold cassava flour. Their many uses include holding bread, foodstuffs, or raw cotton in one of its preparatory stages. Hanging trays keep their contents out of reach of dogs or ants. The *Mosquito* and *Sumo* suspend over the fire the flat withe baskets to hold wooden spoons and stirring sticks. Guiana trays are rectangular, oval, or round, and frequently patterned with geometric motifs developing out of twilling techniques. Edge finishes are varied. Forms interpreted as tray types are mentioned for the *Cuna,* northwest Amazon tribes, *Mojo,* and *Aymara.* The latter's shallow wicker trays may be of Spanish introduction.

**Special household Baskets.**—Among special baskets connected with food getting, preparation, and serving are the following: Wicker stands for pots (Aiarí River tribes); woven rings for calabash stands *(Cayapa)*; for water jars; bottle-necked baskets for farina flour, and hourglass-shaped containers (Guianas); small tubular baskets for storing chili peppers while drying (northwest Amazon tribes); bottle-shaped baskets *(Carajá)*; receptacles for edible ants *(Resigero)*; small waterproofed baskets to serve as cups, dishes *(Haurpe, Aweicoma),* and spoons *(Mojo)*; and forms imitating pottery vessels *(Chiriguano).* A small *Cuna* basket described in the 17th century was said to have been woven so closely as not to require waterproofing. Scoop baskets and trays for handing food to guests are woven in the Guianas.

**Fans.**—Basketry fans are woven by tribes from Ecuador to the Guianas and from Central America south to include some *Guaraní.* Occasionally, fans are used for personal comfort *(Cayapa)*; however, the *Arawak* believe that a woman would lose flesh were she to use one on herself; the greater number are used to fan fires. Besides this use, some Guiana tribes use the fan to smooth, level, and turn over the cassava cake on the griddle.

Shapes of fan blades vary, depending

somewhat upon the form of materials but more upon techniques of construction. Square-blade fans with handles projecting from one corner are the only *Cayapa* type; they are found also on the lower Amazon and upper Xingú together with triangular fans. The rectangular blade is characteristic of Panamanian and *Carib* tribes and *Purí-Coroado;* the shovel-shaped fan is *Arawak,* and the heart-shaped fan is typical of tribes on the Caiarí-Vaupés River.

Almost the only fan materials are palm leaves, the fronds plaited, the midrib included; the *Bacäiri* make some grass fans. *Tupí-Cawahíb* often adorn their fans with feathers; usually decoration is structural as in other basketry, solely the result of technique.

## Basketry fishing gear

Equipment especially constructed of basketry materials and by basketry techniques or modifications of ordinary household shapes, such as the sieve and tray, are used for catching fish. Sizes vary from fence-weirs across streams to small dip nets. Many tribes set conical wickerwoven creels in the weirs (Guiana Indians, *Guarayú, Huanyam*) or dams *(Guarayú, Pauserna, Chiquito, Mojo).* The central *Arawak (Wapishana,* etc.,*)* weave funnel-shaped basketry traps from 6 to 8 feet long and about a foot across the mouth, also smaller traps consisting of one funnel inside another, and spring traps attached to poles.

The *Cayuvava* and other Indians have a strongly made basket form resembling a lampshade, which is useful for catching fish in very shallow water or mud. The basket is thrown down over the fish, which are then taken out through the top opening. Large trays are also woven for the fisherman. The *Chiquito, Mojo,* and *Guarayú* among others, catch eels with baskets of ordinary shapes. *Guarayú* men hold a large oval basket at an angle to the stream bed; assistants beat the water with poles to frighten the eels toward the basket. The *Arawak* and *Guarayú* catch small fish on sievelike trays, by submerging the trays under the aqueous plants, then bringing them up suddenly.

Conical-shaped baskets are landing nets *(Carib, Arawak)*, and larger baskets made for other uses may be attached to harpoon handles and used as landing nets. Basketry dip nets for taking small fish are also reported *(Yahgan, Ona)*. Rushes, bark, and split twigs are worked into crude forms.

Live insect bait is kept in bottle-shaped baskets *(Cayapa)*.

## Basketry objects for personal use

**Covered and telescoping baskets.**—The classic example of a covered basket is the oblong twilled container with hinged lid commonly used in ancient Peru to hold a woman's weaving, spinning, sewing materials, and her small tools and spindles.

Double or telescope baskets consisting of two deep trays, one for body and one for cover, are woven in a variety of forms and sizes with notable success over a wide area. Some of the tribes are the *Chiriguano, Guayaná, Carajá*. More or less flexible hampers with overlapping lids may be furnished with handles (Jamaica). This favorite style comes in round or squarish forms and in different heights and degrees of sturdiness. The *Taino* and West Indian *Carib* make double-walled baskets and place a lining of leaves between the walls to insure against moisture. Telescoping envelopes are reported from the *Cuna*. *Cayapa* hampers as storage containers for clothing and valuables may be drawn up to the rafters; used as traveling bags, they hold a man's mosquito canopy, clothing, face paint, extra finery, and jewelry. *Tule* baskets of this type are small pack baskets which are carried; they are much prized by the women. Characteristic features of telescoping baskets made in the Guianas are the close checker, twill, and wicker weaves and the striking geometrical patterns, especially those developed through manipulation of twilling techniques.

The *Jívaro* make very strong baskets of split rattans. Body and cover are each composed of two separately woven baskets rendered rainproof by interlining the space between them with tough palm leaves. Each pair of baskets is then sewn together around the upper edges, and the cover basket is hinged to the container proper. Anything and everything may be packed in this type.

**Containers for small belongings and trinkets.**—Among baskets woven for special purposes are those in which raw cotton in various stages of preparation is stored and in which spindles, balls of yarn, and sewing supplies are kept. Workbaskets are woven by the *Piro,* by tribes in the Guianas, and on the Amazon. The *Piro* and *Waiwai* make several baskets connected with cotton preparation. One form holds unginned raw stock. The rough framework is thickly lined with palm leaves; near the top is left a hole just large enough for the hand. Such baskets are hung near the roof to keep their contents dry. Ginned cotton is stored in small bowl-shaped baskets; spindles and yarn are kept in larger circular or square baskets. The *Huarpe* make beautiful workbaskets decorated with woolen tufts dyed different colors. The *Cayapa* store spindles in long tubular baskets, and the *Carajá* weave boat-shaped baskets of beautiful workmanship; both types are made to be suspended. Among the most distinctive containers are those in which *Bauré* and *Mojo* women store spindles. The shape is roughly like a wooden shoe with a cord handle across the instep by which to hang it up. Some are twill-woven in an all-over block pattern.

Men and women of certain districts make or may even procure, from other tribes, baskets for personal belongings. Trinkets are carried by *Wapishana* and *Waiwai* women in long pocket-shaped open baskets with narrow mouths. *Cashinawa* women weave small receptacles of bark strips; the *Northwestern Gê* make specially constructed twill-woven receptacles. There is some question as to the aboriginality of splint-ware trinket baskets made by the *Aymara.*

The finest craftsmanship in some tribes appears to have been expended upon trinket baskets worn by men. A *Jívaro* man carries small possessions in a rectangular bag with a flap cover, suspended by a shoulder strap; the *Carajá* weave beautiful hand and shoulder bags,, many of them flexible. Baskets carried by men in some parts of the Guianas are generally square or rectangular forms of the so-called telescope variety; they are distinguished from other forms by a lid which fits down over the top of the basket proper. Guiana weavers make each part of shoulder bags double with a moisture-proof interlining of leaves. The West Indian *Carib* attach their small rectangular trinket baskets by cords to canoe gunwales in case the craft should overturn. The *Waiwai,* experts in making telescope baskets, pass the suspension corder underneath the basket base and thread it through the sides of the lid so that the lid may be moved up and down freely. *Waiwai* weavers often develop elaborate geometric patterns in twill techniques, using dark and light strands of material for emphasis. Guiana trinket baskets may be decorated with loose strings of thick white cotton, knots, and tufts of colored feathers.

Storing of feathers used in decorative work and ornament making and feather-decorated objects is a special concern among some tribes. *Jívaro* and *Carajá* men have baskets for larger pieces of finery; these they hang up on houseposts or suspend from the ridge pole. For feather ornaments the *Carajá* also make long telescopetype containers, and the *Guayakí* plait flexible pouches. Long cane splints held together with spaced twining elements make a foundation which is always covered with bark cloth. The *Tucano* weave an oblong wicker storage basket which they suspend in the community house. Communal treasures and regalia for great feasts, bracelets, necklaces, bone girdles, and feather ornaments are placed in this basket, which can be drawn up to the roof.

"Cover basketry" is the term employed to denote plaitwork built around certain objects. Under this classification come emptied calabashes used as floats for baited fishing lines *(Warrau)*, large jars covered with open basketry the central two-part "bars" between which palm splinters are clamped to form combs (Vaupés River, Rio Negro, and Guiana tribes), blowpipes and clubs *(Macushí, Arecuna*, etc.), spear shafts beautifully decorated with black and white canework *(Carajá)*, bows covered with basketry sheaths *(Tupinamba)*, and handles of clubs.

**Hats, headdresses, and accessories.—** Hats are first and foremost ornamental, and are known only among those tribes influenced to some degree by contacts with White civilization. Plaited eyeshades are worn by the *Carajá* and also openwork hats. "Panama" type straws made by the *Mojo* and *Churapa* after methods presumably learned from the Spaniards, featherbanded straw hats with conical crowns plaited by the Motilones, straw hats of the *Cainguá* and hats of the *Bogotá* appear to be imitations in form and construction. Other forms are the peaked palm-leaf hats *(Warrau)*, and hats of grass straw woven after the style of Panamas *(Chiquitos, Chiriguano*, and *Chané)*.

The *Páez* and *Moguex* make hats by coiling rush or straw and by sewing braid. This last, more common method is followed also by the *Lenca*. Leaves of the sugar palm are cut into strips and braided.

The industry centering around the weaving of the so-called Panamá hat thrives among the

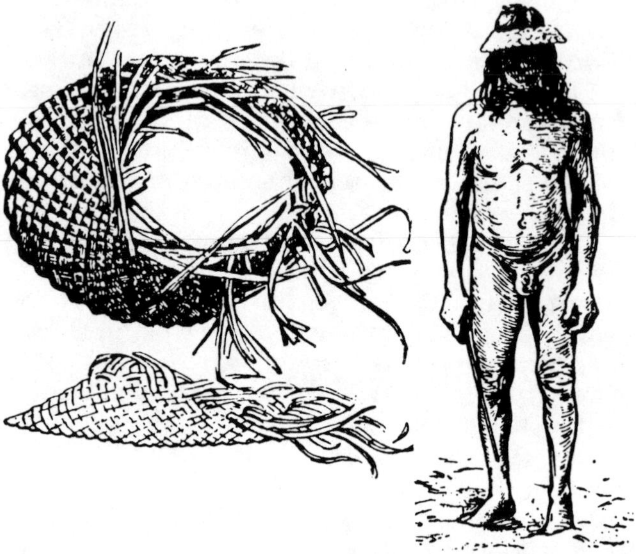

Carajá eye shade made of palm leaves.

*Patuso* in Colombia, in Northern Peru, in Ecuador, and to lesser extent in Central American countries and Jamaica. All grades are made from palm. Weaving the ordinary hat requires 2 to 3 days; finer ones require 10 to 15 days; prices range from 50 cents to $100.

Especially in the northern part of the continent are there tribes who weave basketry bases or light supporting frames for colored feathers. Some Guiana foundations are like broad, flat rings up to 3 inches wide; others *(Bacäiri, etc.)*. are straight-walled coronets. Among *Yamamadí* men feather crown are worn on feast days, among *Jívaro* they are part of dance regalia, and among *Mojo* they have ceremonial significance. The ring or brim-type of headdress (Rio Negro tribes of Vaupés district and the *Arawak* and *Warrau)* consists of a pair of woven circlets with feathers inserted between their outer edges. The coronet type *(Wapishana, Macushí,* etc., and Chaco tribes,) has applied to it a cotton band to which feathers have been affixed. The *Bauré, Mojo, Chiquito,* and *Carajá* have huge feather ornaments mounted on basket frames. The *Mojo* make the largest ornamental headdresses in South America. Added to their principal feature, the arrangement of feathers, are rows of silver tubes.

Much less ambitious headgear is reported from two other areas: *Cayapó* maidens wear narrow fillets of reed to which they bind feathers, and the *Botocudo* contrive simple headdresses of palm leaves, their only basket-making effort.

Among basketry costume accessories are hollow cylinder belts *(Patamona* and *Macushí),* collars woven of fiber and covered with shells *(Jívaro),* and shields of strong wickerwork (Rio Negro tribes).

**Baskets for special uses.**—Basketry cages are made for young birds and animals (Guianas), for monkeys *(Yamamadí),* for parrots (Amazonian Tupi), and for transporting live crabs *(Cayapa).*

Basketry which has a part in ceremonial activities includes the following: The wasp frame constructed in the form of an animal, bird, or fish *(Apalaí, Macushí).* The main part measuring about 6 to 8 inches is wickerwork; the remainder is feather-decorated.

Ornaments carried in the *Caingang* dancer's hand or stuck in the ground are partially dependent upon basketry techniques. Tiny plaited squares and small objects are mounted on stakes.

Some tribes collect the bones of their dead in big, specially constructed baskets; these are either kept in the house *(Moré, Cumana)* or buried *(Caingang, Bororo).* The *Araucanians* sometimes make wickerwork coffins.

**Matwork.** Matwork is important in furnishing both necessities and comforts. The outer walls of some houses are formed of mats. The inner walls of matting form compartments for different families or screen off the bed space of the young girls *(Apinayé)* or the space where a birth is taking place *(Bacäiri)*.

Among the *Aymara* and *Carajá* mats may be used as roofing; in the Chaco they are set up to afford protection from the sun, or they may be woven as the principal shelter material of the hut. Among the *Lengua, Toba, Abipón*, etc., mats are stretched onto a framework of sticks so as to make both roof and side walls. When these tribes move, they take down their mats, roll them up, and carry them to the new location. Very early evidence of mats so used comes from the proto-Chimu bowl depicting women weavers under a mat-roofed arbor.

Mats are housefurnishing, also. They cover the bare earth of the hut *(Paumari, Carajá, Bororo)*; in many tribes they serve as mattresses as sheets of fine quality, and as covers *(Canella)*. Some tribes weave mats for hammocks. The *Canella* make a temporary hammock by interlacing the tips of buritı́ leaflets; the *Cayapa* make two mats for a child's cradle: the larger is the hammock proper, the smaller, placed crosswise, holds its edges apart. The baby sleeps on the smaller mat. The *Bororo* mother rocks her child to sleep in a mat suspended by its four corners. In Mato Grosso and the upper Xingú River district sitting on the ground is usually avoided, and small mats are common possessions. Sitting mats are made and used by fastidious young girls *(Wapishana)* and by fishermen, who expect to stay on a hot river bank for some time *(Carajá)*.

As a temporary protection, stiff mats set just inside the gunwales of a *Cayapa* canoe arch upward to shield children and invalids from sun; small mats serve as "wrappers" to shade the *Apinayé* baby in its mother's carrying-girdle. Among the *Sherente* and *Eastern Timbira* the girdle itself is a mat-like sling plaited of palm leaves. Mats are specially made to cover the contents of the open knapsack (Guiana Indians), and long mats cover drinking troughs (Caiari-Vaupés River).

In connection with food, mats are used to construct storage bins for grains *(Aymara);* as drying sufaces for cacoa *(Cayapa);* as manioc presses *(Bora);* as covers for cooking pots; as platters to serve food *(Patamona, Macushí);* and as strainers *(Huanyam, Bauré, Bacäiri, Carajá).* Some tribes use mats where basket forms would be expectable: the upper Xingú tribes roll feathers up in mats and the northeast Amazon tribes *(Arecuna, Barima Carib, Macushí)* weave mats from which to construct shoulder bags.

Less frequently mats are used in burial of the dead *(Sirionó, Bororo)* and as masks of mummies' outfits *(Canella).* Rafts of the *Mojo* and *Paressí* are oversized mats, as were also the rectangular lug sails mentioned in early reports on Guiana Indians and the sails on modern *Aymara* balsas.

Most tribes make mats for their own needs; *Witotoan* tribes make them for their trades with the whites.

**BEANS** are among the earliest domesticated plants of the Americas and are cultivated by nearly every native community. "Bean" is here applied to edible seeds of the *Leguminoseae* and the plants that bear them, a usage which conflicts with popular terminology in only a few instances.

Pre-Columbians domesticated *Phaseolus* and *Canavalia* spp., peanuts *(Arachis hypogeae),* and *tarwi (Lupinus mutabilis). Phaseolus* domesticates include frijols *(P. vulgaris),* limas and sieva limas *(P. lunatus),* teparies *(P. acutifolius)* and runner beans *(P. coccineus),* whose tuberous roots are eaten as well as the seeds. Various wild legumes supply edible seeds and seedpods, of which *Prosopis* spp. are the most important mesquite *(P. juliflora)* in the Sonoran region and *algarroba (P. chilensis, alba* and *nigra)* in the Chaco and other semiarid South American areas. Since Columbus, various Old World beans have been introduced and frijols, limas and peanuts have been widely adopted in Europe and Africa, but with the arguable exception of peanuts there is little evidence of pre-Columbian diffusion.

Beans fulfill two vital functions. One, like all legumes, they are associated with symbiotic soil bacteria *(Rhizobium* spp.*)* that fix atmospheric nitrogen which in turn becomes available to the beans and to interplanted or following crops. Second, their rather abundant protein (generally 20-25%) "complements" that of many starchy staples; i.e., amino acid deficiencies in each protein are to some extent made up by the other.

The amount of nitrogen added by *Phaseolus* and most other American beans is small, but significant on poor or depleted soils. Indians both interplant and rotate beans with other crops and with fallows, often within the same community. In tropical rain forest areas, however, interplanting is the rule, probably because beans are relatively unimportant there and because pure bean stands would expose the soil too long to the pounding rains.

*Phaseolus* and most other beans complement rather well maize and introduced Old World cereals because the bean proteins are rich in lysine, in which the cereals are deficient. In the ubiquitous maize-frijol combination, tryptophan is still somewhat deficient but protein nutrition is still greatly improved.

Beans were in Aztec and Inca tribute rolls. They still figure in social presentations and in folklore and mythology but far less prominently than maize.

Domesticated frijols are reported from Tamaulipas and Tehuacan Mexico, *c.* 5000 BC, Bat Cave, New Mexico, *c.* 1000 BC, the Mississippi valley after AD 600, and New York State by AD 1100. Domesticated teparies at Tehuacan date from 3000 BC, while sieva limas, runner beans and jack beans *(Canavalia ensiformis)* all appear to be later domesticates in Mesoamerica. The diffusion of these beans into Central America, or their separate domestication, is not at present well documented.

Frijols are generally the most important beans. Teparies are heat tolerant and fast maturing and therefore predominate in hot areas of the Greater Sonoran Desert. They are secondary crops in nearby higher areas and along the southern Chiapas-Guatemala border. Limas are cultivated in warmer climates but are the main bean in only a few tropical locales. Runner beans are scattered through cool, humid parts of the Mesoamerican highlands, especially in Chiapas and Guatemala. Jack beans are widely cultivated but nowhere important. The Spanish introduced large-seeded limas and peanuts from South America as well as many Old World beans, including broadbeans *(Vicia faba)* and peas in cool areas, and chickpeas *(Cicer arietinum),* cowpeas *(Vigna sinensis)* and *Dolichos* spp. in the hot lands.

Among highland Mesoamerican Indians as much as 15-22 percent of the caloric intake is from beans, and the range is not much lower in the American Southwest. The percentage seems to be generally lower but still significant in lowland Mesoamerica. Beans are prominent in explorer's descriptions of eastern North American diets and a tradition of bean eating and specialty bean dishes is still found in Oklahoma and much of the Southeast.

Throughout these regions, beans are mostly boiled without presoaking and flavoring herbs may be added. In eastern North America beans are boiled with green corn or hominy to make succotash. In Mesoamerica, boiled beans are stuffed into tortillas and tamales and are sometimes "refried" with onions, the latter a post-Columbian innovation.

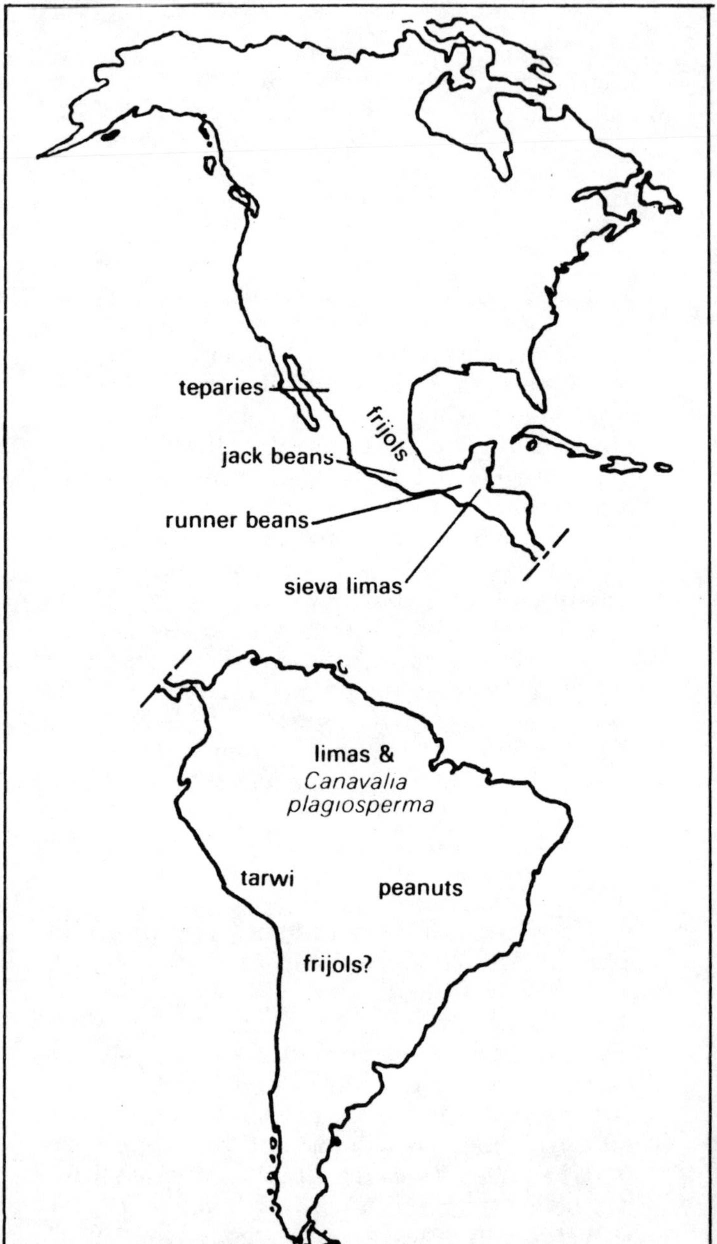


Areas of abundant bean crops in North and South America.

The earliest reported South American domesticated beans are from coastal Peru, large-seeded limas and *Canavalia plagiosperma* before 2000 BC and frijols and peanuts before the Christian era, but none are native to the area. Peanuts come from the Brazilian savanna, the frijols may be derived from either Mesoamerican varieties or wild *Phaseolus* spp. of the Andean eastern slope, and eastern lowland domestication is likely for the limas and *Canavalia plagiosperma*.

Limas and frijols predominate in most tropical lowlands, peanuts on sandy soils, and various Old World tropical varieties are sometimes important. Only frijols continue into temperate zones, e.g. about 5000-9000 feet in the central Andes. Broadbeans, peas and *tarwi* appear at these elevations and replace frijols altogether in the higher *altiplano*.

Beans are most important where maize and/or rice are the main staples: the warm and temperate Andean zones and much of the Caribbean lowlands. The root crop staples remove less nitrogen than maize does and their protein is not so well complemented by that of beans. In the *altiplano, quinoa, cañihua* and barley proteins complement that of potatoes and beans are usually a minor crop. Tropical lowland populations dependent on sweet potatoes and especially manioc rely heavily on animal protein so that beans decline in importance and are occasionally absent.

There does not appear to be the same variety of bean dishes as in Mesoamerica. Beans are most commonly added to stews but are also often boiled by themselves. Many native communities in the Chaco, southern Brazil and the Caribbean coast have adopted the popular beans and rice combination.

There is little likelihood that Old World beans will replace the major American varieties. No doubt this is due to the qualities of the native beans; *tarwi* has been largely replaced by broadbeans and *Canavalia* spp. were probably declining in popularity even before Columbus, but these are bitter, somewhat toxic, types that require long presoaking to make them marginally edible. The development of New World varieties by breeders may cause loss of local varieties but this has not proceeded so far as with many other crops.

DANIEL E. VASEY

**BEAUTY, CONCEPTS OF.** There was a widespread tendency to decorate or elaborate tools and utensils beyond any functional necessity. A pervading interest in body painting, and adornment with clothing and jewelry is evident from earliest times. All of this activity was carried out to make things pleasing to their eyes and the results may be considered to embody their concepts of beauty.

Much of the art was created to fill religious or ritual needs, and motifs were drawn from mythology and cosmology, but the forms were the product of aesthetic choices. Any of their ideas could have been expressed in a number of different ways, but they chose one that was visually satisfying to them, and thus pleasing or beautiful.

There are several hundred distinct art styles, often characterized by inventive and imaginative use of materials, and by exceptional skill in working with the medium.

The Pre-Columbian societies were visually oriented. They gained much of their knowledge of the world by direct observation of the animals and plants that shared it with them. Their oral traditions distilled these observations and were pervaded with images that grew out of their view of life. Their concepts of beauty were developed in the endeavor to make clear visual statements of these images or ideas, using the elements of design—line, color, shape, texture, proportion - to articulate these concepts. They saw the possibilites of colored sand, tree trunks, porcupine quills, feathers, jade, turquoise, gold, clay, stone, grasses and fibers, and developed the skills to use these materials.

What kinds of things were made depended upon the needs of the society. The nomadic cultures made only small portable objects, while the highly stratified city-states needed large buildings, monumental sculpture and elaborate objects of all sorts.

The desire for personal adornment seems to have been universal. Clothing was a matter of necessity in some climates and a matter of choice in others, but usually was decorated in some way. Body painting was widespread. Head deformation was practiced in a few societies, and tattooing and scarification by many. Men and women wore jewelry, sometimes perforating lips, nose, or ears to accommodate ornaments. Materials at hand were used, or sometimes exotic material or finished objects were imported.

Weaving was quite common, using usually cotton, although wool was used in Peru and by the Navaho in later times, and combined with cedar bark fibers by the Chilkat. The south coast of Peru is the best source of ancient textiles, found preserved in burials at Paracas, skillfully made in astonishing variety. Whole garments have been found, but most of our knowledge of clothing styles comes from depictions in painting and sculpture. Feathers were used in clothing and in headdresses and masks. A variety of materials occur in masks, used in dance and ritual, and in burials.

Pottery was almost universal, in a wide diversity of shape and decoration, and is of great importance in dating art styles and in giving archaeologists some idea of the rise and fall, or spread, of various cultures. Painting is found on pottery, both geometric or abstract designs, and narrative scenes, and painting also occurs on walls, on Mixtec and Maya screenfold books, and on animal skins. Some pottery was sculptured into human, animal or vegetable shapes.

Small sculptures, or objects like pipes, tools and weapons with sculptured decoration, have a wide distribution. Monumental scultpture and architecture are confined to the more complex societies. Mounds were built in the eastern parts of North and South America. Large constructions which are not architecture but patterns on the earth, best visible from the air, are found in Peru and in the United States.

All of these things were purposefully designed in accordance with concepts that were of importance to them and resulted in visual statements that pleased them, and perhaps the gods or spirits.

Over time, concepts changed as new peoples came into an area and imposed their ideas. Sometimes cultures declined and disappeared for internal or unknown reasons. As societies flourished and became more stratified, their needs proliferated for large scale building and elaborate ritual or courtly paraphernalia. This led often to the selection of the most talented workers to specialize in weaving, pottery, sculpture or painting. Sometimes, mass production occasioned a lowering of quality, as with some mold-made pottery.

In general, it can be said that concepts of beauty were important to the Indians of the Americas. Their cultures rested on a framework of images. In most times and places, each individual was close to artistic activity, either actively engaged in making something himself or herself, or being familiar with the process by watching others, or certainly in seeing the finished products. Some amount of time and energy had to be invested in making everything, even just the necessities of life, and so some time had to be spent in making aesthetic choices, even though one worked within a general communal style. These concepts of beauty would tend to become deep convictions because they were so bound up with every facet of their existence.

A number of separate cultures are found in North America, shaped in response to different physical environments. Their concepts of beauty were developed in the context of widely varying social organizations and were expressed in the differing materials which were available to them.

The Eskimo used ivory for carving small sculptures and implements. From earliest times the functional objects were decorated with incised lines and circles, harmoniously intergrated with the shape of the piece. In more recent times, engraved pictographic narrative scenes combine with abstract designs. In both drawing and painting, and in sculpture, the significant details or most characteristic forms are abstracted to express the image most clearly.

Northwest Coast Indian art used the abundant supply of wood to fill the needs of their more secure and prosperous society. Wooden houses had painted or carved decoration, as did masks, ceremonial objects and utensils.The tall totem poles are the most complex expression. A rich store of symbols was developed to signify the various totemic animals, and a sequence of animal and human forms was arranged to denote their particular relationship. All of the elements were combined to achieve a clear visual statement, unified by the vertical shape of the treetrunk and by the judicious use of color. These same symbolic forms were used in painting and weaving, as on a Chilkat blanket, where the forms were spread out horizontally in harmonious relationship to the shape of the object. Bold contrasts of color and undulating black outlines translate the different planes of sculpture into a dramatic pictorial design.

The art of the Southwest Indians is primarily two-dimensional and appears on baskets, textiles and pottery. A sharp color contrast and clearly organized geometric or stylized motifs create vigorous rhythmic designs. Navajo sand painting shows this same clarity of conception. The many different compostions use precise outlines and clear colors in primarily rectilinear forms which harmonize with the flat rectilinear ground of the work. The multi-storied Pueblo dwellings exhibit an overall harmony by the repetition of shapes and their relationship to their surroundings. The round ceremonial kivas were decorated with murals in well organized compositions in abstract shapes and a few contrasting colors.

The Plains Indians were nomads whose art appears on small portable objects and articles of clothing, made of painted or embroidered bison hide. A representational style portrays horses and men, intended to tell a story, but pleasing in the distribution of the silhouettes in rows contrasting with large empty areas, and the delicate accents of legs and weapons. Geometric designs with symbolic significance were also used, in varying combinations among the different tribes. Some foreign motifs were adopted, perhaps just because they were visually attractive. Porcupine quills were used for embroidery but were later largely supplanted by glass beads. When the various objects were assembled and worn, the effect must have satisfied their aesthetic sense.

Many different cultures existed at various times in the Eastern United States. These Woodlands or Moundbuilder peoples have left artifacts in various styles, with apparent influences from Mexico in later times. Stone sculpture includes beautifully proportioned and polished banner stones, bowls, pipes, masks and human and animal representations. Pottery vessels have simple shapes with textured decoration, or are modeled into human and animal forms. Only a small quantity of wood sculpture remains. Skillful use of the medium and a three-dimensional conception of simplified naturalistic forms combine to achieve some well-ordered harmonious visual statements. Incised shell ornaments are characterized by a great variety of motifs, but there is a consistent concern for overall design and relationship to the surface. Sheets of mica cut into essentially two-dimensional shapes, such as a hand or a bird claw, are an imaginative use of material to create simple, forceful images.

Important artifacts of more recent times are Iriquois carved wooden masks. Although the images are prescribed by ritual needs, the forms are rythmic and sculptural, very different from the painted Kachinas of the Southwest, or the carved symbolic forms of the Northwest coast, or the often elegant and asymetrical masks of the Eskimos. All the these masks were created to represent and evoke spirits, but may be said to embody the concepts of beauty which prevailed in the various cultures in that they are organized visual expressions which were pleasing or satisfying to them and could not have been interchanged with those of another society.

The formative stage of art in Meso-America is represented by some early pyramids near Mexico City and by the vast quantity of clay figurines found in this vicinity. They are mostly representations of women, expressive rather than naturalistic, with proportions of the body exaggerated and details of dress and adornment carefully noted. There are also objects which are related to Olmec art and are thought to indicate some influence from that civilization which flourished on the Gulf Coast.

The Olmecs had a well-disciplined social organization, based on the veneration of the jaguar or combined jaguar and infantile human. They built pyramids and were accomplished sculptors, making small, carefully finished jade objects and large stone relief and freestanding works. The colossal heads placed around the pyramids are overwhelming in size and scale. They wear helmets pulled down to the eyebrows. Faces are widened horizontally and shortened vertically. They have no necks. The forms are simplified and every detail is directed toward achieving the impression of mass and weight, concentrated in alert watchfulness, a coherent visual expression of the idea of guarding. The seated "wrestler" or ball-player, well-conceived and executed to be viewed from every angle, portrays a man both intelligent and powerful. It would seem to embody their conception of beauty, both as an arrangement of forms and as a statement about man.

Teotihuacan in the Valley of Mexico was the first great city, built by a society organized around the worship of the rain god, Tlaloc. A distinctive style of architecture was developed and vast areas were interrelated along the axis of the Avenue of the Dead from the Pyramids of the Moon and the Sun to the enclosed space in front of the Temple of Tlaloc. His image appears in sculpture, on murals and on the characteristic ceramic vessels with painted decoration in fresco technique. These images were made up of the aggregation of separate symbolic elements and are basically two-dimensional in feeling, as is even the large stone sculpture of the water goddess. Human features are carved on small stone masks of simplified naturalism. The painted murals would seem to indicate that their concepts of beauty included an appreciation of flowers and butterflies, and nature made luxuriant by the rain.

Teotihuacan and Olmec influences were felt by the Maya, but their civilization developed into a distinctive flowering *c.* AD 300-900. They had a large pantheon of deities and a complex social organization. Elaborate programs of building were carried out at their various ceremonial centers to erect tall pyramids topped by temples, stone monuments, ball courts and palaces, resulting in a great variety of local expressions within the general style. Relief sculpture was combined with hieroglyphic writing to portray gods and rulers, always with a wealth of ornamentation and textural contrasts. The murals of Bonampak give us a picture of the highly stratified society with lords, servants, warriors, dancers all elaborately costumed. They are a record of jewelry, textiles, headdresses, musical instruments, featherwork, and show what an integral part of life were art and images. The series of paintings is organized in narrative fashion and records acute observations of varieties of pose, gesture and shape of the human form. This same kind of observation is apparent in a sculptured head from Palenque, being a sensitive portrayal of a Maya ruler whose intelligence and dignity perhaps personified a Maya concept of beauty. Ceramic sculptures from Jaina are small in size but have a monumental quality and seem often to express a feeling of human dignity.

In post-classic times the Maya incorporated Toltec ideas and their art became more rigid and preoccupied with death and sacrifice, as was the later art of the Aztec. Aztec sculpture can be naturalistic in its depiction of vegetables and animals, or conceptual as in the complex design of the Sun stone or in the representations of Coatlicue, but it is always a powerful expressive visual statement. The sculpture of Guerrero is severely abstract, while the Gulf Coast stone palmas and hachas are exquisitely graceful, and the ceramic smiling figures gently curved. Monte Alban with its orderly arrangement of buildings on a mountaintop has yielded expressive incised stone images and ceramic urns with modeled heads of humans or gods surrounded by an array of ornaments applied with remarkable virtuosity. The later Mixtec are noted for the stone mosaic decoration on their buildings at Mitla, their painted ceramics and screenfold books or codices, and for skillfully worked gold ornaments.

The Central American countries were subject to Mexican, Maya and South American influences. Working in stone, ceramics with polychrome decoration, and especially in gold, they evolved a variety of art styles.

In South America, Colombia is known for its excellent gold sculpture, as well as rock cut tombs with multi-patterned painted decoration, and large stone sculpture. Ecuador has some stone sculpture and many different types of ceramic vessels and sculptures, some of which bear some resemblance to those of Mexico.

Textile fragments and engravings of felines, birds and snakes have been found on the north coast of Peru, dated *c.* 2500 BC. At about the time of the Olmecs, *c.* 1000 BC a religious cult emerged in the central highlands, at Chavín de Huántar. It is characterized by large stone buildings and stone sculpture with a recurrent motif of a feline with snake elements and birds. Complex images are composed of many separate parts incised in shallow lines and organized into unified visual statement. These same feline designs spread to the north coast, appearing on pottery and textiles, and to some extent to the south coast.

As this influence waned, local styles became more differentiated. In the south, immense quantities of textiles have been preserved which show consummate skill and knowledge of every weaving technique. Colors and motifs are orchestrated in rythmic variation. More than a hundred colors have been distinguished. Motifs are human and animal. Paracas ceramics and those of the succeeding Nazca style are also characterized by the skillful use of color. They are well made and painted with naturalistic birds and plants, or religious symbols.

The pottery of the north coast, Mochica, is often modeled into sculptural three-dimensional forms, including realistically conceived portraits whose vigorous expressive planes depict the faces of strong and dignified individuals. The narrative scenes which occur on some pottery are unerringly integrated with the shape of the surface and combine silhouette, line and pattern into a clear, harmonious statement.

Around AD 700, another religious cult arose in the highlands near Lake Titicaca and spread its images over the coast. They erected large buildings and massive sculpture, and their stiff angular, remarkably unified Tiahaunaco style has a wide distribution in textiles and pottery.

Shortly before the arrival of the Spaniards, the Inca swept through the land and welded a unified empire, building roads and fortresses. The buildings have an austere beauty because of the simplicity of form, unadorned except for the trapezoidal openings in the facade, letting the monumentality of the perfectly fitted stones express the power and vision of those who built them. Such sites as Machu Picchu show great artistry in harmonizing the architecture with the landscape. The Inca imposed a certain unity of style throughout the empire. Their pottery was confined to a few shapes, with patterned designs of repeated small elements. Some present day viewers dismiss it as inferior or of little artistic value. Others have high praise for the integration of form and function, as in the aryballus, and the sensitively proportioned relationship of the parts to the whole. Beauty is indeed in the eye of the beholder, but whatever beauty is found must be considered to have been the intention of the artist. The most elaborate art, and gold and silver, were devoted to meeting the needs of the court.

Elsewhere in South America, some influences from the Andean civilizations or from the West Indies were felt. Except for the Marajó moundbuilders, there were no highly organized societies. In the Argentine Plains, nomadic groups painted their animal skin coats. In the north, various tribes excelled in basketry, featherwork, bodypainting, or finely made and glazed pottery, and continue to do so today.

Where Indians have been able to live in their accustomed ways, their concepts of beauty can continue to be expressed in traditional fashion. Where they have been dislocated or absorbed into another culture, both their concepts and ways of expressing them have changed.

In general, dress and adornment have remained ways in which they can express their preferences. Pottery, textiles, jewelry, baskets, paintings and sculpture are still being made in various places throughout the Americas. However, as societies stop making everything which they need, the opportunities for expressing concepts of beauty lessen, and the concepts become less clear. Then they become the concern of only the small percentage of the population who endeavor to be artists. As societies stop needing art to express their shared values, it becomes more of a personal expression.

In the past, the Indians of the Americas created a wealth of diverse and original expressions, inextricably set in the context of a particular culture. This art is now receiving the recognition it deserves and is part of the heritage of the Indians which may serve to stimulate present day art. Increasingly, it will become the task of individuals to define concepts of beauty and develop the skills to express them.

FLORENCE F. LIMAN

**BERRIES.** G.L. Vaillant, with the help of A.L. Kroeber's pioneering research, pointed out that Indians of North America had utilized 400 species of indigenous products called "vegetable" in the broadest sense. Hundreds of berries, fruits, flowers, seeds, nuts, stalks, roots, and other parts were mostly gathered wherever found; only a few were cultivated before white men arrived. It would appear that Indians of all the Americas saw little need to cultivate most berries, requiring no regular planting. Incas of the Peruvian mountains ate few wild plant foods, despite their essential vegetable diets; typically, their agriculture comprised potatoes, corn, squash, beans, tomatoes, manioc, and other non-berries. But in the montaña of the Upper Amazon, Incas raised strawberries, blackberries, and raspberries according to early reports. While Mayas cultivated avocados, papayas, and melons, it has been specified they gathered mulberries.

Moving into the North America areas now occupied by Utah and Nevada, the third century Anasazi Indians, revealed by Basketmaker finds, consumed many vegetables and plants, including sunflower seeds, piñon nuts, acorns, berries, and choke cherries. There is no indication that the berries, and choke cherries were cultivated. Sites occupied by Cochise Indians in Arizona and New Mexico showed that early Indians from about 13,000 to 500 BC gathered wild plant foods, including berries. Pueblo Indians were known to gather hackberries, junipers, choke cherries, gooseberries. Dried berries were commonly traded in intertribal prehistoric commerce.

In the Great Basin area, near the Rockies and the Sierra Nevada, evidence points to the eating of raspberries, wax currants, and other berries. Among Digger Culture Indians from about 7,000 BC until as late as the early 1900s among the Piautes and Shoshones, berries were pounded into a paste and dried, particularly for winter storage, along with seeds and piñon nuts.

The Nez Percé and other Shahaptin tribes, mainly in Idaho, Montana, and Washington, added to such staples as salmon and game, commonly gathered roots and berries, for which, again, there is no evidence of agriculture. Northwest Coast Indians ate cranberries, blueberries, and the Saskakoon berry which, William Brandon observes, "contains three times as much iron and copper as prunes and raisins."

The women of western coastal Indian tribes from Alaska, western Canada, and California gathered berries, along with fruits, roots, and tubers. Characteristic of Indian chiefdoms ranging from the northwestern coastal, Mesoamerica, parts of Guatamala, and Venezuela, the parcelling out to specific bands within each tribe would be the work of securing fishing, hunting, and plant foods; each group would channel its take to each chief who would redistribute equitably the foods to all tribe members. Alaskan Tlingit Indians for generations sought out the nagoon berry, related to the raspberry of which one species was called the Arctic raspberry. They were known to mix the berries with a fish grease and fern leaves, which would be stored in the earth.

Plains Indians women throughout the year would pick more than a dozen kinds of wild fruits and berries from persimmons to choke cherries, taking special pride in their task. Well known was the high-protein pemmican, made from pulverized strips of buffalo meat mixed with dried and ground berries and fat, yielding the long-keeping year-round food. Cultivated by the Blackfeet, tobacco was smoked in ritualistic prayers and dances. To counteract the strong taste, tobacco was modified with black berries, sumac leaves, and willow bark.

The Natchez of Mississippi were found by French explorers to have used the policy of distribution of foods by the chief, including wild game, corn, nuts, strawberries, and mulberries. The Natchez divided the year into 13 months, based upon when these various kinds of food were to be found.

Like predecessor Canadian French explorers, Alexander Maximilian in the early 19th century discoverd Indians along the Upper Missouri consuming choke cherries and currants. Maximilian denoted choke cherries as deriving from Virginia, and George Grinnell identified the currants as related to red, yellow, and black varieties also familiar to the Cheyennes and their neighbors. Indian women from Missouri tribes dried a small pear-shaped fruit, about the size of a medium strawberry, adding to it fat and pulverized meat, reminiscent of pemmican.

The wild grapes, esteemed by Missouri Indians, were generally considered superior to grapes found in Illinois. After expressing the juice, the women would boil it until thick, blend it with the wild pear, corn flour, and grated prairie turnip—the *pomme blanche*, the "prairie apple" named by the Canadian French explorers—to mold paste balls. The Mahas Indians in Upper Missouri, as well as the Poncas, Arikaras, and the Mandans on both banks of the Missouri River, depended upon a small unusual tree which yielded a tough wood for arrows and a delicious berry, much like a currant, called a buffalo berry. A trader among the Mandans in the 1830s encountered the berry, and later along the Gros Ventres. Olin Wheeler noticed a yellow variety on the Yellowstone.

The Indian tribes along the Atlantic coast from Florida to Maine and into the Newfoundland areas shared nearly all the varieties of berries found among inland, central, southern, southwestern, plains, and Pacific coastal Indians.

While strawberries had been seen as distant as from Chile, Mississippi, Virginia, and New England, they were not indigenous; but Englishman George Percy in 1607 recorded that Virginia strawberries were "four times bigger and better than ours in England." Although grapes have been observed earlier, they were found in the Great Lakes areas and were discovered growing in profusion in the New York State Finger Lakes area and New England. Some 20 native grapes were seen overall. While seen elsewhere, the cranberries in Massachusetts, particularly in Cape Cod, which were favorite foods of Indians, became a staple of the colonists and a popular berry in the 20th century.

Quite apart from berries as varied foods, Indians utilized certain red and black berry juices for dyes in basket making, cloth weaving, skin and pelt preparation, and paintings. Outstanding artists, Pueblo Indians surprisingly used almost solely earth color sources—clays and minerals—in contrast to their occasional sumac berries for red in basket and cloth weaving, the latter blended with a clay.

OSCAR E. NORBECK
ROLAND E. BURDICK

**BIG HOUSE CEREMONY.** The *Ga'mwij* (all non-English words are Oklahoma Delaware unless otherwise indicated), Big House Ceremony, was the pivotal yearly ritual of the 19th and early 20th century Munsee and Delaware groups of the midwestern United States and the Canadian province of Ontario. Their traditions affirmed that the ceremony was revealed by the Great Spirit to their ancestors in dreams during a period of earthquakes, tornadoes, and volcanic eruptions. Anthropologists Frank Speck and M.R. Harrington, whose fieldwork during the first decades of the 20th century recorded the oral traditions of the Big House were not, however, satisfied with this explanation. Their archival research revealed several 17th and 18th century documentary references to *cantiko* religious dances. The 18th century Moravian missionary David Zeisberger listed a number of separate rituals that were later reported as parts of the *Ga'mwij.* These rituals were probably combined into the Big House Ceremony sometime during the late 18th or early 19th centuries. (One account traced the origin of the *Ga'mwij* to the revelations of a Munsee prophetess in 1805). This process of combining formerly separate rituals into a single rite was termed "ceremony integration" by Speck, who further suggested that this process produced the mass celebrations of "pre-literate tribes," citing the development of the Plains Sun Dance as an example. More recent findings by A.F.C. Wallace on the formation of the Iroquois *Long House Religion* and Hickerson's analysis of the Chippewa *Midewiwin* ceremonial complex have supported Speck's assertion.

Differing geographic locations and kinship affiliations were reflected in variations in the performance of the Big House Ceremony. Speck gathered the most complete account of the ceremony form *Wi·ta pano'xwe,* a member of the Turkey phratry in Oklahoma. (The Delaware and Munsee each had three phratries: Turkey, Wolf, and Turtle).The following outline of the Big House Ceremony largely draws upon both his and other Oklahoma Delaware data.

The *Ga'mwij* was an annual set of rituals celebrated over twelve nights each October. The ceremony was formerly held by each of the three phratries for three consecutive twelve night periods in a permanent log structure known as the *Xijwika'on,* "Big House." The size and frequency of the ceremonies had, however, been reduced to a single yearly observance sponsored by one phratry, with the participation of the other two within the memories of both Speck's and Harrington's informants.

The Big House was constructed of rough hewn logs on an east-west axis. Its dimensions were approximately 40 feet long, 25 feet wide, with a height of 14 feet at the ridge of the roof. Two doors at either end of the east-west axis led into a single room with a hard packed earthen floor. A log post stood in the center of the room, with two carved faces of the Great Spirit gazing at the doorways. Carvings of the faces of ten lesser spirits were sculpted into both the six roof support posts and the four door posts. Each carving was painted red on one side and black on the other. Two fire places flanked the central post, also on the east-west axis. It is important to note all materials of European origin were prohibited in the construction and maintenance of the Big House.

The Big House was the universe in microcasm. The floor was the earth, the four walls the four quarters of the creation, with the heavens represented in the ceiling. The central post was the vertical exis that connected the underworld, the earth and its people, and the further ten spirit levels that led to the home of the Great Spirit.

The oval dance path that curved around the central post and its flanking fires was known as the "Beautiful White Path." The White Path symbolized the path of life and all the cycles of the creation. Life was renewed upon the White Path during each *Ga'mwij,* until death led the souls of the deceased westward through the west door of the Big House to the spirit realm. At that time the Whit Path represented the Milky Way, high road of departed souls.

The Big House was the arena for the recitation of the visions of spiritually blessed persons. Visions, granted by spirits to those possessed of sufficient piety, were the wellsprings of spiritual power. Those blessed with visions were able to invoke the assistance of their guardian spirits so long as they obeyed the caveats accompanying the granting of power. The benefits of spiritual cooperation were both well recognized and avidly pursued.

The purposes of the *Ga'mwij* were to unify the people, avert national catastrophe and sickness, and prevent the destruction of the world. The ceremony was initiated by a spiritually motivated leader, who was then known as *elha'k et,* "one who brings (the ceremony) in." The leader was then assisted by the members of his phratry throughout the ceremony. The leader then selected a speaker, who served as his voice, much as a spokesmen served the secular chiefs. Several *a'cka s,* "attendants," two drummers, and a sergeant-at-arms completed the essential ceremonial complement. Members of the other two phratries were then invited.

The attendants, three men and three women,

prepared the Big House for the celebration. They swept the White Path clear of all contamination, completing twelve circuits around the central post, the men sweeping from the east and the women from the west. Two fires were then kindled by a man and a woman with a traditional fire drill.

The celebrants filled the Big House the first night. They were greeted by the speaker, who then thanked the spirits and told the people of the importance of the *Ga'mwij.* The speaker then handed a turtle shell rattle to the leader, who recited his vision. His chant was taken up by the drummers, who followed him as he slowly danced upon the White Path, followed by anyone who wished to join. The leader handed the rattle to the next person to recite a vision at the completion of his song. This was repeated until everyone who wanted to recite his vision had done so. The evening ended with a meal of traditionally prepared hominy eaten with musselshell spoons.

The leader selected a master of the hunt on the fourth morning to embark upon a sacred hunt to bring back to the Big House venision killed with consecrated traditional weapons. A person dressed as the *Mising,* spiritual Keeper of the Game, was invited into the Big House while the hunters were gone. Coaxed to dance while the drummers sang, this celebration of the *Mising* and other prayer activities thanked the animal creation for their gift of meat. The game brought back by the hunting party was hung upon a pole outside of the Big House, and was presented at the last evening feasts.

The recitation of visions continued until the ninth night, when the fires within the Big House were rekindled, purifying the universe for the coming twelve month year. This rite was followed by the distribution of twelve prayer stickes, the exchange of the crude new drumsticks for two old ones, the measurement of

a line of turtle shell rattles in wampum, which was then distributed to everyone who attended the meeting, and the performance of crying the prayer call, *Ho-o-o*, by two men from each phratry, who were then given a yard of wampum to divide among themselves. This last rite was repeated each evening until the last night of the ceremony.

The women sang their vision songs during the twelfth night of the *Ga'mwij*. Two women, one with red paint and the other with grease, painted the faces of the participants with grease on the right and red on the left. The attendants then repainted the sculpted spirit faces and the remainder of the ritual paraphernalia.

The men resumed the recitation of visions the following morning, and continued until the sun was high. The *Ga'mwij* was then closed by two men appointed to the task. These men led the celebrants for twelve circuits around the White Path, and led the people in giving the prayer call twelve times. A final feast was given, followed by the wampum payment to each of the ritual assistants.

The *Ga'mwij* is an extinct cultural phenomenon. The Canadian Munsee rite succumbed to the missionary fervor of an Anglican Mohawk named G.H.M. Johnson in 1852. Responsibility for the *Ga'mwij* among the Oklahoma Delaware devolved upon to Wolf phratry as interest in the ceremony dwindled. The nativistic elements of the Big House lost currency in proportion to the erosion of traditional cultural values. The last ceremony was held in 1924. Informants stated that poverty drove the people to adopt European values. Poverty was also blamed for the sale of the essential sacred wampum to museums and collectors. The last leader was told he was not to sponsor another *Ga'mwij* "unless the spiritual obligation took possession of his mind with such compelling force that he could not decline his mission." Another ceremony was never "brought in," and the *Ga'mwij* disappeared under the injunction that it not be held simply to maintain the customs of the ancestors.

ROBERT STEVEN GRUMET

**BLACK DRINK**. A drink, so named by British traders from its color, made by boiling leaves of the *Itex cassine* in water. It was employed by the tribes of the Gulf states and adjacent region as "medicine" for ceremonial purification. It was a powerful agent for the production of the nervous state and disordered imagination necessary to "spiritual" power. Among the Creeks the liquid was prepared and drank before councils in order, as they believed, to invigorate the mind and body and prepare for thought and debate. It was also used in the great "busk" or annual green-corn thanksgiving. The action of the drink in strong infusion is puragative, vomitive, and diuretic, and it was long thought that this was the only effect, but investigation has shown that the plant contains caffeine, and the leaves yield a beverage with stimulating qualities like tea and coffee. Excessive indulgence produces similar nervous distrubance. The plant was held in great esteem by the southern Indians, and the leaves were collected with care and formed an article of traced among the tribes. The leaves and tender shoots were gathered, dried, roasted, and stored in baskets until needed. The Creeks made three potions from cassine of differing strength for different uses. In its preparation the leaves were roasted in a pot, were added to water and boiled. Before drinking, the Indians agitated the tea to make it frothy. Tea made from the *Itex cassine* was sometimes used by white people in localities where the shrub grew. Personal names referring to the black-drink ceremony were very common, especially among the Creeks and Seminole. The name of Osceola the noted seminole chief, is properly *Asi-yahóla, 'Blackdrink Singer.'* The drink was called *assi-lupútski* by the Creeks.

**BLOWGUN** is a hollow tube, sometimes simply a length of cane, reed or bamboo, sometimes a double tube-within-a-tube, sometimes two half tubes joined together. Two kinds of ammunition were used: clay pellets, in Mexico, which made the Mexican blowgun the prototype of the school boy's pea shooter; and wooden darts, in South America and eastern North America.

With few exceptions (the Jívaro of the upper Amazon jungles and some other South American jungle tribes) the blowgun, whether the projectile was pellets or darts, was a hunting weapon only, used on small game such as birds. Tipping the dart with the curare or other poison made it effective against peccary and tapir but the amount of poison a dart could implant was not ordinarily fatal to larger game, nor to man, despite exaggerated tales to the contrary.

The blowgun dart is a sharply pointed sliver of well-dried, light wood about 6 in. long, to which is attached, at the proximal end, a wad of wild cotton or similar compressible material. It is against this wad that the force of expelled breath acts to impel the dart. The hunter carried a supply of wadding material with him, along with curare, if that was being used, and "armed" the dart with wadding and curare only when he was in position to shoot. When poison was used the hunter notched the dart just behind the poisoned tip so that it would break off in the flesh of the prey, like a nettle, if the prey succeeded in dislodging the shaft. Darts were carried in quivers with a capacity of from 100 to 200.

Eastern North American, Mexican and Middle American blowgun hunters did not poison their darts. In eastern North America where, in late prehistoric times (for which the use of the blowgun is documented) the principal weapon for hunting and warfare was the bow, the blowgun was a boy's or a sportive weapon.

**BOATS** of some kind were used throughout aboriginal America wherever there were navigable bodies of water. The type of watercraft used varied, depending on a tribe's contact with other Indians, the availability of waterways, and the natural materials available for construction. In some localities as many as three different types of boats were used.

Boats made from animal hide stretched over a wooden frame were widely distributed but reached their highest development in the Arctic. The Inuits used two types, the kayak and the umiak. The kayak was used almost universally by Inuits for hunting and was acquired through trade by their Indian neighbors in Alaska. It was normally covered with seal skin and was a relatively small narrow boat with decking and a pointed bow and stern. The kayak was propelled with a double-bladed paddle which aided in balance, a combination which is still one of the most effective for maneuvering in narrow rough water. The umiak was a larger, undecked, scow-like boat with a much more limited distribution. It was originally developed as a whaling boat used by men with single-bladed paddles and grass-mat sails. In historic times it has come to be used by both men and women for more general purposes.

Hide canoes were used to a small extent in the eastern and western Subarctic and on the Northwest Coast. In these areas bark or dugout canoes were the primary craft, but hide boats were sometimes used for convenience or lack of other mateiral.

The Plains Indians and a few tribes in the Great Lakes region and the Southeast commonly used tub-shaped hide boats, called *bullboats,* for fording streams. Along the Missouri River they were kept on the bank for permanent ferrying, but elsewhere they were usually improvised when needed.

The bark canoe was the dominant boat in the

Subarctic, Eastern Woodlands, and parts of the Northwest Coast and Southeast. Birchbark was the preferred material but in areas where it was not available, less satisfactory barks were used. The bark was sewn together and sealed with pitch over a spruce or cedar frame to form a durable and relatively light canoe. The entire construction process was a complex and skilled task requiring the coordination of several people. Early Anglo-Americans made extensive use of the bark canoe in exploration and fur trading.

The dugout canoe was formed from a large tree trunk by alternately burning and chopping away the charred wood. It lasted longer than the bark canoe but took longer to make and was more difficult to portage because of its weight. Dugouts were used in the eastern United States, some Subarctic and western Arctic areas, and on the Northwest and California coasts. They were adopted more widely by the Indians after the introduction of steel tools greatly shortened the time necessary for their construction.

The Haida built seagoing dugouts capable of providing contact between the islands and mainland of British Columbia over sometimes rough seas. After adoption of steel tools these craft reached sixty or seventy feet in length. They were sometimes joined by a platform to form a double canoe for transporting large cargos.

The balsa was the most common type of boat in California and parts of the Great Basin and Southwest. It was made from long bundles of reeds or rushes tied together to form a craft with raised pointed ends and slightly raised sides. Over permanently navigable water they were used continuously but had to be periodically dried out to prevent waterlogging. Most balsas were probably between ten and fifteen feet long, were poled along rather than paddled, and were used mainly for fishing, ferrying, and shortrange transportation.

Simple rafts were used by many tribes in North America but were nowhere of great importance, usually being improvised to ford streams. Cane rafts were used by a few Southeastern tribes. Log or pole rafts were used much more widely and are the only type of craft known in parts of the prehistoric Southwest.

A plank boat is reported to have been used by the Indians on the coast of southern California and the nearby Santa Barbara Islands, but nowhere else in North America. It was made of pine planks overlapped slightly at the ends, tied together, and sealed with asphaltum. The bow and stern were pointed and higher than the sides, and lengths are reported from eight to thirty feet. The craft was manned by two to fifteen men and propelled with double-bladed paddles stroked alternately on either side.

The canoe was of major importance in South America to the Tropical Forest peoples, but among the other tribes its use was limited and its construction primitive. Many tribes lacked canoes simply because they did not live on large streams. At the same time, they often purposely avoided large rivers because stronger, more aggressive, and definitely more aquatic-minded Tropical Forest peoples occupied them.

Canoes were absent among the *Tehuelche* and *Puelche* of the almost streamless Pampas, though in the Pampas and among some Chaco tribes the bullboat was occasionally used. Other tribes lacking canoes were the *Guayakí*, *Caingang*, *Bororo*, *Purí-Coroado*, *Tapirapé*, *Sirionó*, *Nambicuara*, Guiana tribes, most of the *Northwest* and *Central Gê*, and many of the Chaco tribes. The *Bororo* and *Botocudo* adopted dugouts in the historic period.

Bark canoes were used by tribes living peripheral to the Amazon Basin on its headwaters, by the *Suya*, *Mura*, and upper Xingú tribes, and by the Archipelagic peoples. The last, however, adopted the dugout early in the historic

Balsas on Lake Titicaca.

period, and later the plank canoe. Dugouts were apparently native to the *Guató*, many of whom virtually lived in them, and to the *Guahibo* of the Orinoco, the *Carajá,* some of the Chaco tribes, and the *Charrua*. Under Andean influence, the *Huarpe* made reed balsas.

**BONE AND HORN CRAFT,** the utilization of the bones, antlers, shells, teeth, beaks, and hoofs from a multiplicity of animals as material from which tools and implements were made and decorated, was widespread among American Indian peoples, appearing in every region. These materials were especially important to Indians who lived in sparsely wooded areas. Not surprisingly, the Indians of the Northwest Coast were the creators of a great variety of objects made from horn and bone substances. The earliest carving tools used in cutting and carving the materials were fashioned from stone; with the colonial influence, metal tools were introduced which made bone and horn carving and incising much easier for the artisan and led to an extensive development of techniques.

Bone and horn from whatever animals were indigenous to each particular region were used. Various parts (small teeth, claws, bones, and tusks ) of birds, shellfish and small animals were used decoratively, in the form of costume ornamentation, necklaces, armbands, and belt ornaments. Large pieces of bone and horn were used widely. The Northern Indians shaped these materials into arrows, harpoons and hunting implements, pipes, knives and other utensils, musical instruments, and even used them in constructing houses, boats, and sleds. Decorative carved scents on pieces of bone and horn were made after metal tools were introduced to the Indians.

Although the craft developed most predominantly among Northwest Coast and Eskimo Indians, who used bone and horn from whales,

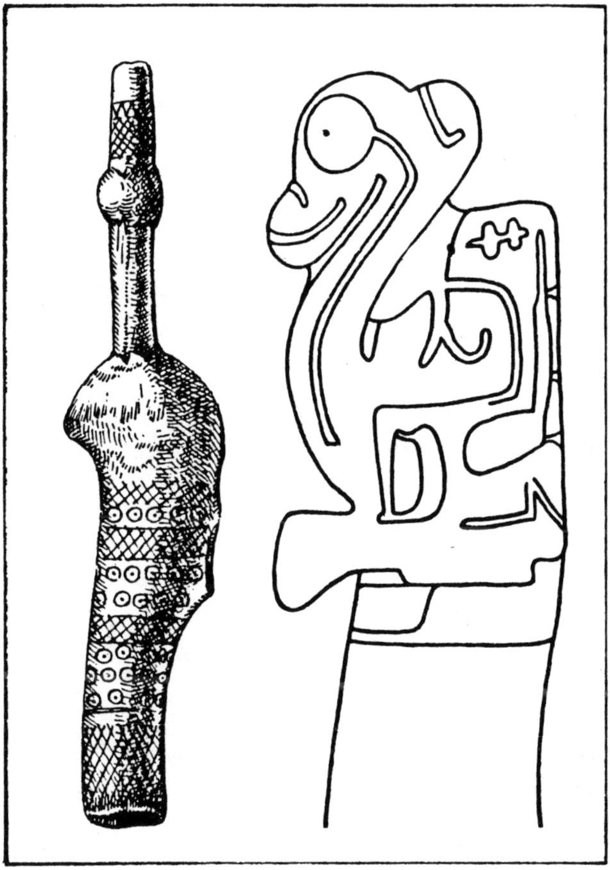

(Left) bone horn. (Right) Cupisnique carved bone handle.

seals, reindeer, moose, bear, deer, and walrus, Indians inhabiting the other areas also used the bone and horn of whatever animals were available. Again, implements for hunting and cooking, musical instruments, and ornamental objects were created. Some dramatic examples of decorative use were the Plains Indians' hide clothing ornamented with carved elk tusks and some Pueblo Indian silver jewelry inlaid with shell and horn. In the Central and Eastern areas, horn and bone were also used to create farming tools. Some engraved human bones have been found in mounds in the East.

**BOW AND ARROW.** Before the Discovery the bow was in use throughout the Western Hemisphere; from the Arctic to the Terra del Fuego. Though an active trade was carried on between various regions and over suprising distances, as proven by the archaeological recovery of exotic flints and obsidians, most of the aboriginal bows were made from local materials which, in turn, had a definite influence upon bow design.

In short, where was no typical American Indian bow. In an overview, such as this, the best approach is to describe the various kinds of bows used in the Americas by their construction rather than by geographical areas. First, however, a description of how bows work and what makes them shoot.

A bow is essentially a two armed spring spanned by a string. In its most simple form it is made from a single piece of wood, more or less trimmed to shape so it can be drawn without breaking. These bows, made from one piece of wood, are known as "self bows". In a well designed self bow the arms, or limbs, are carefully tillered so that each does its proportionate share in flexing, and contributes correspondingly to the cast of the arrow. As the bow is drawn, the half of the bow-arm away from the archer (the back) is under compression. Therefore, the wood cells in the belly of a self bow tend to collapse slightly, which results in a permanent set in the bow stave; it becomes "bow shaped". This set in the stave of a self bow is called "following the string" and is quite normal. Fortunately, it usually progresses only so far and then stops.

There is a limit to how far an arrow can be drawn in a bow. If it is drawn too far in a self bow the wood grain on the back will feather up, or the limb itself will splinter. To reduce this danger, it was the custom among European bowmakers to carefully follow the grain on the back of the bow and never cut across it, since that would induce a weak spot. One unfailing characteristic of native American bows is that they whittled out their bows with no concern whatever about violating the grain on the back.

Within certain limits, and everthing else being equal, the shorter the bow the greater the cast of the arrow with the same length of draw. With a self bow made by an expert bowyer from a superior bow-wood, it will be found that the bow is on the point of breaking when the length of the draw is one half the length of the bow. This bowdraw ratio of 2 to 1 is as low as is practical with a self bow. In exceptional instances it can be reduced even lower, but, for all practical purposes, a 2 to 1 bow-draw ratio is as low as one can reasonably expect to go. For practical working self bows this ratio must be raised to about 2.2 to 1. When examining a self bow of native manufacture, it is safe to asume that its ratio was not below 2.3 to 1, if that.

The average length of draw is around 28". There for, the shortest theoretical self bow length with a 28" draw would be 56" between the nocks, and the ideal length for a working self bow for the average man would be around 62". It follows that a bow three times the length of draw of 28", or 84", is not powerful bow, as is commonly supposed, but a sluggish one. It cannot be otherwise.

An examination of the bows in the storerooms of any American Museum reveals Native bows ranging all the way from excellent to exceedingly poor. Anthropologists are in the habit of excusing the poorly designed bows by saying that they were adequate to the needs of their owners. This is an assumption which cannot be granted, for the instantaneous acceptance of the gun by every Native tribe or group disproves that specious apology. In the history of mankind, his weapons have been his means of survival, and he has always striven to increase their effectiveness — and his probable span of life.

This does not mean that we should judge an aboriginal bow against contemporary European or modern examples, but within their own framework or reference. A poorly designed, ineffective weapon made where good bow-wood is easily available, should be recognized for what it is. Another bow with no better cast, but made by a Copper Eskimo from caribou antlers or driftwood, backed with sinew cords, is a triumph of human ingenuity and should be hailed as such.

In the following discussion, native American bows fall into two basic divisions: (1) the self bow and (2) the simple composites. The simple composites, in turn, were (a) the reflexed, sinew-backed wooden bows, known as the reinforced; (b) the Eskimo bows made with antler or driftwood bellies and sinew-corded backs; and (c) the sinew-back horn bows of the High Plains.

The self bow was used throughout the Western hemisphere except in the more forbidding portions of the arctic, but, because of limitations on space only the aboriginal bows east of the Mississippi, and on the Amazon will be discussed here.

Our Museums are full of 19th century bows accumulated from Indians living between the Mississippi and the Atlantic, but most of them are degenerate specimens, made well after the introduction of the gun. Few deserve even a second glance. An authentic aboriginal Indian bow from this region is now in the Peabody Museum at Harvard, and was taken from an Indian shot while ransacking a house in Salisbury, Massachusetts in 1660. It is a well designed self bow of hickory, 65" between the nocks and 67-1/8" overall. It measures 1-3/16" x 15/16" wide at the grip, 9/16" x 1-7/8" at the midpoint of the upper arm and 3/8" x 3/4" wide just below the upper nock.

Saxton Pope (1923:353) secured the dimensions and an outline drawing of this bow from Professor Kroeber in 1920, made an exact replica from a dense grained well-seasoned piece of hickory and found that it had a weight (the number of pounds required to pull the string) of 46 pounds at 28 inches of draw, and a cast of 173 yards. His conclusion was that "it is soft and pleasant to shoot and could do effective work either as a hunting or a war implement."

It is reasonable to assume that the 16th century English explorers knew what they were talking about when they found that the bows along the Eastern seabord varied in performance from region to region, for it must be remembered that the English longbow was being phased out at that time and any man with pretensions to military experience, had been raised in its use. Captain John Smith, for instance, had a very poor opinion of the native bows around Jamestown, for he reported that the maximum range was about 120 years (1907:104), whereas James Rosier (1906) speaks of shooting a bow which would do effective work at that distance — which was an entirely different matter!

The bow pictured by John White during his stay at the Roanoke colony between 1585 and 1587, look suspiciously like English longbows. Did he draw what he saw, or what he thought he saw, when he painted "An Indian Chief" or "A Warrior of Florida" (Lorant, 1946)? Since the arrow held by the latter looks exactly like an Old English broadhead depicted in an early 15th century painting of St. Sebastian (Pope, 1923: 376) at the University of California, Berkeley, some do not think they can be depended upon.

The only surviving painting of the forty two made by the Frenchman, LeMoyne, on the Florida coast in 1564, has a bow in it, but it is

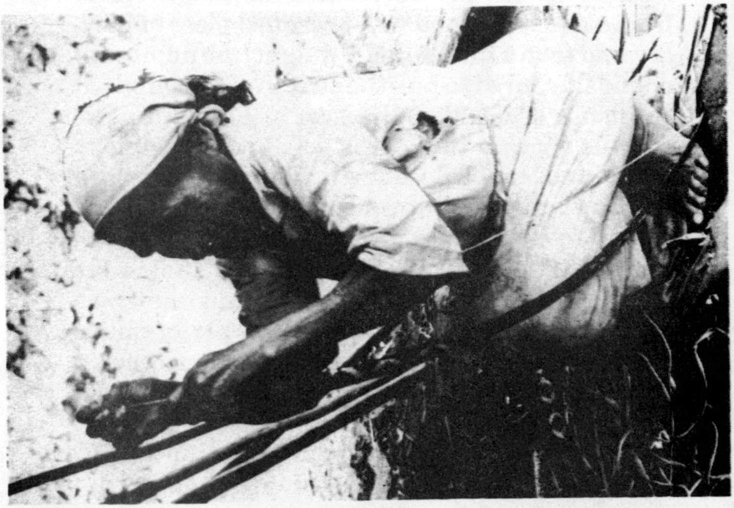

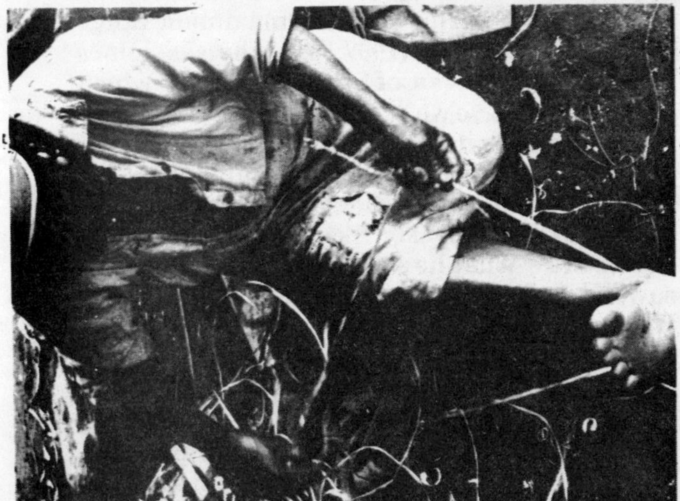

Guarani woman preparing the string for small bows (visible in the background) that the Indians make near São Paulo, Brazil

impossibly club-like (Lorant, 1946:32). The same can be said about most of the engravings made by de Bry from Le Moyn's lost paintings. However, for some unknown reason, one of de Bry's engravings after Le Moyne has bows in it which have all the ear-marks of having been drawn accurately and on the scene.

In this picture, "Saturiba Goes to War" all the bows are relaxed, exactly as one would expect them to be when the warriors were in council. There are two forms of the self bow shown: the ordinary D-bow and the double -curved. These double-curved self bows (Fig. 1 ) are a North American characteristic. Various reasons for the double-curving have been discussed at length (Hamilton, 1972:46-48), but no satisfactory explanation has yet been advanced for they buck in the hand when shot and are not as accurate as the ordinary D-bow. However that may be, here we see these typical aboriginal American bows in de Bry's engraving.

Furthermore, the D-bows, as well as the double-curved, are about what one would expect to be carried by men who hunted and fought on foot. They would be about shoulder high, and their proportions are correct. Therefore, one is inclined to accept these bows as truly representative of those used in that area at that time, even though it is hard to explain how de Bry managed to get them engraved.

There is a bow which is remarkably similar to the double-curved bows shown by de Bry. It is made of Osage orage; 60½" long overall, 59½" between the nocks rectangular in cross-section, 1½" x ¾" at the grip, 1 ⅛" x ⅜" at midarm, and 11/16" x ⅜" just below the nocks. The belly is slightly rounded and the back flat, with no attempt to follow the grain. It is double-curved. Some years ago it was tried out. Its weight was almost 50 pounds at 26" of draw and it cast a field arrow, slightly more than an ounce in weight (30 grams), 159 yards. It bucks badly in the hand and is not pleasant to shoot.

This bow was picked up some eighty years ago among the Five Civilized Tribes, and was probably brought into Oklahoma when they were removed from the Southeast. It is not a true aboriginal bow, but it is evidence that in some areas of the Southeast a good effective bowmaking tradition persisted long after the Discovery.

We cannot speak too intelligently about the arrows used east of the Mississippi at that time because none of them have survived. In 1565 John Hawkins (1906) was on the present Georgia and Florida coast and made the folowing observation:

> "In their warres they use bowes and arrowes, whereof their bows are made of a kind of yew, blacker than ours, and for the most part passing the strength of the Negros and Indians, for it is not greatly inferior to ours. Their arrowes are also of a great length, but yet of reeds like other Indians, but varying in two points, both in length and also for nocks and feathers, which the others lack, whereby they shoot very steady."

Percy (1907) speaks of an arrow an "elle" (45") long with which an Indian shot completely through a small English target (shield),

> "which was strange, being that a Pistoll could not pierce it. We seeing the force of his Bowe, afterwards set him up a steel Target; he shot again and burst his arrow all to pieces. He presently pulled out another Arrow, and bit it in his teeth, and seemed in a great rage; so he went away in a great anger."

Bows in South America ranged from 12 feet in length, as reported among the Siriono on the Amazon by Metraux (1945: Vol. 5:230) to 4½ feet among the Ona (Bridges, 1949:376) in Terra del Feugo . . Holmberg (1950:14) reports that the average Siriono bow was between 7 to 9 feet, with the longest measuring 9 feet 7". Holmberg records that the outer layer of the chonta palm was used by scraping it down with molusk shells before it could dry out. When finished it was roughly oval in cross section, about 2" in diameter at the grip, tapering down to about ¼" at the tips. There were no nocks. The bow lasted about a year before it became so dry it was useless. From time to time it was soaked in water to prolong its life.

The archaeological team of Clifford Evans and Betty Meggers found similar bows among the Wai Wai in British Guiana (Hamilton, 1972:52-56) with arrows ranging from 70" to 81" in length and weighing from 2¼ to 2½ ounces, while the Robert Waggoner collection (p. 55) had arrows of reed averaging 60" in length and weighed from 1½ to over 3 ounces. The Wai Wai arrows used two feathers, radially applied, and the ones in the Waggoner collection were tangentially mounted, which means that two whole feathers were lashed on opposite sides of the butt end.

On the Amazon reeds were used almost exclusively for arrow shafts, with sometimes elaborate forshaft-points made from hard woods or bamboo. Excessively long arrows, as well as bows, seem to be characteristic of the rain forests even though Heath and Chiara (1977:142) in their excellent study found bows less than a meter in length among the Taulipang, and the longest among the Yanomami was only 7 feet 3 inches (2.22 meters). On the other hand, they found the average length of the Taulipang arrows to be 46" (1.17 meters) while the Yanomami average was 6 feet, 7 inches (2 meters). Incidentally, the longest Wai Wai bow they found was only 6 feet, 8 inches (2.03 meters) with an average length of 6 feet, 5½ inches (1.97 meters). They give no lengths for Wai Wai arrows.

Certainly, none of the bow lengths reported by Heath and Chiara could be called excessive; their measurements indicate that there has been a tendency toward shorter bows during the years intervening since the earlier studies were made, but the popularity of the long arrow has persisted.

### The simple composite

No true composite bows were made by the American Natives, but were confined to Eurasia. The better Asiatic composites have a bow-draw ratio considerably lower than 2 to 1, and were built upon a thin strip of wood, which served as a foundation, upon which were glued a belly of horn and a back of sinew. The purpose of the horn belly was to withstand the tremendous compressive stresses imposed by the sinew back in the extremely low bow-draw ratios of the Turkish and Persian bows. A detailed discussion of the mechanics of the Asiatic composite will be found in Klopsteg (1947) and Hamilton (1972:70-84). Suffice it to say here that the Asiatic composite, as perfected by the Turks, has never yet been equaled by modern engineers utilizing atomic age materials, and that dried sinew from tendons of a deer is the most elastic substance known in Nature.

### The Eskimo bow

Though antler was used in an emergency when constructing a bow among the Eskimo, the best were made from driftwood. The purpose of the antler or wood was to serve both as a skeleton, or frame, for the bow as well as the belly. The power of the bow — its cast — was derived entirely from the sinew back, which, because of the subzero temperatures encountered in the Arctic, was applied in the form of a complicated arrangement of sinew cords. John Murdock, who wrote one of the first detailed studies of the Eskimo bow (1884), and the most interesting, thought that the method of applying these lashings dictated the area from which they came. This idea has not stood up, but that in no way detracts from this fine pioneering study.

The Eskimo bow works on the same priciple as the Asiatic composite; the belly simply acts as fulcrum over which the sinew back is stretched, and the various forms taken by the Eskimo bow show its direct relationship to the more sophisticated form in Asia. Obviously, the concept of the composite moved Northward from the steppes of Asia into the Arctic areas and thence across Bering Strait into Alaska and across Canada into Greenland (Hamilton:1970 and 1972:70-88).

The Eskimo bow is perhaps the most ingenious solution of an impossible problem ever made by primitive man, for the resulting bow was surprisingly serviceable. Saxton Pope (1923:338) tested a Type IV bow about 53" long and having a belly of Douglas fir. The weight was 80 pounds at 26" of draw, and the cast was 180 yards. Not bad at all, especially when you consider that old bow had lain unused for years in a museum storeroom.

## The reinforced wooden bow

The reflexed, sinew-backed, wooden bow had reached full development by the time the Spanish first reached our Southwest, for Espego (Hammond and Rey, 1929:57), who made his reconnaissance in 1582-83 into New Mexico describes the bows of the Otomoacos Indians as being "Turkish, all reinforced and very strong". Obviously, the term "Turkish" all referred to their appearance when braced, which, to the casual observer, would remind him of the composite bows they had seen in the hands of the Moors in Spain.

With the introduction of the horse and the flowering of the Plains Indian culture, the need for a short bow for use on horseback became imperative, and the reinforced bows, such as those used by the Otomoacos, were ideally suited for modification into a short bow and still maintain a reasonable length of draw; certainly longer than was possible with a self bow.

We have no way of knowing how long the average Otomoacos bow was originally, but since one could now ride close to a buffalo or an enemy before releasing the arrow, a shorter cast and, hence, a shorter draw were acceptable. Any good bow-maker could make a satisfactory modification practically on notice.

The Plains Indian culture extended into the third quarter of the 19th century so there are many of these reinforced horse bows in our museums, as well as the arrows shot in them. The arrows are almost uniformly short; the average permitting a draw of only 22" to 24". The sinew lining on the back of the relexed wooden bows would allow a bow-draw ratio af around 2 to 1, so a bow length of from 44" to 48" between the nocks is indicated. A description of a typical reinforced Plains bow bears this out.

This particular bow was collected from the Apache. It is 44½" long overall and 43½" between the nocks, which in this instance are two notches cut into the sides of the stave. The stave is of white oak, a surprising wood for a bow, rectangular in/cross section. The center of the grip is 22" from the upper tip and measures 15/32" x 3/4". Eleven inches from the two tips the arm measures 1-1/32" x 5/8"; one inch below the upper nock the arm measures 11/16" x 17/32"

The sinew backing, or lining, appears to be about 1/16" in thickness, but it may be greater toward the center since the back of the bow is slightly rounded. The backing goes over the tips and down on the belly side to the nocks where it is whipped down with sinew thread. Other whipping is applied here and there at points where the maker felt the backing might come loose. The backing is extremely hard and looks like the bark on a young hickory sapling.

The reflex, measured from the back of the grip to a straight line drawn from tip to tip, is 5-3/8"

There are, of course, variations in these bows. They seldom have notches; the nocks are usually formed by wrapping sinew about an inch below the tips until a ridge is formed against which the bowstring can rest. The belly is usually flat, and the back and sides can be square across or rounded, but the better examples have flat backs, are between 42" and 45" in length, and they have a reflex of 5" to 7" which has been maintained through an untold number of shots with little or no deformation.

From what has been said about the self bow and their tendency to follow the string, it is natural that questions should arise as to why these relexed bows with lower bow-draw ratios did not also deform. The final answer has not yet been determined, but it has been discussed at length elsewhere (Hamilton, 1972:60-61).

Suffice it to say that the reinforced Plains bow was remarkably well adapted to hunting and fighting on horseback and, next to the horn bow, was the most effective offensive weapon on the plains until the invention of the cap and ball revolver.

### The horn bow; The American composite

The horn bow, or the American composite, was also a triumph of primitive invention. Unlike the Eskimo bow, there is no evidence whatever that the Asiatic composite contributed in any way to its development, but that it was strictly an independent American Indian invention which suddenly made its apprearance on the High Plains along with the advent of the horse. The horn, which made up the belly of this bow, is easily identified, veen when reduced to fragments, and would last for centuries in the middens of the old Indian villages on the upper Missouri where it was much in evidence in the mid 1800s. However, those pieces which have been found were intermingled with gun caps, bottle glass and similar post-contact debris (Hamilton, 1972:93). So far, there is no evidence whatever that the horn bow existed before 1700, at the earliest, and everthing indicates that it was developed by some red skinned genius to compliment the horse in hunting and fighting. Today these bows are rare; an estimate is that there are not over fifty of them extant.

Briefly, the belly half of the bow-lamb is composed of horn while the back half is composed of sinew in a glue matrix. The horn belly is flexible enough to bend with the draw, but, unlike wood, is pratically noncompressible yet still rigid enough to maintain the structure of the bow while counteracting the tremendous compressive forces imposed upon it by the sinew back in the draw. It must be emphasized that the cast is a result of the two countereacting forces; the tension built up in the back at full draw opposed by the noncompressible belly. In spite of statements to the contrary, horn alone will not make a pratical bow; there must be a back of sinew to get any cast.

There were two kinds of horn bow; those made with an elkhorn belly and those using the horn of the mountain sheep. Powell (1875:128), Wilson (1919:107), Henry & Thompson (1897:713-4), Lowie (1924:246). Bradbury (1904:107), Kurz (1937:78 and 93), and others all mention the bighorn bow, but superficially, Catlin (1857:Vol 1,32) so misunderstood the horn bow that he makes no mention of the sinew and argues that it was made from a bone from the jaw of the sperm whale.

The elkhorn bow did not fair so well in the written accounts. The artist, Alfred Jacob Miller (1959, 1968: 7) was the only eyewitness who left a worthwhile account of the elkhorn bow, but more can be gained from his comments than from all the rest:

> "The bow he carries in his hand is remarkable; it is made of Elk-horn with sinew strongly cemented on the outer side . . . The bow unstrung is directly the rerverse in form to that when strung; a diagram will explain it."

Unlike the others mentioned above, including Catlin, Miller was fascinated enough with Indian archery to examine the bow in detail. He makes repeated references to it in his notes (1959):

> "Now if an Elk-horn was carried to the smartest Yankee we have, with a request to make a bow of it, the probability is, that, for one, he would not find it convenient to attempt it" (p.7).
>
> "While Indians are resting in camp, one of their amusements . . . . is a trial of skill with the Elk-horn bow . . . ."
>
> "With an Elk-horn bow, they sometimes drive an arrow completely through a Buffalo, its propelling power being greater than that of a Yew bow. In the Buffalo chase it is most effective. . . . ."(p. 60).
>
> " . . . . . and from the Elk-horns they make their most efficient bows." (p. 140)

> "They secure the skins . . . .used for leggins, and of their horns, measuring over five feet, they construct their best bows." (p. 158)

Aside from a few of his pictures, and the above comments,.we have practically nothing else from which to judge the actual performance of these remarkable bows, for the other references given above are practically useless, dealing primarily in superlatives and not specifics. The actual mechanics of the horn bow are easily understood by anyone familiar with the Asiatic composite (Hamilton, 1972:71-82), but we would also like to know how an Indian with only a skinning knife and, perhaps, a hatchet could make such a remarkable weapon. We would also like to know something about its cast and its bow-draw ratio.

Tiet (1927:97-98) devotes a few paragraphs to describing how the Coeur D'Alene made a bow from a single piece of ram's horn. It is very good as far as he goes, but concludes by saying that the sinew, after being applied to the back, was cut practically through every 5 centimeters or so "at right angles to the length of the bow stave." This must be in error, for it would be self defeating, to say the least, to cut the sinew at any point.

He does state that the back, when finally applied, was from 5 to 10 millimeters (.2" to .4") thick and that it took from 20 to 30 deer leg sinews to make one back.

The most complete account of the making of both the bighorn and the elkhorn bows is to be found in the field notes of Gilbert L. Wilson, made when studying the material culture of the Hidatsa, and is based upon a narrative by Wolf-Chief recalling the method followed by his father Smallankles. Wolf-Chief was fifteen years old at the time and it took over two weeks to make a bow.

This account, describing how both bows were made, is in the files of the American Museum of

Natural History, New York, and has never been published, but a summary, furnished by courtesy of the Museum, will be found in Hamilton (1972:94-96).

There would have been no object in expending the extra effort to make a horn bow if it had not resulted in a better cast, but we will probably never know exactly what it could do. However, assuming that the proportions shown in Miller's painting are reasonabley accurate, the probable bow-draw ratio can be estimated at around 1.71 to 1 (Hamilton, 1972:100). This is by far the lowest ratio achieved in the Western hemisphere. The horn bow could not possibly have equaled the Asiatic composite in cast, but it was still a most remarkable achievement by American bowmakers emerging from the stone age.

T. M. HAMILTON

## REFERENCES

Bradbury (1904). Bradbury's Travels in the Interior of America, 1809-1811 *Early Western Travels*, 1748-1846, Vol. V Reuber God Thwaites, editor. The Arthur H. Vlark Co.

Bridges (1949). *The Uttermost Parts of the Earth.*

Catlin, George (1857). *Illustrations of the Manners, Customs, and Condition of the American Indians.* London.

Hamilton, T.M. (1970). The Eskimo Bow and the Asiatic Compostite. *Arctic Anthropology*, Vol VI, #2, pp 43-52.

(1972). *Native American Bows* George Shumway Publishers, York, Pa.

Hammond, George P. & Rey, Agapito (1929). *Expedition into New Mexico made by Antonio de Espego,* as revealed in the Journal of Diego Perz de Luxan.

Hawkins, John (1906). The Voyage Made by Mr. John Hawkins, 1567-1568. *Early English and French Voyages, 1534-1608.* Henry S. Burrage, editor. Scribner's 1906.

(1906). The Third Voyage by Mr. Hohn Hawkins, 1567-1568. *Early English and French Voyages, 1534-1608.* Henry S. Burrage, editor. Schribner's.

Heath, E.G. and Vilma Chiara (1977). *Brazilian Indian Archery.* The Simon Archery Foundation, Manchester Museum. England.

Henry and Thompson (1897). *New Light on the Early History of the Great Northwest.* Edited by Elliott C. Coues. New York.

Holmberg, Allan R. (1950). *Nomads of the Longbow.* Smithsonian Institution, Institute of Social Anthropolgy.

Klopsteg, Paul E. (1947). *Turkish Archery and the Composite Bow.* Evanston, Illinois.

Kurz, Rudolph Frederich (1937). *Journal of Frederich Kurz.* Bulletin 115, American Bureau of Ethnology.

Lowie, Robert H. (1924). Notes on Shoshonean Ethnography *Anthropological Papers of the American Museum Natural History, XX, III.* New York.

Metraux, Alfred (1945). *Handbook of the South American Indians.* Bureau of American Ethnology, Bulletin 143.

Miller, Alfred Jacob (1951). *The West of Alfred Jacob Miller.* Edited by Marvin C. Ross University of Oklahoma Press.

Murdoch, John (1884). A Study of Eskimo Bows in the U.S. National Museum. *Smithsonian Annual Report, 1884.*

Percy, George (1907). Observations of Master George Percy, 1607 *Narratives of Early Virginia, 1606-1625.* Lyon Gardner Taylor, editor. Scribner's.

Pope, Saxton (1918). *A Study of Bows and Arrows* University of California Publications in American Archaeology and Ethnology. Vol. 13.

Powell J.W. (1975). *Exploration of the Colorado River of the West and its Tributaries.* Smithsonian Institution.

Teit, James A. (1927). Salishan Tribes of the Plateaus *45th Annual Report.* Bureau of American Ethnology.

Wilson, E.N. (1919). *The White Indian Boy.* Revised and edited by Howard R. Driggs Yonkers-on-Hudson.

---

**Parts adapted from *The West of Alfred Jacob Miller*, by Alfred Jacob Miller, with an account of the artist by Marvin C. Ross. Courtesy Walters Art Gallery, Baltimore.** 

**BOXES AND CHESTS** were made for a wide range of purposes by many tribes, expecially in the Arctic and on the Northwest Coast. They were particularly valued for carrying and storing materials which required protection against crushing, moisture, and cold temperatures.

Large wooden boxes and chests were common on the Northwest Coast in Canada and Alaska where woodworking of most kinds was the most advanced. Because of their weight and bulk in transport, they were primarily used by more sedentary tribes, especially in areas where timber was readily available. Boards of redwood, red cedar, and other easily worked woods were cut, shaped by a grooving, steaming, and bending process, and sewn together at the joints with sinew or spruce root fibers. The pattern of the sewing was sometimes first carved out so that the finished surfaces were smooth. Depending on their intended use, the boxes and chests were then often elaborately carved in relief and painted. They were made for such purposes as carrying water, boiling food with hot stones, storing food, clothing, and other materials, and as caskets.

The Eskimos carved a great variety of highly ornamented small boxes of wood, bone, and ivory. These were often made with cords attached for carrying them on the person and were of special value for protecting materials

A box used to hold dried bees by the Inuit of Point Barrow.

from the environmental extremes of the Arctic. Their utility was increased significantly with the Eskimos' adoption of tobacco and gunpowder.

Boxes of wood and other rigid materials were used in scattered areas throughout the rest of North America. The Yurok of California, for example, used wooden boxes for storing valuables, and the Sioux and Pueblo Indians used them for storing feathers. In areas where containers were primarily made from bark, hide, or woven materials, many had a shape and rigidity near that of wooden boxes. Box-like cases made of parfléche or stiff-dressed rawhide were widely used by Plains and Rocky Mountain tribes. One common form was flat and about two by three feet and painted with symoblic geometric designs. These were usually made in pairs and were convenient for carrying food, clothing, and other materials on horseback. Smaller medicine or feather cases, roughly cylindrical in shape, were used for holding feathers and other personal and ceremonial objects.

Inuit wooden box for whaling amulet.

**BREAD.** Wherever corn was a staple of the diet of the Indians among the Southern, Meso, and Northern American tribes, so too bread became a basic food.

Although primitive corn has been found in the Tehuacán caves south of Mexico City dating from some 7,000 years ago, and in both Bat Cave in New Mexico and in pre-Inca graves some 5,000 years ago, it can only be postulated that ground corn was made into bread at that time. Among many diggings in the Americas, grinding stones have been unearthed, pre-dating these con finds, which might have been used to grind nuts, seeds, or even corn, or both. Grinding stones, similar to those discovered relatively recently, had become familiar to the Spaniards who saw Indians pulverizing corn kernels to fashion the paste for making bread. The base stone, often hollowed to retain kernels readily, the Spaniards called the metate; the held-hand stone, the mano. These stones served much like a pestle and a mortar. While some finds have revealed wooden grinding implements, it appears that the metate and mano accompanied the dissemination of the knowledge of corn cultivation.

When white men first observed the customs of the Indians, they recorded that the Incas shaped the corn meal paste to bake unleavened, flat bread in ashes. While Indians in many parts of the Americas incorporated corn as kernels, as ground corn, or as corn cobs in various religious rites, the Incas ate a sacred corn bread during their Solemn Feast of the Sun, made by the Virgins of the Sun, as a part of their adoration of the Sun God.

The Mayapan people utilized a griddle, ingeniously fashioned with a rough underside to distribute the heat evenly over the smooth upper side on which tortillas were baked. The Aztecs continued to use the clay or stone baking griddle. The Aztecs and Mayas alike consumed large quantities of tortillas daily. The latter were described as having regularly eaten 20 large sized tortillas at evening meals.

Southwestern Pueblo Indians perpetuated the corn tortilla-type bread baked on clay or stone slabs, and corn cakes baked in ashes. Everywhere Indians raised corn, throughout the southern, central, and eastern areas of North America, essentially the same kinds of corn breads were baked.

While the Aztecs have cultivated amaranth pigweeds which they ground and baked into flat cakes, they were unique in departing from exclusively corn meal cakes or bread. North American Indians experimented widely in baking breads from ground nuts, seeds, and tubers. California Indians baked acorn flours. In a cave near Kenton, Oklahoma, flat and circular cakes made of acorn meal were found, mixed with wild cherries or plums; the cakes appeared to have been perforated for stringing, perhaps for drying them. Waldo Wedel remarks that even though acorn cakes were found, no corn cakes were found despite the fact that corn cobs were present in the cave.

In and adjacent to Death Valley, the Koso Indians pounded and ground the stalks of the common reed, *Pragmites*, to toast cakes made from the flour. Indians on the western slopes of the Rocky Mountains dug out kouse roots, which were ground into thin cakes. The "dough" was spread out one foot by three feet and laid upon poles for baking over the fire. Indians living in parts of New York State, Ohio, and Michigan, ground sunflower seeds to make mush for baked cakes. Timucuan Indians of Florida made bread from coontie roots, from which arrowroot is derived.

During the 17th and 18th centuries, Spanish, French, and English explorers and settlers encountered myraid variations among North Indians using corn, nuts, vegetables, seeds, and combinations to make breads. They would be cooked by baking in ashes, on griddles, or boiled in water. An Iroquois "leaf bread" used the corn husks to hold the corn meal paste to cook the rolls in boiling water. Navajos made essentially the same bread, calling it descriptively "kneel down bread." Westen Indian recipes called for piñon nuts; others used hazelnuts. Cherokees combined beans with cornmeal. Early New England colonists learned from the Indians to mix pumpkin and corn meal for still another bread. Persimmon paste, chestnuts, sunflower seeds, and acorns were also used in that area.

The New England settlers found the Indian corn dough would never adhere easily as would their familiar wheat and rye flour. And even though the Mayas had created a "margarine" from cacao seeds, there is no indication that it was used to bind the corn paste for baking their tortillas. Had the Mayas applied their margarine to corn baking, it certainly would have been transmitted to North American Indians. However, the Indians throughout North America learned quickly to adapt colonial housewives' use of yeast in making corn breads, and today's Indians add baking powder and shortening. Like white families, Indians in New England would mix corn meal with wheat or rye flour (transplanted from England and cultivated readily here), to provide the gluten lacking in corn, to help the cakes and breads to rise.

By the time John Russell Bartlett's classic *Dictionary of Americanisms* was first issued in 1848, the language was enriched with new words related o corn bread stuffs—mostly derived from Spanish or Indian roots. Among such words were: hoe-cake (literally baked on a hoe, for want of a griddle); johnny-cake (sometimes mixed with pumpkin pulp), which the *Shorter Oxford English Dictionary* suggests may have come from "Shawnee cake"; corn-dodger; cornpone; tortilla; tamale; and bannock, surprisingly a Scottish import, originally oatmeal rather than corn meal cakes, and adopted by many Indians. Not only in bestowing new elements in vocabulary, it was also and especailly the Indians' unleavened corn bread which initiated a new food to the Old World, and inscribed it indelibly upon the white man's alien culture.

OSCAR E. NORBECK
ROLAND E. BURDICK

**BREECHCLOTH** (also breechclout; loincloth) is the garment worn as a protective genital covering by men (and in some tribes, occasionally by women) under the outer clothing, or as a solitary adornment, somewhat similar to "shorts." There were as many shapes and forms for this covering as the materials used for its manufacture. Usually, they were of Y- or T-shapes, sometimes tailored to fit, or as a simple fold-over rectangular length of material with or without a self-belt. The long strip went between the legs, and was folded up and over a belt which held it in place. Most were of animal hides, or woven over vegetal materials such as bast, cotton, yucca or (following the introduction of sheep) wool. Generally, the garments were plain, although appliqué and interwoven decoration was common, most particularly for those ritual or ceremonial garments which frequently became very ornate. Almost all woven breech-cloths were produced on the backstrap or waist loom.

To itemize the various New World tribes who used breechcloths would be to inventory well over two-thirds of the known groups; only in the tropical regions where nudity was customary, or in a few peripheral areas, was the garment unkown—and even many tropical peoples used it simply as a matter of physical convenience. Until the coming of the European, the main reason for the breechcloth seems to have been the physical protection of a vulnerable, sensitive region, rather than for purposes of modesty.

In South America, the prehistoric Peruvian weavers created magnificent breechcloths from llama, alpaca and vicuña wool, often shaped in an hour-glass form for comfort, and frequently elaborately decorated to fit the social position of the wearer. The ancient Marajó Island women made and wore beautifully-formed and decorated trangular pubic coverings of clay, called a *tanga*, which was not unlike the shell and ceramic coverings found in other parts of prehistoric and contemporary America. In more recent times, breechcloths were woven of various basketry fibers, *e.g.*, among the Atacameño, while other tribes made use of yucca or *caraguatá* fiber; these were usually pounded to soften the fibers for greater comfort. Barkcloth was a favorite substance in those regions where this substance was manufactured. The Macushí wove corded cotton loincloths for their menfolk, as the Carib, while the Carajá loincloth was made of thick bark fibers (indeed, the Carajá girl is given a long fringed belt at the time of her weaning, as a ceremonial gesture). Tucano loincloths are commonly made of long strips of cloth *chambira* fiber, frequently painted in colorful designs.

Some garments were quite large; the wide belts worn by the Jívaro covered the entire loins as a wrap-a-round band, while the Cayapa made bark-cloth "trunks", similar to our own shorts (probably due to European influences). The Mundurucú interwove feathers into their loincloths, thereby producing brilliantly colored garments; on the other hand, the Puelche wore simple horsehide coverings.

In Middle America, modeled and mold-made clay figurines from Mayan sites clearly demonstrate the ornate loin garment common to the ancient Mexican-Guatemalan region, and suggest the widespread existence of remarkably elaborate, long woven garments which were often embellished by colorful decorations, and rectangular, with plain ends or on occasion decorated with paint, quilling, or beadwork. Under their thick fur garments, the Eskimo wore a thin sealskin G-string, since the warmth of their well-insulated homes required the shedding of the bulky garments indoors.

Donning of the breechcloth was tantamount to becoming an adult in many tribes, and was often accompanied by special ritual. Among the Inca, the December ceremony known as *Warasikoy,* "putting on the loincloth," was accompanied by the bestowing of a new name, the offering of sacrifices, and the piercing of the boy's ears. Following such a ceremony, the individual was regarded as a full-fledged adult warrior. Although it was a decorative and important garment, intensely personal in character, the loincloth also had a special, obvious, significance of its own: the well-known episode in which Black Hawk, the Sauk chief, ripped off his loincloth and publicly slapped it across the face of Keokuk to show his profound contempt, is a dramatic demonstration of this latter.

F. DOCKSTADER

**BREWING.** Fermented fruit juices (wines), fermented seeds or grains (beers), and fermented honey or saps (meads) were all known in aboriginal America. These beverages were not continuous in distribution nor did they extend to the extreme northern and southern limits of the Americas.

Fermentation is a natural occurence and does not need man's consistent experimentation in the same way that plant domestication did. It is likely that pre-agricultural hunting and gathering bands of the warmer, moister middle hemisphere were the first to experience this natural chemical action and put it to use. Plant sugars and starches and natural ingredients were found in many of the foods upon which early hunters and gathers depended. Wild fruits, berries, tree saps, tubers, and honeys contain natural sugars or starches which, when combined with moisture, warmth, and the action of yeast, provide many natural opporutnities to experience the effects of fermentation.

The Andean *chicha* beer is prepared by mixing a mash of masticated or pulverized corn with water and allowing it to ferment. The Sirionó, on the eastern Andean slopes, prepare corn meal, manioc, and sweet potato into beers by letting the mash stand in water and honey for about three days. The Jivaró process sweet manioc by boiling the tuber until it is soft. One half of the softened tubers is then mashed and the other half is chewed and spit into a bowl, where the mash is allowed to ferment for a day or so. The Cariban Waiwai prepare their bitter manioc beer by taking chunks of cassava bread, dipping them into water, and laying the pieces aside for several days. The action of the bread, water, and other conditioning agents such as banana mash, crushed seeds of gourds, or nuts work together to produce a stout beer.

The Makiritari farmers brew their *yaraki* beer by allowing the decomposed tubers or bitter manioc mash base and herbal additives to ferment in hollow logs for several days. Honey mead, common among a number of tropical forest tribes, is prepared by the Caingang of Brazil in hollow cedar troughs, which are filled with water and honey. Hot stones are put into cylindrical baskets and crushed fern stems are added, after which the froth is allowed to stand until it bubbles. The milk of a palm nut is sometimes used instead of water in the fermenting mixture.

The Maya *balché* honey beer is made by pounding pieces of the Lonchocarpus tree with sticks until softened. The shreds are then put in a jar with water and a portion of honey. The mix is then allowed to sit for three days until it turns a yellow color.

*Pulque,* the popular native beer of Mexico, is made from the liquid sap of the maguey or century plant. Just before the plant sends forth its central flower-bearing stalk, the central part of the plant is removed, leaving a natural receptacle. Juices drain from the leaves and drop into this "cup". The extracted sucrose juices have added to them a portion of already-fermenting *pulque.* The whole mixture is then allowed to continue fermenting for a period of 10 or 12 days. It needs to be drunk within 24 to 48 hours after completion since it spoils quickly after that.

Cactus fruits such as tuna or prickly pear and the sahuaro are prepared into a pulp or syrup, mixed with equal portion of water, and fermented in jars under a low, steady heat for at least two days. Such beverages must be drunk almost at once or they lose their intoxicating quality and spoil. The native corn beers such as *tesvino* of the Tarahumara and *tulipai* of the Apaches are made of juices pressed from corn stalks or green corn sprouts, soaked in water, and heated over a slow burning fire.

The intoxicants, for the most part, are related to ritual and are generally prepared under ritually controlled conditions. Hunting peoples may use these ritual beverages to assist them in obtaining spirit-power helpers. Among agriculturalists, community intoxication is frequently related to the success of the rain-making or increased ceremonies. In all cases, beers, wines, and meads serve social functions in that they promote solidarity of groups.

**BUILDING MATERIALS.** The building materials of the Indians of North America were used to construct dwellings classed as community houses and single, or family, dwellings. The typical community houses, as those of the Iroquois tribes, were 50 to 100 ft. long by 16 to 18 ft. wide, built of poles and with sides and triangular roof covered with bark, usually of the elm; the interior was divided into compartments and a smoke hole was left in the roof. A Mahican house, similar in form, 14 by 60 ft. had the sides and roof made of rushes and chestnut bark, with an opening along the top of the roof from end to end. The Mandan circular community house was usually about 40 ft in diameter; it was supported by two series of posts and cross-beams and the wide roof and sloping sides were covered with willow or brush matting and earth. The fireplace was in the center The leading examples of community houses the large, sometimes massive, many-celled clusters of stone or adobe in New Mexico and Arizona know as *pueblos*. These dwellings vary in form, some of those built in prehistoric times being semicircular, others oblong, around or inclosing a court or plaza. These buildings were constructed usually in terrace form, the lower having a one-story tier of apartments, the next two stories, and so on to the uppermost tier, which sometimes constituted a seventh story. The masonry consisted usually of small, flat stones laid in adobe mortar and chinked with spalls; but sometimes large balls of adobe were used as building stones, or a double row of wattling was erected and filled in with grout, solidly tamped. By the latter method, known as *pisé* construction, walls 5 to 7 ft. thick were sometimes built. The outer walls of the lowest story were pierced only by small openings, access to the interior being gained by means of ladders, which could be drawn up, if necessary, and of a hatch way in the roof. It is possible that some of the elaborate structures of Mexico were developed from such hive-like buildings as those of the typical pueblos, the cells increasing in size toward the south. Chimneys appear to have been unknown in North America until after contact of the natives with Europeans, the hatchway in the roof serving the double purpose of entrance and flue.

Other forms, some community and others not, are the following. Among the Eskimo is the *karmak,* or winter residence, for which a pit of the required diameter is dug 5 or 6 ft. deep, with a frame of wood or whalebone constructed within 2 or 3 ft. above the surface of the ground and covered with a dome-shaped roof of poles or whale ribs, turfed and earthed over. Entrance is gained by an underground passageway. The temporary hunting lodge of the Labrador Eskimo was sometimes built entirely of the ribs and vertebrae of the whale. Another form of Eskimo dwelling is the hemispherical snow house, or *iglu,* built of blocks of snow laid in spiral courses. The Tlingit, Haida, and some other tribes build substantial rectangular houses with sides and ends formed of planks and with the fronts elaborately carved and painted with symbolic figures. Directly in front of the house a totem pole is placed, and near by a memorial pole is erected. These houses are sometimes 40 by 100 ft. in the Nootka and Salish region, and are occupied by a number of families. Formerly some of the Haida houses are said to have been built on platforms supported by posts; some of these seen by such early navigators as Vancouver were 25 or 30 ft. above ground, access being had by notched logs serving as ladders. Among the N.W. inland tribes, as the Nez Percé, the dwelling was a frame of poles covered with rush matting or with buffalo or elk skins. The houses of the California tribes, some of which are above noted, were rectangular or ciricular: of the latter, some were conical, others dome-shaped. There was also formerly in use in various parts of California, and to some extent on the interior plateaus, a semisubterranean earth-covered lodge known among the Maidu as *kūm.*

The most primitive abodes were those of the

Paiute and Cocopa, consisting simply of brush shelters for summer, and for winter of a framework of poles bent together at the top and covered with brush, bark, and earth. Somewhat similar structures are erected by the Pueblos as farm shelters, and more elaborate houses of the same general type are built by the Apache of Arizona. As indicated by archeological researches, the circular wigwam, with sides of bark or mats, built over a shallow excavation in the soil, and with earth thrown against the base, appears to have been the usual form of dwelling in the Ohio valley and the immediate valley of the Mississippi in prehistoric and early historic times. Another kind of building material in use in Arkansas before the discovery, was a rectangular structure with two rooms in front and one in the rear; the walls were of upright posts thickly plastered. With the exception of the Pueblo structures, buildings of stone or adobe were unknown until recent times.

The building materials of some of the tribes of the Plains, as the Sioux, Arapaho, Comanche, and Kiowa, were generally portable skins (tent or tipis), but those of the Omaha, Osage, and some others were more substantial. The building materials of the Omaha are fully selected and preparted posts together in a circle, and bound firmly with willows, then backed with dried grass. The entire structure was covered with closely packed sods. The roof is made in the same manner, having an additional support of an inner circle of posts, with crotchets to hold the cross logs which act as beams to the dome-shaped roof. A circular opening in the center serves as a chimney and also to give light to the interior of the dwelling; a sort of sail is rigged and fastened outside of this opening to guide the smoke and prevent it from annoying the occupants of the lodge. The entrance passageway, which usually faces eastward, is from 6 to 10 ft. long and is built in the same manner as the lodge. An important type is the Wichita grass hut, circular, dome-shaped with conical top. The frame is built somewhat in panels formed by ribs and crossbars; these are covered with grass tied on shingle fashion. These grass lodges vary in diameter from 40 to 50 ft. The early Florida houses were circular with dome-like roofs. The frame was of poles; the sides and roof were covered with bark, or the latter was sometimes thatched. The Ojibwa usually constructed a conical or hemisphereal framework of poles, covered with bark. Formerly caves and rock shelters were used in some sections as were formerly constructed in natural recesses or shelters in the cliffs, called *cliff-dwellings.* Similar habitations were in use to some extent by the Tarahumare of Chihuahua, Mexico. Cavate houses with several rooms were also hewn in the sides of soft volcanic cliffs; so numerous are these in Verde Valley, Arizona, and the Jemez Plateau, New Mexico, that for miles the cliff face is honey-combed with them. As a rule the women were the builders of the houses where wood was the structural material, but the men assisted with the heavier work. In the Southern states it was a common custom to erect mounds as foundations for council houses, for the chief's dwelling, or for structures designed for other official uses.

The erection of houses, especially those of a permanent character, was usually attended with great ceremony, particularly when the time for dedication came. The construction of the Navajo *hogán,* for example, was done in accordance with fixed rules, as was the cutting and sewing of the tipi among the Plains tribes, while the new houses erected during the year were usually dedicated with ceremony and feasting. Although the better types of houses were symmetrical and well proportioned, their builders had not learned the use of the square or the plumb-line; the unit of measure was also apparently unknown, and even in the best types of ancient Pueblo masonry the joints of the stonework were not "broken."

The Indian names for some of their structures, as tipi, wigwam, wichi-up, hogan, and iglu, have come into use.

## SOUTH AMERICA

Logs and poles are the principle building materials throughout the Amazon and in the Northern Andes. The logs are not elaborately prepared for use. The bark is usually removed, and some of the larger logs may be split into several longitudinal sections. Uprights have a fork left, or are notched at the top to receive the ridge poles or house beams, but notching at the sides is rare. Cut-out joints or nails were not employed but the house beams and posts were lashed together. In the Andes logs were used for roofing materials, food lintels, and as wall binders, but most building was with clay or stone. One site in Nazca Valley has numerous rows of forked logs set upright in the sand.

Mud or clay was a common building material on the Coast of Peru and was also used extensively in the Highlands. The *Aymara* and *Uru-Chipaya* still build with cut-out sods, without further modification since the grassy roots in the sod serve as a binder. Puddled-clay, or tapia, is commonly used today as well as in pre-European times. The clay, tempered with grass, sand, or gravel, is stomped between two board walls to form large blocks. These are not moved, but rather are built in position where they are dried by the sun into a concrete-like hardness. Some of the blocks at Chan Chan ruins measure 1½ m. by 60 cm. by 80 cm.

Clay is most frequently used in the form of sun-baked adobe bricks, which vary greatly in size and shape. The manufacture is essentially the same, however. Fine grained clays are mixed with a temper of sand, grass, gravel, or broken pieces of pottery. The clay is then molded either by hand or by mold into the desired shape, and exposed to the sun for drying. Hand-made conical adobes, or variants thereon, are quite common in the earlier periods. Some are true cones, with a flat base about 15 cm. in diameter, 40 cm. in length, 6 cm. at the pointed end. Some are more like truncated cones, or even cylinders rounded at the top. Others approach a hemispherical shape. The term odontiform is applied to conical adobes which have a somewhat wedge shape. The second type of hand-made adobe is a true hemispherical shape, with one side flat and the other curved. A third type is described as cobble-shaped; i.e., lumps of clay modeled by hand into crude balls which vary in size from a double fistful up to about the size of a head. Small, cubelike adobes are a fourth type. A fifth is the rectangular or square adobe made in a board or cane mold. The variation in size is enormous. At one early Mochica site the average adobe is 39 by 25 by 15 cm. At Chan Chan one group of adobes averages 28 by 17 by 11 cm. The *Inca* period rectangular adobes average 80 by 20 by 20 cm. Such variation does not indicate period differences, since in many sites adobes of different sizes are contemporaneous. A final adobe type is the so-called sugar-loaf, which is a rectangular block, convex on one side. Some of these measure 50 by 30 by 15 cm.

To some extent the adobe types can be arranged in a chronological series, although much of the variation is only an indication of local preference. In general, the adobes of the earliest periods on the Coast of Peru are hand-made variants of the conical shape. A sequence is well established on the North Coast where Coast Chavín Period conical adobes are stratigraphically earlier than the rectangular mold-make adobes of the Mochica Period. On the South Coast of Peru, small conical adobes are characteristic of the Nazca Period. These are replaced later by the coble shapes, and ultimately, in the Late Periods, by rectangular forms. In the *Inca* periods, the rectangular and the sugar-loaf types are in general use. The tapia type construction was known in the Early Periods, but was never used extensively until the Late Periods.

Unmodified stone was a common building material in the Central Andes. Water-worn cobble stones were employed as foundations; buildings were made of the rough mountain stones which split off in irregular shapes; and large natural slabs and boulders were utilized without modification. However, in much of the building the stones were split for better fitting, or the stones were dressed and polished. In the building techniques rough stones were used as foundations for adobe walls; stones were set in a crude clay mortar, a technique known as pirca construction. The dressed-stone constructions rarely employed mortar or cement of any kind.

The precise techniques of stone dressing are not accurately known, although much of the process can be reconstructed from indirect analysis. The stones were shaped by pecking with hammers, principally of hematite, and then smoothed by patient rubbing and grinding with sand and water. Round chisels have been found with which holes could be drilled to aid in the splitting of the stones. There is some evidence that the splitting was aided by filling these holes with water and allowing it to freeze. In many of the irregular stone walls around Cuzco, the stones must have been quarried in the rough, and ground to final shape in situ. Part of this grinding was undoubtedly done with the wall blocks themselves; that is, by rotating one of the upper row of stones on a lower one in order to grind a flat contact. As a result of this process, the upper stone gets a slightly concave surface, the lower one gets a slightly convex surface, thus acting as a binding joint. In some of the better walls, the top of the tier was ground flat before the next tier was started. In brief, whatever the amount of dressing of the blocks at the quarry itself, the final finishing was done during the process of building the wall.

## Building techniques

This discussion of building techniques is largely limited to the archeological periods in the Central Andes, since it is difficult to summarize the principles involved in the building of the large Amazonian frame houses. To be sure, the building of these houses would depend on reasonably accurate floor plans. Distances must have been measured by pacing or with special poles, and right angles must have been estimated. It is known that the rafters and beams were first spliced temporarily and, later, more permanently lashed. Some of the houses employed a considerable number of posts and beams in the frame. For example, one house in the northwest Amazon had 6 heavy central posts, 10 secondary posts, 72 roof poles, 76 transverse connecting poles, and 560 bundles of thatch. Undoubtedly some of the house builders were specialists, but whether professional architects existed is not known.

The *Inca* had architects and specialized masons who planned and supervised the construction of public buildings. Probably such specialists existed in much earlier times, judging by such elaborate centers as Chavín de Huántar in the North Highlands of Peru and Tiahuanaco in the Highlands of Bolivia. For example, the Castillo of Chavín is a three-story building with interior galleries, rooms, and ventilation system. The whole building must have been carefully planned and constructed under close supervision. Presumably, the ground-floor galleries, vents, and rooms were first built up with rough stones and roofed with slabs, then the exterior facing wall of dressed stone was made. The spaces between the interior galleries and rooms and exterior facing walls was next filled with rubble, and the foundation for building the second floor was thus completed. It seems probable, both at Chavín and at Tiahuanaco, that mass labor was employed only to assemble materials, and that the actual construction work was done by specialists.

The selection of materials for a construction depended in part upon geographical location. In general, Coast buildings were of adobe; important Highland buildings were of stone. This is not a question of the availability of materials, since stone is abundant on the Coast and adobes can be made in the Highlands. It may reflect a desire for durable buildings, in which case a consideration of the amount of rainfall would be important. For example, the *Inca* used adobe in their Highland house construction, but most of the important public buildings were made wholly or partly of stone. The *Inca* were acquainted with many stone masonry styles, and the selection of a particular technique seems to have depended on the use and purpose of the walls. The gray yucay limestone was utilized for the great polygonal blocks in the foundations of Sacsahuaman. The green Sacsahuaman diorite porphyry was used for polygonal blocks in walls where great solidity was desired. Elsewhere it was employed only for corners. A black andesite was used for the rectangular blocks of some of the finest constructions.

The large building stones used were moved on log rollers by crews of men using pry bars of bronze or wood, and pulling with ropes or slings. Protuberances and indentations were left on the blocks for purchase for the pry bars. The protuberances also served for attaching the slings which were needed not only for dragging the stone to the construction site, but also to aid in the grinding when it was fitted in the wall. The indentations and protuberances on the blocks were either removed in the final grinding process, or they were left as decorations. The large stones were raised into position by means of earth ramps, some of which can still be seen. The *Inca* had a name for the plumb bob, although the use made of it is unknown. Perhaps a level was made with an equilateral triangle and a plumb bob, since it is certain that a level of some kind was known. The techniques of moving and

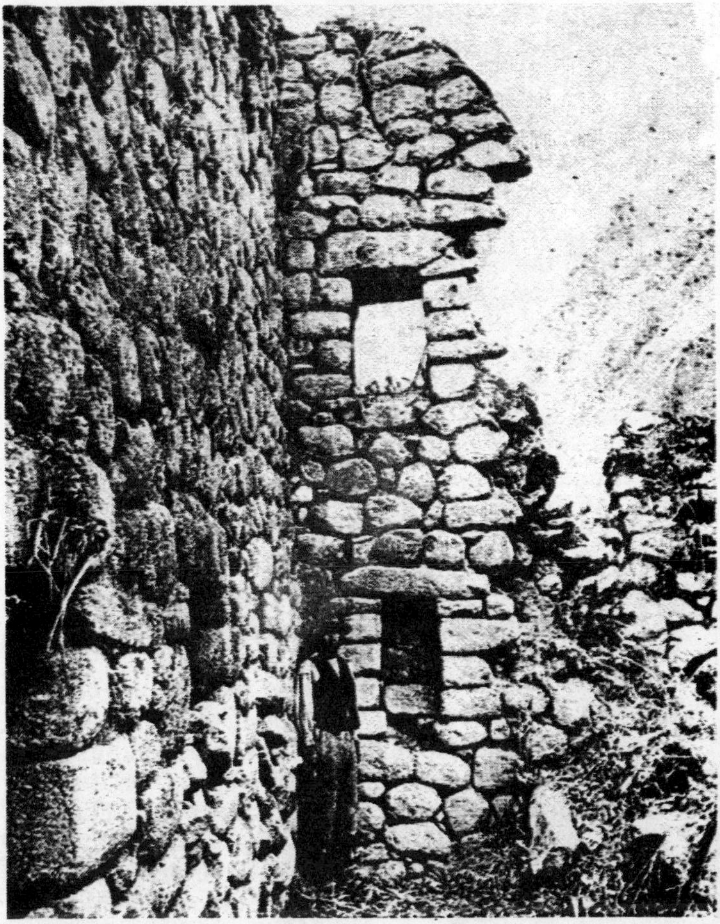

Example of coursed masonry at Macchu Picchu.

placing large stones were known in the much earlier periods, judging by the buildings constructed.

The nature of the terrain was a major consideration in the Certral Andean architecture. Natural rocky outcrops served as the central cores of some pyramids, and the rest of the building conformed to the countours of the terrain. Cliffs were utilized in building a fortress; large surface boulders effected tha plan of construction; and natural caves were incorportated as a building feature. The preparation of a solid foundation was a basic requirement in erecting a building. The surface dirt of a site might be cleared away to the base rock below, or a foundation of solid stone would be carefully laid as a support for the upper, and less durable, walls. On the Coast the foundations for high adobe walls were usually made of rough stones or cobbles. Likewise, in the Highlands, foundation walls of carefully cut and dressed stone were capped with adobe construction. As mentioned above, the weight of the stones in a wall was usually sufficient to hold it together, even without the use of mortar.

In the buildings, particular attention was paid to the facing walls. Even in a well-built solid wall, careful fitting is found only on the facing surface, whereas the back side is apt to be quite irregular. A common type of wall consists of a fitted facing with a fill behind. This was used mainly for terraces. Free-standing walls may be double-faced, with a rough stone or rubble fill between. Facing walls are made of rough blocks, polygonal blocks and squared blocks. At Chavín, the walls are made with horizontal rows of slabs, alternately thick and thin. At Tiahuanaco the walls are composed of uprights placed at intervals with fitted small blocks between them.

Some of the large adobe constructions on the Coast are nothing but irregular piles of adobes with carefully finished facing walls. However, some adobe pyramids, like the Huaca del Sol at Moche, are composed of a series of columns of piled-up bricks. Some adobe constructions have a series of overlying facing walls. A cut in one of these revealed eight superimposed walls, and certainly suggests different building periods. In fact, some of the interior facings had been coated with clay and painted. Actually, most exterior walls of adobe buildings were covered with a clay plaster which was either painted, or carved into relief, arabesque designs.

The corners of all buildings were carefully made. In the stone buildings, the corners might be made of dressed and fitted stones, although the rest of the wall was of rough stone. The corners of adobe buildings were often reinforced with cross poles. Special attention was also paid to the construction of niches, windows, and doorways. The lintels were commonly single-dressed slabs, or hewn wooden beams. The niches and doorways in the *Inca* buildings were trapezoidal in shape, namely, narrower at the top than at the bottom, and served to reinforce the walls. In some adobe buildings, the lintels for the niches and doorways were composed of three poles, cord wrapped, and coated with clay. The niches of the house sites at Chiripa had lintels made of unreinforced adobe blocks.

In buildings of any height, the walls were usually battered. This was also true of the higher tarrace facing walls and gave them better strength of retention. Many of the higher walls had set-backs, like broad steps, which often gave and over-all effect of a stepped pyramid. In others, the structural steps were so narrow that they conveyed only an ornamental effect. In many of the adobe buildings, the bricks were laid in "English bond," i.e., alternate rows of headers and stretchers, which increased the solidity of the construction. Algarrobo logs were also used as binders in some of the higher adobe pyramids. They were laid close together at right angles to the face of the wall. In stone buildings, long slabs were sometimes used in the same fashion.

In the adobe masonry, the bricks were laid in courses, although usually irregular. In any case, extensive vertical joints were always avoided, both in adobe and stone walls. There was no coursing in the polygonal *Inca* stone walls; rather, the strength of the wall depended on the irregularity of the joints, the careful fitting, and the weight of the stones. The *Inca* masons who used the unit-sized dressed slabs and blocks attempted to achieve a coursed ashlar technique, but even here the lines usually wavered or broke. At Chavín, the facing walls which alternated rows of thick and thin slabs, never achieved true coursing. However, although the principle of coursed masonry was never mastered, the fact that the walls of adobe and stone have stood for centuries in a country noted for earthquakes is mute testimony to the solidity of their construction.

The use of joints for careful stone fitting is characteristic of both *Inca* and Tiahuanaco architecture. The *Inca* mason cut out a projecting ledge from one block which interlocked with a corresponding ledge on the adjacent block, or a projecting tenon was fitted into a sunken joint of another stone. As previously mentioned, most of this type of fitting was done in situ, but at Tiahuanaco, such joints seem to have been planned in advance. Many dressed stones have tenoned margins for fitting. Uprights in the facing walls have cut-out niches intended to receive and secure the adjacent smaller blocks. Many of the stones have square orifices into which a projecting squared tenon of another block will fit. The flat slabs for the temple floors have slight depressions cut out for the bases of the uprights. All of this suggests planning, even though the final fitting was done in situ.

The use of copper cramps for joining stones was a unique characteristic of Tiahuanaco masonry. T-shaped slots were cut out of the margins of two adjacent stones and specially cast copper cramps were fitted into them. Although such cramps would not support the weight of the blocks, they would prevent them from shifting position. Another jointing technique at Tiahuanaco consisted of drilling two holes in adjacent stones and cutting a groove between. Melted copper was then poured into the holes and the groove and allowed to solidify as a cramp.

Mortar or cement was not employed in the best stonework constructions, but in the adobe buildings, a crude sort of clay binding cement was used. In the earlier periods, the cobblelike adobes were set in cement, but the conical adobes were not. Instead, in building a wall of conical adobes, the first double row was laid point to point. The second row was laid on top of this, base to base. Thus the shape of the adobe itself was utilized to form double thick solid walls, with a flat, battered outer facing. In many of the *Inca* stone walls, the edges of the blocks were beveled. This seems to have been only an ornamental device, with no structural significance. Some of the *Inca* walls were curved, so that the dressed-stone had to be cut to fit an arc. The lack of the principle of the true arch has already been mentioned. However, the *Inca,* and perhaps others in the Central Andes, employed the corbeled arch. Roofs of small houses were made in this manner, in which flat slabs are projected inward and weighed down at the back. The flat mountain stones were particularly adaptable.

**BULLROARER** is a thin, rectangular piece of wood, attached to a leather thong or a rope that may have a wooden handle to facilitate whirling the wooden piece to produce a buzzing sound. Other names for bullroarer were lightning stick, whizzer, and whizzing stick. They were widely used in the Americas, and varied in size, being six inches to two feet long and ½ inch to two inches wide.

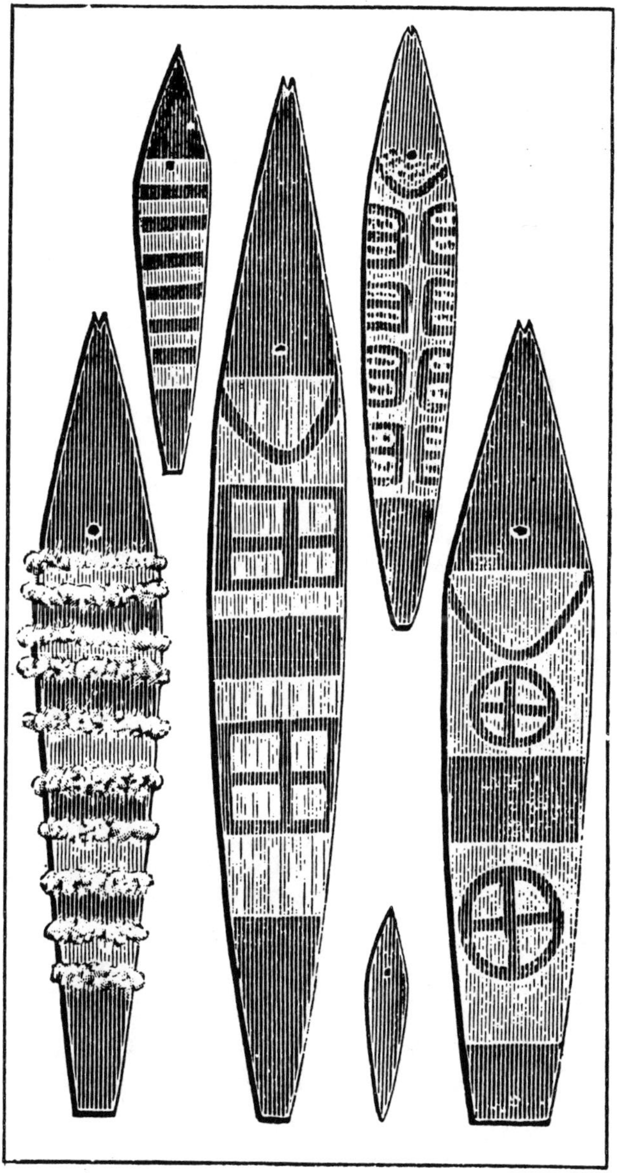

Bullroarers with various clan designs.

The Hopi thought of the bullroarer's whizzing noise as that of the wind that brings rain storms. The Navajo believed it to be the voice of the thunderbird, and a representation of the thunderbird often appeared on it. These two tribes made bullroarers from wood that had been struck by lightning, and, as well as others who lived in arid regions, used the bullroarer to bring rain. But in areas with plenty of water, bullroarers were intended to communicate with the wind, seeking dry weather.

Among the Northwest coast Kwakiutls, the bullroarer was symbolic of spirits and ghosts.

**BURIAL CUSTOMS.** Death is universal phenomenon. It is part of nature as much as birth and growth are. For all human societies, it also remains an unknown: Why death? What after death? Ineluctably faced with death, human societies have devised ideas and practices to deal with it. Mortuary rituals are the cultural expressions given by a social groups of their ideology and attitudes concerning death. Thus, though death is a natural phenomenon, mortuary ritual transforms it into a social phenomenon.

Mortuary riturals can be conceived as consisting a burial customs and of mortuary rites. Burial customs are the technical practices associated with death: as such, they provide for the disposal of the body of the deceased. Mortuary rites are the symbolic counterpart of burial customs:

> "They consist of the execution of a number of symbolic acts that may vary in two ways: in the form of the symbols employed and in the number and kind of referents given symbolic recognition." *

---

* Binford, L.R. *Morticary Practices*, SAA memoirs, 1971

Most of the time, especially in an archaeological context, one depends on burial customs only to interpret the mortuary rituals of a given society. Although a lot can be learned about the society and its attitudes towards death though burial customs, a knowledge of its mortuary rites greatly expands this understanding. Actually, although closely related, each set of events, the technical and the symoblic, responds to different needs and motivations.

Mortuary rituals are social practices. As such, events and symbolism associated with death cannot be dissociated from the cultural system of which they are but an expression. Knowledge of its dynamics is thus necessary to explain such specific practices.

Though death is a universal and unique phenomenon, mortuary rituals have considerably varied through time and space. This variation, as we shall try to illustrate among the American Indians, is generally understood as the result of ecological, social and ideological factors. Environmental and climatic characteristics can affect such practices as the type of burial, the time of exposure of the body, the fact that he will be cremated instead of buried, the place in which he will be buried, the nature of the funerary offerings, etc. In turn, many aspects of mortuary ritual are closely related to economic and social factors: age, sex, relative rank of the social position occupied by the deceased within his group and the community at large.

In the remainder of this piece, we shall give an overview of mortuary rituals among the American Indians. They give evidence of a long and complex history of beliefs and practices related to death. This history goes back to at least 6000 BC, time at which we find one of the first archaeological evidence for human burials in Mexico. In the valley of Tehuacan, Puebla, Mexico, from where we have chosen our example, seven individuals were found in three sites dating to *c.* 6000 BC: a single extended burial of an adult male; two multiple burials, one consisting of two children whose heads had been removed and exchanged, the other consisting of three individuals, a burned elderly male, a somewhat younger female and an infant flesh burial, finally a cremated adult female. Thus we are informed that, even at this early period, the American Indians had developed a set of beliefs and practices in relation to their dead and that there existed variation in their burial customs. Very little can be inferred, in this case, concerning the meaning of these customs. Archaeological and ethnographical evidence from later periods allows us, however, to document and interpret the complex practices and beliefs associated with death among the American Indians.

Although a great deal of variation of a linguistic and social nature exists between and among them, American Indians share certain beliefs concerning death that show some degree of cultural homogeneity.

The American Indians have a strong belief in life after death. They have conceived of death as a form of passage between two ways of life. The deceased is perceived as a possbile intercessor between the natural and the supernatural universe. Everywhere he is engaged in a network of relationships which keeps on operating: it is in this way that death is a social phenomenon. The rituals are thus greatly influenced by the position of the deceased in the social network.

The afterlife, in its material expression, reproduces the conditions of life on earth and is thought to take place in the same environment, with the same mode of subsistence, and within the same social and ideological systems. The only difference is that it is an immaterial version of it. In other words, a dichotomy is believed to exist between the material and spiritual components of all inanimate and animate beings. Linked to this belief is the importance given these spiritual components, in the power they have to influence the living, at all times, even after they have separated from their material counterparts. Many practices associated with death are thus aimed at making the spirits happy and favorably disposed toward the living.

Examples of burial customs are as numerous and diverse as there are American Indian ethnic and linguistic groups. The dimension of time adds to this diversity since we are dealing with more than 8000 years of mortuary practice. We have chosen to present examples from three types of American Indian societies: hunting, agricultural and state societies. They represent the main types of socio-economic adaptation realized by the American Indians previous to the arrival of the Europeans at the end of the XVth century. Today, most of these Indian groups are more or less integrated into modern American industrial society. Their burial customs, as much as the rest of their culture, have been strongly influenced by the European colonial and now ruling groups. To avoid the problem of isolating what is Indian and what is European, the accounts given here will rely heavily on historical and even prehistoric evidence.

## The hunters of North America

Nomadic populations of North America (Montagnais, Naskapis, Crees, Algonquin) share a certain number of constant features in their mortuary rituals. The after-life occurs elsewhere but in a context similar to that of the living. Caribou, beaver, snow and hunting are part of this other life but always in some ethereal way. Their existence is never material; the souls of the hunters wear souls of snowshoes and walk in the soul of snow; they are armed with the souls of specific tools and they hunt the souls of moose. It is thus a copy of the real universe and the belief in it determines specific behaviors. Thus the deceased will be given daily utilitarian objects so that he may arrive safely in the world of his ancestors. To release the souls from these, certain groups will bury while others will ritually kill (break) these offerings. Still others will cremate their deceased. These variants, identified ethnographically and archaeologically, are seen as more or less different techniques to meet the same end. Food is also sometimes given to the deceased to accompany him in his last voyage. Sometimes he will even be offered a farewell dinner at the burial. However, relatively few objects are usually left with the deceased. Only very seldom is he given more tools than the few objects are usually left with the deceased. Only very seldom is he given more tools than the few he used or he liked best; no house, very seldom a canoe or showshoes, no additional clothes, little or no food, sometimes a dog, only objects linked to his hex, etc. are given to him. Most of the time only the tools that would allow him to make these are provided.

The souls themselves are blue prints of human beings. They have arms, senses and all the properties of the natural system. They are nevertheless relieved from their material aspects and as such, become potentially threatening. This is one of the reasons why the deceased are so well treated and why the rituals aim at having them leave this world as quickly as possible. As an additional precaution, one now avoids pronouncing the name of the deceased.

Underneath this apparent homogeneity, there exist a great deal of variability in burial practices, related to age, sex status, type of death, season, etc. So much so that each ethnographic description of individual ceremonies appears relatively unique; each grave excavated by the archaeologist has its own peculiarities. These graves may be more or less deep and contain the remains of one or several persons. The skeletons may be placed in an extended or in a flexed

Dakota scaffold burial, with framework of tipi in the background. Possibly another corpse is inside the ring of tipi stones.

position, the body may be buried very shortly after death or sometimes after it has started to decompose. Offerings may be abundant or absent, ornaments simple or sophisticated; there sometimes are large quantities of red ocher in one grave while in the one next by there is none. The orientation of the body can also vary. Some burials show that careful attention was given to its arrangement while most cremations are rather careless.

Mortuary rituals, as exemplified in these groups, are determined by several factors that go from the pressure of common traditions and beliefs to idiosyncratic expression.

## The Iroquoians of North America

Among the Iroquoians as among the nomads, death was ritualized; mortuary rites would begin as soon as the individual felt his time had come. He would then offer a farewell meal to show his courage and his contempt for death. Aftert death, his body would, in most case, be buried in foetal position, after having been carefully wrapped in fur, and placed in a bark coffin with many grave goods. Several variants of this pattern existed however. Thus, young children were buried along paths, the bones of dead captives were thrown in middens, and people who died by drowning or freezing were fleshed: their skin was burnt and only their bones buried. There also were periods of mourning, taboos on names, etc. One of the most spectacular events of the Iroquaian universe was the feast of the dead, practiced by the historical Hurons; the ritual may even go back to the Pickering culture. On this occasion, before definitely abandoning a village (this happenned every 10 to 15 years), the majority of bodies individually buried were exhumed and their remains were cleaned. A large trench was then dug and lined with beaver skins. The bodies were solomny reburied after several days of feasting. It is only after this ritual of friendship and solidarity that the population definitely abandoned the village.

Among the Iroquoians, perhaps even more than among the nomads, death was the occasion to express one's friendship, one's generosity and one's spirit of self-denial. Brebeuf says about them:

> "You might say that all their exertions, their labors and their trading, concern almost entirely the amassing of something with which to honor the dead. They have nothing sufficiently precious for this purpose; they lavish robes, axes and procelain in such quantities that, to see them on such occasions, you would judge that they place no value upon them; and yet these are the whole riches of the country. You will see them often, in the depth of winter, almost entirely naked, while they have handsome and valuable robes in store that they keep in reserve for the dead; for this is their point of honor. It is on such occasions they wish above all to appear magnificent."*

Looking back at the societies of hunters and gatherers and the societies of farmers of North America, we can say that they share the same fundamental beliefs, the same fear of souls that were just freed, the same will to give them all the necessary things for the trip to the country of the ancestors, the same desire to express, when death occurs, their solidarity beyond the divisions of clans, moieties or lineages, the same wish to express a fundamental identity. Each culture, however, expresses this message in forms as varied as they are restricted in distribution, so that an inventory of this would be virtually infinite. This variation is expressed

---

* Twaites, R.G. *Jesuit Relation and Allied Documents.* Burrows Brothers, Cleveland

as much at the level of certain beliefs (ex: world of souls represented by the Milky way or a subterrannean world) as at the level of the participants in mortuary rites (ex: parents, designated persons, shaman etc.), the mourning period (more or less long and demanding), the clothes of the deceased, the way he is exposed, the disposal of his goods, etc.

## Pre-Columbian state

Mesoamerica and the Central Andes are the only two pre-Columbian cultural areas in the New World to have developed a social-political system that can be difined as state. The Aztecs (Mesoamerica) and the Incas (Central Andes) are their last representatives before the Conquest. An extensive record of their customs and achievements is available through ethnohistory and archaeological documents.

The Aztecs were masters of a huge empire. Their society was highly stratified with a ruling class composed of soldiers and priests; the rest of the society was divided into closed groups of merchants, farmers artisans and slaves. Religion, a very powerful tool for the ruling class, served to perpetuate this stratification. Customs and beliefs concerning death were very precisely codified and organized. There existed two kind of treatment of the dead: cremation and flesh burial. Only under specific circumstances were people buried; all individuals whose death was caused by the gods of rain or water were buried: these included the victims of drowning, of diseases like gout, leprosy and dropsy, those struck by lightning, and those offered as human sacrifices to these gods. These people were buried with grains of *huautli* on their face, a club in their hand and with decorations of paper. Women who died in childbirth were buried in the patio of a temple dedicated to a group of feminine deities, the Ciupipiltin. Children were generally buried next to corn granaries. Apart from these exceptional cases, most people among the Aztecs were cremated. The deceased was burnt with a dog, his companion. Dressed in his best clothes, he was placed in a flexed position, his knees drawn up to his chin, and covered with several layers of cloth tied with ropes. This funerary bundle was then cremated on a special funeral pyre that was being watched by the elders; the cremation was accompanied with funerary chants. The ashes and bones were then placed in a jar with a piece of jade, the precious stone, symbol of life. The jar was buried in the house in the case of a layman, or in the temple of Huitzilopochtli in the case of chief. When the deceased was an enemy or a sacrificial victim, he often was beheaded and his head served as a trophy. In Tenochtitlan, for example, the ossuary of Huitzompan contains more than 62,000 skulls.

After leaving this world, the deceased went to various places connected with specific gods, depending on his status in the society and the circumstances surrounding his death. The universe of the Aztecs consisted of thirteen higher heavens and of nine lower heavens. Most people, those who had been cremated, went to the ninth layer of the underworld—Mictlan, where they led a life similar to that on earth. Offerings were given to the deceased at fixed intervals during four years, which was the length of time he was thought to take to reach his last abode. People whose death was caused by the gods of rain went to Tlalocan, which was the first sky of the underworld. Children went to the 13th sky—Tamoanchan. Sacrificed warriors and women who died in childbirth went to the upper skies where they accompanied the sun in his daily round. Four years later, the warriors were transformed into hummingbirds. Burial customs among the Aztecs, as we have tried to show, varied in relation to the position of the individual in the society and conformed with beliefs strongly embedded in the state religion.

The Inca developed their empire at approximately the same time as the Aztecs—XVth and XVIth centuries. Their society was also highly stratified.

For the Incas, the afterlife was the continuation of life on this earth. Also basic to their religion was the belief that the deceased were often transformed into supernatural beings who could influence the living. That may explain the importance given to ancestor worship and to the cult of the dead. Not only did the Incas conceive of an afterlife but they also believed in reincarnation; an ancestor would come back to earth, in the form of one of his descedants. For that reason, it was customary to give to a newborn the name of one of his ancestors. That may also explain why the deceased were buried in foetal position.

Reincarnation was possible, however, only if the remains of the deceased were well-preserved. To that effect, great care was taken to prepare the body before it was buried. After removal of the viscera, the body was embalmed with herbs and probably resin and honey. Generally speaking, mortuary ritual faithfully reproduced the structure of Inca society: rituals were accordingly much more elaborate for the Inca and the nobility than for the commoner. In the first case, the deceased was embalmed and dressed in his best clothes. His wives and servants were killed, embalmed and placed next to the deceased sovereign. All of them wer exposed on a platform during a month, during which fasting and lamentations were the rule. After this time, the deceased and his retainers, wrapped in clothes, were buried in a vault—*pucula*. He was given mortuary offerings in great quantity: food and chicha beer, pottery and gold or silver vessels and some of his personal ornaments and implements. The mourning period would last a few months after the burial proper. On the coast of Peru, the deceased was also wrapped in clothes and buried in deep graves in dry desert sand. In all cases, the main objective of the burial customs, in the highlands as well as on the coast, for rulers and commoners, was to insure the preservation of the bodies of the deceased, as demanded by the ancestor cult. The details of these rituals were ecologically and socially determined.

In conclusion, one should stress the fundamental beliefs that underlie the customs related to death among the American Indians. Mainly, death is a transitory state between two lives. It is not the end, it is a passage into another existence, into the world of ancestors or of spirits. There is no break between the two lives. On the contrary, the presence and power of the spirits are strongly determinant of events in the world of the living.

The examples given here have shown that these ideas about death are expressed in various ways by different American Indian cultural groups. Some of this variation can be interpreted as either as the result of specific historical conditions, or in ecological terms, or again, in social terms; some remain unexplained. Burial customs are an intergrated complex within cultural behavior, a specific way chosen by a human group to express and justify its beliefs.

LOUISE I. PARADIS
NORMAN CLERMONT

* * *

# C

**CALENDAR SYSTEMS** of the Indians north of Mexico were based directly on the natural cyclic phenomena of their environment, particularly on those phenomena critical to subsistence. Their calendars were never developed to the advanced stages of those of the Indian civilizations of Mexico and Central America. Apparently no tribe north of Mexico had a true calendar: a single integrated system for reckoning the year and its divisions over long periods. Those aspects of the cycles of day and night, the moon, sun, and seasons, important to Indian life, were usually reckoned independently, occasionally correlated, and often acknowledged and celebrated in religious ceremony.

The day was recognized as a basic unit of time by all Indians. There is no record of prehistoric naming systems for days, but days were counted by methods such as notching a piece of wood, tying knots in a cord, or taking one stick per day from a bundle of predetermined numbers.

The year was determined directly on the basis of the sun and seasons rather than by a calculated number of days. The time designated as the beginning of the year varied. Many tribes observed it about the time of the vernal equinox, and some observed it in autumn. The Kiowa observed it about October first, the Hopi in November, the Carrier in January, the Creek in July or August, and the Zuñi at the mid-point of the sun's journey between the summer solstices, or about December nineteenth.

The lunar cycle, or "moon," the Indian's equivalent of our month, usually began with the new moon or the conjunction of the sun and moon. Many tribes named the moons and correlated them with the year. Most counted twelve moons to the year, and some, such as the Cree and the New England tribes, counted thirteen. Eskimo tribes often designated twelve periods, roughly corresponding to our months, by characteristic phases of climate and animal or plant life. To the Eskimos of Ungava Bay, Canada, for example, the approximate equivalent of May was the time of fawning, and December was the time of ice formation. Some tribes adjusted for the discrepancy between lunar and solar cycles. The Creeks are reported to have counted twelve and one-half moons to a year by adding a moon every two years. An unspecified tribe of the Sioux or Chippewa is said to have added a "lost moon" every thirty moons.

The seasons as determined by cyclic patterns of the sun, climate, plant life, and growth and migration of animals were of utmost importance to the Indian. The seasonal divisions recognized varied with the geographical location and the means of subsistence of the tribe. Among the more sedentary and agricultural tribes especially, much religious and ceremonial activity was attached to seasonal cycles. Usually the four seasons — spring, summer, autumn, and winter — were recognized and named. Tribes in some areas, many in the Southeast, for example, recognized five. Some tribes of the Northwest Coast divided the year into equal summer and winter periods.

Tribes kept chronological records by various methods. The Salish and neighboring tribes of the Northwest Coast kept biographical records by tying knots and colored markers in a string. Often started by the mother for a child at its birth, the string would serve as a record of the child's age and the important events in its life. Some tribes kept a year count after an important event by means of a notched stick. The Kiowa and some other Plains tribes often kept chronological records in the form of pictographs drawn spirally on animal hide, each symbol representing a significant event of a season or year.

Little record exists of prehistoric Indian calendars north of Mexico. In many respects they were probably held sacred or secret, and the introduction of the

Anglo-American calendar eventually altered or replaced the traditional Indian methods. As a result, our knowledge of Indian calendar systems is very incomplete, and many of them may have been more complex than is now thought.

## MIDDLE AMERICA

Mexican and Mayan calendrics are exceptionally complex. It has been shown that the sacred calendar of 260 days was based on such sophisticated calculations that its astronomical base has long been unrecognized. Furthermore, it has been suggested that cycles recorded in the Mayan astronomical table known as the Dresden Codex represent a pre-Columbian astronomer's attempt to tie the synodic periods of Mercury, Venus, and Mars (taken as 117,585, and 780 days, respectively) to the sacred 260-day calendar ($9 \times 260 = 2{,}340 = 20 \times 117 = 4 \times 585 = 3 \times 780$). Solar eclipse prediction may have utilized the observed regularities, such as the phases of Venus, which are described in the Dresden Codex for a period of almost 104 years.

Whatever their methods, Mayan astronomers inherited or developed excellent methods for eclipse prediction, an achievement that could hardly have been accomplished without an accurate knowledge of the moon's minor perturbations. It is possible that the stakes shown on temple platforms in Mexican codex drawings indicate the existence of a system of measurement of the moon's solstices by means of the nightly resetting of stakes, much in the manner that megalithic astronomers of Western Europe appear to have developed for studying the moon's minor perturbations as early as 2000 BC.

Such calendric and observational skills indicate highly accurate observation methods and tools, records, and calculations. Studies carried out in various American areas afford a fortunate opportunity to determine precisely which celestial objects and events were most important to Native American astronomer-architects. It has been established that the rise-set orientations of the sun, moon, Venus, Capella, and other significant celestial objects were meaningfully observed by early astronomers using sight lines from Mesoamerican temple openings to distant markers, and that complexes such as Group E at Uaxactun served to determine solstice and equinox events. The study of a reversed Group E complex at Dzibilchaltun and other sites in Yucatan indicate that observation of solstice sunsets was also of interest.

American archaeo-astronomy is seriously handicapped by the delay in establishing a scientifically substantiated correlation between Mesoamerican and Gregorian calendars. Before the development of archaeo-astronomy, it was thought that since solar and lunar eclipses tend to repeat themselves, it was impossible to determine the correlation from astronomical data alone. The problem may, in fact, be more complex than it has been considered. Conceivable changes in the length of the year and other considerations have not been taken into account in certain retroactive calculations of solar eclipses. In a recheck of the Dresden Codex data, it was noted that construction of accurate tables of astronomical intervals contained in the codex required the recording of many observations of eclipses and planetary positions, some of which may have been recorded earlier than previously realized.

## SOUTH AMERICA

A certain amount of star lore is found among all tribes in South America, and everywhere some constellations are recognized and named, frequently after spirits. Some tribes determine the annual cycle by observation of the stars and the constellations. Others observe the movements of the sun and the moon for time divisions. The organization of such astronomical observations into a calendrical system is, however, rarely found. This may be due to the poor information available. The best material is on the calendrical system of the *Inca* at the time of the Conquest, and even this is very sketchy. Consequently, there are radically different opinions about the nature of the *Inca* calendar and the observations on which it was based.

Some authorities believe that the *Inca* kept a record of months and years on their knotted-string quipus. Some of the combinations of numbers on certain quipus do suggest time records. However, this would not be a recorded calendar but rather a form of mnemonic device for remembering past events. Many attempts have been made to demonstrate that the Andean people recorded calendrical dates. Some of the claims are fantastic, others more reasonable. It has been suggested, for example, that the low relief designs on the "Gateway of the Sun" at Tiahuanaco have calendrical implications. Such an interpretation is not illogical, since the stone-carving design is clearly of a religious nature and thus perhaps associated with a ceremonial calendar, but there is as yet no evidence that these designs represent a sequence of years with convential symbols such as those on the *Maya* dated stones in Central America. Another much debated design is that found on the so-called Echenique plaque. This is a gold disk with hammered relief design. A feline face in the center is surrounded by a series of design units, some of which are repeated four times, others twice. Although the design is definitely not a recorded calendrical date, it might well be a symbolic representation of the four seasons, or, as suggested by some, of the solstices and the equinoxes.

It is probable that the intensive agriculturists of the Central Andes were long interested in calendrical observations, and that ceremonies were linked with these. Al least, by the *Inca* Period, the ceremonial calendar and the agricultural calendar were clearly related. Some of the early archeological temples are definitely oriented with the cardinal points, and some have suggested that these sites were used for astronomical observations. For example, it is claimed that the main temple of Calassasaya at Tiahuanaco has its eastern stairway situated so as to mark the equinox when observed from the center of the temple. It is likewise pointed out that the corners of the temple, when observed from the same spot, mark the solstices of the sun. Such work is interesting and suggestive, but will probably never lead to a reconstruction of the calendar.

In the *Inca* period, certain specialists of the priest group made solar observations, but there is considerable confusion about the methods employed. One method, described by the chroniclers, made use of four (sometimes eight) small square masonry towers which were built in a row along the skyline. The two center ones were placed close together, the outside ones farther apart. Observations on the setting of the sun behind these towers were taken from a raised platform in the great square of Cuzco. When the sun passed the outside tower, about the month of August, it was time to sow the early crops. When, in September, the sun was framed by the two central towers, it was time for general sowing. Some claim that such towers were used to observe the solstices. Others state that towers were erected along the skyline to mark the beginning of each month. Actually, there is little evidence that the towers were used for anything except setting the sowing dates and perhaps checking the basic lunar calendar. Some of the chroniclers state that the equinoxes were observed by the shadow of a pole set upright in a circular space. This suggestion has led to the identification of certain rough rocks as sun dials. The rocks are flat on top and have a short upright projection in the center. These rocks have been found at Machu Picchu and other sites and are called "intihuatana." They may well have had some symbolic meaning, as part of the sun worship religion, but they could not possibly have served as sun dials, since the upright projection is too short, and the flattened surface is rarely horizontal.

The *Inca* calendar was based on observation of the movements of the sun and moon, but just how the two were reconciled is by no means clear. The solstices and equinoxes may well have been observed, but they do not stand out prominently in the calendar itself. The months were lunar and not exactly adjusted to the solar year. The discrepancy of 11 days between the 12 lunar months and the solar year may have been adjusted, as some authorities claim, by inserting 6 extra days at random throughout the year, and adding 5 days at the end of the year. Other authorities state that the calendar was arbitrarily adjusted when it was too far off.

The calendar was both agricultural and ceremonial. Each of the 12 months had a special name, each was associated with certain important festivals, and each was correlated with the agricultural cycle, in terms of planting, cultivating, rain and harvest. The ceremonial calendar began in December.

Knowledge of other calendrical systems is scanty indeed. The *Aymara* are said to determine the solstices by observing the position of the sun in relation to six geographic points, but it is specifically stated that the equinoxes are not observed. In all probability the *Aymara*, like the *Inca*, once had a lunar calendar, since it is known that the moon and its phases governed all aspects of their agricultural cycle. Cieza de Leon (1554) states that the *Aymara* had a year of 10 months, but this is not confirmed by any other writer. None of the month names has survived, but months were probably named after important events in the ceremonial calendar.

Scattered references to the Chimu peoples mention an annual cycle based on the time of appearance of the Pleiades, whose constellation was also the patron of agriculture. This suggests a somewhat different type of calendar. In the Madre de Dios country, of the upper Amazon, the *Araona* and *Caverna* had a lunar calendar of 12 months to which a decimotercio was added every 3 years. The calendar was probably borrowed from the *Inca*. The years were counted by means of grains of corn and the moons were counted wih pebbles. There is little direct information about and calendar for the *Chibcha* of Colombia, although it would be logical to suppose that it existed. The *Chibcha* had a September maize harvest ceremony, and two New Year's rites, one for the March and one for the June moons.

**CATS**. The relationship between Amerindians and the continents' indigenous and introduced feline population is one which is not well illuminated by the existing archaeological and ethnographic records.

Our knowledge of the importance of felids to Amerindians is limited in part by the differential investigation of the subject in the archaeological sequences of the American continents. The relationship between humans and cats is manifest most clearly in the artistic traditions of the indigenous American peoples, and this subject has been most thoroughly investigated in Mesoamerica and South America.

In North America, the topic of human/felid relationships has not been subject to the same intensity of investigation. Available zoogeographic and cultural data indicate a higher degree of interaction between the jaguar (*Felis onca*) and the native North American populations than has been previously supposed. Because the jaguar figures so prominantly in the cultures of the Americas, the history of its relationship to human beings is of seminal importance in the discussion of felid/human relationships through time in the Western Hemisphere.

Aside from several late Pleistocene and early Holocene cave deposits where human and jaguar remains have been found in dubious association, no clear evidence of the jaguar exists in human contexts until about AD 500. At this time, representations of a spotted cat are found incised on bone in Hopewellian burial mounds in Ohio.

It appears that felids have from the start assumed a more important role in the mythological and artistic aspects of the cultures of the American Indians than figuring in any significant way in their diet. This is a characteristic shared with the other carnivores which as a group are assumed to have contributed relatively little to the subsistence systems of native American peoples. This trend is reinforced by the fact that beginning with our first direct knowledge of human/felid associations, the nature of this relationship is expressed in artistic media, folklore and tales in ethnographic cases, rather than in the food-refuse middens of the peoples concerned. Undoubtedly, the larger cats of the American continents were hunted in aboriginal times, but ethnographic accounts indicate such action was taken to reinforce the hunting prowess of the pursuer or to obtain the cat's hide and other body parts for manufacture into items of clothing or personal adornment.

In spite of the jaguar's importance, other wild felids appear in the faunal assemblages recovered from many North American sites. The bobcat or lynx (*Lynx rufus* and *Lynx canadensis*) and the mountain lion or puma (*Felis concolor*) were apparently hunted for much the same reasons as the jaguar. The 14th century pueblo of Grasshopper in east-central Arizona has yielded awl-like implements and tubes made of *Lynx* bone. Similar felid bone tubes, presumably used for personal adornment, occur at Pecos, New Mexico in archaeological contexts dating to *circa* AD 1250 to 1540. Non-artifactual remains of the mountain lion (*Felis concolor*) were also found at Pecos. It should also be pointed out that small quantities of both *Lynx* and *Felis concolor* remains are known from many sites in the United States, but again their presence is probably a result of ritual activity or non-subsistence hunting.

As has been mentioned earlier, the amount of data relating to the association between humans and felids is greater in Central and South America than anywhere else in the Western Hemisphere. Once again, it is the jaguar, or another smaller member of the family Felidae, the ocelot (*Felis pardalis*) that are of particular importance in this regard.

One of the earliest major cultural manifestations south of the Rio Grande was the Olmec civilization whose heartland centered on the Gulf Coastal Plain of Mexico in what is now southern Veracruz and Tabasco. It is in a discussion of the Olmec culture that one begins to see the prominent role of large cats in the developing cultures of Mexico, Central, and South America. From archaeological contexts throughout the Olmec sequence (*c.* 1500 to 100 BC), "...archaeologists had known about small jade sculptures and other objects in a distinct and powerful style that emphasized human infants with snarling, jaguar-like features."*

This theme is characteristic of Olmec art and is indicative of the degree to which jaguars were considered mystical. One interesting interpretation of these artistic motifs that combine both human and feline features is the contention that these representations may depict victims of the genetic condition known as Down's Syndrome which produces in human infants many of the characteristics common in Olmec art such as sharp, fang-like teeth (a result of ectodermal dysplasia), a broad, flat face, short nose and epicanthic fold. Additionally, many victims of the syndrome acquire serious malformation of the hands which in some cases result in broad, claw-like fingernails. The resemblance of many of these features to those of felids, particularly the jaguar, may account, at least in part, for the apparent Olmec notion that a special class of humans had the ability to take on the physical characteristics of the jaguar, not unlike the central European tales of lycanthropy.

Further to the south, and later in time, the Classic Maya (AD 300 to 900) murals at Bonampak in Chiapas depict a series of prisoners being tortured under the apparent direction of an authoritarian figure wearing a jaguar-skin cloak and holding a symbolic staff of authority which is also decorated with jaguar hide. It should be mentioned that in later times just prior to Spanish contact in the 16th century, the jaguar figured prominently in the symbolic system of the Aztec people in the region around present-day Mexico City.

Perhaps the clearest cultural expression of human/felid relationships comes from the South American continent where there emerged on the northwestern coast in modern Peru and Bolivia, a series of dynamic cultures that culminated in the Inca empire about the time of Spanish contact. The artistic traditions of these cultures are particularly useful in assessing the relative importance of felids in the various aspects of their lives

---

*Coe, M.D. *Mexico*, Praeger Publishers, NY.

as primary evidence, such as reports on faunal remains recovered from archaeological sites, are generally lacking form this area.

Work on the Chavin culture of Early Horizon Peru (*c.* 1200 to 300 BC) represents one of the best syntheses of form and meaning in early South American art. Analysis of South American artistic traditions, as expressed mainly through textiles and ceramics, indicates the predominate image of the cat represented by the jaguar. While one may be cautious to point out that the felid motif expressed clearly as a jaguar is not particularly common in Chavin art, the possibility that both jaguars and pumas are represented is present.

Later in time, during the Late Intermediate Period (*c.* AD 900 to 1476) the Ica artistic style is in part characterized by felid motifs.

Elsewhere in South America the nature and extent of human/felid associations is poorly known. Archaeological evidence for such relationships is generally lacking and the ethnographic data on the use of felids by humans is similarly scarce.

There is no evidence that indicates any of the indigenous Western Hemisphere felids have ever been domesticated. The earliest firm record we have for the introduction of the European domestic cat (*Felis domesticus*) dates to AD 1623 when it is recorded that the Catholic missionary, Gabriel Sagard, travelled with a pet cat during his stay among the Huron Indians in the Georgian Bay area of Lake Huron, Ontario. While isolated instances such as this form our earliest record of the domestic cat in the Americas, it was never imported *en masse* until the mid-18th century when entire colonies, such as Pennsylvania, were innundated by rodent pests. After the close of the 17th century, historical accounts of domestic cats in the Americas are quite common and indicate the cat had become an integral aspect of European communities and thus well-known by the Amerindians of the time.

Modern ethnographic accounts of the use of felids by the native peoples of the Americas are not in abundance. Data indicate that indigenous peoples in the Western Hemisphere continue to utilize felids in a variety of ways, particularly in Central and South America. As in the past, the trend seems to be toward functional applications of felid products in articles of adornment and other artifacts rather than as primary food sources.

It is clear that Amerindian utilization of indigenous Western Hemisphere cats is a phenomenon of considerable antiquity. The unique behavioral characteristics of felids undoubtedly contributed to their incorporation into the symbolic worlds of many native American peoples.

JOHN W. OLSEN

**CAT'S CRADLE** is the common name for a wide range of cord manipulations, also known as "string figures." The former usually applies to those uses primarily intended for children's amusements, while the more formal or ceremonial activities are known by the latter name. Usually regarded largely as a game, the basis of the figures is normally made from a single loop from which the various forms are developed in sequence, often becoming remarkably elaborate and complex. While most frequently performed by one person, using the hands and teeth, adults also enjoy the same, occasionally playing it as a two-person, four-hand activity; less frequently, four persons play with two on each side, devising forms or challenging the opposing pair. Skill, rapidity of motion, and visual balance of the figures are important, but universally, the most highly-regarded quality seems to be the degree of inventiveness displayed by the player in devising new forms of interpretations. Strangely, the game is rarely used as a basis for gambling.

The remarkable variety and widespread occurrence of cat's cradle has engaged the interest of many scholars, interested in the psychological implications of the game, or the wide range of anthropomorphic or zoomorphic identifications given to many of the figures. While the game is not regarded as sacred by most peoples, it does have religious overtones in certain circumstances; the Arctic Eskimo, for example, use string figures to ensnare the sun during summer solstice rituals, in an effort to hold it from continuing on its rounds.

The use of string figures is known through the world; almost no tribe or group has been encountered to whom the game is not familiar. In the New World, the practice seems particularly rich among the Arctic Eskimo and the Navajo of the Southwest and certain South American tribes—although this may simply reflect the degree of interest of a limited number of scholars. But it does seem evident that these peoples developed a tremendous range of forms, names and customs involving the game. Some Indian tribes incorporate names of local flora and fauna by which to identify certain string forms, others do not. A surprising degree of parallel development can also be traced whereby the players from various regions have developed a sequence in common with others—often to the extent of parallel names.

The Navajo believe that the game was taught to them by the Spider Women; the Zuñi claim that theirs came from the Spider Woman also, but that she taught it to the grandmother of the Twin War Gods, and that the designs represent the netted shield of the Holy Children. Other tribes of North America have evolved forms too numerous to list ranging from the Kwakiutl and Salish of the Northwest to the Cherokee and Creek of the Southeast, and the California tribes to the Eastern Woodlands peoples of the Atlantic; no area is known to have lacked the game. Some uses are unusual, *e.g.*, the custom of divining the sex of unborn babies (among the Wailaki and Southern Paiute), or some amusing forms which involve physical tricks, *e.g.*, the "trap" figure which actually catches and holds the person's finger playing opposite.

In Middle America, the Mayo, Huichol, Cora, Yaqui and Maya are among those tribes whose string figures have been studied; the Carib and Arawak of the Caribbean are thoroughly conversant with the game, and carried it back-and-forth between the islands and the southern continent.

Several South American tribes are particularly inventive in the game, most particularly as reported among the Patamona, Warao, Makushi and Wapishana, as well as all of the tribes of the Guianas; they along with the Chaco Indians have a rich nomenclature and string-figure vocabulary. More than 800 figures have been recorded among the various regions of the world by scholars interested in the pastime; one of the most active was Alfred C. Haddon, a turn-of-the-century British anthropologist and field ethnographer who devised the system whereby these interesting figures can be permanently recorded in written form.

FREDERICK DOCKSTADER

**CAVES AND ROCKSHELTERS** and other similar natural geological structures have been utilized since Pleistocene times by Native American groups. Although geology and topography were limiting factors in the natural occurrence of such features, where caves and similar structures were present and available, native utilization was usually extensive. The actual role, and degree of importance, of caves and rockshelters has also varied somewhat from a regional and temporal standpoint. Generally speaking, caves were utilized for shelter during the earliest (Paleo-Indian and Archaic) periods. In subsequent eras, though shelter is still an important usage, cave sites often took on a more ceremonial function for many native peoples.

### Paleo-Indian period

There is considerable controversy over precisely when the first inhabitants of the New World crossed over the Bering Land Bridge from Asia. Some archaeological evidence suggests that more than one migration may have taken place; certainly the Pleistocene climatological conditions would have resulted in the opening and closing of the Bering passageway more than once during the Wisconsin Glaciation (*c.* 70,000-7000 BC).

Archaeologically there is increasing evidence of a very early pre-Projectile Point Native culture present in the New World well before 10,000 BC. Curiously, the strongest proof for this crude lithic horizon occurs in South America, with more debatable traces now known from both Middle and North America.

By about 10,000 BC the widespread manufacturing of stone lance (or projectile) points commensed and, as such, clear evidence of Paleo-Indian presence begins in North, Middle and South America. During this Pleistocene era the usage of caves and rockshelters for temporary shelter and habitation is pronounced and extensive. Not only are lithic fragments and worked stone tolls found from cave floors, but often the remnant scraps of bone of now extinct Ice Age fauna.

In North America, early evidence of cave utilization is concentrated in the far western and eastern mountain ranges of the United States. In the west, a prime example of late Pleistocene habitation is evidenced at the Wilson Butte Cave in Idaho. Here a lengthy intermittent occupation of the cave, running from historic times back into the Pleistocene has been recovered. Lowermost (and earliest) levels of the cave have produced crude flint scraps (blades, burins and biface tools) which were made by Paleo-Indians of about 12,500 BC. At the site of Mummy Cave in the Rocky Mountains of Wyoming, archaeologists have evidence of Native utilization of this large alcove from at least 7,200 BC at the very close of the Ice Age. A long history of habitation by projectile point using hunters has been documented.

In eastern North America, two recently explored cave sites have begun to produce equally early signs of usage. The Dutchess Quarry cave site in New York has produced lithic evidence of Early Man and a radiocarbon determination of *c.* 10,500 BC. Further south, in Pennsylvania, the Meadowcraft Rockshelter has yet another long history of use, with earliest human evidence dating to 13,000 BC.

In all of North America, however, it is in the southwest region that the greatest concentration of Early Man cave sites seem to have been located. Sites like

Ventana Cave in Arizona and Tularosa Cave, Cordova Cave, Bat Cave and Sandia Cave in New Mexico have very early dates of first utilization and show long records of employment (often as long as 10,000 years or more).

Still further south, in Middle America, two well-known Mexican sites, Lerma Cave in Tamaulipas and Coxcatlan Cave in Puebla, have produced evidence of man in association with Pleistocene game. Coxcatlan Cave, an exceedingly important site in the subsequent Archaic Period, has indirectly dated evidence suggesting usage by Native peoples by *c.* 9,000 BC. Lerma Cave has a carbon-14 date of 7,700 BC in one of the lower levels of the cave (though not the deepest) and lacks evidence in its early horizons of any form of projectile points. The stone tool assemblage is composed of primitive scrapers, choppers and blades, and lacks any evidence of projectile points. In its pre-7,000 BC levels, then, Lerma Cave may have proof of the controversial pre-Projectile Point Culture.

The earliest and most provocative Paleo-Indian indications of cave utilization in the New World come from Ayacucho, Peru. Here several cave sites recently excavated by archaeologist R. S. MacNeish present the strongest proof to date for the existence of a very early Pre-Projectile Point horizon in New World cultural development. At Pikimachay, or Flea Cave, for example, MacNeish has strong evidence for the direct association of primitive looking stone tools and the bones of extinct animals. Carbon-14 dates range between 12,200-17,600 BC. Unlike many Pre-Projectile Point sites, the Flea Cave finds have strong provenience data.

Other well-known Paleo-Indian sites of South America include Los Toldos Cave Gruta de Cadonga and Cueva de las Indies (Argentina), Lauricocha Cave and Guitarrero Cave (Peru), Eberhardt Cave (Chile), and El Abra Cave (Colombia); all have dates ranging from 10,000 BC. The Lagoa Santa and Coufins Caves of eastern Brazil have recently produced carbon-14 dates of about 18,000 BC. Excavations in the last century at the latter sites, plus Eucaliptus Rock Shelter and Marciano Cave have produced human skeletal material which may belong to Early Man. From the very tip of South America, at the site of Fell's Cave and Palli Aike Cave in Patagonia (Chile), Early Man was present no later than 11,000 years ago.

### Archaic Period

By about 7,000 BC there is a gradual end to the colder Ice Age climate, and the disappearance of most Pleistocene fauna. Native groups began undertaking alternative lifestyles (adaptations) t the new emerging (modern) flora and fauna. This period of adaptation, from about 7,000-1,000 BC is marked, in the archaeological record, by an increase in woodworking and food grinding implements, often of ground and polished stone, and by evidence of greater, more diverse exploitation of the new Archaic environment. Although the ecological adaptations varied somewhat from region to region, the overwhelming indication from the archaeology suggests that man was exploiting new settings largely (or totally) ignored by the Paleo-Indian predecessors. Archaic cave sites are, again, numerous.

In western North America the Great Basin area of Utah, Nevada, and Southern Oregon contain numerous Desert Archaic cave sites, some which were occupied from the very end of the Paleo-Indian period until historic times. These sites served as the temporary encampments of small bands of semi-nomadic Archaic natives who cyclically migrated throughout the harsh exerophytic Great Basin zone in search of plant and animal food supplies. Sites like the Leonard Rock Shelter, Humboldt Cave, and Lovelock Cave in Nevada, Danger Cave, Hogup Cave in Utah, or Fort Rock Cave in Oregon retain evidence of Archaic transhumence and intensive exploitation of a rugged desert environment.

Due to the dry, arid climatic conditions, and the sheltered settings of these Great Basin sites, preservation of normally perishable remains is often remarkably good, resulting in a much more detailed archaeological picture than elsewhere in North America for the Archaic Period. Aside from the generally durable Archaic items, like milling stones and handstones, more perishable items like vegetable fiber cordage used for snares, feathered duck decoys, fiber bark cloth, rabbit fur blankets, twisted and coiled basketry, twined moccasins and sandals, fish nets and fish lines with hooks, have all been uncovered, and suggest the richness of cultural remains which once existed.

In the eastern United States the Graham Cave, Missouri and the Modoc Rock Shelter, Illinois, both retain evidence of Paleo-Indian remains overlain by Archaic habitation. Both sites are deeply stratified, as are most western Archaic caves, and have radiocarbon dates ranging from the end of the Pleistocene into the Archaic. These sites are seen, then, to be important transitional sites between two major native cultural patterns and revealing crucial data on the changing subsistence adaptations of natives during this era. As in the west, eastern Archaic sites have produced not only milling stones but projectile points, various scrappers, choppers and polished stone implements. Subsistence was diverse with deer, raccoon, opossum, bird, fish and shellfish remains common at many eastern Archaic sites. Such fauna would have been complemented by gathering and processing of wild vegetable plant foods (nuts, seeds, etc.). Although preservation is generally not as good as that of Great Basin counterparts, the eastern Archaic cave sites reveal similar patterns of a rich material culture and a greatly intensified exploitaton of the natural environment for subsistence support.

Archaic Period cave sites of Middle America have produced some of the most detailed archaeological and paleo-botanical evidence known for the New World transition from hunting-gathering lifestyle to agriculture and year-round sedentism. In Mexico, in the small Tehuacan Valley of Puebla, in a setting similar to that of the North American Great Basin, a series of sites, especially Coxcatlan, Purron, San Marcos and El Riego caves, have documented the earliest appearances in the Americas of several important domesticated plant foods. Of particular significance is the evidence from Coxcatlan Cave of the earliest cultivated corn (*Zea mays*) by about 5,000 BC. Corn, or maize, following increasing hybridization, becomes the principal food crop of Native New World peoples. With food production originating in Mesoamerica, the evolution to substantially larger and more complex human social units commensed. Again, preservation of organic plant and animal remains on the dry cave floors of the Tehuacan Valley aided greatly in reconstructing this gradual, but tremendously important cultural evolution.

Evidence from South American caves during the Archaic Period is not nearly as abundant as during earlier eras. This may be, in pat, due to inadequate archaeological sampling rather than being an accurate reflection of actual absence of Archaic sites in the south. In Ayacucho (Peru), however, we see a similar trend to that earlier seen in Mesoamerica, with maize being adopted at some time after 4,000 BC and probably having been diffused southward from Mesoamerica. As in Mesoamerica, with the growing importance of maize farming to the economy, permanent habitations of increasing size occur more frequently in the more fertile valley floor regions rather than in the cave areas of hillsides and mountains. Consequently, there is a recognizable decline in cave dwellings by late Archaic times as an apparent result of the adoption of agriculture by Native groups, and a shift to open site living.

**Post-Archaic Period**

With the emergence of village-farming communities, first in Mesoamerica, and shortly thereafter in South and North America, we find caves employed less for habitation. However, in many areas of the Americas cave locations took on a more ceremonial function (for burials, ritual deposits and caches,rites of passage, and other religious-cult practices).

In North America, some of the Archaic cave sites continue to be utilized for lengthy periods. Some, like Lovelock Cave in Nevada, are utilized less for habitation and more for ritual activities like burials (often with grave goods) and occasionally for "caching" (apparently a seasonal storage of valued articles to avoid the need for transporting such goods). The site of Salts Cave in Kentucky has shown a very early and prolonged Native interest in the mining of crystaline mirabilite (a cathartic) and gypsum (for its white pigment deposits). Both Salts Cave and Mammoth Cave show utilization well beyond the Archaic era. In Montana, Pictograph Cave is noted for its rock engravings but also has an archaeological sequence running from Paleo-Indian times until the Protohistoric Period.

In Mesoamerica, the concept of the underworld was intimately connected with Mesoamerican deities (particularly the Death God) and with cave rituals. Ritual use has been revealed through the presence of sometimes quite elaborate cave paintings. Several early Olmec (*c.* 1,000 BC) wall paintings are known from the Oxtotitlan Cave and Juxtlahuaca Cave in Guerrero, Mexico. At the sprawling highland Mexican site of Teotihuacan archaeologists have recently discovered a cave-tunnel beneath the massive Pyramid of the Sun. The cave had a series of interconnected chambers, was utilized for religious rites, and was covered over (*c.* AD 250-450) by the earliest pyramidal constructions. It is most probable that the location of this cavern determined the site for the subsequent construction of the huge pyramid atop which was a major temple for Teotihuacan.

Elsewhere in Mesoamerica, it is quite clear that the lowland Maya utilized caves for various purposes during the Classic (AD 300-900) Period and later. In the Maya Mountains of Belize sites such as Las Cuevas, Eduardo Quiroz Cave and Rio Frio Cave E, and the Gruta de Chac, in Yucatan, have produced signs of ritual Mayan water collection. In such caves the slowly dripping cave moisture was considered ritually pure ("virgin water") and sacred for ceremonial rites. Occasionally caves were utilized for the disposal of the dead and as ossuaries. The Copan and Cuyamel Caves of Honduras were employed as such burial repositories.

In South America, also, caves were recognized as sacred places for some Post-Archaic cultures. At the Intihuasi Cave and at Ongamira Cave in the central sierras of Argentina, Paleo-Indian and post-Archaic deposits (with pottery, jewelry and other artifacts) are known. In Peru and Brazil caves and rockshelters show signs of intermittant usage, though only rarely for long-term habitation. Cave sites are common in the Andes Mountains, and a number of cave sites are known which have been actually published on the topic. As early as the Early Horizon, the site of Chavin shows some architectural features which suggest an artificial "cave." These deep structural galleries appear in later Peruvian sites as well. Some cave sites were clearly employed for post-Archaic Period burials (often in the form of mummies). The Late Horizon culture of the Inca are also reputed to have employed caves, particularly for interrments.

PAUL F. HEALY

**CHILDBIRTH CUSTOMS.** Native people who lived in North, Middle, and South America at the time of contact with Europeans probably originated in Asia. Scientists now think that there were several migrations from northeast Asia across the Bering Straits between approximately 28,000 and 12,000 years ago. Descendents of these early migrants pushed southward, reaching Tierra del Fuego at the southern tip of South America not less than 3,000 to 5,000 years ago. Various groups of people settled in different environments and eventually developed variations in sociopolitical organization. Nevertheless, there was a tendency to retain certain Asiatic traits. Some of these traits included similarities in physical type, languages, tools, skin-working, shamanism, puberty and death rites, various other rituals, and certain customs related to childbirth.

For the most part, childbirth customs with an Asiatic orgin among Indians in the New World included restrictions or *taboos* and other magical acts which were carried out before, during and after childbirth. The point of these rituals was to insure the well-being of mothers and infants. Often fathers, other relatives, and shamans played important roles in the magical observances surrounding childbirth. This was especially true for South America, where the participation of fathers in the *couvade* was almost universal (*see also* CHILD REARING).

Unlike some native people, such as those in Australia and Melanesia, New World native peoples were familiar with the basic facts of human reproduction. This was demonstrated by the almost universal distribution of the couvade in South America, and by the fact that there are no recorded cases of Indian people denying the physiology of human reproduction.

**Limitations on fertility**

Generally speaking, Indian people greatly desired children and looked forward to their arrival. However, in California, the Great Basin, and elsewhere in North America, as well as in South America, herbal contraception sometimes limited the fertility of native groups. Permanent sterilization of woman by herbs has been reported for the Woodlands and Great Plains of North America, and elsewhere. And, the number of native offspring who reached maturity was often limited by abortion, infanticide, and a high rate of infant mortality. Because infant mortality was generally high throughout the New World, it is likely that abortion and infanticide had little effect on the overall population of native groups. In fact, most of the infants encountering this fate probably would have died anyway from malnutrition and other causes.

Abortion has been reported for all areas of the New World, but the frequency of abortion varied from tribe to tribe. Some groups did not practice it at all. Abortion was normally the personal business of women, and was not considered a crime. Motivations for abortion included economic and social factors such as insufficient food or the desire to prevent illegitimacy (although illegitimacy was not as stigmatized among Indians as among Europeans). Techniques for inducing abortion varied, but could be grouped into three equally-distributed types: mechanically-induced abortion, drug-induced abortion, and exercise-induced abortion. Infanticide was likewise reported for all areas of the New World, but not for all tribes in all areas. This practice was usually regarded as a necessity rather than a crime. It was most often carried out when a mother died and her baby could not be fed, where obtaining food was a problem, or when babies were deformed. Rates of infanticide were highest for areas where obtaining enough food or enough protein was difficult, including the Arctic, the Subarctic, the Great Basin, northeastern Mexico, and tropical South America.

Among the Ojibwa (Chippewa), who were Algonquian-speaking hunters, gatherers, and trappers of northeastern North America, abortions were frowned upon. However, they were sought by women who were single, whose husbands were incompetent providers, or who simply wanted abortions. The most common method of inducing abortion was to drink a tea made from the bark of a certain tree. Other methods included lifting heavy objects, straining, and jumping from high places. Spontaneous abortions sometimes occurred after a fall or when women worked too hard, as when chopping wood. Products from spontaneous abortions were given the same funeral and burial rites as adults, while those from self-induced abortions were buried in the ground, under the floor of the mother's wigwam, or under the roots of the tree which had provided the bark for the tea which induced the abortion.

Among the Arapaho, who were Algonquian-speaking hunters of the North American Plains, women stated that they never induced abortion, and that they used herbs to prevent miscarriages caused by hard work or accidental injuries. Sometimes, Arapaho women were sterilized by exposure to the fumes of certain herbs while they drank an extract made from these same herbs. However, once a child was conceived, the Arapaho made every effort to ensure its birth.

The Ona, who were Chon (Tshon)-speaking hunters, gatherers, and fisherpeople of the island of Tierra del Fuego at the southern tip of South America, used no contraceptives or abortifacients, and left no clear record of infanticide. By contrast, the Mapuche, who were Araucanian-speaking farmers of central Chile, practiced both abortion and infanticide and used approximately a dozen different abortifacients made from plants. As was often the case among native groups elsewhere in the New World, the Mapuche disposed of deformed infants and one of a pair of twins. This was accomplished by drowning or by suffocation with mud.

Among the Yanomamo, who were Yanomamo (Shiriana or "Waika") speaking slash-and-burn cultivators, hunters, and warriors of southern Venezuela and northern Brazil, infanticide, especially of female infants, was very common. The Yanomamo apparently suffered from overpopulation combined with a shortage of complete food proteins. They therefore preferred male babies who would grow up to become hunters and warriors who could feed and defend their villages and replace men killed in battle. Since couples preferred a male as their firstborn, women practiced selective infanticide until they produced a "firstborn" male. Yanomamo mothers also killed their babies at birth regardless of sex if they were breastfeeding. This was done because mothers assumed that the new infant would probably die from lack of food, and it seemed wiser to maintain a baby who had already proven the ability to survive than to risk losing both babies. Yanomamo women practiced abortion in order to avoid killing a newborn, and when husbands ordered their wives to abort because they suspected that an unborn baby was not theirs. Abortion was straightforward—a woman lay on her back while a friend jumped on her belly in order to rupture the amnion. Yanomamo babies who had already been born were disposed of by strangulation with vines, by standing on a stick placed across the infant's neck, by tossing infants on the ground or against a tree, or by simply abandoning them after birth. Sometimes, women who felt that they could no longer care for a child simply stopped feeding it. Birth control for the Yanomamo consisted of abstention while a woman was pregnant or nursing. Nursing was normally continued for at least three years.

For purposes of comparison, it is useful to examine fertility control in at least one Siberian tribe in an area where some of the ancestors of New World native peoples may have originated. Some Siberian tribes, such as the Chukchi, who were Paleosiberian-speaking marine hunters and reindeer breeders of northeastern Siberia, and the Koryak, who were Paleosiberian-speaking marine hunters, reindeer breeders, fisherpeople, and hunters of eastern Siberia, have been recorded as having high birth rates. However, the Kamchadal (Itel'mens), who were Paleosiberian-speaking fisherpeople, marine hunters, and gatherers of the Kamchatka Penninsula in northeastern Siberia, attempted to control their fertility. On the one hand, Kamchadal women who hoped to become pregnant ingested spiders and human umbilical cords together with a certain grass. On the other hand, abortion by abdominal trauma or vaginal amniotomy was widely practiced. These techniques were carried out under the supervision of older women who specialized in abortion, and frequently caused the death of the mother. When unwanted infants did not die before birth, Kamchadal mothers strangled them or fed them to the dogs. Kamchadal women could induce permanent sterility by drinking an infusion made from a certain grass.

## CHILDBIRTH CUSTOMS OF REPRESENTATIVE INDIAN GROUPS

Descriptions of the childbirth customs of a representative cross-section of New World native groups provide a comparative picture. Throughout both continents, people believed that childbirth was surrounded by supernatural powers, but also that it was a normal process which should be accepted with stoicism. In many cases, women continued to perform their daily tasks until just before childbirth. Widespread magical observances, such as food restricions for one or both parents and prohibitions for the mother against being frightened or seeing anything which was deformed were thought to insure the safety of mothers and infants. Midwives were often present at delivery, and the preferred position for labour and delivery was frequently kneeling or squatting. However, in the Southwest, California, and the Northwest Coast areas of North America, sitting was preferred, and in tropical regions of both continents, women often gave birth in a supine position in hammocks.

**North and Middle America**

Among the Athapaskan-speaking hunters, fisher-people, and gatherers of the Western Subarctic of North America, pregnant women observed food taboos which often became more stringent as pregnancy progressed. For the most part, birth was considered the business of women and occurred in a special area prepared for that purpose. For example, the Upper Tanana dug a shallow pit for childbirth near the family dwelling and lined this with grass. These pits were covered with huts only in cold weather. The Ingalik padded the benches of their houses with grass, and women gave birth indoors while men were excluded.

Western Subarctic women were normally assisted by one or more female relatives while they crouched or stooped over a pit. Sometimes an assistant supported a woman in labour, and sometimes the woman gripped a horizontal bar about three feet high which was attached to upright poles at both ends. Placentas were buried or hung in a tree deep in the woods. Some tribes believed that if dogs ate the placenta, the mother would become sterile. If a birth was difficult, shamans were brought in to sing. Death in childbirth was not unknown.

Newborn Western Subarctic infants were washed or wiped clean with moss, diapered with moss or dry grass, and wrapped in a rabbitfur blanket or placed in a moosehide bag lined with rabbitskin. Many Western Subarctic groups used dried pieces of the umbilical cord as charms to protect the health of infants. Until babies were able to walk, they were carried on their mother's backs in birchbark seats or in carrying straps.

A Western Subarctic child's well-being was thought to depend on the careful management of taboos and restrictions for both parents. Thus, mothers who had given birth in birth huts remained inside of these huts for several days, and most Western Subarctic women were obligated to restrict their activities for approximately twenty days following childbirth. Some Western Subarctic groups required new mothers to observe the same taboos at birth as they had observed at puberty.

Among the Ingalik, Upper Tanana, Kutchin, and other Western Subarctic groups, both parents observed the same post-partum taboos. For example, Ingalik couples observed food and sex taboos and did not work for twenty days. During this time, Ingalik fathers wore old clothes and covered their heads with parka hoods whenever they went outdoors. Western Subarctic babies were nursed for at least three years, or until another child was born.

The Micmac, who were Algonquian-speaking hunters, gatherers, and fisherpeople of the Gaspe Penninsula of Quebec, Newfoundland, and the Maritime Provinces of Canada, were representative of the Woodlands style of life in northeastern North America. The Micmac were extremely fond of children, and considered them central to the success of any marriage. However, Micmac parents also attempted to control their fertility. Plant medicines for curing sterility and inducing abortion were used, and older people warned that women who had sexual relationships with too many men would become sterile. However, if such women changed their ways, they might be able to conceive.

During pregnancy, Micmac women observed proper behaviour in order to ensure their own health and the health of their infants. Elaborate care was taken during the first three or four months when unborn babies were known to be susceptible to crippling and blemishes. During this time, relationships with people and animals were handled with great care. For example, lack of courtesy to a witch might cause a "bad wish" in the form of a patch of fur on the infant. Similarly, mockery of handicapped people or animals would cause a child to be born with the same handicap. Harelipped, fox-faced, or mooseheaded babies were known to be born to women who teased these animals. Sometimes, fathers had a profound influence on their unborn offspring, as in the case of one father who teased a seal, and then had a son born with a flipper in place of one hand. Micmac women who touched themselves on the face or who gripped their elbows with their hands while craving a specific food might cause their babies to be marked on the face or elbows with spots shaped liked the desired foods. Seeing people maimed by fire was thought to produce babies with pulpy, fiery-red faces. Since it was felt that one of a pair of twins would turn out badly, twins were considered abnormal. Mothers of twins were compared to female dogs, and were certain to have bad luck.

Micmac women could assure an easy delivery by proper preventative measures. Thus, it was necessary for pregnant women to go straight through doorways because hesitation in doorways would cause babies to become caught in the mother's "doorway" during birth. For the same reason, pregnant women were obliged to rise immediately upon awakening. Jewelery encircling the body or anything tied around a woman's waist would cause babies to be born with their umbilical cords wrapped around their necks.

If labour began when a Micmac woman had gone alone to the bush to gather wood, she handled the birth by herself, and returned to camp with a bundle of wood on her back and her baby in her arms. When travelling by canoe, a woman in labour might ask to be put ashore. There, she went into the woods alone. After a short while, she returned with her infant and continued her share of the paddling. Micmac women who began labour while they were in camp were usually assisted by one or more older women, who were paid for their services. An example of payment during historic times was the knife used to cut the umbilical cord.

During labour, Micmac women assumed a kneeling or squatting position and grasped the centre pole of the wigwam. Normal labour was said to last about two hours. If labour lasted too long, a woman's hands were tied to the centre pole of the wigwam and her ears, nose and mouth were stopped up. The midwife then pressed hard on the woman's sides in order to force the baby to be born. When this technique failed, a shaman was called in and given tobacco to offer to the spirit which was interfering with the birth. In historic times, salt was placed in the mother's cupped hands and she was asked to blow on the salt as hard as she could in order to expel the placenta. The placenta was then thrown in the fire; the faster it burned, the fewer the afterpains.

Regardless of the temperature of the water, Micmac babies were washed in a nearby stream immediately after birth. They were then made to swallow bear grease or seal oil, wrapped in soft skins, and bound to a cradleboard. Cradleboards were always placed or carried in an upright position. Boys were diapered by passing the penis through a hole in their wrappings, while girls were diapered via a little bark trough which led to the outside of the wrappings. Powdered dry-rotted wood or moss was also placed under the rump. This was changed daily.

Many Micmac babies were born in a caul or viel, which was considered fortunate. These babies were smart, had the power to foretell the future, and would escape the hazards of drowning, fire, and warfare. Since pieces of cauls protected other people as well, Micmac soldiers purchased them from owners or the parents of owners as recently as World Wars I and II.

When a Micmac baby's umbilical cord fell off, it was buried in a spot which would assist the baby's future career. For example, when placed in a tree, the cord would cause a boy to become a good hunter. It was said that if an umbilical cord was burned, its owner would always be searching for it by poking in the fire.

Micmac babies were nursed for two or three years. Since women could not feed or carry more than one child at a time, nursing mothers who became pregnant used a "secret" drug to produce abortions. When weaning began, both parents placed chewed meat in a child's mouth. It was said that in order to wean her child, a Micmac mother watched the moon. When the moon was in its dark phase, she stopped nursing. By the time the moon reappeared, her baby had forgotten the breast.

The Ojibwa (Chippewa), who were Algonquian-speaking hunters, gatherers, and trappers of the woodlands of northeastern North America, also attempted to control their fertility. Sterility could be produced by an herbal drink, but sterile people were not esteemed. To induce pregnancy, Ojibwa wives or both spouses used several extracts concocted from plants. It was claimed that these remedies were always successful.

On the other hand, children who were spaced too closely together were considered a disgrace.

For the most part, the Ojibwa stated that conception occured as a result of intercourse. However, it was known that twins, babies born in cauls, with patches of grey hair, or with teeth, notched ears, or birthmarks were reincarnated elders whose ghosts had entered the baby's body at the time of conception or soon afterwards. A baby's sex could be predicted by the contour of the mother's abdomen. There was no general preference for girls or boys, but it was said that daughters were more likely to care for aged parents.

Depending on the group of Ojibwa, food restrictions and taboos for pregnant women and their husbands were strict or relaxed. Violation of these rules was known to affect the birth process, as well as the anatomy, physiology, and personality of the unborn child. For example, women who ate lynx would have difficulty during childbirth because lynx had difficulty giving birth; women who ate raspberries, blueberries, or blackberries would have babies with marks the colour of these berries; women who ate popped rice would have babies with difficulty breathing; and women who ate porcupine meat would have babies with stuffy noses, or who were clumsy, crippled, clubfooted, pigeon-toed, headstrong, difficult to train, hateful, or temperamental. Ojibwa mothers were encouraged to eat venison, wild rice, lake-trout, and whitefish, but not to eat too much, since this led to large babies and difficult births. There were also many behavioural taboos transmitted by older people. If followed, these taboos would lead to success, but if violated, they would lead to harm. Included were such taboos as not turning over in bed because this would cause the umbilical cord to become wrapped around the baby's neck, not gazing at deformed people or animals, and not tormenting any animals, including flies. Pregnant women were expected to work hard at all normal tasks, such as chopping wood, because this kept the child loose and insured an easy delivery and normal expulsion of the placenta. Expectant mothers were told not to enter wigwams other than those of close relatives, and not to accept food or gifts from anyone other than close relatives, lest jealous people direct bad medicine at their babies.

In wintertime, childbirth usually took place inside of the family wigwam. In warmer weather, it often took place in a private spot away from the wigwam. Since all Ojibwa women seemed to know how to handle childbirth, women in labour were usually assisted by their close female relatives. Men were present during labour and delivery only when women were unavailable when help was needed.

At the onset of labour, an Ojibwa woman drank an herbal mixture which eased her pain and facilitated the birth. Women in labour were encouraged to continue working and moving around until their pains became quite severe because this made the birth process easier. Furthermore, childbirth was considered a normal event to be taken in stride. Like the Micmac and most other North American tribes, Ojibwa women preferred to assume a kneeling position during the final stages of labour. In historic times, Ojibwa women who had become accustomed to kneeling found that together with conventions for modesty, this preference made it difficult to accept non-Indian medical procedures for childbirth.

Traditional Ojibwa women braced themselves during laobur and delivery in several ways. One of these ways included pulling on a moosehide or fibre strap or rope which was tied to the trunk or limb of a tree. More recently, ropes were tied to the rafters of a house. Another way of bracing involved kneeling and then leaning against and grasping the centre pole of the wigwam in such a way that a woman's elbows were on the opposite side of the pole. It was said that the more a woman in this position used her arms, the less pain she encountered. Yet another method of bracing involved grasping a sapling which was placed horizontally across two forked side-poles. In historic times, horizontal poles were often nailed to the inside of a house, or chairs and boxes were used.

Attendants during childbirth practiced modesty to the point of covering the mother with a large sheet of buckskin. Later, these conventions of modesty made Ojibwa women reluctant to deal with white physicians, especially if they were men. Traditionally, male or female shamans were consulted only when it seemed that a mother might die. Shamans were paid with buckskins, items of clothing, or kitchen utensils.

Death of Ojibwa mothers during childbirth was fairly common. One account stated that this was often due to an improperly-expelled placenta, especially if the placenta was pulled or hurried so that pieces remained behind and the mother developed an infection. Herbal beverages which aided labour and delivery were also thought to aid in expelling the placenta, but additional herbs were used when needed.

When herbs combined with a woman's willpower were unsuccessful, women stretched, pressed their abdomens with their hands, and tickled their throats in order to gag. If these remedies failed, special midwives were consulted. Certain midwives were said to be able to deliver stillbirths and to remove leftover pieces of the placenta or the entire placenta with their hands. Traditionally, the placenta was hung near the main trunk of a tree at a height which would not be reached by animals. More recently, it was buried or burned.

Newborn Ojibwa infants were bathed in a solution of boiled herbs in a special birchbark container. This bath was known to encourage strength, and could be repeated whenever mothers wished. Babies were then wrapped in squirrel and weasel hides from the waist up, packed in dried swamp moss covered with rabbit skins from the waist up, packed in dried swamp moss covered with rabbit skins from the waist down, and placed in birchbark containers or tied to cradleboards with buckskin over wrappings and thongs. A newborn infant's nose and ears might be pierced so that ornaments would be inserted, but this was said to have no significance other than decoration. Shortly after a successful birth, the baby's family and their friends gathered for a feast where tobacco pipes were smoked.

Indians of the Great Plains of North America followed widespread North American customs with respect to childbirth. Plains Indian women assumed a kneeling position and were assisted by one or more midwives, one of whom cut the umbilical cord. The placenta was normally wrapped in hides and hung in a tree. The umbilical cord was dried, placed in a decorated skin bag, and hung around the infant's neck (*see also* CHILD REARING). Plains Indian babies were not always bathed immediately after birth. Instead, they might be dried with dry-rotted wood powder or moss and placed in a hide bag stuffed with moss. They were often nursed for four or five years.

Among the Blackfoot, who were Algonquian-speaking hunters of the northern Plains, large families were very common. Women who were several months pregnant wore a broad, adjustable rawhide belt for support while they worked and rode horseback. If labour began while a Blackfoot band was travelling, the woman dropped back, gave birth, and rejoined her band about two or three hours later. When bands were camped, birth took place inside the family tipi with one or more women and an elderly midwife in attendance. Blackfoot women in labour grasped one of the poles which supported the tipi while an assistant held them around the waist. They were also given an herbal drink which eased their pain and facilitated the delivery. The midwife in attendance handled the actual delivery, and then laced the mother in her rawhide belt.

Newborn Blackfoot babies were washed, diapered with moss or soft, dry-rotted wood, and wrapped in soft skins. Significantly, cradleboards were less common among the Blackfoot than among other North American tribes. Pieces of a Blackfoot baby's umbilical cord were put aside to be dried and placed in a decorated buckskin case. These little cases were made in the shape of snakes for boys and lizards for girls because it was known that lizards and snakes never became ill, and had long lives. Blackfoot mothers often resumed their normal duties the day after childbirth. Like many other Plains tribes, they nursed their babies for four, five and even six years, or until they again became pregnant.

Among the Interior Salish, who were a group of Salish-speaking hunters, fisherpeople, and gatherers of the interior of British Columbia in Canada, pregnant women and their husbands observed many taboos. For example, in order to prevent babies from being deformed, pregnant women were not allowed to see anything which was ugly or deformed. There were also a large number of taboos surrounding the preparation and consumption of food.

Immediately before giving birth, women from all of the Interior Salish tribes went into seclusion. Lillooet women were assisted by midwives, but unless labour was difficult, women from the other tribes gave birth alone or with the help of their husbands. Various accounts state that Interior Salish women worked until just a few hours before childbirth, handled births with relative ease, and resumed their normal activities a few hours later. Fathers removed taboos which had been placed on them by bathing immediately after a birth. Some restrictions for mothers were also removed at this time, but others were added and observed for several more weeks.

The Kwakiutl, who were Wakashan-speaking fisher-people of the west coast of British Columbia in Canada, felt that the first nine months of development before birth were central. During this time, both spouses observed strict taboos in order to insure the health of their baby. For example, Kwakiutl fathers avoided birds and seals with blood on their heads, seals with singed fur, and all things which had been injured by humans. Then, everyone who was concerned with a baby's welfare participated in the same taboos and ceremonies after its birth. For example, Kwakiutl midwives and relatives uttered prayers asking that the baby be spared from harm.

Among the Hopi, who were Uto-Aztecan-speaking farmers of the American Southwest, couples continued to have intercourse throughout a woman's pregnancy. This was compared to the principle of crop irrigation, and helped make childbirth easier. However, people who walked in front of a woman in the advanced stages of pregnancy could cause a difficult delivery.

During pregnancy, Hopi women were prohibited from holding children on their laps or breathing into the faces of small children lest these children waste away; they were not allowed to tan or dye hides lest they injure their babies and spoil the hides; and they could not look at snakes lest their babies crawl up instead of down during delivery. Husbands of pregnant women were not allowed to injure any animal lest this also injure their babies; they were not allowed to cut off the foot of any living creature lest this cause babies to be born club-footed or without hands; and they could not tie a rope tightly around the necks of sheep or burros lest this cause the umbilical cord to become looped around their babies' necks.

Hopi women carried water, ground corn, and otherwise worked industriously throughout pregnancy. This kept them trim and prepared them for labour. Men rubbed their wives with weasel skins and fed them raw weasel meat in order to help babies be like weasels and slip out swiftly during birth.

During labour, Hopi women were assisted by a medicine man, a midwife, and sometimes also by female relatives. The medicine man massaged the mother's belly and moved her baby into the correct position for delivery. The supernatural power in his hands helped the woman a great deal. The woman then knelt on the floor on her hands and knees over a pile of sand which had been especially prepared for the birth, and pushed downward. The medicine man, midwife, and other assistants took turns standing over the woman and helping her to push down. If labour was difficult, heavier pressure was applied, but a woman's body was never "opened" in order to save her baby.

Hopi midwives cut the umbilical cord, folded it over, and tied it approximately a finger's length from the naval with a piece of string made form the mother's hair. This kept fresh air from entering the baby's belly and causing death. The baby was then wrapped in a cloth and placed near the fire.

Immediately after delivery, Hopi mothers were given juniper tea to drink and juniper twigs to chew. This hastened expulsion of the placenta. If necessary, the midwife tugged gently on the placenta cord while an assistant stood behind the mother, held her around the waist, and shook her. The mother might also be instructed to stick her fingers down her throat and gag until the placenta was completely expelled. Once the placenta was expelled, the mother sat on a low birth stool by the fire and allowed her blood to drip onto the sand below. Another drink of juniper tea helped to cleanse her womb. Soon, the midwife bathed the mother in yucca suds, wrapped her in a blanket, fed her warm cornmeal mush, and helped her to lie on her side in front of the fire. This sideways position helped to fit the mother's pelvic bones back into place. The midwife then placed the placenta in an old basket, swept up the sand and added this to the basket, sprinkled the basket with cornmeal, and asked one of the assistants to throw the basket on the placenta pile at the edge of the village. It was important that no one ever step on a placenta because this would cause the person who did so to become ill.

As soon as a Hopi mother was settled and the various by-products of delivery had been removed, attention was focused on the baby. The baby's aunt (mother's sister) or another close female relative was summoned, and she came joyfully in order to assure good luck and a cheerful spirit for the baby. In her arms she carried cornmeal, two ears of white corn, water, a piece of yucca root, and baby wrappings. After greeting the baby with tender words, she bathed it, rubbed it with ashes from juniper or sage brush in order to make its skin smooth and its hair grow in the right places, and pierced its ears and tied them with thread. She then rested the baby on her bare knees and announced its identity and membership in its mother's clan. Then, she placed the baby's arms at its side, wrapped it in a warm baby blanket together with a cedar bark diaper, and laid it in a wicker cradle. Following this, she sat for a long time in front of the fire with the cradle on her knees. Finally, she laid the cradle on the floor next to the baby's mother and placed an ear of white corn on each side. One of these ears represented the baby, while the other represented the mother.

Very early the next morning, the aunt drew four horizontal lines on each of the four walls of the birth chamber. These lines were made with cornmeal and represented the "house" within which the mother must remain for twenty days. Every five days, one layer of the lines would be removed during a small ceremony of bathing and prayers to the sun. After the lines had been drawn, the aunt fed the mother corn cooked with juniper twigs, and perhaps also unsalted gravy or milkweed. This helped the mother's milk to flow freely.

Before the sun had risen, women from the Hopi Sun Clan propped two poles against the eastern door of the birth chamber and covered these poles with a blanket. This prevented the sun from entering the birth chamber until the baby had been presented to the Sun God. That same morning, many meighbors came to congratulate the mother. They brought food and expressed good wishes for the baby's future. The baby's godmother then bathed the baby, rubbed it with juniper ashes or special clay, and presented it to the mother for breastfeeding.

It was said that Hopi babies were very wise and realized when their milk was being stolen. Thus, when Hopi mothers had no milk, their babies were fed by women who did not have nursing babies of their own, lest these other babies become nervous and sick over the theft of their milk. Babies whose mothers had no milk might also be fed finely-ground sweet corn mixed with stewed fruit juice, or a little unsalted gravy.

Each morning, Hopi babies were unbound and removed from their cradles, bathed, rubbed with baby ashes, rediapered with fresh cedar bark, and rebound to their cradles. In addition, their cedar bark diapers were changed three or four times a day. Nursing always took place while Hopi babies were still bound to their cradles. In order to hide crying from evil spirits, saliva from a baby's mouth might be rubbed on the nape of its neck.

When a Hopi baby's navel cord fell off, it was tied to an arrow which was thrust into the ceiling of the birth chamber. If the baby died, this arrow provided a resting place for the baby's spirit until the spirit was able to re-enter the mother's womb and be reborn.

For twenty days after childbirth, Hopi women followed many rules. During this time, all of their food was cooked in juniper leaves, cold or salty food and beverages were avoided in order to prevent blood clots from forming in their wombs, and the birth chamber fire was kept going at all times. Since the birth chamber fire belonged to the new baby, it was not used to light other fires lest the baby become upset over the theft of its fire. If the birth chamber fire accidently went out, it was rekindled immediately and the number of that day was not counted. No food was cooked in the coals of this fire, since that would cause the baby to meddle with fire when it grew older.

Hopi fathers were prohibited from having sexual intercourse with their wives for forty days after childbirth. To do so caused another baby to be formed from the blood which remained in the mother's womb. This could worry the existing baby so much that it might be ruined for life. Husbands who attempted intercourse with their wives during that time were diciplined by the wife's sisters and clan sisters. Intercourse with women other than a man's wife was also known to cause the baby to become ill.

Native tribes of the southeastern United States observed many taboos with respect to childbirth. The Cherokees, who were Iroquoian-speaking farmers, hunters, fisherpeople, and gatherers, were the largest nation of Indians in the American Southeast at the time of contact with whites. They believed that babies resulted from a mixture of substances from both parents. Conception was thought to occur only after a mutual climax, but parental substances might mix at any time. If these parental substances mixed soon after intercourse, babies were born earlier than if the substances mixed several months later.

As soon as Cherokee women realized that they were pregnant, they informed their families, their friends, and the community. Then, accompanied by their husbands and a native priest, they visited a spot near water where the priest foretold the sex of the baby, its health, and its progress. These visits were repeated at regular intervals. At the same time, women drank an herbal mixture meant to insure an easy delivery and the health of their babies.

Cherokee women were subject to many food restrictions throughout pregnancy. Among these restrictions were rules against eating squirrels because squirrels climb up trees and might encourage babies to climb up instead of down during birth; against eating speckled trout lest babies be born with birthmarks; against eating rabits lest this encourage babies to have large eyes or to sleep with their eyes open; and against eating salt because salt makes flesh swell. Like Micmac women, Cherokee women avoided loitering in doorways during pregnancy because this was known to cause babies to descend slowly at birth. They likewise avoided anything tied around their necks because this caused umbilical cords to become wrapped around their babies' necks.

Southeastern women usually gave birth in menstrual huts in the company of one or more midwives. Newborn infants were dipped in water or anointed with water from a nearby creek or stream, rubbed with bear oil in order to toughen their skins and discourage insects, and then nursed. Bear oil treatments were continued throughout infancy.

Twins born to tribes in the Southeast were regarded as likely to have special powers and to become priests or witches. This was especially true of the younger twin. Girls and boys were treated differently from the moment of birth. For example, girls were wrapped in deer or bison skins, while boys were wrapped in cougar skins. Soft moss served as a diaper. Most Southeastern tribes used cradleboards to shape the skulls of infants, and this was said to enhance vision.

Southeastern fathers fasted for four days following childbirth. Mothers could not prepare their husband's meals, sleep with them, or even touch them for approximately three months after giving birth. At one month of age, babies were bathed in fresh water; in winter they might be rolled in snow to make them strong. Southeastern babies were nursed on demand, and were weaned when mothers again became pregnant.

Among the ancient Aztecs, who were Nahuatl-speaking farmers with a state-level society in the Valley of Mexico, pregnant woman received attentive care. News of a woman's pregnancy was the signal for rejoicing in both families. A banquet was held in the pregnant woman's honour, and she was placed under the protection of the goddesses of fertility, health, childbirth, and midwives. With great ceremony, family elders then selected an appropriate midwife. The midwife went to her client's house and examined the client's belly in order to see how the baby lay. She instructed the pregnant woman's household to give the woman anything she wanted, and explained taboos which the woman and her husband must follow. For example, pregnant Aztec women were not to become angry or frustrated; they were not to chew chicle lest their babies' mouths swell to the point that the babies could not nurse; they were not to look at red objects lest their babies be born askew; they were not to view an eclipse without an obsidian knife next to their skin lest their babies be born with a harelip; and they were not to venture out at night without a bit of ash hidden in their clothing lest they be frightened by ghosts. Aztec fathers were not to encounter phantoms lest their babies be born with heart disease.

An Aztec midwife was generally in charge of her client's household during childbirth. She prepared the food and steam-baths, massaged her client's belly, and if necessary, administered medicines which caused strong contractions. One of these medicines was made from a plant, while the other was made from the tail of an opossum. When things did not go well, the midwife shut herself in a room with her client and prayed to the goddesses of childbirth. If a baby died *in utero*, the midwife dissected it with a flint knife.

Aztec midwives cut the umbilical cord and then spoke to each newborn baby at length. Boys were instructed to become fierce warriors, while girls were instructed to become good housewives. Then, babies were washed while the midwife prayed to the goddess of water to purify their lives.

Successful births led to a complex series of ceremonies for an Aztec family. Older women of the family thanked the midwife, who responded with a poetic speech. Special orators greeted the baby and distributed presents, while another group of elders answered the orators with elaborate speeches. The new mother was compared to a goddess, while her baby was compared to a necklace, a rare jewel, and an exquisite feather. The glorious history of the baby's family was recounted in exact detail. Meanwhile, the baby's father summoned a magician from the local clan temple. With elaborate care, the magician studied a horoscope some twenty feet in length in order to determine whether the baby had been born under good or bad signs, and the lucky and unlucky days in its life (see illustration). Later, the midwife presented the baby with its name during an elaborate baptism ceremony.

Aztec women who died in childbirth were carried by the sun to his palace in the heavens. These women were considered to be as honourable as warriors who died in battle or as religious sacrifices. A deceased woman's body was first washed and dressed in her best new clothes. It was then carried by her husband to the courtyard of the temple of goddesses called "the heavenly women," where it was buried at sunset. Accompanying the husband on the way to the courtyard was a procession of all the midwives and older women of the area, each of whom carried a sword and shield and made the battle cries of warriors. As the procession wound along the streets, warriors and students from the local college tried to steal the woman's body. Later, warriors also tried to steal the body once it had been buried. Aztec warriors believed that the hair and middle finger of the left hand of a woman who had died in childbirth gave them great strength and blinded their enemies when carried into battle.

**South America**

In native South America, childbirth customs involved a variety of magical observances. These observances were focused on mothers and babies, but could also be extended to fathers and other relatives concerned with a baby's welfare. The *couvade* (*see also* CHILD REARING) was nearly universal in South America. This custom involved a series of taboos for the father, and sometimes also for other relatives. These taboos were followed before, during and after childbirth. They usually included restrictions on food and sex, but could also involve restrictions on hunting and other activities. In extreme cases, South American fathers remained quietly in their hammocks, and even re-enacted the process of childbirth. In each case, the couvade symbolized magical ties between parents and children and was meant to insure the survival of infants. Some South American tribes extended the couvade to their dogs. In that case, owners abstained from foods and certain activities during the pregnancy and post-partum periods of valuable female dogs.

Native women in South America gave birth in a variety of positions. In some tribes, childbirth took place in hammocks. In others it took place in kneeling, squatting, or half-sitting positions, or while grasping a kind of crossbar of frame which was erected for the event.

South American Indian women were often assisted by female relatives and their husbands during labour and delivery. In some cases, skilled midwives were available. For example, among the Inca, who were Quechuan-speaking farmers with a state-level empire which extended from mid-Ecuador to mid-Peru, midwives moved babies into the correct position for delivery by massaging women's bellies. Inca midwives were even able to produce abortion by this technique. Among the Mapuche, who were Araucanian-speaking farmers of central Chile, midwives handled difficult deliveries with plant medicines, manipulation, and surgery. If necessary, Mapuche midwives practiced cephalotomy, or surgical dissection of the baby's head.

Among the Sirionó, who were Tupí-Guarani-speaking hunters, gatherers, and cultivators in Eastern Bolivia, it was agreed that pregnancy was related to sexual intercourse, However, the exact details of conception were unknown. Babies were thought to be minature replicas of themselves from the moment of conception. Thus, they simply grew in size and could be encouraged to grow by sexual intercourse throughout pregnancy.

The Sirionó did not practice abortion or infanticide. In aboriginal times, miscarriages were rare. Those miscarriages which did occur were known to be caused by the breaking of food taboos, overwork, or extreme fright. The remains of miscarriages were discarded without ceremony while both parents underwent three days of mourning rites which resembled the rites for successful births. As part of these rites, parents wore feathers in their hair and were scarified on the legs.

A Sirionó woman realized she was pregnant when she no longer menstruated and her breasts began to swell. Sometimes, she dreamed the news about being pregnant. Pregnant women were allowed to eat all vegetables, fruits, and fish, but were required to abstain from eating certain meats. For example, they could not eat coati meat lest babies be born with sores and very long heads; they could not eat howler monkeys, macaws, or guans lest babies cry too much; they could not eat armadillos lest babies inherit the armadillo's tendency to be afraid; they could not eat night monkeys lest babies inherit this animal's tendency to stay awake all night; they could not eat anteaters, porcupines, or honeybears lest babies be born clubfooted, they could not eat turtle eggs lest they have miscarriages or die in childbirth; and they could not eat jaguars lest babies be stillborn. Sirionó fathers were prohibited from eating many of the same animals, but in reality tended to observe only the taboos on howler monkeys and anteaters. Husbands and wives were also prohibited from eating double manioc roots or double ears of corn lest these foods produce twins. They were likewise prohibited form eating twisted or deformed plants lest babies be born clubfooted. On the other hand, Sirionó mothers were encouraged to eat tapir and peccary meat because these animals were strong and industrious. Women continued to work at all normal tasks until just before delivery.

Sirionó women gave birth in their hammocks inside of the large communal huts constructed by each band. Labour lasted from one to three hours. If laobur began during the day, the husband went hunting to look for an animal to use as a namesake for the baby. Since hunting was impossible after dark, babies born at night might be named after a personal characteristic.

At the onset of labour, a Sirionó woman completed the preparations for childbirth by herself. These preparations involved using a digging stick to loosen the soil beneath her hammock and stringing a rope above the hammock. A woman might also spread ashes over the softened soil beneath her hammock. She then reclined in her hammock for the duration of the labour.

Sirionó women received no assistance during labour and delivery except when twins were born, or when husbands lit small fires at night for extra visibility. Births were well-attended by women and children, but not by men. A crowd of female observers always gathered around a woman's hammock and spent the time discussing their own experiences with childbirth or speculating about the sex of the baby.

At delivery, Sirionó babies slid headfirst off the strings of the mother's hammock and onto the soft earth a few inches below. The shock of falling to the ground was enough to induce most babies to breathe. Mothers then got out of their hammocks and knelt to one side of their babies on their hands and knees until the placenta was expelled. This normally took about ten minutes. If a woman had difficulty expelling her placenta, she was pounded on her back until the placenta appeared. The woman then picked up her baby and began to clean it. At the same time, she pressed the baby's hips inward and its head from front to back in order to make it beautiful. Soon, the mother bathed her baby in a calabash shell full of water and offered it her breast.

In order to acknowledge paternity, Sirionó fathers were obliged to cut the umbilical cords of their newborn babies with a bamboo knife. If babies were born at night when their fathers were nearby, fathers immediately cut the umbilical cord. If babies were born during the day, it was necessary to wait until their fathers had returned from hunting. In either case, the ritual was the same. The father first bathed, and then squatted on the ground next to his baby. While the mother held the umbilical cord, the father cut the cord with a bamboo knife about ten centimeters from the placenta. As the mother continued to hold the cord, the father cut off a piece about fifteen centimeters long and tied this to the underside of the mother's hammock. This kept the baby from crying. The remaining twenty centimeters or so of cord were left attached to the baby and were not tied. The father then retired quietly to his hammock and began his role in the couvade.

Since no one else was allowed to do this, Sirionó

mothers cleaned up all evidence of childbirth. This was done as soon as the baby was washed and fed. The mother buried all such material in the ground or placed it in a basket which was later discarded in the bush. She then continued to sit on the ground and tend her baby for several more hours before retiring to her hammock.

Siriono babies were thought to be profoundly linked to their parents for at least three days after birth. Since they were also highly susceptible to illness and death during this period, they were affected by everything their parents did. Thus, parents of a newborn Sirionó baby remained close to their hammocks and refrained from going outside unless absolutely necessary. In addition, the parents were subjected to a number of food taboos. For example, they could not eat coati or jaguar meat lest their baby contract sores; they could not eat paca lest their baby's hair fall out; and they could not eat papaya lest their baby contract diarrhea.

On the day following the birth of a Sirionó baby, the parents were subjected to an important purification ritual. This ritual removed old blood and helped to keep the baby well. As part of the ritual, both parents were scarified on the legs with the canine incisor of a rat squirrel. Before being scarified, each parent took turns puting on coati teeth necklaces, and winding the baby's new sling around their necks. For this occasion, the baby's sling was died with red dye called urucu. The parents' legs were then scarified, washed, and covered with urucu. The same day, the baby was given a haircut in the traditional Sirionó style. The baby's hair which had been cut off was then incorporated into a necklace worn by the mother.

Two days after the birth of a Sirionó baby, both parents received identical decorations. These decorations were applied by a co-wife or potential wife of the husband, and were extended to all members of the family who were closely related to the baby. As a first step, the parent's hair was cut and decorated with feathers. Then, urucu-dyed string was wound around their arms, legs, and necks. Finally, urucu was smeared on their arms, legs, and faces.

On the third or fourth day following the birth of a Sirionó baby, parents and all others with a close relationship to the baby underwent rites which officially ended the couvade. During these rites, all participants were smeared with urucu. The parents were also given quill necklaces. Then, the parents and all others undergoing these rites took ashes from a dying fire and went our into the bush to gather firewood. For the first time, the mother carried the baby in its new sling. She also carried a calabash shell full of water out into the bush and then brought it back to the hut. As the group walked, they scattered ashes along the trail. When the group returned to their hut, a new fire was built with the wood they had collected in the bush, and the mother bathed her baby in the calabash shell full of water which she had carried out into the bush and then brought back to the hut. As soon as these rites were completed, both parents resumed normal behavior.

The Jívaro, who were Jívaro-speaking gardners and hunters at the foot of the Andes in Ecuador and Peru, understood the relationship between sex and pregnancy. People estimated that a woman would give birth about a year and a half after marriage. This same interval was estimated for subsequent births. Jívaro women used plant abortifacients, but the only method of contraception was sympathetic magic. To combat sterility, Jívaro women drank the powdered leg-bone of a fox dissolved in Manioc beer. It was said that families like to have a son first, and then a daughter. This provided a hunting partner for the father as soon as possible.

During pregnancy, Jívaro women often felt cravings for special food. Unlike anyone else, they sometimes ate small amounts of pottery clay or earth taken from anthills. During the last week or so of pregnancy, they were forbidden to eat certain birds.

A Jívaro woman was assisted by her husband and her mother during childbirth. In wet weather, childbirth occurred inside of the house, but in good weather, it occurred in the privacy of a woman's garden. Women in labour squatted on a clean banana leaf and hung their arms over a crossbar. This crossbar was about two and one-half feet high and was supported by two sidepoles. While one assistant held a woman's arms, the other helped her to push down. At delivery, Jívaro babies were received onto the banana leaf which had been placed below the crossbar.

Unlike most South American Indians, Jívaro fathers did not participate in a strict couvade. Instead, they were allowed to go hunting and to carry out other normal tasks. However, they were also required to observe certain restrictions on food and sex. For example, until babies could walk, fathers avoided all plant and animal foods containing "magic stuff" or power. Since these foods affected a baby's spirit, they could easily harm the baby by becoming associated with the baby's father.

If a Jívaro man had no other wives, he was obligated to do most of his wife's work for about two weeks after childbirth. Thus, he worked in his wife's garden, dug manioc and washed it in a nearby stream, and fetched water. Meanwhile, his wife rested for about two weeks and was allowed to do only little cooking. It was believed that women who did not rest after childbirth would contract lengthy illnesses. Food taboos for both parents after the birth of a baby included animal viscera and certain birds. The Jívaro believed that if either parent engaged in extramarital sex while their baby was small, the baby would die.

Infanticide among the Jívaro was not common. It was practiced only in case of deformity, and by some unmarried women. In either case, it was carried out by simply crushing babies with the foot.

Newborn Jívaro babies were wrapped in a loose cloth. When this cloth became soiled, a clean section of the cloth was dipped in water and used to wipe the baby. After this, the baby was wrapped in a fresh cloth. Soiled baby cloths were washed, dried over the fire, and reused.

Jívaro babies who cried too much were thought to have a fever. This fever could be cooled by bathing the baby in lukewarm water. If crying awakened mothers while they were asleep, babies might be scolded or slapped.

A few days after birth, Jívaro babies were given a mild hallucinogenic drug. This enabled them to see a protective vision which would aid their survival. Drug treatments were often repeated whenever babies became ill. About the same time as the first drug experience, Jívaro babies were given a name. A few days later, all babies had their ears pierced.

About two weeks after giving birth, Jívaro mothers returned to work in their gardens. Since this work was difficult, babies were left at home in small hammocks near their mother's beds. If babies cried, they might remain unattended until their mothers returned. Daughters four years of age and older were often given the job of watching babies while women worked in the gardens. In that case, babies who cried might be picked up and sung to or fed a little chewed manioc.

The birth of a new baby did not cause Jivaro mothers to wean older children. Thus, mothers often nursed children of different ages. Wet nurses were unknown. Mothers who did not have enough milk chewed boiled manioc and fed this to their babies along with a little beer. Weaning took place when a child was six or seven years old. To wean children, Jívaro mothers smeared hot pepper on their breasts.

Among the Aymara, who were Aymara-speaking farmers of Bolivia and Peru, birth control was not practiced and abortion and infanticide were frowned upon. However, unmarried woman occasionally practiced abortion by drinking a strongly laxative tea or rolling heavy stones across their bellies. Infanticide was practiced only on deformed babies. In that case, babies were simply allowed to die.

Aymara women recognized pregnancy by the absence of menstruation. Pregnant women did not follow strict food taboos, but they were required to observe important restrictions on behaviour. For example, they were not allowed to see dead people or animals lest their babies become ill; they were not allowed to visit cemetaries or to handle human bones lest babies be born deformed; they were not allowed to handle wool lest they have hairy babies; and they refrained from weaving lest the winding of yarn cause their babies' umbilical cords to become twisted.

Dreams and coca leaf divination were used to predict the sex of an Aymara baby. In case of doubt, magic combined with offerings to a shrine produced the desired sex. Among the Bolivian Aymara, cooking utensils placed under the mother's bed produced a girl, while farm implements produced a boy.

Aymara women gave birth inside of the main house of their family compound. They were assisted by their husbands, and by female relatives and professional midwives. Among the Aymara, midwives were elderly people of either sex who were paid for their services.

The day of an Aymara baby's birth determined its success throughout life. When labour began, the baby's health was assured by passing glowing coals around the house. To ease delivery and protect the mother and baby from evil spirits, a knife was thrust into the floor near the doorway of the house.

Aymara midwives moved babies into the proper position for delivery by massaging the mother's belly and tumbling her in a blanket. If labour was slow, the mother was given medicine to make it proceed faster. No medication was given for pain.

Aymara mothers did not remove their clothing during the final stages of labour, but crouched and were supported by their husbands or female relatives. Immediately before delivery, a woman's belt was tightened above her belly, If newborn babies did not breathe, midwives breathed down their throats. The baby's umbilical cord was cut with an obsidian knife and tied with cotton string. It was then supported by a string tied around the baby's neck, and the navel was covered with a cotton pad. To speed expulsion of the placenta, the mother's belt was tightened. If the placenta did not appear of its own accord, the midwife pulled it out. Mothers were then rubbed with herbs to prevent them from catching cold.

Aymara midwives divined a baby's future by floating a piece of the placenta in a basin of water. Placentas were considered dangerous and liable to injure the hands and eyes. Thus, once a placenta had been disposed of, the hands of people who had handled it were covered with llama fat and red ochre. In parts of Bolivia, placentas were covered with flowers and buried in a shady location along with miniature farm implements for a boy, or tiny cooking utensils for a girl. In Peru, placentas were placed inside of two new pottery bowls and burned. The ashes were then buried in a shady location or used as medicine. Aymara midwives received extra pay for disposing of placentas.

About six to twelve hours after birth, Aymara babies were nursed for the first time. They were then fed whenever they were hungry. Aymara babies were not bound to cradles, but were diapered with old rags and wrapped with a belt. They were then carried in a cloth slung over the mother's back. Diapers were changed about two or three times a day. On the first day after birth which was considered fortunate for this event, babies were washed by the midwife or by a relative.

Unlike most South American Indians, Aymara fathers did not participate in a couvade. In Bolivia, Aymara mothers did not go into confinement after childbirth, but in Peru, they were confined to the house for a week. During this time, the waste products of mothers and babies were placed in a hole in the floor of the house near the doorway. Throwing these wastes outside in the sun was known to make babies ill. At the conclusion of confinement, all blankets and other articles contaminated by the birth were washed. Water was poured into the hole near the doorway and the hole was filled. In addition, the mother's house and clothes were disinfected with the smoke of certain herbs. For a full month after childbirth, these mothers were prohibited from washing with water. They were then required to wash their hands and hair with a special solution of herbs.

The Timbira were a group of Gê-speaking farmers, collectors, and hunters in northeastern Brazil. Among some of these groups, parents observed a number of taboos as soon as women realized they were pregnant. Many of these taboos concerned food. Childbirth took place in a couple's platform bed, which was partitioned off for the occasion.

During labour, Timbira women were assisted by elderly female relatives. Husbands were sometimes present, but gave no direct help and avoided looking at their wives. More often, husbands speeded delivery by walking around the hut.

Timbira couples participated in couvade regulations which were common in that geographic area. For

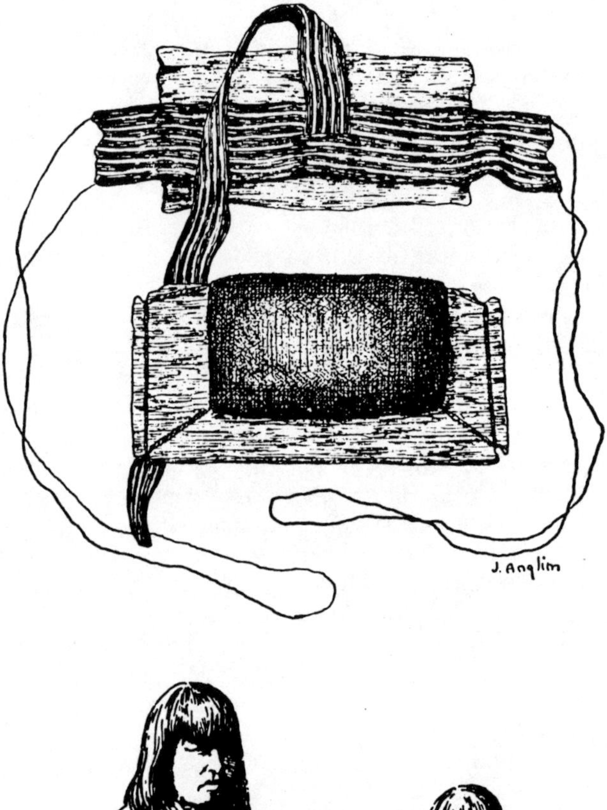

*Handbook of South American Indians.*

Panoan (Shipibo) mother and children. The head of the infant is undergoing artificial deformation by use of a device illustrated above.

example, until a baby's navel cord fell off, both parents remained quietly in their compartment inside of the matrilineal family hut. During this time, the parents used scratching sticks, refrained from painting or decorating themselves, avoided cutting their hair, and did not eat meat. Fathers were especially prohibited from working hard or otherwise exerting themselves. Since these observances insured the safety of the baby, they were also extended to all other men who had recently had sexual intercourse with the mother. Thus, as many as four men might simutaneously observe the couvade after the birth of a Timbira baby.

Among the Mataco, who were Mataco-speaking collectors, hunters, gardeners, and fisherpeople of the GranChaco in South America, abortion and infanticide were common. Unmarried women induced abortion or committed infanticide as a matter of course, while married women practiced abortion during initial pregnancies because this was thought to help future deliveries. Abortions were induced during the third or fourth month of pregnancy by abdominal trauma. To effect this, a friend beat or pressed on a woman's belly until the baby was dead. Twins were often killed at birth because they were considered a bad omen, and also because it was difficult for Mataco women to nurse more than one baby at a time. Sterility was thought to be due to an obstruction in the uterus. Since this was caused by sourcery, it was difficult to cure.

As soon as a Mataco woman realized she was pregnant, both parents abstained from foods and activities which would harm their baby's health, influence its character, or cause a difficult delivery. Birds, certain animals, and certain parts of animals were included in the list of foods which were taboo.

During labour, Mataco women were assisted by female relatives and friends. An older woman squatted on the ground while the woman in labour sat on her thighs. To ease her pain, the woman in labour gripped a pole which was positioned in front of her. Delivery usually took place in this position. Difficulty during labour was known to be due to sourcery or negligence on the part of the husband. When labour did not go well, assistants pressed on the lower part of a woman's belly. Umbilical cords were not cut until the placenta had been expelled.

Information on the couvade for Mataco fathers is incomplete, but it is known that men in other tribes in the Gran Chaco participated in a strict couvade.

The Ona of Tierra del Fuego (see above) were aware of the relationship between intercourse and pregnancy. It was felt that intercourse throughout pregnancy was necessary for babies to develop. Women gave birth in a half-sitting position and then placed newborn babies in a special hide sack (*see also* CHILD REARING). There was no requirement for Ona mothers or babies to bathe, but mothers often washed themselves with wet clay after delivery. Babies were nursed whenever they were hungry.

For about a month after childbirth, Ona mothers abstained from certain foods. Fathers simply ate as little as possible. An Ona baby's dried umbilical cord was placed in a small pouch. Then, when the baby was old enough to walk, the father caught a certain bird and held it while the baby tied the pouch around the bird's neck. The bird was then placed in the baby's hands, and the baby was instructed to let it go. As the bird flew away, it was said that all birds of that species would protect the baby for the rest of its life.

KATHRYN T. MOLOHON

**CHILD REARING**. Before contact with Europeans, Indians of North, Meso, and South America displayed a wide range of cultural patterns. Variations in child rearing practices among different groups were often linked to needs created by differences in ecology, economic structure, and social organization. Occasionally, individualized child rearing practices were simply the result of tradition.

In general, primary care of infants and very young children was assigned to a child's biological mother, who was then frequently assisted by others in the immediate and extended family group. People who belonged to band-level, tribal, or chiefdom societies tended to lavish great affection on children, and to handle them with ease. Often, as for example among the matrilineal Pueblos and Navajos of the American Southwest, or among the matrilineal Tlingit of the Northwest Coast of North America, children had more than one social mother upon whom they could depend for affection and support. In such cases the biological mother's brother often played a strong role in discipline, in the transmission of important cultural traditions, and in the inheritance of property.

**Cradles and slings.** In band-level, tribal, and chiefdom societies, the management of children tended to be organized around the need for Indian women and men to remain economically productive while caring for children. One of the most visible indications of this principle was the cradleboard or "cradle", an ingenious device providing warmth, safety, and security (see illustrations). Indian cradles also allowed infants to ride or be placed at approximately eye-level with adults, and thus to observe adult activities from a sophisticated viewpoint. Since New World peoples are thought to have originated in Asia, it is interestng to note that cradles similar to those of North and South American cultures have been observed among native peoples of Siberia, including the Mansi (Voguls), who were Ugrian-speaking settled hunters and fisherpeople of the Ob River Basin in northwestern Siberia, the Nivkhi (Gilyaks), who were Paleo-Siberian-speaking fishing and marine-hunting people of the Amur River region and Sakhalin Island in southeastern Siberia, and the Evens (Lamuts), who were Tungus-speaking reindeer breeders and hunters of northeastern Siberia. Just as North and South American Indians often used special cradles for transporting children on horseback, the Evens had special cradles for transporting infants on the backs of reindeer.

Among Indians of the North American Subarctic, the East (including the northeastern Woodlands), the Plains and Prairies, the Plateau, and parts of the Northwest Coast, cradles usually consisted of a flat board or framework with a footrest and head hoop or bow. Such cradles could be carried on a mother's back via straps over her shoulders or forehead with the infant facing backwards. These cradles could also be leaned against a wall, hunt from a house post or tree, and carried on a horse. On the Plains, thick pieces of stiff rawhide were sometimes substituted for wooden cradles. Birchbark cradles which seated an infant with its legs hanging free were common among groups living in the North American Subarctic, including Athapaskan-speaking hunters and gatherers of the interior of northwestern Canada and Alaska. In California, the Great Basin, the Southwest, and parts of Mesoamerica, cradles often consisted of flat frameworks of plant stems or reeds which were woven or laced together like basketry. In parts of the Northwest Coast, babies were carried in boxes made of doweled and sewn boards, or in dugout wooden containers. Finally, in southwestern Oregon and northern California, a basketry seat which allowed an infant's legs to hang free was commonly used.

In South America, cradleboards were represented in designs on pottery from the early archaeological periods of Peru. The Inca, who were Quechuan-speaking agriculturalists with a state-level empire reaching from mid-Ecuador to mid-Chile, used cradles consisting of a board or slatted back with four low feet. Folded shawls provided cushioning, and two hoops crossed over an infant's head and another over its feet so that blankets could be draped over the cradle without danger of suffocation. Inca cradles either rested on their feet, or were carried on mothers' backs by shawls tied over their chests.

The Ona, who were Chon (Tshon)-speaking hunters, gatherers, and fisherpeople of the island of Tierra del Fuego at the southern tip of South America, placed newborns in a baby sack constructed from a rolled hide lined with furs. They also made special eyeshades for babies. At the end of three months, Ona babies were placed on ladder-back cradles. The nearby Tehuelche, who were Chon-speaking hunters of Patagonia, used two kinds of cradles. One of these was flat, was apparently of ladder-back construction, and could be swung from the roofs of skin tents by thongs tied to each of its four corners. The other type was a curved wicker cradle used for transporting children on horseback.

The Araucanians, who were a group of Araucanian-speaking agricultural tribes in central Chile, used both portable cradleboards and basketry cradles suspended from the ceilings of houses. The portable cradles of at least one tribe in this group, the Mapuche, had head hoops and were constructed of two longitudinal arms connected by either boards or netted frameworks. The Huarpe, who were Huarpean-speaking agricultural-

Drawing by George Catlin of a Seminole mother and her infant. Note the charm or toy suspended from the head hoop of the cradle board.

ists, hunters, and gatherers of western Argentina had cradles in which infants slept, and which were also used for transporting infants on women's backs by way of straps passing over the forehead.

When cradleboards were used, Indian infants could be wrapped, bound, or tied in various ways. Together with footrests, head hoops provided protection in case cradles fell. Also various coverings could be draped or tied over head hoops in order to provide protection from the weather. When their upper wrappings had been untied in order to free their hands, infants often played with toys attached to their head hoops (see illustrations). Head hoop toys included rattles, bones, animal teeth, feathres, shells, plant cones, strings of beads, items of pottery, various games, including some with parts which slid back and forth across the hoop, and teethers and pacificers. Among the Ojibwa (Chippewa), who were Algonquian-speaking hunters, gatherers, and trappers of northeastern North America, as well as among other Woodland groups, tiny birchbark cones filled with hard maple sugar were sometimes placed in a cluster of unfilled cones and hunt where an infant could put them in its mouth. Gifts from people who had important relationships to an infant, such as those who had given it a name, as well as charms to ensure an infant's health and well-being were likewise attached to the head hoop. For example, an important Ojibwa charm was a decorated case containing a child's umbilical cord. This charm provided wisdom, and was kept for lifetime. Among the Pawnee, who Caddoan-speaking prairie farmers and buffalo hunters of the Kansas-Nebraska area of the United States, as well as among the Ojibwa, small charms representing spider webs protected babies from harm. Finally, cradles were often decorated with paintings, carving, beadwork, and other forms of ornamentation. Among the Iroquois, who were Siouan-speaking farmers and warrriors located below Lake Ontario and the St. Lawrence River in the United States and Quebec, as well as among other eastern North American groups, floral designs on cradles or other artifacts were influenced by contact with Europeans, especially the French (see illustration).

In regions where it was too hot to wrap infants, such as much of Mesoamerica, the Circum-Caribbean, tropical South America and the Gran Chaco (central plain) of South America, infants were often carried in woven or net slings and kept in hanging cradles or hammocks inside of the house. For example the Bororo, who were Gê-speaking hunters, gatherers, and fisherpeople of the upper Paraguay River in the eastern Brazilian highlands, used mat cradles suspended by four cords from the roof beams of houses which were then rocked via a fifth cord by mothers as they worked. Examples of the use of hammocks as cradles included the Omagua and Cocama, both Tupí-Guarani-speaking slash-and-burn cultivators, hunters, and fisherpeople of the upper Amazon River, as well as tribes living in the Pilcomayo and Bermejo River areas of the Gran Chaco.

Among some groups, such as Nahuatl-speaking people in central Mexico, slings for transporting infants were (and still are) represented by a kind of shawl or "rebozo". Slings could also be a type of blanket. Children in slings were carried either on the back, or in front over one hip. For example the Carib, who were Cariban-speaking fisherpeople, hunters, and farmers of the northern coast of Venezuela and the Lesser Antilles, wove circular baby slings about 23 to 31 centimeters wide which were carried over the mother's right shoulder and under her left arm. Young children then sat in the loop of these slings facing their mothers.

**The Couvade.** Generally speaking, native people in the New World greatly desired children, but were faced with the fact that many of their offspring would not survive. In addition, a large number of Indian cultures assumed an important mystical bond between parents and children. This bond was most clearly reflected in *taboos*, or strict rules which applied to parents (and sometimes to other kin) before, during, and after the birth of a child, and which were accompanied by explanations regarding the survival and long-term welfare of children. The most common of these taboos dictated which foods parents could and could not eat for specific periods of time. Restrictions for mothers on the consumption of meat were especially common. In fact, food restrictions and other taboos for Indian parents following the birth of children were so common throughout the New World that some scholars have speculated that they may have been universal.

One of the most interesting of these customs was the *couvade*, a term taken from the French word *couver*, meaning "to hatch". The couvade involved symbolic participation of fathers in pregnancy, labor, delivery, and in the post-partum welfare of infants. Although extreme forms of the couvade did not occur in North America, native groups in the Great Basin and California practiced what might be termed a "semi-couvade". In South America, the couvade was almost universal. There, the observation of a series of taboos by fathers before, during, and after the birth of children was often regarded as an expression of powerful bonds between fathers and the souls of their offspring. As a result, fathers were prevented from doing anything which might harm infants until they were strong enough to endure strain and avoid various dangers. For example, among the Bakairi, who were Cariban-speaking fisherpeople, collectors, farmers, and hunters of the upper Xingu River in Brazil, the bond between fathers and children was expressed by the word for infants, which translated means "little father".

Mystical bonds between parents and children did not always end with the completion of rites surrounding the couvade. For example, among the Sherente, who were Gê-speaking farmers, collectors, hunters, and fisherpeople of the upper Tocantins River in Brazil, married men and women were required to observe marital taboos when their parents were ill under the assumption that failure to do so would further damage their parents' health.

A clear example of the couvade occurred among the Guarayú, who were Guarani-speaking farmers, hunters, and fisherpeople of the upper San Miguel and Blanco Rivers in eastern Bolivia. Guarayú fathers of newborn infants slashed themselves with an agouti tooth (young boys were often scarified or bled in order to make them strong), smeared their bodies with genipa (a black dye) or stained their feet and articulations with urucú (a red dye), and stayed quietly in their hammocks for three days, during which time they ate only small fish. The Guarayú felt that an infant's soul followed its father everywhere he went, and that the tiny soul might encounter harm if a father exerted himself too violently. Among the Guarani, who were a widely-distributed group of Guarani-speaking slash-and-burn farmers, gatherers, hunters, and fisherpeople located in approximately the area encompassing eastern Paraguay and southern Brazil, fathers stayed in their hammocks until their infants' umbilical cords had fallen off. During this time fathers loosened their bows and refrained from making tools or weapons, from hunting, and from setting traps lest these activities harm their offspring. Among the Tupinamba, who were a series of Tupí-Guarani-speaking slash-and-burn farmers, collectors, hunters, and fisherpeople distributed along the Brazilian coast from the mouth of the Amazon River to the state of Sao Paulo, fathers of newborn infants lay carefully wrapped in their hammocks for several days lest they catch cold and impair the health of their offspring. During this time fathers were visited by friends who brought gifts. Couvade rites lasted until a child's navel cord fell off, and included continued confinement and taboos on meat, fish, and salt for the father. Once the navel cord had fallen off, fathers could walk about, but were still required to avoid violent exertions such as felling trees lest these exertions harm their offspring. For baby boys, claws of ferocious animals, small bows and arrows, and bundles of grass symbolizing future enemies were attached to their little hammocks, which were in turn suspended between two war clubs. Baby girls were given capivara teeth to make their own teeth hard, and were presented with a gourd and cotton garters. Tupinamba fathers also performed special rites to insure their children's future success. So that sons would become good hunters and fishermen, fathers took a male baby's carrying sling and placed it in a miniature trap as if it were game, shot at it with a small bow and arrow, and covered it with a fishing net. So that infants would be fertile and produce a large number of children of their own, fathers sliced their infant-s dry umbilical cords into small pieces and tied each piece to one of the main house posts. If Tupinamba fathers were absent or deceased, these rites were performed by the mother's brother or some other close maternal relative. Throughout the period of the couvade and related paternal obligations, Tupinamba mothers observed strict food taboos.

It should be noted that mystical relationships between parents and children were also found in Siberia. For example among the Buryat, who were Mongolian-speaking pastoralists and hunters of southern Siberia, parents who were rearing children became *naydji*, or intimately related to a shaman.

**Naming.** Native peoples in the New World (and in Siberia) frequently attached great significance to names. In both North and South America, names often represented important categories of property which could belong to social units as well as to individuals. They could also carry or transmit various kinds of power. The importance of names was often shown in rules regarding their inheritance, as well as by ceremonies and activities surrounding the naming of infants and young children. In North America, infants were often presented to the public during a naming feast or ceremony where they received at least one name. Later. children might receive several more names.

In North America North of Mexico, there was a strong tendency for parents to name children after distinguished people in hopes that this action would transfer the personalities of distinguished men and women to offspring. Although hereditary was important, donors of names were not necessarily relatives. Young children were sometimes awarded hereditary nicknames, and then later received serious hereditary names when serious names were able to denote actual achievements. Often, both types of names were received from a single donor. Since distinguished people normally acquired a series of names through time, young people received considerable status by being awarded such names as a "package".

As an example of some of the naming practices, North America Ojibwa children might have several names. These names had different meanings and were acquired in different ways. There were dream names given to children (and sometimes to adults) by a namer, dream names acquired by an individual (usually as the result of a vision during puberty), namesake names given children by parents, names of clans or kinship groups, common names or nicknames (which were often humorous), and pleasant-sounding names which had no special meaning. The first type of name was acquired during a public ceremony where an infant received power and an associated name from a namer chosen by parents shortly after birth. Namers who performed these ceremonies were persons who had received important power during dreams and could transmit this power to others. Power transmitted by namers provided children with a personal source of strength, support, and protection, and encouraged a long and healthy life. Such power could be called upon indefinitely, but could not be transferred by the recipient to anyone else. Often, parents with a sick child who had not yet received a "power" name hastily summoned a namer in hopes that powe transmitted by the namer would save their child's life. By contrast, Ojibwa namesake names were not bestowed by ceremonies, and were not associated with the transmission of power. Instead, they represented the naming of offspring after people whom parents respected and admired.

Among Indians of the North American Plains, infants normally received a name at a feast shortly after birth. During this feast, names were given by adults of the same sex who were known for supernatural power. Namers took infants in their arms, prayed to a spirit on behalf of their "godchildren", and announced a name taken from an episode or character which had occurred in a personal vision. Great warriors sometimes named children after one of their famous war exploits. If children became ill, another namer would be asked to supply a new name.

In Mesoamerica, names were usually determined by the date of an individual's birth. For this reason, they did not involve the same traditions as those found in North America. By contrast, the situation in South America was more like that of North America. Among South American Indians, names were often considered important personal property and were closely interwoven with the rest of an individual's culture. Names were frequently acquired or inherited through special rules, and their acquisition often involved ritual and public ceremonies. Particular names could lead to special circumstances, such as participation in specific ceremnies or membership in a given moiety. Like North American Indian names, South American Indian names were not always the property of individuals, but could belong to social units. In addition, nicknames were widely employed.

Among Indians of the Gran Chaco or central plain of South America, children were named after birds, animals, places, or some identifying personal trait. Names for children were often suggested to parents by events in real life or in dreams. Among the Mataco, who were Mataco-speaking collectors, hunters, gardeners, and fisherpeople of the Gran Chaco, fathers named children who were two or three years of age after an object or animal which had occurred in a dream, or perhaps after words or sentences which had been uttered by characters in these dreams. The Mataco were reluctant to reveal personal names, and often told outsiders that they had no names. Among the Toba, who were Guaicurú-speaking residents of the Gran Chaco with an economy similar to that of the Mataco, a child's relatives gathered in the presence of a shaman after its navel cord had fallen off. An older man then recited a series of names until the shaman located one which was appropriate and which represented the name of an ancestor who was reincarnated in the person of the infant. Following a pattern which was widely-distributed among New World groups, and which reflected both the power vested in personal names and their intimate connection with bearers, the Albipón of the Gran Chaco (who were linguistically and economically similar to the Toba) felt that addressing an individual by a "real" or personal name was a grievous insult which had to be avenged. Among the Guarani of approximately the region encompassing eastern Paraguay and southern Brazil, personal names were not divulged because they were considered to be a kind of soul. The Apapocuva-Guarani felt that babies were reincarnated ancestors. Thus, a shaman was summoned soon after the birth of a child in order to identify the returning spirit, and through supernatural power, obtain a magical substance to be rubbed into the infant's body. Names conferred during infant baptism referred to mythical beings or objects on the horizon from which an infant's soul had come. Children were closely identified with dieties of the Upper World, and were sometimes given miniature symbols of their divine namesakes. In case of danger or illness, Guarani names were changed in order to separate adults and children from destructive influences or disease, and a new baptism ceremony was performed.

**Discipline in smaller Indian societies.** In many smaller Indian groups and villages, children were of such great interest to everyone, and child rearing techniques were so standardized that anyone might legitimately discipline, feed, care for, or demand an errand from any child who happened to be in the vicinity. As a rule, children in these groups were disciplined by verbal statements, public opinion, gossip, ridicule, and occasionally, threats of supernatural sanctions. Also relatives outside of the immediate family group often helped parents with more severe forms of discipline. Although children were normally taught physical endurance as a matter of personal pride and survival, physical punishment was rarely used. For example, among the Ona of the Tierra del Fuego region, children seldom cried. Following a pattern which was widespread among New World native peoples, Ona mothers nursed infants and small children whenever they indicated that they were hungry. Ona elders frequently gave children detailed lectures regarding socially-acceptable behavior which included warnings about self-respect, family tribal pride, a shortened life, and even actions by the Supreme Being, Temáukel. Ona boys and girls were separated and closely supervised from a very early age. The nearby Yahgan, who were Yahgan-speaking marine gatherers, marine hunters, and fisherpeople of the southern coast of Tierra del Fuego and the adjacent archipelago, likewise rarely used physical punishment. Instead, children were corrected verbally or were sent out of the family hut for a day. Elders frequently administered moral lectures to children, who were obligated to listen even when they were not eager to do so. Boys and girls were kept separated after the age of seven. As another example, the Tehuelche of the Patagonia region indulged their children and seldom employed punishment. Likewise, the Gé-speaking Botocudo of eastern Brazil, who were hunters and gatherers who later adopted agriculture from Brazilian colonists, seldom punished their children physically. Instead, Botocudo mothers threatened naughty children with ghosts, jaguars, and "white" people (Brazilian colonists).

Among the Comanches, who were Uto-Aztecan-speaking hunters and warriors of the North American Plains, children were managed by advice, counsel, and commands regarding correct behavior and tribal law. Comanche children were not punished physically, but were disciplined by persuasion, example, and threats. Young babies soon learned that crying did not necessarily lead to gratification. Youngsters were told how to behave not on the basis of right and wrong, but because a particular act was either advantageous or disadvantageous. They were encouraged to consider their own personal pride, to observe that brave, generous men and industrious women were publically admired, and to imitate widely respected behavior. When children misbehaved, older people sometimes disguished themselves as ghosts, and adults mentioned Big Cannibal Owl, a cave-dwelling creature who ate bad children during the night. Forceful discipline was often delegated to relatives outside of the immediate domestic unit. As an example of this, one Comanche warrior recalled whining when he was a small child to the point where his mother called in an older classificatory sister. The sister simply dragged him into a tipi by a rawhide thong around his neck and threatened to hang him from the top of the tipi if he did not stop whining. According to the old warrior's memory, this technique was highly effective.

Agricultural Indian groups, or those where agriculture was an important part of the economy varied greatly in the application of physical punishment and other forms of discipline for children. This may have been partly due to the effects of agriculture on population size, density, and distribution, as well as to the strategic availability of complete proteins, land, trade routes, and other resources.

Among the agricultural Pueblo Indians of the American Southwest, the mother's brother was a major disciplinarian, and formal village disciplinarians were also used on a regular basis. For the first two years, a Pueblo Indian child's life was relatively free. However, about the time Pueblo children learned to walk, this pattern was reversed. They were then encouraged to be industrious, to endure discomfort without crying, to avoid wasting food, and so on. In case they did not behave properly, parents mentioned ogres and giants or katchinas (village disciplinarians) who visited the Pueblos on a regular basis and were known to carry away children who nagged, cried, were disobedient, or who otherwise misbehaved. When these masked and costumed personalities arrived bearing their whips, children hid inside of houses, but were permitted to look out through partially-opened doors and windows. Parents with particularly mischievious or difficult children arranged beforehand for the disciplinarians to visit their homes, find their children, and threaten to carry them away unless promises to reform were followed by genuine improvements in behavior. Meanwhile, other children who were nearby watched and heard this performance, and were as impressed as the center-stage participants.

Among the Creek, who were Muskhogean-speaking agriculturalists of the Alabama-Georgia area of the

United States, parents did not strike or whip children. Instead, mothers punished children by scratching their legs and thighs with a pin or needle until they bled. Some mothers kept the jawbone of a garfish, which had two teeth, entirely for this purpose.

Among the Chama, who were a group of Panoan-speaking slash-and-burn farming, hunting, and fishing tribes of the Ucayali Valley in eastern Peru, misbehaving children were whipped or threatened with jaguars. Chama fathers sometimes frightened disobedient youngsters with a disguise made from banana leaves and a calabash mask. The Iquito, who were Záparoan-speaking slash-and-burn farmers, hunters, gatherers, and fisherpeople of the Peruvian Montana, also frightened recalcitrant children with masks. The Tucuna (Ticuna), who were Tucunan-speaking slash-and-burn farmers, hunters, gatherers, and fisherpeople of the northwestern Amazon region, used physical punishment which included the external application of nettle flowers grown for this purpose. Among the Tupían-speaking Witoto, who were also slash-and-burn farmers, hunters, gatherers, and fisherpeople of the northwestern Amazon region, children were physically punished but not frightened. The Cariban-speaking tribes of the northern coast of Venezuela and the Lesser Antilles were described by one source as never punishing small children under the assumption that punishment would make them die.

Traditional Mapuche Indians of the south central Chile region rarely chastized boys because it was thought that this action would cause them to become base and cowardly. Instead, boys were praised for self-assertion. Fathers took sons to drinking feasts, and were pleased when they demonstrated vigorous drinking and love-making ability. More recent observations state that stories with a moral were used to educate Mapuche children, and that boys seven years of age and older were counselled and instructed by grandfathers each evening. Even more recently, boys of about eleven were required to pay a formal visit to the cacique (community headman) and prove their knowledge of etiquette. At about the age of sixteen,

Tehuelche girls' puberty rite dance held by firelight.

boys were required to demonstrate oratorial ability. Finally, misbehaving Mapuche children were sometimes mildly drugged with ground *Datura stramonium* seeds and then lectured while in that state of mind.

Occasionally, observations of contemporary customs lend important clues to pre-contact behavior. Contemporary Mapuche children are disciplined primarily by their mothers, who often scold children but rarely punish them physically. Few distinctions are made between rewards and punishments for pre-subteen girls and boys. Lazy youngsters may be punished by being assigned extra work, or by being left to watch the house and animals while the rest of the family goes visiting or makes a trip to town. Girls remain in close association with their mothers until they marry, while sub-teen boys begin a lifelong association with their fathers and are treated like adult males. As a general statement, contemporary Mapuche children grow up within extended family arrangements which are part of a distinctive cultural setting. Each family has older members who play the role of grandparents. Grandparents speak to children in the Araucanian language, reinforce moral values, and provide important training through stories about traditional Mapuche culture. As a rule, parents tend to be "lenient" and "permissive," while children appear to want to meet parental expectations and perform as well as adults.

**The use of praise.** The "leniency" and "permissiveness" which is often mentioned in the literature on New World native peoples may be a relative phenomenon. That is, where children were managed and disciplined by groups of adult kin living in face-to-face communities alongside of others who led the same lifestyle and agreed upon standardized child rearing techniques, supervision was often so continuous and control so complete (even when this did not appear to be the case) that physical punishment was seldom necessary. In addition to the presence of a relatively large number of people who watched and commented upon every move children made, and the delegation of serious punishment (which might have caused resentment towards parents) to disciplinarians outside of the immediate family unit, many Indian groups made extensive use of praise. This is especially clear in the literature on North America, which stresses the use of praise for all ages, and particularly for children. Furthermore, the phenomenon of extensive public praise seems to have traversed economic and political organization, as it was found in many different types of societies. For example, among the Micmacs, who were Algonquian-speaking hunters, gatherers, and fisherpeople of the Gaspé Peninsula of Quebec, Newfoundland, and the Maritime Provinces of Canada, the family of a boy who had killed his first game animal invited all people in the vicinity to a feast. During this feast the young hunter's game was distributed to guests, who responded with praise and joyful singing. Among the Crow, who were Siouan-speaking buffalo hunters and warriors of the Montana-Wyoming area of the North American Plains, fathers constantly praised sons during bow and arrow contests. Crow fathers also sponsored many feasts in honor of their sons where friends made speeches of praise and predicted future success for the sons. One observer stated that among the Shawnee, who were Algonquian-speaking farmers and hunters of the Ohio Valley in the United States, children learned that good behavior earned rewards, while incorrect behavior brought sanctions. A few words of praise from adults were coveted prizes which children eagerly pursued. At the same time, Shawnee children treated physical pain with indifference. A particularly bitter punishment for a Shawnee child was to have some of their faults mentioned to a visitor or friend. Among the Natchez, who were Algonquian-speaking agriculturalists with a series of villages on the lower Mississippi River in the United States, old men supervised and praised young boys as they practiced shooting arrows at bundles of grass thrown in the air. When Natchez warriors had finished describing past glories and had received applause during public ceremonies, boys were encouraged to tell the assembled crowd what they expected to achieve in the future, and were then praised as if they had already accomplished these feats. Among the Zuñi, who were Penutian-speaking Pueblo farmers of the American Southwest, children were praised for every successful act, including proper social etiquette and the correct terms of greeting when visiting. Among the Nootka, who were Wakashan-speaking fisherpeople of the Northwest Coast of North America, young boys were encouraged to imitate well-known orators before an assembled group of elders. These elders offered encouragement, and predicted that the boys would accomplish great things in the future. Among the Yanomamo, who were Yanomamo ("Shirianá" or "Waika")-speaking slash-and-burn cultivators, hunters, and warriors of southern Venezuela and northern Brazil, young boys who demonstrated warrior-like fierceness by striking their fathers were rewarded with cheers from all adults in the household.

**Discipline in state societies.** In the large state societies of Meso and South America where there were formal schools (see the example of Aztec schools given in the above illustration), children were normally managed within individual households and by personnel in institutions providing specialized training. Thus, techniques for managing and disciplining children differed from those of smaller Indian societies, and were often what might be considered "harsh" or "non-permissive". Among the ancient Aztecs of the Valley of Mexico, recalcitrant children eight years of age and older were handled with strong admonitions and physical punishment ranging from pricking and scratching with maguey spines, to exposure to night cold in the mountains, to being bound and placed in mud puddles. It is likely that the first of these practdices was the most common. For purposes of comparison, note that contemporary Nahuatl (Aztec) speakers of central Mexico discipline children five years of age and older with much of the spirit of the ancient Aztecs. "Spoiled" children are thought to result from a lack of strict discipline. Both mothers and fathers apply physical punishment for lack of obedience, lack of responsibility, bad manners, and mistreatment of younger siblings. Youngsters who talk back may be slapped on the mouth by their mothers.

Among contemporary Mixtec Indians of the states of Oaxaca, Guerrero, and Puebla, Mexico, whose ancestors once dominated that area, children are physically punished by their mothers and other kin for lack of obedience, lack of response, and repeated misdemeanors. Other forms of punishment include threats, shaming, descriptions of witches and strangers who steal bad children, and bitter herbs which are also used for weaning. Rewards for children include affection, statements of appreciation, food, and small gifts.

Among the ancient Maya, who were Penutian-speaking agriculturalists with an empire of city-states distributed in Honduras, Guatemala, British Honduras, and Southern Mexico, daughters were strictly disciplined by their mothers. Girls who behaved improperly or who did not work hard received lectures, were pinched on the ears, or had red pepper rubbed in their eyes.

Among the ancient Inca of the Peru, Ecuador, and Chile regions, children were punished in proportion to age and degree of transgression. Inca fathers were often punished more severely than their children under the theory that they had neglected their first duty to the state, or that of educating children to respect the law. Since the application of Inca law was instantaneous, and punishment was severe, Inca children were described by one observer as so well-disciplined and obedient that they resembled pet lambs.

**Economic contributions.** For the majority of Indian cultures, there was a common division of labor between men and women, where women attended to domestic functions while men hunted, worked, travelled, traded, and negotiated matters outside of domestic units. Thus, as Indian children grew old enough to become economically productive, girls were trained by mothers and other female relatives in areas of economic production assigned to women, while boys were trained by fathers and other male relatives in areas of economic production assigned to men.

In order for women and men to remain economically

productive while caring for children, children in many Indian societies were taught as early as possible to respect adults, to avoid interfering with adult activities, and to learn by quietly observing and imitating adult skills. However, when adults in these societies were free to deal with children, they tended to display great affection and to give children their full attention.

As Indian children grew older, they normally began to participate in the economic life of their cultures at a level commensurate with ability at any given age. The average age which the literature on North, Meso, and South America gives as the beginning of serious economic contributions on the part of Indian children is between seven and eight, with rapidly increasing contributions as children mature. However, this age can vary. For example, among the Alacaluf, who were Alacalufan-speaking marine gatherers and hunters of the southern Chilean archipelago, children who had just learned to walk gathered and roasted mussels for their own consumption. By age four, Alacaluf children could manage shellfish spears, spent many hours hooking mussels and sea urchins from canoes tied to the shoreline, and cooked nearly all shellfish which they consumed. One observer noted that Alacaluf children were allowed to do more or less "as they pleased," although the observer speculated that they were likely punished whenever they contradicted parental wishes.

Among the Sirionó, who were Tupi-Guarani-speaking hunters, gatherers, and cultivators of eastern Bolivia, the collection of edible forest products was an activity in which both men and women participated. Thus, Sirionó boys and girls became proficient at locating and gathering wild plant foods as early as possible.

Before a Sirionó boy was three months old, his father made him a miniature bow and arrows. By age three, Sirionó boys could handle these tiny bows and arrows and had begun to practice shooting skills. By age eight, Sirionó boys had usually secured a small game animal or bird, and began accompanying their fathers on hunting trips. At first a boy went with his father on only about one short hunting trip per week, but as he became accustomed to the jungle, his hunting excursions became longer and more frequent. As he watched and imitated his father and helped carry game back to the camp, a boy perfected such important hunting skills as the ability to imitate the sounds of all animals in the forest. When he killed a game animal of any importance, a Sirionó boy was decorated like a mature hunter and received considerable public recognition. By age twelve, Sirionó boys were established hunters who could supply their own households with meat.

Before a Sirionó girl was three years of age, her father made her a miniature spindle for spinning cotton thread. Little Sirionó girls played "house" by making cotton thread, twining bark-fiber string, and manufacturing baskets and pots. They also helped their mothers shell maize, carry water, and raost wild fruits. By about the age of eight, Sirionó girls were proficient at spinning cotton thread, twining bark-fiber string, weaving baskets, and at performing most of the other tasks assigned to adult women. At about age twelve, Sirionó girls were ready to assume their full share of adult responsibilities.

Among contemporary Navajos, who are Athapaskan-speaking herders and farmers of the American Southwest, children who have just learned to walk may participate in herding by standing at gaps in the fence and diverting any sheep who are trying to escape. By age three, Navajo children participate in herding on an active basis and have begun to practice roping. Four and five year olds help pen sheep, and boys and girls of six and seven accompany older siblings and parents out onto the range with the herd. Navajo youngsters begin riding horses as soon as they can sit on a horse along with adults or older siblings, and at about age nine are able to handle tame horses by themselves. By their early teens, boys are able to drive horses into watering pens, and once trusted to go off by themselves on horseback, are considered adults. Navajo girls also learn roping and riding, but spend more time helping women with domestic tasks. Girls may also learn to weave wool rugs which can be traded for credit at local trading posts or sold at fairs.

**Toys and games.** For most Indian children in cultures outside of the great state societies of Meso and South America where there were formal schools, the distinction between play and learning to work was not clearly defined. As a general rule, the toys and games of Indian children represented activities which provided training for adult life. Throughout much of North, Meso, and South America, little boys practiced shooting toy bows and arrows, played with toy fishing boats and otherwise rehearsed skills which were assigned to men, while little girls played with dolls, made small baskets or tiny items of pottery, and otherwise imitated domestic tasks assigned to women. Often, boys re-enacted battle scenes while girls and boys cooperated at "playing house." As Indian children played, the young of various animals and birds were their frequent companions.

A child's first weapon, doll, or miniature household item was usually made by a parent or other adult relative and presented to the child with a geat deal of affection. Later, children might construct their own toys under the supervision of adults. As they grew older, Indian children were generally discouraged from depending on adults for toys or helping in making toys, and instead were encouraged to participate more directly in the economic lives of their families and communities.

KATHRYN T. MOLOHON

**CLOTH**. Pre-Columbian cloth, while it was made, is difficult to find in some areas; because of weather conditions, it deteriorated rapidly. In temperate climates, charred cloth, cloth impressions on ceramics (accidental and deliberate), and cloth in contact with copper objects have been the only evidences of textile manufacture found in archaeological digs. In contrast, early cloth has been found frequently in graves in the extremely arid coastal deserts of western South America.

**Plant fibers**. A variety of materials were used by Native Americans to produce cloth. The fibers of *Apocynum* (Indian hemp and dogbane), milkweed

(*Asclepias*), moosewood (*Dirca palustris*), nettle (*Urtica*), as well as shredded cedar (*Juniperus*), basswood (*Tilia*), and mulberry (*Morus*) bark, milkweed down and down feathers of birds were used in North American cloth manufacture. Often, fibers from two or more sources might be combined and there is evidence of trade along the eastern seaboard in raw materials—northern tribes with southern tribes. Cotton was grown in the American Southwest, in Mesoamerica and in South America. Fibers from the leaves of Spanish-bayonet (*Yucca*) and of maguey (*Agave*) were used to make coarser fabrics in Mexico.

**Animal materials.** Hair and sinew "threads" were used in cloth manufacture. Mountain goat fur and dog hair were utilized to weave Chilkat garments along the Pacific Northwest Coast. Bison hair was braided to make some Plains items. After the introduction of sheep, wool became popular, particularly in the Southwestern United States. Rabbit fur was common in early Mexican cloth. The hair of llamas, guanacos, and vicuñas was and is used in Andean weaving, that of the vicuña being especially soft and, therefore, prized.

**Carding and spinning.** While cotton and wool fibers can be teased or combed to straighten them out and many Indian weavers now do use carding combs (similar to wire brushes) for this purpose, the straightening can be, and was, done by hand, removing seeds, dirt and foreign matter in the process. In eastern North America, threads and yarn were usually spun by twisting fibers between palm and thigh. Aztec and Southwestern (notably Hopi) weavers put completed yarn on a "whorl spindle," a long rod with a small circular flywheel, the whorl. To spin, the person rolled the rod with yarn attached on the thigh, wrapping the spun yarn around the spindle shaft. Among Andean peoples, a spindle was rotated and dropped, the yarn spinning as the woman stood or walked. As the rotation slowed to a stop, completed yarn was attached to this "drop spindle" with a half-hitch and the process repeated.

**Dyeing.** A variety of native dyes and natural mordants were used in dyeing, depending on available tribal sources. Many wild plants yield colors when boiled, varying in shading with the choice of mordant, quantities of mordant and dye-stuff used, cooking time and the type of heating vessel. Some mineral dyes were also known and used; the blue in Chilkat cloth, for example, was derived from a copper salt.

**Fingerweaving.** Probably a very old means of textile making, known on several continents, was by fin-

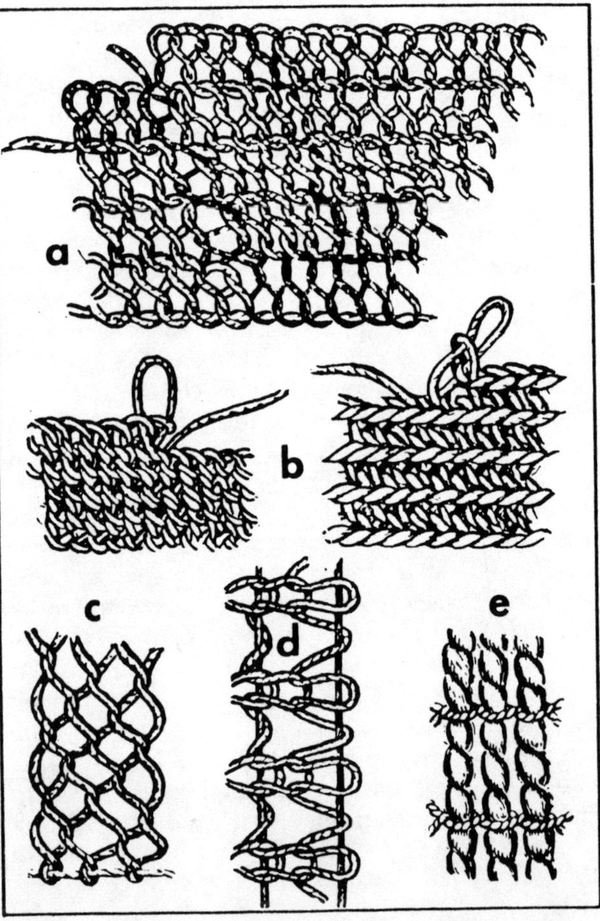


Technique of bags and netting of the Gran Chaco: (a) Mataco; (b) Choroti; (c) Ashluslay; (d) Mataco; (e) Ashluslay.

gerweaving, also called plaiting or braiding. Fiber strands were woven in and out by hand. Rather than being parallel or perpendicular to the edges of the cloth, yarns were diagonally aligned. Fingerwoven objects, usually rather narrow pieces of cloth, were common in the eastern Woodlands, the Great Lakes area, the Southwestern United States and Central America.

**Looms.** Looms varied. Long narrow objects such as tump lines, sashes, belts and garters might be woven on a simple loom, stretching the long warp threads from a fixed object to the weaver. Wider cloth was usually woven on an upright loom, two posts with two horizontal beams attached at the top and bottom between the uprights. Warp threads (the threads which run the length of the finished cloth) were strung between the two horizontal beams.

In plain weaving, the back and forth yarns or threads, called wefts, are introduced in a regular in-and-out arrangement, switching to out-and-in in the following weft row. On the loom, one stick was used to separate even warps from odd warps, simply bringing it downward closer to the weaving while a flattened stick "batten" was inserted to widen this shed, or separation of warps, even more.

Another stick was attached to every other warp by a continuous cord looped around these warps. The stick was pulled toward the weaver to make the other shed. Such looms are presently used by Navajo and Hopi weavers. The Hopi have been weaving cloth for at least twelve hundred years. The same type of loom was used by other North American weavers, by Andean and probably by Mexican weavers. Compared to modern looms, this simple Indian vertical loom could not produce long fabrics, as there was no mechanism developed to store and later bring additional warp into play. Weft, rather than being on a shuttle that slides across the entire shed, was kept either in yarn balls or wound around sticks that served as "bobbins." Often, designs were worked in by laying several different colored weft yarns through different sections of one shed (across a row); the cloth then is properly called a tapestry.

**Advanced techniques.** Weavers in the Southwest, in Mesoamerica, and in the Andean area could also produce twills and brocades. Some garments worn in the Southwest which appear to be embroidered, such as Pueblo Kilts, are actually cottons with a woolen brocade. A woven-in secondary weft of wool creates the design pattern. The Peruvians were particularly partial to an open-work, gauze-like cloth.

Embroidery in loop stitch and in stem stitch was highly developed. Reserve dyeing (tie-dyeing; ikat; batik) was known in the eastern United States as well as Mesoamerica and the Andes, but was primitive compared to development of these techniques in some other world cultures. American Indians in North America, Mesoamerica, and South America made objects by netting, suggestive in some cases of crocheting; however, true knitting or crochet were unknown.

**"Loose warp" weaving.** Woven textiles could also be made with loose warps supported from a horizontal cord or beam. This type of weaving was all done by hand. Loose warp weaving was common on the Northwest Coast. In making a robe or similar piece of cloth, warps not being worked at the moment were wrapped in waterproof animal membranes. Mountain goat wefts were twined around each and every shredded cedar bark warp manually. Such weaving took enormous amounts of time to produce a finished piece of cloth of the size desired. No wonder woolen trade goods were quickly accepted by these people. Clothes fashioned from these trade woolens were then usually decorated with white mother-of-pearl button, also obtained from the same traders.

**Woolen "trade" goods.** European textiles were presented to Indians or used in trade for furs or other valued commodities. In the earliest period of contact in North America, trade cloth included heavyweight woolen fabrics from Kersey and Gloucester in England and from Duffel in Belgium. In the early nineteenth century, the woolen used most frequently in Indian trade was a coarse, poorly dyed "strouding" made in Stroudwater, England, and usually scarlet red or dark navy blue in color. The dyeing was such that pieces of the textile were often used as a dyestuff by Plains tribes to color their porcupine quills, the quills in turn being used to embroider designs on articles of clothing. In like manner, red baize, a felt-like woven fabric traded with the Navajo, was often unraveled and the yarn used in Navajo weaving or as a source of dye for native wool.

**Cotton trade goods.** Cotton fabrics for trade were usually in bolts 38 to 40 yards long. Sateen, a glossy cotton, was used in occasional Plains women's dresses and men's shirts. The most popular cotton goods were the printed calicoes. To illustrate their distribution, Iroquois women made calico "overdresses"; Seminoles—both men and women—had complete costumes in calico. By the mid-nineteenth century, calicoes were frequent among Prairie tribes.

With the introduction of the sewing machine at the beginning of the twentieth century, Seminole women began sewing narrow strips of solid-color cottons together, recutting and sewing to produce very colorful pieced garments (sometimes called Seminole "patchwork").

**Silk.** Silk ribbon was always popular. A wide variety of colors were introduced by traders. Ribbon was often used for bindings on garments, around cuffs and neck openings. Small lengths were decorative additions on shirts and headdresses. Ribbon bands were often the only decoration on Plains breechclouts. Ribbon might be braided into or wrapped around braids of hair. The Osage and their neighbors cut and sewed ribbon to a popular woolen "list cloth" to create beautifully ribbon-appliqued garments. Appliqued clothing is still popular in this area of the United States, the basic fabric now a woolen broadcloth.

**Velvet.** Velvet was well-liked in the northeastern Woodlands and among Great Lakes area tribes. It was often used as trim around collars, for vests, caps, bags and other articles; it accentuated the simple beaded white designs of western Great Lakes tribes. In the American Southwest, Navajo women have long used velveteen, a cotton short-pile velvet, in making skirts for themselves and shirts for their husbands. And there seems to be nothing as wonderful as a dark velveteen shirt against which to wear a piece of Navajo turquoise and silver jewelry.

**Conclusion**

Cloth has played a major role in the life of the Native Americans for milennia. Europeans introduced sheep as a source of a completely different fiber. Later came trade goods of wool, cotton, linen, and silk, together with thread and needles, scissors and thimbles. Indian clothing and its manufacture were forever changed. The robe which once took over a year to make was replaced by a garment that took a few days to put together and decorate to the wearer's satisfaction. Cloth is an interesting facet of the kaleidoscopic heritage of the American Indian.

RONALD P. KOCH

**CLOTHING** of the Indians of the Americas was fabricated from a wide variety of raw materials, usually indicative of the most common animals or plants of the habitat. Animal skins were often used, either with the hair left on, which was common in winter wear, or with hair removed. In some areas plant fibers were spun, dyed and plaited or woven into textiles, sometimes rather crudely, often with highly developed craftsmanship. Climate generally determined the minimum amount of necessary clothing, though the specific culture determined the type of clothing and the maximum amount.

Decoration was quite variable. Wing and tail feathers and down of a wide selection of bird species were highly favored. Noteworthy examples include turkey plumes used in capes and headgear in the eastern woodlands of North America; eagle feathers for many objects among Great Plains tribes; flicker feathers, common in ceremonial clothing of central California. Masks and hide objects were painted; leather, stained; cloth, dyed. Porcupine quills were used extensively to embroider shirts, dresses, leggings, moccasins and robes, especially on the northern and central Plains. Other adornment included the use of bones, hair and fur, claws and hooves, teeth, shells, seeds, nuts and fruits, and grasses. Traders introduced beads, metal objects, new fabrics and ready-made clothing.

**Breechclouts, aprons, loincloths.** The simplest clothing consisted of skins or pieces of cloth wrapped around all or part of the body. A long narrow piece of material could be tucked through the crotch and held in place, front and back, by a belt; this was the breechclout. One or two aprons might be worn over the lower trunk. The apron could vary widely; one small apron might barely shield the pubic area. Double aprons sometimes completely overlapped one another at the thighs. One isolated Mexican tribe wore triangular aprons, the apexes joined in the crotch and superficially resembling a breechclout. Ceremonial aprons of one Amazon tribe are completely made of beads. Material wrapped around the waist over the lower trunk only formed a loincloth.

**Wrap-arounds.** Longer skins or pieces of cloth around the waist created a man's kilt or woman's wrap-around skirt. Simple "fringe" skirts were fabricated from grass-like plant fibers, pendant feathers, or skins cut into narrow fringes. Noteworthy for the use of fringe skirts were the early inhabitants of California; women often wore skirts of rushes. Men of one southern California tribe wore a feather skirt in a "Feather Dance" costume.

**Robes, capes, mantles, ponchos.** A robe was merely a larger skin or blanket wrapped around the entire body or the upper trunk only; the robe was worn by most native American people. Natives of the Great Plains were very fond of a bison robe for winter wear. A cape or cloak was a garment knotted around the neck, the knot either in front or above one shoulder. Like the robe, the front-knotted cape was widely distributed throughout the Americas. Mantles, as we shall use the word, were simple uncut clothing pieces worn around the entire torso, under one arm and over the opposite shoulder, holding the upper end with a pin or by knotting. Mantles were usually belted at the waist and occasionally pinned on the open side. Women of the Pueblos of the Southwestern United States fre-

Arapaho ghost shirt (1897).

quently wore mantles. Another simple garment was the poncho, a skin or cloth with a neck slit, worn as a shirt or blouse.

**Leggings.** Wrap-around leggings—material wrapped around the legs and held in place with garters—while not common, have been recorded. Usually leggings were made from skins sewn into more or less tubular covering for each leg. These were held by thongs or part of the basic legging material attached to a belt. The legging could be left as is, or the leather outside the stitching might be fringed. The bottoms might be cut straight across horizontally or, among some tribes, made into "tabs." Short leggings were often worn by women.

**Dresses.** Double aprons might be worn in such a way that, in appearance, they resembled a wrap-around dress, though actually unsewn. The simplest sewn dresses were of one skin fashioned as a wrap-around but stitched at their junction. Other dresses were made of two skins, one in front, one in back, stitched at the sides, often with sleeves of other skins. Or dresses might be created from three skins: front, back, and a poncho-like yoke piece, often long enough to allow for sleeves or sleeve-like projections.

**Shirts.** Sewn shirts were frequently made like the two-skin dress. The simplest men's shirt, worn on the North American Plains, was simply two uncut skins sewn together at the shoulder and loosely tied together at the sides and below the sleeves. Eastern Woodlands and Pleateau shirts, in contrast, were cut, somewhat shaped and sewn together at the sides and under the full length of each arm. The idea of the vest was probably introduced by Caucasians.

**Footwear.** In Arctic and temperate areas where footwear was a necessity, it varied considerably in basic construction. Fur-lined boots or combination boot-leggings or boot trousers were a winter necessity for Eskimos and Aleuts. Hide boots were common in chaparral (dense shrubbery) areas. Sandals were worn by the tribes of California, the Plateau-Basin region, Central America, and of the Andes. Moccasins might be either soft-soled or hard-soled. In the typical soft-soled form, the entire foot was covered with tanned leather, the bottom usually being brought up arond the foot, "puckered," and the edges sewn, either together or to a separate upper vamp. Another soft-soled moccasin form was developed from one piece of tanned hide, the edges stitched together at one side of the foot. A hard-soled moccasin was made with a sole of rawhide and tanned leather uppers; more properly, this could be called a true shoe.

**Mittens.** Mittens were vital in the Arctic and in cold southern South America. Elsewhere, handwear was uncommon.

**Headgear.** Fur caps or skins of fur worn over the head were common in colder climates. Otter fur turbans were frequent in the Southeastern United States, and the otter turban was well-accepted by Prairie tribes after its introduction. Masks for ceremonial purposes varied. In the eastern United States,

Full feather headdress and costume of the Northern Cheyenne, Montana (1907).

masks or carved basswood or of braided cornhusks are well-known among the Iroquois tribes of New York State. Carved cottonwood masks and tabletas were common in the Southwest Pueblos. Very elaborate masks of carved red cedar were created by Pacific Northwest Coast artists. Masks were and still are carved in Central America. Tribes in the Valley of Mexico and in the Yucatan-Guatamala region prepared elaborate ceremonial headdresses incorporating woven basketry, carved wood, feathers, flowers and mineral materials to represent a pantheon of Gods. Andean peoples wore knitted caps, woven cloth turbans, long narrow turban-like bands, or basketry helmets.

**Tailored clothing: the Arctic.** Waterproof clothing of northern North America, worn by Eskimos and Aleuts, is made from seal skins, tailored, fitted together, and stitched very carefully. The seal hides were prepared by masticating, the chewing process adding a great deal of fat to the Eskimo diet. Other Arctic clothing was fabricated from caribou skins. Apparel items in this harsh environment usually included a well-made fur-lined jacket, often with a hood over the head. Arctic hide shirts were tailored in a variety of patterns; a hooded shirt formed a parka. A pieced shirt was sometimes made from many ground squirrel skins, like a modern furrier's creation, by the Aleuts and some Eskimo tribesmen. Parkas made from animal intestines were prepared in a few tribes.

Triangular genital coverings, like underwear, were made from hides by certain Eskimos. Trousers, resembling old-fashioned knickerbockers, were worn by both men and women. Some were cut like pants; others, like leggings with a separate piece set in between the leggings—a stitched-in breechclout. In summer, Arctic clothing was one-layered with the hairside worn outward. Wintertime wear was of two layers, hair inward.

Boots were also an Arctic "must." Occasionally, either leggings or hide trousers and boots were combined. The trouser combination might be called hose. The leggings-boots usually are worn as "waders" over other clothing. Many Eskimo tribes also make "snow suits," often for children to wear, combining shirt and pants in a single garment.

Mittens and snow goggles formed from slitted pieces of wood or from walrus ivory were necessary in the winter season.

**Eastern Woodlands.** In the northeastern United States, including Great Lakes area tribes, loincloths were commonly worn. Capes and kilts or wrap-around skirts were typical of the Iroquois tribes of New York and the Lenape of Delaware and New Jersey. Throughout the Eastern Woodlands, men's leggings were front-seamed. Short leggings, reaching up to the knees, were worn by women in the wintertime in the Northeast but were rare in the Southeast. Moccasins, which were puckered, were decorated with moosehair embroidery, shells, shell beads and feathers. Early European artists depicted wampum-like beads on Indian garments and in one early painting of Pocahantas, turkey feathers. Trade glass beads were readily accepted from white traders. The Iroquois used white beads almost exclusively in beaded edgings and designs. Designs called sky-domes and celestial-trees were Iroquois favorites. Other Great Lakes tribes developed very characteristic, beautiful beaded floral designs on clothing. Ribbon, introduced by traders, was very popular for edgings and, among Prairie tribes, was developed into attractice appliqued garments.

Double aprons and shoulder capes, wrap-around skirts, or mantles were all worn in the southeastern United States. Fringed skirts were once worn by tribes in a narrow band along the Atlantic coast from New York to Florida, those in Florida often being made from Spanish moss. The Seminoles of Florida have, in recent years, produced very elaborate pieced clothing for personal apparel and for tourist purchase.

**Plains.** On the North American Plains the ubiquitous bison robe, furred in the winter, hide only in the summer, was often decorated with symmetrical line, hourglass-like, or circular "sun-burst" designs. Men usually wore hide two-skin shirts on the northern and central Plains, but such shirts were probably not worn

Arikara warrior.

on the southern Plains. Leggings on the Plains were usually side-sewn. A wrap-around legging may have been common on the northern Plains in the early life of these people. Prairie tribesmen, transitional in dress between woodland dwellers and the Plains people, wore both front-sewn and side-sewn legging styles.

There is some controversy concerning the antiquity of Plains breechclouts; these coverings, while common in the historic period, may have been less frequent earlier. Perhaps an apron or aprons were worn instead by Plains men. Women wore short leggings on the Plains.

An older woman's dress of the northern Plains resembled a slip, with sleeves attached separately. The two-skin dress later was favored by most women on the northern Plains as well as by Plateau women. A three-skin dress was worn by Dakota, central and southern Plains women. Soft-soled moccasins were worn in the northern part of the area, but hard-soled types were more common throughout the Great Plains. On the southern Plains, women often wore high-topped skin boots.

Perhaps the best known American Indian headdress is the Plains eagle feather war bonnet. The bonnet was originally earned by an individual as recognition for a number of valorous acts, and was quite rare. Single eagle plumes worn in the hair were much more common.

Plains clothing decoration was with feathers, paints, stain and dyes, and embroidery using porcupine and bird quills. Accessory clothing pieces were made from hair pipes (long bone beads), tails, small animal skins, claws (often, grizzly bear), teeth (elk teeth were very popular), hooves, horns, shells, fruits and nuts. Beadwork flourished on the Plains after the introduction of glass trade beads, both on hide garments and later clothing of trade textiles. Beadwork designs were usually geometric. Choice of bead colors, sizes and shapese, as well as of designs used, varied from tribe to tribe.

**Southwest.** The Pueblo people, with a long history in the American Southwest, were and are noted weavers. Men wore embroidered cotton kilts and women, mantles and capes. The hard-soled moccasin was perhaps first developed by ancestral Pueblo people. Women wrap long strips of leather arond the lower legs, the leather incorporated with their moccasins. Ceremonial carved masks and headdresses were elaborate and varied.

The Navajo people, later arrivals in the Southwest, developed great skill in weaving blanket tapestries. Men often wore blanket-ponchos. The Navajo and the Apaches also wear simple hide ponchos. Navajos learned silverworking techniques from the Spanish and have become highly skilled in this craft, creating masterpieces in the precious metal which often incorporate pieces of locally mined turquoise.

**Northwest Coast.** The tribes of the Pacific Northwest Coast, from southern Alaska to Washington, wore skins or wove mountain goat or dog hair as well as shredded cedar bark into capes such as the famed "Chilkat blanket," double aprons, ponchos, mantles and, occasionally, wrapped leggings. A woven rain poncho of shredded cedar bark was worn by both men and women. Designs used for decoration were elaborate totemic figures such as beavers, bears, whales, sharks, ravens, eagles and thunderbirds. Cedar was carved into very intricate masks, often with moving parts and interchangeable pieces, beautifully painted, and perhaps decorated with abalone shell, shredded bark or feathers. Hats were woven of reed, spruce roots or shredded bark, the shape varying from tribe to tribe. Such headgear was necessary in their rainy environment. A cap was also sometimes made of an ermine skin, folded somewhat like a high overseas cap and worn on dress occasions. Generally these people went barefoot, but occasionally wore a pucker-toed soft-soled moccasin. The breechclout was unknown to them until recent times.

**California.** The men of California, a well-populated region in pre-Columbian times, wore loincloths; the women, double aprons, fringed skirts, or mantles. Decorative earrings of incised bird bones and necklaces of shells were common. Hats were made from basketry; hairnets were also known in the area. Ceremonial clothing in central California often included very spectacular "Big Head" dance headdresses, bands and belts—all of flicker feathers.

**Plateau and Basin.** In the arid region between the Sierra Nevadas and Rocky Mountain cordillera, early clothing was simple. Women wore double aprons, the back apron larger than the front, or fringed skirts. Men wore a folded skin loincloth around the hips. Ponchos might be very simple, or cut and stitched to form short sleeves. Later clothing of the area took on many of the characteristics of Plains clothing. Fur headbands were worn. Nez Percé women are known for their distinctive basketry hats. Strips of rabbit pelts were sometimes woven into blankets by the desert dwellers. Both pucker-toed and foldover soft-soled moccasins were worn.

**Central America.** Clothing among the peoples of the Valley of Mexico and of Guatamala-Yucatan was quite similar, as observed both in sculpture and in real-life. These civilizations had well-developed weaving techniques, preparing cloth from cotton, *ixtle* (maguey), palm and yucca fibers and the hair of animals (especially rabbit hair). A wide selection of mordants and dyes were known, including cochineal (derived from an insect) and a purple dyestuff derived from a clam, reminiscent of Phoenician purple. Men wore a long cloth wrapped several times around the waist and brought through the crotch and hung in front. This could be termed a combination loincloth-breechclout, called a *maxtli* by the Axtecs or an *ex* by the Maya. A large rectangular garment, the *tilmatli*, could be worn as a man's mantle or as a man's cape. Aztec and Maya men often wore this cloak tied over one shoulder.

Women wore a *nagua*, or wrap-around skirt. In modern usage, the sides of the wrap-around skirt are sewn together to form a wide tube; the waist is gathered in a wide variety of folding methods, depending on the tribe. A *quechquemitl,* or neck garment, is made of two cloth rectangles attached to one another in several ways, but leaving a neck opening. The *quechquemitl* was probably originally a ceremonial garment, but is very popular today in northern Mexico. A *huipil*, probably originally a poncho but later stitched at the sides to form a sleeveless blouse or longer dress, was and is worn throughout Mexico and Central America.

Early Central American men and women wore *cactli* sandals. Adornment items included emeralds, carnelians and other gemstones, shells, pearls and jewelry of gold, copper, jade and turquoise. Jewelry included mosaic-inlaid items, bead necklaces, earrings, lip plugs, bells and occasional nose ornaments. Goldsmithing was well-developed in Panama, with many early gold objects passing in trade to Mexico before Mexicans learned the smith's art. The Mayan people probably never did develop metalworking arts. Turbans were popular. Ceremonial masks and headdresses made from reed, wood, plant fiber papier-mâché and from feathers were common. The most prized feathers were tail plumes of the male quetzal (resplendent trogon), very long and iridescent green. Flowers were worn in garlands or as part of masks. Objects were embellished with fine feather mosaics, such featherworked pieces being prized by people with whom the Mexicans traded.

**Andes.** Many villages developed in the Andean highlands and along the fertile river valleys that flowed west from these mountains to the Pacific. While these communities were independent, not united until conquest by the famous Inca family, their clothing was quite similar. The Andean people were outstanding textile workers, weaving first from alpaca, llama and vicuña wool, later from cotton. Like the Mexican people, they had a wide assortment of mordants and dyes. Unfortunately for comparative purposes, few Mexican textiles have been preserved, while many fabrics survived in arid desert graves of coastal Peru. The variety of techniques the Andean people used and the superb quality of finished articles are truly remarkable.

Men's clothing consisted of either a breechclout, the *huara*, or genital aprons—square, triangular, or shaped—held by a belt; a poncho-like tunic, or *unku*, of varying size, sewn down the sides; and a blanket-like *yacolla*, worn either as a cape or as a mantle. A bag, or *chuspa*, to carry coca leaves and lime was considered another necessity. Aymara men of Bolivia wear a knitted cap, or *chuco*. On the southern Peruvian coast, a large feather-decorated basketry helmet was common. Other Andean men wore wrap-around cloth turbans or a similar long, narrow, knitted headband, the *llauto*.

Men's jewelry consisted of gold, silver or copper ornaments: disk-shaped earrings that "plugged" into holes in the earlobes; bracelets; nose ornaments (hole pierced in the nasal septum); necklaces; and breast ornaments. Necklaces of human teeth and feathers were also popular.

Andean women wore a mantle, the *anacu*, held together with *tupu* pins over one shoulder and down he open side and with a sash, or *chumpi*, at the waist. Ladies wore a cape, the *lliclla*, held by a *tupu* and a head cloth, the *ñañaca*. Women wore pubic aprons; men typically wore a hide penis sheath, sometimes tying this in an upright position with a thong attached to a waistband.

Tribes of both the pampas and the colder areas in the south wore garments of skins, bark, bird skins, or finger-woven hair or feathers as robes, mantles or capes. Guanaco and fox pelts were especially favored. Belts and pubic aprons were common for both men and women. Among the Chaco of central South America, both men and women wore wrap-around skirts. Occasionally boots or guanaco skin leggings might be observed but were uncommon.

Even in the coldest areas of the continent, perhaps the only concessions to the weather were the wearing of crudely constructed one-piece seal-skin moccasins stuffed with grass, and hide mittens.

All over South America, other than in the Andean region, adornment was more noteworthy than actual clothing. There were necklaces of shells, bones, feathers, braided sinew, and very popular pig tusks. Caps and headdresses were formed from bright bird plumes. Anklets and bracelets wre made from braided leather or grass. Ear plugs and nose and lip ornaments are common in Amazonia, but absent further south. Some

Amazon Basin tribes also glue feathers to their faces and to their bodies.

### Conclusion

The introduction of machine-made goods had profound effects on the clothing of native American people. Cloth was made into garments or ready-made clothing was worn. Beads, sequins, and metal objects were used in adornment. Needles and knives made garment-making easier. New skills such as metalworking created a plethora of new ornaments. Before the advent of European trade, materials were those readily available in the immediate area—furs and skins of local animals, fibers from plants near at hand, rocks and minerals. Particularly valuable objects were traded tribe-to-tribe for long distances. Macaw feathers, for example, were used by Pueblo people; dentalia, or tooth shells, from the Pacific were prized by Great Plains tribes. Andean gold found its way to Mexico.

Clothing forms changed gradually from one culture area to its neighbor. New styles, materials and techniques slowly spread to other regions from their place of origin. Yet skilled observers could identify native source very specifically by a single small clothing item. Both everyday dress and ceremonial costume provide fascinating subjects for the student of native American peoples.

RONALD P. KOCH

**CORN DANCES**. Corn was the premier plant food produced by Indian farmers and therefore had a major relation to their lifestyle and their economy. As such it entered deeply also into their religion, becoming a subject of ceremonies and dances. Corn or maize was probably developed as a domestic food crop somewhere in Central America or Mexico, most likely in Guatemala, at least by 2000 BC and probably much earlier. By the time of the coming of Columbus it had been bred and re-bred into many varieties to be growable in many climates and habitats from dry deserts to wet jungles, from cold coniferous forests to hot tropical savannahs, and also high up on the mountains.

**General characteristics**

Corn dances were found almost wherever corn was grown, from the plains of Patagonia, and the forests of southern Chile north through much of South America and most of Central America to the southwestern United States and then east and north to the Dakotas and to the St. Lawrence River in Quebec. The dances were almost completely religious in nature, as the successful growing of the corn crop was vital to the life of the Indian farmers, and times of drought or otherwise bad conditions for the corn were traumatic periods of near-starvation. Many of the dances were likely derived from such bad times and came to symbolize the efforts of each tribe to propitiate higher powers and make sure such disasters did not occur again. Thus a legend of the Delaware actually stated that during such a period the elders of the tribe counselled together to devise a dance ceremony to protect their people from such catastrophes. In many such dances the waving of the corn in the wind, its graceful symmetry and marvelous growth, were emphasized in the dance steps or other movements of the arms and body, while the deep beat of the drums symbolized the thunder and the tintinabulation of the rattles or gongs spoke of the good rain coming.

When a hunting and gathering tribe partially gave up its nomadic life for the more settled life of farming, symbolically the male element of the chase and war, identified among many American Indians with the eagle, became gradually tamed by the female element of growing things, symbolized by the corn maidens or corn goddesses. In another mythic meaning, gentle Mother Earth began to civilize Father Sky of the sun's blazing heat, the lightning's fiery spears, the wind's roaring and the rain's pelting in torrents. We can think of Mother Earth reaching up with her waving plants to meet the rain and sunlight of Father Sky, and the two joining together to fertilize the land and produce growth. But growth without fruition, corn without corn cobs, brought disaster to the Indian farmers, as sometimes happened because of disease, insect pests or other dangers. To the Indian this often meant that he had done something wrong, either through bad thoughts and actions or through imperfect performance of the ceremonies and dances. In some legends of North America this is put quite poetically in stories of the shy young corn maidens having to run away because of bad thoughts and actions on the part of the people so that they never become fertilized nor come to fruition in the form of the corn cobs, whose symbolic partner is the mature woman, the bearer of children.

All these ideas and others similar are often expressed in the dances. The corn dances are given at different times of the year, sometimes in the spring as encouragers to the corn to grow, other times, as at the winter solstice, to call the corn back to life from the death of winter, and, most joyously of all, as festive celebrations in the fall when the crop has been good and food is plentiful.

## Regional variations

**North America**. North of the Rio Grande the warlike or Father Sky-like nature of the men's way of dancing is probably more emphasized. Like the jagged lightening, the men step up and down much higher and more vigorously than the women, who usually dance demurely with their feet scarcely rising above Mother Earth, as if they can only have strength by closeness to Her, yet both men and women dance in harmony. The violence of the men seems to beckon down the rain, while the sucking-like motion of the bare feet of the women appears like it is trying to pull the plants up out of the earth.

In the southwest, at such pueblos as the Zuñi and San Domingo, the male-female combination grows in strength hour after hour so that the watchers feel as if the very air is charged with power. They are not surprised when often after such a performance the desired rain falls.

Among the southwest Pueblos Koshare dancers put both ghostly and humorous elements into the Corn

Dances. These men are usually painted all over white with black spots, but often with other colors on an arm or leg, and act as both clowns and warners while supposedly being spirits of past ancestors who are invisible to those present. The other dancers act as if they do not exist. The Koshare dancing is often made up of such leaps and gyrations as at times to appear unbelievable. As warners they not only poke awake sleepers, warn those who break rules, and pick up objects dropped by the regular dancers, but also act as rescuers of small lost or hurt children. The humorous tricks they pull are actually meant to emphasize by contrast the deadly seriousness of the other dancers.

The so called Busk or Green Corn Dances of the southeastern tribes, such as the Natchez, the Creeks, Cherokees, and Choctaws, generally happened at the time of the first harvest of the corn in lkate August. Besides being harvest dances, they also were thought of as a time for purifying, in which useless things were thrown away or burned, the whole village cleaned up, old fires put out and, after three days or so of fasting, new fires were started, and both men and women were purified by taking a special drink that caused vomiting and other internal cleansing. Then followed several days of dancing, with different dances, such as the turkey dance of the women, a tadpole dance to symbolize "new life," and so on. Besides a march down to the river where the men dived in to each retrieve four sacred stones, the Busk was finally finished by a Mad Dance, which symbolized the last chance the people had to act wantonly, for after that they must act with decorum and purity. During the Busk all bad feelings were supposed to be ended, old debts forgiven, and a new era of peace and goodwill started.

The Bread Dance of the Shawnee of the Ohio Valley was given at the time of first planting, in mid-May. The Shawnees usually used slow and dignified steps, the men and women dancing either intermingled or in separate lines, the changing lines and circles beautifully managed and designed. Later the women danced with a peculiar twisting motion of both feet. Between dances there was often fun and repartee as both men and women would claim to have done the best dancing and so won the competition.

At most North American Corn Dances old chiefs or medicine men often gave speeches, warning the people and their children to be good and honorable and to help each other and the tribe.

**Mesoamerica.** Probably the main Corn Dance of the Aztecs of Mexico involved a woman who was dressed up beautifully in embroidered clothes and red sandals, with a turquoise disk necklace, and a brilliant headdress of green and crimson quetzal plumes. The Sacred Quetzal Bird's long beautifully emerald tail feathers represented the growing corn all through Mexico and Central America. The woman herself symbolized the goddess of corn, *Xilonen*. In her hand she carried a magic rattle and a shield. In the dawn, after a sleepless night, the men formed lines, all holding aloft stalks of corn called *totopantli*, to represent the harvest. The women followed *Xilonen* and everybody began to dance and sing, the symbolic goddess shaking her rattle, as she led the way to the Temple of Tineopan, where the priests blew on their horns and conches and the priestesses banged the two-toned gongs to create a terrific din. As usual with the Aztecs, such ceremonies had to end with a human sacrifice and the representation of the Goddess *Xilonen* lost her head to the swish of a gold-handled knife, symbolizing the corn losing its heads before being eaten.

The ancient Maya of Yucatan and Guatemala were generally not so bloodthirsty with their dances. Perhaps their most unusual corn dance came in certain years when there was a scarcity of water and a great abundance of corn sprouts, when the Mayan priests turned to a god called *Yax Cocay Mut*, "the green firefly pheasant," and called on the old women of the tribe to perform a spectacular dance done on stilts, three feet or more high, after which they offered to the god dogs made of pottery with food placed on their backs. This was supposed to help the corn produce.

In western Panama the Guaymi tribe of the mountain country had an even more spectacular dance at the time of the planting of the corn, called the Balseria by the Spanish, in which two lines of men took turns whirling six foot long sticks and then throwing them at each others' legs, which made the opposite side dance to escape them. The dance, if done properly, they said, would help the corn grow and give a good crop.

**South America.** The great Quechua and Aymara tribes of western South America, the back-bones of the Inca Empire, probably put on the most spectacular corn dances of their continent. The first was given in the month of Capac Raymi (December) and was part of the major religious ceremony of the whole year, in honor of Pachacamana—the Earth Mother. Everybody in the Inca Empire, including the Incá himself, always preceded by a contingent of Sacred Sun Virgins, took part in the dances in the streets, and in the temples.

In the month of Aryihua (April), the "Month of the Corn Ears of a Thousand Colors," there was another great harvest festival at which a Sacred White Llama was dressed in bright red cloth, hung with Big Ear ornaments, surrounded by royal attendants, and given coca and chicha (a corn drink). Fifteen ordinary llamas were sacrificed to give honor to it, and then the dancing began. This usually consisted of men playing on drums and horn pipes while the women danced in circles, first in one direction and then in the other, but sometimes the men, blowing their panpipes, also danced in circles. The tunes were very haunting and beautiful.

## Contemporary situation

Where agricultural tribes are still clinging to their ancient culture and religion or some elements of it the Corn Dances are still yearly events. This is particularly true of the Pueblo tribes of Arizona and New Mexico and the Quechua and Aymara of South America. Usually the dances and ceremonies are somewhat simplified over what they used to be, or changes have been made. For example, the Aymara in South America now kill the Sacred White Llama at the time of the dance instead of letting it live and die of old age as was done in the ancient times. Other dances have been corrupted because of too much alcoholic drinking.

Thus the Balseria or Stick Game Dance of the Guaymi of Panama was so ruined by liquor that it often turned into a drunken brawl.

In the modern pluralistic Indian societies, particularly in North America, where there are so many people of mixed blood from different tribes, corn dances have not been as popular as war, hoop and round dances, etc., because the corn dances are directly associated with unified tribal efforts to produce a successful corn crop.

VINSON BROWN

**COSMOLOGY**. The basic characteristic of the Indian socio-religious system appears to have been an excessive interest in the movements of the heavenly bodies, in particular Venus, and a catastrophic cosmology involving the destruction of previous world orders. Such religious rituals as human sacrifice and the sacred ball game (*tlachtli*) were closely tied to cosmic events. The *Popol Vuh* and other native texts clearly express a relationship between a dread of recurring disasters and propitiatory human sacrifice, including the decapitation of the ball game losers. The legendary ball game in which Hunter and Jaguar Deer win out over the Lords of Hell can be interepreted as referring to the advent of the present Sun and Moon, stated to be the successors of those of earlier, catastrophically destroyed world orders. Many of these disaster-constructs clearly held an almost equally important place among the peoples of North and South America from whom there are no written records and less systematic information with regard to cosmic myths.

**Regional variations**

Such strong similarities of cosmology and of astronomical practice as are evident in different areas of the Americas suggest a common point of origin. They may represent, however, an attempt by various peoples to record traumatic experiences commonly suffered over the entire continuum and to keep a close check on celestial events. It may be argued that roughly similar astronomical observatories and observations might result from the objective astronomical facts that are on display nightly. Longitude, latitude, and time, however, strongly affect the events that could have been observed. Moreover though the objective astronomical facts may have been roughly the same as similar latitudes and dates, the subjective interpretation of these events and the mental constructs built on them—such as zodiac and solar and lunar calendars—should not be the same unless contact between the peoples had taken place. In fact, similar architectural practices and a similar use of astronomy for the timing of agricultural and other rituals extend over a wide range of latitude as do various of the subjective constructs.

The early development of Native American astronomy cannot as yet be closely pinpointed as to time or place, but it is significant that, in general, the regional variations in architectural traditions, cosmologies, and subjective astronomical constructs are more a matter of degree than of kind. A continuum exists between the intense astronomical concern evident in the Mesoamerican high cultures and the practices that can be detected in the North American Southwest and in the Mound Builders areas of the Midwest. The remarkable beauty and variety of Mayan and Mexican architectural structures, as well as the enigma of the abandonment of the sacred centers, has long intrigued archeologists and astronomers.

**Cataclysms on Earth**. Mesoamerican archeoastronomy and ethnoastronomy may help solve a question upon which scientists are divided—*i.e.*, whether the Earth has in reality undergone catastrophic events within historical times. A large-scale comparison of Mesoamerican site destructions between 1500 and 600 BC and a systematic study of Mesoamerican astronomical records of early planetary movements, should be of use.

One especially notable feature of Mesoamerican ceremonial centers, the ball court, has long been thought to have been associated with a solar cult, but may instead show a significant association with Venus. Evidence has been produced to demonstrate an association with Venus by comparing iconography on the four walls of the ball court at Tajin (dated AD 1000) with a legend in which the planet-god comes down to earth, indulges in a sinful love affair, suffers, dies, and is transformed. The Caracol at Chichén Itzá also appears to have had significant alignments with regard to Venus.

The sacred ball game may have commemorated a cosmic catastrophe in which, as the epics specifically state, a former world age ended and the present one began, the successful ball game players (Hunter and Jaguar Deer) becoming the present Moon and Sun. It is not uncommon for the heroes of an astronomical myth to end up as celestial bodies, but rarely is the process terminating a world age as explicitly described as in the Mesoamerican epics and legends. The Mesoamerican cosmology of world ages ended by cosmic destruction parallels the sequence of events outlined in a hypothesis of the history of Venus. In that hypothesis, Venus entered the solar system as a comet, and the Earth passed through the tail of this comet in 1400 BC, after which Venus reapproached at dreaded 52-year intervals until in 700 BC it came into collison with Mars, and was propelled to its present, safe orbit. Whatever the explanation, clearly the catastrophic legendary materials and the anomalies of the Olmec site destruction must be explained. Although the objective reality of the cosmic disturbances described in Mesoamerican epics is not yet scientifically studied, mathematical analysis of possible orbital changes, based on findings from space exploration and on astrophysical hypothesis, indicates that such a celestial dislocation as is described in the *Popol Vuh* and in the *Ipuwer* papyrus is by no means impossible. Studies of Venus observations made by ancient Mesopotamian observers also suggest that the early behavior of Venus was erratic. Ancient descriptions and iconographic representations of Venus suggest that the planet had a much greater size and brilliance than at present. Clearly the Mesoamerican, Mesopotamian, and Egyptian observations and cosmologies, as well as the *Ipuwer* documents, should be made the subject of a comparative study. The "errors" reported may lie not with the observations of the ancient astronomers but in the assumption that present planetary orbits may be taken as models for those of earlier periods.

The destruction of early American ceremonial centers, similarly, should be compared with that of Bronze Age site destructions elsewhere, and equated with geological and other evidence of tectonic and volcanic events. One scholar's suggestion that Mesoamerican cultural discontinuities may be attributed to the collapse of a theocracy that had shown itself unable to control destructive celestial events is worth consideration. It must be noted, however, that Olmec construction dates are suspect, due to the possibility of contamination during large-scale combustion attributable in a hypothesis of cosmic disaster. *Trez Zapotes*, for example, yields a quite improbable date of 9000 BC; its early levels are sealed with volcanic ash. Also, asphalt lumps have been noted at San Lorenzo. Clearly the Olmec site destructions are of importance with regard to Bronze Age site destructions elsewhere.

The classic Mesoamerican cultures flowered so late that textual references and astronomical notations may well contain information with regard to the actual and objective events that were the basis for Mesoamerican and other legendary and epic accounts of the destruction that ended the last world age and brought about the present orbits of Sun and Moon, Venus and Mars. It may not be coincidental that the events described in American accounts are strikingly similar to those described by *Ipuwer*, half a world away. In short, Mesoamerican and other ancient historians may have been romancing or they may have been recounting ancestral stories and eyewitness accounts of events that did indeed happen in the "real world out there."

**COTTON**. Native American cultivation of cotton extended from the *Hopi* and the Rio Grande pueblos of New Mexico to Central Chile, Tucumán, and Paraguay. In North America, the limits of its cultivation fell significantly short of the areas climatically suited. Cotton was not cultivated by the tribes of the south, notwithstanding the favorable soil and climate. (The cotton blankets seen by De Soto's troops on the lower Mississippi were said to have been brought from the West, possibly from the far-off pueblo country of New Mexico and Arizona.) Although New Mexico and Arizona seem less favorable to its cultivation, cotton has been raised to a considerable extent by the Pueblos, especially the Hopi, from time immemorial, and cloth, cord, thread, and seed are commonly found in ancient deposits in caves, cliff-dwellings and ruined pueblos throughout that region.

The Hopi are now the only cultivators and weavers of cotton, their product consisting chiefly of ceremonial robes, kilts and scarfs, finding their way through trade to many other tribes who, like the Hopi, employ them in their religious performances. In the time of Coronado (1540-42) and of Espejo (1583), Acoma and the Rio Grande villages in New Mexico, and the Pima of southern Arizona also raised the plant, until about 1850; but the introduction of cheap fabrics by traders has practically brought the industry to an end everywhere among the Indians, the Hopi alone adhering to the old custom of cultivating and weaving it, and that chiefly for ceremonial garments. In ancient Hopi and Zuñi mortuary rites, raw cotton was placed over the face of the dead, and cotton seed was often deposited with food vessels and other accompaniments in the grave.

In South America, the Andean populations were supplied with cotton in quantity from both flanks of the Andes. In the arid coastal lowlands much cotton was grown by irrigation. In both *Inca* and pre-*Inca* coastal sites there is found, in addition to the cotton textiles, a good deal of cotton in the seed (both the large naked and tufted seeds, probably *barbadense* at Ocucaje, for instance). On the eastern flank the Yungas of the Antisuyo were noted producers, as were, farther north, the Chachapoyas-Moyobamba and Quijos-Canela regions.

In aboriginal Venezuela the district of Tocuyo produced coarse cotton piece goods, from which the name "tocuyo" passed into wide Spanish usage for coarse cotton cloth. Very fine thread is found in Peruvian textiles; at the other extreme twine and cordage were made from cotton; especially in areas lacking the coarser fibers of cabuya and maguey. The natural fiber colors, white, tawny brown, red, and green are known. Seeds were not generally used for food, but had medicinal uses.

Both in the New and the Old World the cottons grown before the industrial revolution were mainly

Distribution of cotton during the Inca period.

perennials, annual forms making their appearance where seasons did not admit perennial habit. In higher latitudes, with long summer days, an annual, more herbaceous form tended to replace the perennial form. Where winter cold was encountered, only the annual forms, it appears, could exist. In the polar parts of the range, therefore, annual forms should have prevailed, and it is from such margins probably that the sea island and upland cottons were selected. Early historical references to annual cottons in the New World are lacking.

Geographically, there are two large species of New World cultivated cottons: *Gossypium barbadense*, and *G. hirsutum*. (Genetically, there is a third, *G. tomentosum*, endemic to Hawaii, which is "generally further removed from *G. hirsutum* than *G. hirsutum* is from *G. barbadense*").

With regard to *barbadense* the situation is well clarified. Here belong Peruvian and some woody Brazilian cottons. Its aboriginal range included the West Indies, the Caribbean mainland, coastal Peru, and the Brazilian lowlands. In its most ordinary form, that of a vigorously branching shrub, *barbadense* is restricted to low latitudes (short-day habit).

Prehistorically, the *barbadense* complex appears to have been almost wholly South American, meeting the North American *hirsutum* complex only in lower Central America and in the West Indies.

*G. hirsutum* in the large sense extended aboriginally from the Colorado Plateau in the north (archeologically), southward along the Pacific coast to the Tumbes area of Peru (Boza), across the West Indies and along the northern shores of South America into northeast Brazil. Its major area was Middle America, both mainland and island, and its South American penetration appears to have been principally from the northern shores southward, and along the coast.

**COUP** designated the formal token or signal of victory in battle by North American Plains Indians. Coups were usually "counted," as it was termed—that is, credit of victory was taken, for three brave deeds, killing an enemy, scalping an enemy, or being first to strike an enemy either alive or dead. Each one of these entitled a man to rank as a warrior and to recount the exploit in public; but to be first to touch the enemy was regarded as the bravest deed of all, as it implied close approach during battle.

Among the Cheyenne it was even a point of bravado for a single warrior to rush in among the enemy and strike one with a quirt or gun before attempting to fire, thus doubly risking his own life. Three different coups might thus have to be counted by as many different persons upon the body of the same enemy, and in a few tribes four were allowed. The stealing of a horse from a hostile camp also carried the right to count coup. The stroke (coup) might be made with whatever was most convenient, even with the naked hand, a simple touch scoring the victory. In ceremonial parades and functions an ornamented quirt or rod was sometimes carried and used as a coup stick. The warrior who could strike a tipi of the enemy in a charge upon a home camp thus counted coup upon it and was entitled to reproduce its particular design upon the next new tipi which he made for his own use, and to perpetuate the pattern in his family. In this way, he was said to "capture" the tipi. Warriors who had made coups of distinguished bravery, such as striking an enemy within his own tipi or behind a breastwork, were selected to preside over the dedication of a new tipi. The noted Sioux Chief Red Cloud stated in 1891 that he counted coup 80 times.

**COURTSHIP CUSTOMS**. Basically there is only one generalization that should be made about the customs and cultures of Native Americans in precontact or aboriginal and early historic times, and that is that they were characterized by much linguistic and cultural diversity. This is also true of customs of courtship and marriage, where the primary generalization that can be made is that for most tribes marriage was a normal, expected, and often mandatory state of affairs where it was expected that every person would marry.

In some societies adult status was dependent upon marriage and parenthood. The actual forms of courtship and marriage ranged from informal and casual practices, like those of the Eskimo, to formal and structured patterns, like those of the Natchez in the Southeast and of the Northwest Coast tribes. This discussion will be limited to customs of the North American continent, although similar practices may be found among the native populations of Middle and South America.

To illustrate the range of marriage customs found in North America, a brief description of Eskimo and Northwest Coast practices will be given. For the Eskimo, marriage was a cooperative relationship between males and females that was built up over a time of cohabitation during which children were born and ties of economic interdependence and cooperation developed with both sets of kindred. Courtship was casual; a young couple from groups with no existing relationships of mutual aid began having sexual relations, and if they were compatible, they would remain together. There was no formal ceremony. Permanence and stability in the relationship came with the birth of children. Polygynous marriages were permissible if the male was capable of supporting more than one wife. While the economic balance and division of labor made marriage necessary, this same economic balance of property rights helped make marriages last. However, marriages were brittle, ending through disagreements, strife, and involvement with other men. Most marriages were dissolved due to sexual rivalries; indeed, most male rivalries were over women and sexual adjustment and dominance predominated in interpersonal relations.

Northwest Coast tribes could be regarded as falling toward the other end of a continuum of formality and structure in marriage customs. Here virginity appears to have been valued, as virginal brides were dowered and constantly chaperoned. A girl was considered marriageable after her puberty ritual, and the most desired quality in a bride was industriousness. Marriage arrangements were made by the groom and the bride's family. The suitor brought gifts to her family; he might sit at the door of her house for a period of days while he was insulted and sent on errands by her family. Following the successful bargaining over bride price, which might include skins, canoes, fish, and oil, the wedding was celebrated with a feast and a potlatch. When the bride went to her husband's canoe, she walked on a carpet of skins that were part of her dowry. Sororal polygyny was practiced, with bride price paid for each bride. In a society oriented toward the accumulation of wealth and social status, the more wives a man had, the more wealth he could accumulate. Marriages were not easily dissolved; divorce was rare, especially in families of chiefs.

### Criteria for selecting a bride

Certain criteria in selection of a bride seem to have been fairly common in North America. In societies where there were girls' puberty rituals, the girl had to have gone through the ritual before she could be considered marriageable.

One universal criterion in spouse selection was blood relationship; all Native American societies practiced some form of kin group exogamy, although this ranged from nuclear family (Eskimo) to class (Natchez), with clan, lineage, and moiety exogamy found most commonly. The Natchez system probably was the most unique. There were two exogamous social classes, the nobility, divided into Suns, Nobles, and Honored Men, and the commoners, called the "Stinkards" by the French. The nobility were required to marry Stinkards; the children of women of the nobility had the status of their mothers in this matrilineal society, while the children of fathers of nobility and commoner mothers moved down one step in the social scale: Suns became Nobles, Nobles became Honored Men, and Honored Men became Stinkards. Kinship criteria also included cross-cousin marriage as a preferred form of marriage in some societies. In matrilineal systems, patrilateral cross-cousins often were preferred marriage partners.

Among the Navajo, Algonquins, and tribes of the Southeast and Northwest Coast industriousness and competence were also valued traits in a bride. Other traits with more limited distribution included health, social position, age, observation of menstrual taboos (Southeast), and beauty and chastity (Plains). Among the Plains tribes, it was not the young men who were expected to do the heavy work of tanning and preparing hides and making tipi covers, but older married women. Hence beauty was more important among Plains tribes in selection of a bride than was industriousness. Chastity in a bride was also not commonly a critical factor in choosing a bride. It was found primarily among the Plains tribes and in the Northwest Coast; among the latter, it was usually found in conjunction with the factor of social class. Among most tribes, premarital sexual freedom was accepted and expected behavior. The Catawba had a class of "prostitutes," attractive young women who offered their sexual favors for a fee, which was then turned over to the chief. There was no social stigma attached to this "occupation"; after several years of prostitution, the women married, had families, led normal lives, and were not looked down upon.

Actual courtship among Native Americans, in which young men wooed young women, was relatively rare. It was found among the central Algonquins and some Plains tribes, where during the summer young men wooed young women with flutes, love songs, and gestures. Generally, however, marriages were arranged by the families, particularly if bride price was involved. For example, in the Southeast, the young couple had no choice in the selection of their marriage partners. Once a boy had received his adult name, after he had performed an act of bravery, he was ready for marriage. His bride was selected by the female members of his clan and his maternal uncles, and they made the arrangements with the bride's clan. Among the Plains tribes, where chastity was honored and girls chaperoned, men married only after they had achieved some degree of social position through war exploits of counting coups and stealing horses. The horses were necessary for the gift made to the bride's brother, who made the arrangements for the marriage.

In the Southeast, Northwest, and northern California, where bride price was found, it was necessary to legitimate the marriage and often for purposes of social status as well. It was usually found in conjunction with bride service for those who could not pay the bride price, although bride service without bride price occurred among the northern Algonquins like the Slave, Dogrib and Yellowknife. In some societies the groom's family gave gifts to the bride's family. Among the Navajo, horses or livestock were given; on the Plains, horses were given to the girl's brother; among Great Lake Algonquins, meat was the gift; and among the eastern Algonquins, the gift was wampum. Gift exchanges were found in California (among the Pomo they were pledges of good will between the two families) and on the Plains. Dowries were uncommon, found primarily among Northwest Coast tribes in conjunction with status and virginity.

Spouses could also be acquired through inheritance, through the practices of the levirate and the sororate, which usually occurred together. These practices were found in the Southeast, California, and among some of the Plains tribes.

**Marriage rituals**

Some tribes had little or no ritual accompanying marriage. Among the Zuñi, where marriage arrangements were made by the groom and the bride's father, if the girl agreed to the marriage, the couple would go to bed and then the bride washed the groom's hair. Four days later, she took a basket of corn to her mother-in-law, and they were considered married. Among many California tribes, like the Mohave and the Luiseño, there was no bride price, gift exchange, or ceremony. Marriage simply involved cohabitation.

Among most tribes, however, there was usually some form of ritual to mark the transition in status in the life cycle, usually involving a feast. Among the Southeastern tribes this was a secular and economic event that was also necessary to seal the union. It involved breaking an ear of corn in two and planting two reeds and then a trial period for the marriage until the next Busk (Green Corn ceremony). The Navajo ceremony was held in the hogan of the bride's parents after they had received the gift of livestock. The ceremony involved a ritual meal of corn mush eaten from a new wedding basket (colloquially called "dipping the corn") with the bridal couple symbolically feeding each other and then passing the basket to the guests. An older man, usually a singer, exhorted them on the responsibilities and spiritual aspects of marriage, and then the guests shared a feast of mutton and coffee.

Elopement was an alternative escape to arranged marriages, common in societies where there was little choice to the individuals involved.

**Marriage forms and practices**

While the actual form of marriage was usually monogamy (serial monogamy in the case of some Puebloans), polygyny, generally sororal polygyny, was frequently the preferred form of marriage. It was found among the Athapascans, the Northwest Coast tribes (where it was related to social status and wealth), the Iroquois, the Algonquins, Plains tribes, Eskimo, Basin-Plateau tribes, and in the Southeast. Polyandry is reported to have occurred among some of the northern Athapascans (Slave, Dogrib, Yellowknife) and in the Basin.

Post-marital residence practices were frequently related to the kinship system. Matrilocal residence practices were frequently related to the kinship system. Matrilocal residence usually was found with matrilineal descent systems (southern Athapascans, Southeast, Iroquois, and Pueblo) and was also usually associated with mother-in-law avoidance. Virilocality was found among the tribes of California, the Northwest Coast, and the Algonquins.

While premarital sexual freedom was generally the rule among Native Americans, post-marital chastity was universally required, except in cases where wife-lending or wife-hospitality occurred (among the Natchez and the Eskimo, and here it was permitted only when the husband offered the sexual favors of his wife to persons he selected). Adulterous women often were physically punished, by having the tips of their ears or noses cut off, for instance. Among the Algonquins they were disowned by their husbands; among some Plains tribes they were subjected to rape by all men of the band or tribe, and divorce was frequently the result. Sometimes the male partner might be killed as well.

**Dissolution of marriages**

While death was the one universal way of ending marriages, attitudes towards divorce varied. Divorce was easy and common in the Southwest, California, and the Plains, although steps would be taken to prevent it. Among the Southwestern tribes it was often the women who instituted divorce proceedings by placing the husband's possessions outside the hogan or pueblo, an indication that the marriage was over. It terminated when he took his possessions to his home. In the Southeast, Northwest Coast, Plateau, and among the Iroquois, however, divorce was both rare and difficult.

Grounds for divorce were varied; adultery or infidelity was the most common, followed by childlessness or barrenness. Other reasons included inability to resolve differences, laziness, nagging, and incompatibility.

RACHEL A. BONNEY

**CRAFTS** have traditionally held an unparalleled position in Indian life. The creation of both functional objects and objects of ceremonial significance is an important aspect of all Indian cultures, although the specific kinds of crafts differ from region to region. The physical environment of a tribe determined those peoples' needs; the variety of objects created by craftspeople was based on the kind of life led by the individual tribes. For example, Indians whose subsistence was dependent on agriculture and who therefore led rather sedentary lives utilized pottery vessels with greater frequency than the more nomadic hunting peoples who created containers from hide. Coastal dwellers of both the Northwest Coast and the East lived in areas that were heavily forested; therefore these peoples developed significant carving skills in wood, while desert dwellers used wooden objects less frequently, giving wooden objects greater value. With the advent of inter-tribal trade and the influence of white settlers, the North American tribes were no longer limited to indigenous materials and began to transcend the barriers imposed by their environments.

An aesthetic value common throughout Indian cultures was the artisan's appreciation of the material used in his or her craft, and the relationship between that material—whether stone, clay, horn, wood, or plant—and the objects which were created. Because of the pervasive belief in the unity of all things, there was great respect for each region's natural resources, and whatever spiritual powers those resources were believed to contain. Often, especially in the process of creating objects to be used in ceremonial contexts, the artisan would take great pains to ritually insure that the spiritual forces contained in the original material be successfully transmitted into the final object.

Good craftsmanship has traditionally been a part of the Indian culture, and the Indian artisans' sensitivity to the balance of content and form is crucial. Functional objects of everyday use, such as dishes, knives, blankets, and clothing were created with great care. Often, notably among Northwest Coast Indians, a chief's high status was maintained by his ownership of great amounts of such utilitarian objects as well as the more symbolically significant totem poles. Even today, Indian artisans of the Southwest are awarded prizes for their crafts at the annual competition in Gallup, New Mexico. Craftspeople were carefully trained, usually instructed by older artisans in both the physical and metaphysical understandings of the creative process. In some tribes, the position of artisan was hereditary, inherited by sons and daughters of artisans.

There is a rather strict distinction made in most tribes between crafts made by women and those made by men. Carvers of both wood and stone objects are men; most weavers, potters, basket-makers, beadworkers, and costume-makers have been women, although there are some exceptions. In general, the majority of objects used for ceremonial purposes were created by men and the more sedentary kinds of crafts were created by women, as women's lives were traditionally oriented around staying at home. Neither category eclipses the other in importance, however, as ceremony was heavily integrated into the pattern of daily life.

The major traditional crafts of Indians are carving (in wood, stone, bone, and horn), baketry, weaving, pottery, painting, jewelry, quillwork, beadwork, and rock art. Materials were often combined on a single object, as in the Hopi kachina dolls—carved figures which are painted wood, frequently decorated with feathers and beads as well as hide masks. In general, artisans of each geographical area developed distinctly different stylistic ways of treating similar objects. For example, therefore, it is not at all difficult to distinguish between Hopi and Papago baskets, Northwest Coast and Navajo blankets, and carved figures of all cultural areas. Decorative patterns were also interrelated, and often the decoration found on textiles (blankets and fabrics) is derived from decorative patterns on basketry. Pottery patterns in the Southwest frequently have been influenced by Spanish artifacts.

Geographically, the area cultivated by the Indians north of Mexico can be divided into major culture regions—Northwest Coast and Arctic, California, Southwest, Plains, and East—each of which exhibits strengths in different crafts.

Eskimo art (crafts of the Arctic region) is essentially composed of objects carved in wood, ivory, horn, and bone. This craftsmanship was primarily exhibited in functional objects which were decorated in either a highly naturalistic style, consisting mainly of human and animal figures carved in the round, or a more two-dimensional geometric system which was made up of patterns combining lines and circles and abstracted figures. In Alaska, wooden masks were carved, painted, and decorated with feathers for use in ceremonies.

Artisans of the Northwest Coast were also dependent on wood and their creations were extraordinary both in size and in importance. The totem poles covered with figures carved into the huge blocks of wood were created as significant symbols reflecting the hierarchic social system operating in that area. Family lineages were represented by the use of animal and human figures which indicated the wealth and prestige of the owner. The fronts of houses were often painted with abstracted animal symbols for the same social reasons. Most Northwest Coast artisans created functional objects; their decorative carving and painting were made to fit the demands of these objects. Smaller objects with animal and human figures in the same style were carved in horn and ivory, and these same motifs were incorporated into canoes, baskets, blankets, clothing, furniture, tools, and implements used in cooking. The Chilkat blankets of the Tlingit incorporated into weaving the patterns common to carving and painting.

Chilkat blanket, a unique form of blanket woven by the Tlingit, is perhaps the most significant craft of these people of the Northwest Coast.

The Chilkat blanket is woven form mountain goat wool or dog hair on a crudely designed loom, where the single warp beam is cedar. The blankets are five-sided, and have a pointed base and straight top edge. Since weaving is traditionally the work of women in the Northwest Coast area, Chilkat blankets are woven by women. They are, however, designed by men who are also the carvers and painters of the more dramatic Northwest Coast crafts. The decorative scheme is therefore quite consistent with the decoration of less static craft forms, such as carving and painting.

The blankets are highly decorated in the traditional Northwest Coast manner, which is made up of a stylized complex flat pattern. The major design elements of this culture are carefully architected into the blanket forms: all available space is covered, an animal or human figure is shown as though split into two symmetrical halves, and the use of x-ray views and eye joints (the repetition of circles) is included. The blankets share the same mysterious ambiguity of content with other Northwest Coast crafts. Anthropomorphic and zoomorphic forms are divided by lines which show the figure simultaneously frontally and in profile. The figures are made confusing to the observer by the addition of "filler" material: circles and geometric shapes which have questionable symbolic implications. Scholars speculate that their full meanings are known only to the weaver and original owner of the blanket.

The blankets are brightly colored. The older blankets were woven in natural colors: yellow, black, and blue; yarns dyed with European pigments found their way into Chilkat blankets only as trade and interaction with the non-Indian peoples grew.

In the north, the naturalistic treatment of form was translated into a more abstracted stylistic treatment wherein animals were distinguishable from one another through the inclusion of certain key identifying features. The central tribes were more naturalistic, and, as in dancers' masks and costumes, were created to convey an impression of the infusion of the supernatural force into the physical object.

The objects created by Plains artisans were equally as functional; however as their lives revolved around buffalo hunting, buffalo hide was the most commonly utilized material. It was sewn into containers, especially parfleches; clothing; tipis; drums; and shields, and was decorated either by polychromy painting or with embroidery. Objects were embroidered with porcupine quills and later, with glass beads obtained by trading with Europeans; painting was, however, the more extensively used form of decoration. Some wooden and stone objects used in ceremonies were also painted and decorated with beads, feathers, and quills. Both geometric and naturalistic styles were common in painting and embroidery, and were often invested with symbolic significance, as was the choice of colors used.

Pueblo Indians of the area now known as the Southwestern United States were quite diversified. Basketry, jewelry, pottery, carved figures, mural painting, sand painting, and blankets were all created, since the area was not limited by one material. Most decoration—whether painted, woven, or carved—was traditionally geometric, and frequently was religiously symbolic; however much of the decoration was abstracted from naturalistic forms. There are as many varieties of pottery and basketry as there are tribes in the Southwest. Navajo rugs and blankets are also found in a diversity of styles. Hopi, Zuñi, and Navajo jewelry all utilize the same materials—silver, coral, turquoise, and sometimes shell—but have quite readily distinguishable characteristics. Sand painting and mural painting were both based in ceremonial traditions; sand paintings, which are made by using many colors of dry materials in forming symbolic figures of humans, animals, plants, and celestial bodies to appeal to spiritual forces, rarely survive after their ritual use is completed.

Crafts of tribes of the East were quite varied; few examples still exist, however. Body ornamentation, including painting and tattooing, was prevalent and was widely utilized for ceremonial purposes. Other ornamental objects were made of wood, shell, dopper, and even stone. Clothing was decorated with animal skins, feathers, and hair. Utilitarian objects were carved from wood and painted in bright colors: human and animal figures (often larger than life-sized) in decorated villages. Small stone figures were also carved. Baskets, woven in colored materials, were decorated with geometric designs. Pottery was often decorated with figures of living things.

The current interest in Indian culture and crafts has led to a greater appreciation by non-Indians of these objects, and to a deeper understanding of the philosophies of the people who created them. This increased popularity brings with it a tendency toward creating crafts solely for sale to the tourist or collector trade, rather than for use as a part of everyday life. It has, more encouragingly, also led toward the recognition of Indians as individual craftspeople, and has opened up new areas in art to Indians, such as pottery.

## Pottery

Pottery, which has been developed to an incomparable level of sophistication among some Indian tribes, occupies an especially prominent place in the study of Indian crafts. Pottery making was not common to all Indians. Since it was impractical for nomadic people to transport breakable clay pots and jars as they travelled and desert and coastal dwelling peoples had other materials (wood and plants) from which to carve and weave containers. Areas in which pottery was significant were those regions in which a sedentary agriculturally dependent culture survived. For the areas in which pottery making was prominent, most particularly the pueblo Southwestern United States and the Mississippi Valley and Gulf region, its development from prehistoric times (*c.* 300 BC) through the present has resulted in spectacular craftsmanship.

Potters have traditionally been women, since the craft is considered a sedentary one. It has only been in the past twenty-five years, with the recognition of individual potters and artisans, that a few notable men have become potters. Pottery containers were used extensively in cooking and eating, and as vessels for carrying and storing waters and foods. The variety of elements that comprise the making of pottery—the clay, temper (material which is added to the clay to prevent its cracking in the drying and firing stages), size and shape of the pot, its decoration and ultimate use—insure the uniqueness of each piece of pottery. It is interesting, however, that very strong stylistic features have evolved which make pots of each tribe (and often of individual potters) easily distinguishable from one another. Most pottery was created for functional everyday purposes, but some tribes did create pottery solely for ceremonial usage or for commercial trade.

The three methods of pottery making were coiling, modeling, and molding the clay. Coiling has been the predominant method, especially as American Indian potters traditionally have not used a potter's wheel or a kiln. In making a coiled pot, the potter formed the base and then added coils made from rolled out balls of clay, connecting the coils by rubbing or pinching their ends together. This method was the most popular in the southern half of North America, the area in which most

Indian pottery was produced. Modeling a pot consisted of building the rectangular sides of the pot onto the base, pinching them together at the edges of contact. In molding, a pot was constructed around another pot or basket or even a hole in the ground whose form was being followed by the shape of the new pot. Except for the pottery of one Eskimo region, the earliest pottery in the northern half of the continent was modeled or molded, but the coiling technique of the southern half soon became a prominent method of pottery construction in this area too. Often, paddles and anvils were used both in smoothing and shaping the pots, and in applying decorative stamps or designs to the exteriors. Other decoration was made by incising the clay with geometric and often symbolic designs of living organisms. Coloration of pottery was frequently employed.

The potter dug the clay out of the ground. Her tempering materials included sand, crushed stone, and shells. The pot was hand-built from the mixture of clay, temper, and water; once it was shaped, the pot was left in the shade to dry. It was then scraped and smoothed with a stone (although the Navajo potters used corncobs as a smoothing tool) and moistened with slip. If the pot was to be painted, pigments originally ground from minerals (with the exceptions of a black color sometimes used in the Southwest which came from a weed, and the poster paints used by the Tesuque and neighboring Santa Domingo Indians) were applied with a brush made by chewing the end of a yucca stem until it was malleable. The basic colors, using the mineral-based pigments, were black, white, tan, off-white, yellow, red, and orange. Only rarely were glazes employed, and when used they never covered the entire pot. In fact, the base of an Indian pot is always left unpainted and unglazed. The pots were then baked in clay ovens heated to temperatures of 1200-1500°F, or in open or covered fires.

The pottery of the Southwestern United States, particularly that of the Pueblo Indians, is considered to be the most revealing recording of the life and artistic behavior of the inhabitants of that area. Pottery has been produced in this region for an impressive amount of time (*c.* 300 BC to the present). The forms and decorative aspects show the variety of uses of pottery by the people of the Southwest throughout this span of time. The adherence to traditional shapes and decorative elements is a profound expression of the Indians' belief in the continuity of life and their respect for tradition. Pottery is one of the few crafts in which the influence of non-Indian cultures has not caused tremendously reckless changes in the quality or conception of the crafts.

The three major traditions in pueblo pottery were the Mogollan, Hohokam, and Anasazi. The Mogollan bowls and round narrow-necked jars were quite simple in form. The earliest Mogollan pottery was molded, but the coiling technique was used. First the potters scraped the coiled exterior surface until it became smooth, but later the coils around the neck of the jars were left unscraped. In this early stage of Mogollan pottery the usual red or brown color was supplanted by the use of reduction firing, a process in which the amount of oxygen is reduced in firing, thus causing a blackening of the pottery. Although the inclusion of geometric patterns was not unknown, undecorated simple pottery was the hallmark of this stage. Hohokam pottery, uniquely lacking in protuberances, was made in a multitude of shapes. The "Gila-shouldered" jars are the largest pots ever made in the Southwest. The famous Mimbres paddled coiled bowls and pitchers were covered with black ornamentation painted on a white background. The majority of these were decorated with complex geometric patterns, but later some were painted with stylized life forms: figures of people, fish, toads, lizards, birds, dogs, insects, and other animals. Other Hohokam vessels were tan, gray, or red, or a combination of these colors. The first polychrome painting on pottery was introduced in Hohokam pots with the use of yellow pigment. The Anasazi pottery tradition was by far the most diverse, the pottery of different regions showed many variations of form and decoration. Following the Mogollan tradition, the early Modified Basketmaker vessels were coiled and scraped; and in the same tradition, some potters even left the neck coils unscraped. Early pottery had black designs on gray, or white or red or orange. The ornamentation was simple geometric line patterns. In the Developmental Pueblo stage which followed this early period, coiled pots were made in which thc coils were not smoothed over, as well as the plain gray pottery. Most of the decoration was black painted on white or red, and utilized innovative geometrical variations incorporating not only simple linear designs but also step motifs, spirals, meanders, triangles, dots, scrolls, and complex interwoven patterns. There was some geometrical treatment of life forms. The great regional variety in pottery was a characteristic of all stages of Anasazi pottery making. Modern pottery for the most part, has adhered to the forms and decorative elements of the three traditions, particularly the dominant Anasazi.

Hopi pottery, the most outstanding of all pueblo pottery,.is still created for utilitarian purposes in almost every village of the three Mesas. Like their ancestors, the contemporary Hopi use the bowls for cooking and serving and the jars (*ollas*) for storing food and water. Many of these vessels are undecorated and are brown or gray or a variegated orange.

The decorated pottery, made in First Mesa, is famous for its complex treatment of space and form. The low wide bowls and short bulging jars are covered with curvilinear patterns reminiscent of earlier pottery yet increasingly innovative. The potters' control of line can be seen in the geometric shapes and abstracted (often beyond recognition) representations of animals or parts of animals, lightning, rain clouds, and kachina figures. Bowls are decorated on the inside, sometimes with additional repeating geometric patterns appearing in a band on the exterior of the rim. Interior decoration can be either symmetrical or asymmetrical, commonly employing a variety of linear curves and stylized birds. Bcause of their shape, the jars are decorated on the outside. Banding begins just below the area at the top of the jar. The geometric pattern on the band can be repeated across the jar, or the band can be divided in several ways: into two symmetrically ornamented halves; into anywhere from four to six parts either of equal or unequal size, and decorated wtih repeating parts of equal size which are filled with one of three design patterns. The colors are usually black on tan; red, black and white on red; or black and red on tan. Very often the clay used by Hopi potters does not require a temper. The bowls and jars are commonly quite thin and smoothed.

The clay of the Zuñi has always been heavy, by contrast, although the surface of Zuñi pots appears smooth. In addition to the bowls and ollas, for about 100 years the Zuñi have made pottery owls. Bowls are no longer made and jars are not produced in any quantity today, although the owls are commercially successful. The owls are painted with black over a white base; the feathers and wings and round open eyes are painted in a conventionalized manner. The jars are divided vertically between the neck and body by a horizontal band, referred to as a "life line." Based on a legendary belief that the potter's spirit should not be trapped inside her pot, the life line is broken at one point on each jar to insure that the spirit will have a way to escape so the pottery will not die. The painted decoration was much less refined in Zuñi pottery than in Hopi. Zuñi jar decoration is made up of geometric elements: simple squares, diamonds, hooks, scrolls, step patterns, and rosettes; as well as representations of birds and deer. The painting on modern jars has degenerated considerably in both quality of work and treatment of space. Zuñi bowls were decorated, like their Hopi counterparts, with an internal geometric elaboration of lines and a band around the external rim containing a simple repeating unit of geometrical forms. The interiors of the bowls were designed so that a complicated band covering the deepest part of the bowl was beneath a more simply designed thinner band. The more complex larger band utilized a combination of the same geometric elements seen in jar decoration.

The pottery of the Rio Grande pueblos has gained great notoriety in the 20th century, for it was in San

Ildefonso where Maria Martinez and her husband Julian developed the matte-polished pottery, which is the single most important innovation in modern Indian pottery. Through the 19th century the pottery of this area had been made for everyday use in cooking and storing food and water. Geometric decoration was black (sometimes with red) painted on white or off-white, or black on red, and a monochromatic pottery of all-red or all-black was also produced. In the early 1920s, Maria and Julian Martinez arrived at a process by which a stylized matte design on a highly polished background was created. Best known in its all-black form, it has also been adapted for monochromatic pottery in red, light blue or gray, rose, tan, or combinations of white matte on polished tan or red backgrounds. Carved pottery was also developed at San Ildefonso and has been incorporated into the matte-polished ware. Potters in the nearby Santa Clara and San Juan pueblos have followed Maria Martinez' technique and have enjoyed similar commercial rewards. Often, the matte-polished pottery of Santa Clara is indistinguishable from that of San Ildefonso. There are two shapes, however, which are distinctly Santa Claran: the dual-necked "wedding" jar and the jar with a singularly high neck and wide mouth. In addition, small animals and some vases with handles were made in Santa Clara. Santa Clara pottery frequently features ornamentation made by depressing dull objects into the clay, rather than painting on the surface of the clay. San Juan pottery incorporates incising into monochromatic pottery. Santa Domingo pots both in bichrome and polychrome have large geometric curvilinear designs. Zia pottery combines stylized birds and deer with leaves on a field of swirls and pointed shapes. The Acoma pottery, perhaps the most refined of all Rio Grande area pottery, has also the thinnest walls of all Southwestern pottery. No Acoma bowls have been made other than for comercial use in the past century. Acoma pottery decoration, black painted on orange tones, has two styles: naturalistic and geometric. The naturalistic style shows large birds separated by plant-like swirls, eating flowers or berries. The geometric style consists of a pattern of angular linear shapes (with the frequent addition of scallops and curves) which covers the jar. Recently an emphasis on linear hatched squares and diamonds has been popular. Cochiti jars and bowls are crudely shaped and painted in a relatively simplistic way, leaving large areas of pastel yellow or pink background between the large black figures of animals and humans. The unpainted pottery of Taos and Picuris are difficult to distinguish from one another. Potters from both pueblos use a clay containing mica, so that the resulting jars and bowls (and in Taos, bean pots) are shiny. The only ornamentation is the occasional indentation around the rim of these brown or gray pots. Their appearance is much closer to Navajo and non-pueblo pottery. For the two centuries before they became familiar with poster paints in the early 1920s, Tesuque and Jemez potters created lovely pots with simple shapes and flowing linear designs. Since the first quarter of this century, however, this pottery has degenerated into a glaring example of the effecct of commercialism on art. Not only do the potters of these pueblos now make jars and bowls in miniature (useless for utilitarian purposes), but they also break another tradition by painting them with brightly clashing commercial paints in blocky solid shapes. The pots continue to be commercially successful, either due to or in spite of their garishness.

Of the non-pueblo pottery, the most outstanding has come from the Mohave, Maricopa, Pima, and Papago. Most other non-pueblo Indians produced only crudely formed and decorated cooking pots. Mohave jars and bowls are simply shaped and decorated with angular patterns of lines with solid shapes filled in. Some jars are topped with human heads modeled onto the jar. Mohave modeled toads, made of thick clay and covered with red spots, are also popular. Maricopa pottery, the most sophisticated non-pueblo pottery, is usually red or red with black geometric ornamentation and has been highly polished. Pima and Papago tribes, excellent basketmakers, are no longer prolific potters. Traditional pottery of these tribes were red or black

wide-mouthed ollas decorated with linear and solid shapes, used for storing water. Contemporary Papago and Pima pottery consists of small jars, square or rectangle boxes, bowls, and ashtrays, all created and decorated with curvilinear lines and forms and sometimes even flower patterns, for commercial use.

None of the non-pueblo pottery comes close to matching the sophistication and elegant vitality of Hopi pottery, in form or decoration.

The Mississippi Valley and Gulf area of the United States was the second productive pottery-making region. Again, pots were used for cooking and storing food and water. Often, pottery was unpainted and decoration of these modeled jars and bowls took the form of incising or stamping the clay before firing, or engraving the hard clay walls after removing the pot from the oven. Sometimes holes were poked into the clay or roughly textured fabrics were pressed against the soft clay to form an impression from the weave. In addition, effigy figures of humans, animals, and plants were common decorative elements modeled onto the utilitarian vessels and pipes. Vases were quite colorful. Not infrequently, effigy figures themselves were modeled. If painted, southeastern pottery was usually red, or red decoration was painted on pots of white or tan. There were also some monochromatic black or brown pots, and some white based pots with black decoration. Thse painted designs, like their stamped, incised, or engraved counterparts, were both abstracted naturalistic forms or, more frequently, geometric. Southeastern pottery employs a more curvilinear treatment of design than does the pottery of the Southwest. The shapes of the pots, from the Mississippi to Florida, such as the three-legged ones, were influenced by trade with Europeans and West Indians.

The only other area in which pottery was mildly significant was in Alaska. There, fired pottery with designs made by stamping curvilinear patterns or impressing cord into the soft clay have been found ranging in age from 1000 BC to AD 900. There was a lack of pottery in the Pacific states and Northwest Coast. What little pottery came from southern California was most likely influenced by that of th nearest Southwestern Indians. The Iroquois of the mid-Atlantic region made some simple cooking vessels and pipes.

The influence of non-Indians and commercialization on the pottery of the Indians has had a variety of effects. Most obvious is the degeneration of traditional styles and decorative forms, as seen in the popularity of miniature bowls and jars in the Southwest and the use of poster paints by the Tesuque and Jemez. With the advent of the railroad and through increased trade, non-Indians also encouraged Indian potters to model clay to resemble animals (the Zuni owls and Mohave toads) because they were easily salable. For the same reason, new forms such as ashtrays, candlesticks, square boxes, and individual plates and saucers were created. The increase in travel and trade made it easier for Indians of one tribe to become familiar with the forms and designs of potters of other tribes, and the distinctions between tribal styles began to fade as they were copied and modified. The most encouraging effect of 20th century commercialization upon Southwestern potters has been the recognition of individual potters' contributions to the development of modern pottery. By valuing a pot with the potter's signature on the bottom more than an unsigned pot, white traders and collectors have introduced the element of financial success into the potter's feeling of pride in her careful artistry. At times, this recognition has influenced potters to attain levels of fine craftsmanship.

## Latin America

When the Spaniards first landed on Mexican soil, one of their greatest sources of amazement, among the many marvels of the New World, were the beautiful pieces of craftsmanship which the Indians used in their religious ceremonies, daily wear and personal ornaments. The praise rendered toward these objects by many of the chroniclers is proof that this art deeply impressed the Spaniards and its influence was a determining factor in the formation of the new American culture.

The samples of native craft which Cortés sent to

Europe brought forth phrases of admiration from many of the well-known figures of the Old World, such as this one of Durer's: "... I also saw the things that were brought to the King from the new land of gold: a sun, six-feet wide, made of pure gold, and also a moon, of the same size, in silver; further, several curious weapons and missiles; many strange garments, beds and all types of articles for human use, all of this more beautiful to behold than miracles. So precious were these objects that they were valued at one hundred thousand florins. And as for myself, I have never, in all the days of my life, seen things that so delighted my heart. For I saw among them wonderful works of art and was astonished at the subtle ingenuity of the men in those distant lands. I cannot say enough about the things which were before my eyes."

Although future artisans were obliged to adopt new aesthetic and ideological concepts in their work, the spirit of those ancient artists has endured up to our times. Thus the arts that the Spaniards introduced from Renaissance Europe acquired, in this new land, new life, new outlines, new essence. Sculptors and builders, both Indian and mestizo, created architectural forms of the most extraordinary baroque art, all impregnated with the spirit of their ancestral deities.

Potters, members of one of the most traditional and important of craft groups, ceased making ceremonial earthenware (at least in the eyes of the church and its spies) and soon adopted European and Chinese techniques. They thus succeeded in creating the new hand-varied ceramic work which is seen today. The great mass of Mixtec silver and goldsmith was absorbed almost in its entirety by the church for the fashioning of religious objects of gold and silver; only a small number of silversmiths remained who were dedicated to the making of feminine ornaments and jewelry, and relics which the people offered to their patron saints in gratitude for some favor. The gold and silver crafts went into decline when the influence of the church was limited by the Reform laws, and it was not until this century that they regained importance with the flourishing of new silver centers.

One of the handicrafts which underwent almost no change in style was that of textiles—the costumes of today are almost identical with those worn before the Conquest. However, new industries were established, such as that of the rebozo, possibly Oriental in its origin, and the sarape, derived from the Spanish shawl of the Jemez region.

Textiles and ceramics are the two most widespread crafts in Latin America.

There are several large pottery centers in various regions whose wares have an ample distribution. Such is the case of the pottery made in Tonalá and Tlaquepaque, Jalisco; the so called "talavera" or mayolica whose origin is undoubtedly Chinese and which is made in Puebla, Dolores Hidalgo, Guanajuato and Aguascalientes; the glazed earthenware from Oaxaca; the earthen pans and jars for cooking from Puebla, Texcoco, Tecomatepec and Metepec in the State of Mexico. Other ceramic centers sell their products within a certain limited area near the production center, such as Patamban, Purépero, Huantzito, Tzintzuntzan, Capula and Sta. Fe de la Laguna, in the State of Michoacán; Encarnación and Atemajac, in Jalisco; Tolimán and Amayaltepec, in Guerrero; Actlán, Huaquechula, San Mateo Acteopan and San Martin Texmelucan, in Puebla; Ocotlán in Tlaxcala; Huatusco in Veracruz; Ocotlán, Tehuantepec, Coyotepec and Atzompa in Oaxaca; Amatenango, in Chiapas; Tepakan in Campeche, and Ticul in Yucatán.

Ceramic products are fundamentally domestic in their purpose: cooking bowls, jugs and jars to carry or drink liquids, plates, etc. Used for ceremonial purpose are candlesticks, urns, and incense holders. There is, however, an interest in aspect of ceramics which is of great importance to the people: toys. These are made mainly in Tonalá, Jal., Metepec, Méx., Huaquechula and Acatlán, Pue., Huatusco, Ver., Amayaltepec and Talimán, Gro., Coyotepec, Atzompa, Juchitán and Tehuantepec, Oax., and in Ticul, Yuc. In spite of the fact that the mestizo population regards toys as such, for the indigenous population these have a deep ritualistic significance. They are made for such occasions as the Day of the Dead, Corpus Christi, Holy Week and Christmas.

These "toys" are very similar to the clay figurines whose significance is still not clear, which were made in Mexico more than three thousand years ago. Although they served a religious purpose, they did not always represent gods. Thus, the present "tangu-yu" of Juchitán and Tehuantepec, brightly colored clay dolls and horsemen on strange mounts, are placed on the altars on New Year's Eve, side by side with the patron saints. The toys from Metepec for the most part represent religious personages such as the Three Kings, St. James, Archangels, the Virgin Mary, Adam and Eve, etc. But the most popular and deeply-rooted toy in Mexico is that relating to the Day of the Dead (All Souls Day). Imagination runs wild in such objects as skulls whose lower jaws move by pulling a thread, skeletons which, by pulling another string, emerge from tombs, or whose joints move by springs, or "dance" at the slightest movement. All these toys of the dead, plus a variety of other ceremonial objects made of clay, paper, palm leaf, flowers, wood, sugar and bread constitute the most important elements in the Mexican cult of the dead.

Lacquer work is another craft which goes back to ancient pre-Hispanic times when it was used not only on gourds, but also on ceramics and onyx. The basic method is to apply many coats of color mixed with a resin extracted from a certain insect and a drying oil. Techniques differ according to the region. In Uruapan, Michoacán, the inlaid technique is used, i.e., carving out the design on the lacquer and then filling in with the chosen colors. This is the original method as can be seen on archaeological objects painted in "cloisonné." In other parts, a black, red or white lacquer base is applied and the design drawn on top with a brush. The main lacquer centers today are Uruapan and Pátzcuaro, in the State of Michoacán; Olinalá in Guerrero and Chiapa de Corzo in Chiapas.

Blown glass is another important handicraft which was introduced from Europe. Large factories exist in Mexico City, Guadalajara, Puebla and Texcoco.

Basketry, even earlier in origin than ceramics, is another significant craft. The principal production centers of baskets, cordage and hats are found among the various Otomi groups in the State of Hidalgo, the Chochopopolocas in southern Puebla, in the central region of Guerrero, south the Balsas River, and among the Mayas on the Yucatán peninsula where the famous "Panamá" or jipi japa hats are made.

Leatherwork, another industry of note, is best exemplified by the huarache or sandal, and the saddle. The largest production centers are Guadalajara, León, Puebla, Mexico City, Oaxaca and Mérida. The saddles made in Puebla are veritable works of art for their richness in decoration.

Amozoc, in the State of Puebla, excels in the making of objects of forged iron such as spurs with a blui tint, buckles, iron work for saddles and other charro accessories, machetes and cutlery.

Jalisco, Guerrero and Oaxaca are also famous for their machetes, those of Oaxaca being particularly beautiful for their engravings and inscriptions such as "if this snake bites you, there is no remedy at the drugstore," or "don't expose me without reason or put me away without honor," etc. In Santa Clara del Cobre, near the famous pre-Colombian copper mines of Hinguarán, Michoacán, the "beating" method is used on this metal: hammering the pieces of copper and shaping them into pots, jars, flower holders, fruit bowls, plates, etc., of lovely and elegant lines. In Puebla, Mexico City, Cuernavaca, Toluca, Guanajuato, Guadalajara and Taxco, tin is shaped into lanterns, candle-holders, mirror frames and other decorative objects.

Although Mexico is a country that produces an infinite variety of precious woods, these are employed to a comparatively small degree in the popular arts and crafts. Such objects as inlaid boxes for keeping rooster blades are made in Jalostotilán, Jalisco; jewel cases and chocolate beaters in Campeche and Yucatán; in Teocaltiche, Jalisco, and Uruapan, Michoacán, the wood is worked by turning and the use of bone applications is common. Furniture for popular use is made in Parcho, Mich., Puebla, Tehuantepec, Oax., and other places in southeastern Mexico. Dance masks and carved religious figures are made in Jalisco, Michoacán, Guerrero, Querétaro, Guanajuato, Chiapas and the State of Mexico.

In recent years, the artisans of Taxco have combined silver with precious woods such as rosewood, ebony and mahogany in the making of salad bowls, jewel cases and a variety of lovely brooches and bracelets. Colonial furniture of pine or white cedar is also mass-produced in Taxco.

And so, whether it be in the clothes he wears or the candy he eats, in the festive toys or the solemnity of his religious festivals, the Indian is always surrounded by beauty. For this reason, almost ten percent of the rural indigenous population is made up of artisans. Among the rural population, craftwork is as much a basic activity as agriculture. The latter insures the daily sustenance, while the former is the only means of obtaining a cash income without having to sell or transfer the crop. Thus, the Indian, in this productive pastime, lovingly and with no thought of praise, surrounds himself and his society with the beauty his spirit requires.

**CRIME AND DELINQUENCY**, the violation of principles of social control defined by the rulers, is one of the most difficult subjects in the study of Indians in the Americas. Official crime and delinquency figures cannot be accepted as an accurate index of the actual level of criminal activity for the general population, much less for any one area or the members of any particular group comprising a small proportion of the national population. Some categories of crime, usually the less serious from the rulers' point of view, are inevitably underrepresented in official records and are sometimes dramatically affected by changing standards of law enforcement. Other behavior which a subject group may consider criminal, such as witchcraft, is missing altogether from official records. In addition to these standard pitfalls in the study of crime, criminal records for Indians may also be biased by the way in which justice is administered to this group in comparison to other groups, and broad generalizations about Indian crime are likely to be of limited value because of the differences from one tribe to another and between reservation and non-reservation Indians of the same tribe.

Perhaps because of these serious problems with sources, few aspects of Indian crime have been studied in a thorough and convincing way. The few general treatments of Indian crime based on official statistics such as those published in the *Uniform Crime Reports* suggest higher crime and deliquency rates for North American Indians than for the general population, especially after 1967; on the order of three times the rate for black Americans and ten times the rate for white Americans. Most Indian crimes were misdemeanors and other petty offenses, but Indian crimes against persons (e.g. homicide) and alcohol-related crimes also were substantially higher than for the general population, up to twenty times higher on some reservations. Indians have had the highest rate of arrest of any racial group in the U.S. for alcohol-related crimes and urban crimes. Simple drukenness has been a far more common cause of arrest among Indians than among other racial groups, this may be partly the result of bias in the administration of justice, although most studies find that Indians have a high rate of alcoholism and cirrhosis of the liver, and that alcohol is an important factor in other criminal offenses including homicide and suicide. The generally high Indian arrest rate also should be tempered by the fact that black Americans have higher arrest rates for the serious crimes of homicide, rape, assault, burglary, larceny, and robbery; and some Indian tribes and reservations have reported crime rates at or below the national average. (Since Latin American crime statistics usually do not identify Indians specifically, no comparisons can be made on these points.)

Crimes against property seem to be proportionately less important for Indians than for other groups. Summary figures suggest that Indians commit about twice as many crimes against persons as against property; the proportion is reversed for the general U.S. population. This pattern of Indian crimes against persons over crimes against property is repeated for the few communities of Mesoamerica that have been studied, and seems to be a pattern with considerable historical depth in the highland Indian regions of Latin America.

For North American Indians, homicide, suicide, and juvenile delinquency have received the most attention. They provide the basis for some tentative observations about Indian criminality and comparisons to the few studies of Indian crime in Latin America.

Homicide is perhaps the only social act almost universally regarded as a crime by rulers and subjects throughout the Americas since the arrival of Europeans. It is, therefore, the only category of crime for which the written documentation can be accepted with some confidence. Homicide has been studied for a number of reservations and rates have been compiled for a group of twenty-four reservations states, mostly west of the Mississippi River. Several characteristics of Indian homicides are shared with the general population. Roughly three-fourths of all homicides were committed by men, and the high points in age of offenders are the young to middle adult years. In the rate of homicide, however, Indians depart from the general population. Crude homicide rates for Indians in these studies prior to 1967 generally have been about three times as high as rates for the general population; age-adjusted rates have been three and one-half to four times as high (the Indian age-adjusted rate between 1959 and 1967 varied from 19.6 to 26.6 per 100,000 per year). Following 1967, the rates of Indian homicide jumped substantially and homicide is now the eighth leading cause of Indian death, following accidents, heart disease, cancer, influenza and pneumonia, diseases of early infancy, stroke, and cirrhosis of the liver. The apparent incidence of homicide before 1967 may not be especially high compared to earlier periods. Recourse to homicide, commonly an end result of feuding and retaliation, is documented for various tribes before the establishment of reservations.

Homicide cannot readily be studied for Indians as a

group in Latin America, but a few community studies suggest that, while some villages are anti-homicidal and record only occasional violence, homicide rates are generally high (ranging up to 251/100,000 per year) and that political homicide is the main reason for high homicide rates in Indian areas of Mexico, Guatemala, Peru, and Bolivia. For Indian communities of Mexico that have been studied, people kill over blood revenge, factionalism within their communities, and jealousy over the suspected adultery of wives. These patterns seem to be fewer and clearer than the circumstances surrounding homicides among North American Indians in the twentieth century.

Historical studies of the patterns of homicide in Indian regions of Mexico based on numerous trial records are beginning to suggest relationships between Indian violence and peasant values and the conditions of life in the countryside. In these exceptional circumstances of personal and political violence, features of the society that are taken for granted in everyday life, such as social values, sometimes rise to the surface of consciousness. Social patterns of homicide have been studied for two regions of eighteenth-century Mexico: the Mixteca Alta region of Oaxaca in southern Mexico along the trade route from Mexico City and Puebla to Guatemala; and central Mexico, the hinterland of the colonial metropolis at Mexico City.

In looking closely at the setting and personal relationships in homicides, central Mexico and the Mixteca Alta traced somewhat different patterns. In most ways, the central Mexico homicides reveal a richer and less predictable variety of patterns. They spanned more evenly all levels of social relationships from husbands and wives to neighbors to officials to outsiders. The motives ascribed in the offenders' declarations in central Mexico often amounted to vague statements about passions and uncontrollable forces without clear reference to rules of social relationships among members of the community which were typical of the offenders' declarations in the Mixteca Alta cases. The central Mexico killings more often involved alcohol (although alcohol was present in less than half of all homicides for both regions) and the setting was more often a tavern. Disputes that led to violent deaths in central Mexico more often involved economic conflicts such as disputes over stolen property, unpaid debts, and damage to cropland or livestock.

Two features of central Mexico killings are especially distinctive. One is the "fighting words"—the insults exchanged before a lethal attack. Virtually every insult imaginable is documented as a prelude to at least one central Mexico killing. Many of these insults have in common a strong macho tone, pungent with the intent to defame and humble through verbal combat. Rather than being literal accusations, they were figurative insults of the grossest kind. The other special feature of peasant homicides in central Mexico is the weapons used. They were often deadly by design—especially firearms and long knives. Mixteca Alta villagers, on the other hand, tended to use whatever was at hand at the time of attack (rocks and knives) and their fighting words wre literal accusations rather than figurative insults.

These regional contrasts between central Mexico and the Mixteca Alta suggest some important differences in the social characteristics of the Indian villages and the differing effects of subordination within the colonial system. Patriarchy and male dominance were, at least in the formal sense, common to Indian villages in both regions, as they were to most Indian groups in the Americas, but the homicide evidence suggests that self-assertive and less sociable forms of manliness so characteristic of lower-class life in modern societies were diluting community-oriented values in central Mexico in the late eighteenth century. Accompanying this mixture of individual responsibility to the community and self-expression and self-interest were two other developments: a modern form of *caciquismo* or local boss rule and the beginnings of the modern pattern of political homicide.

Suicides by North American Indians are said to be numerous compared to the general population although inter-tribal rates vary from a relatively low believe that crime rates have increased among Indians since contact with and subordination to Europeans. The reservation setting and missionary activity contributed to new uncertainties, geographic isolation, chronic seasonal unemployment, and social disorganization as well as a kind of legal protectorate for tribal groups. Division of tribal lands into family plots at the end of the nineteenth century discouraged patrilocality which, in the case of the Nez Perce Indians of Idaho, has been part of a process of declining aboriginal communal discipline and marital instability. The nuclear family, a weak cultural institution in these Indian societies, has not effectively replaced the declining community in controlling drunkenness, interpersonal violence and other unlawful behavior. In sedentary Indian societies of Spanish America, by contrast, reservations were not instituted and, in spite of great changes imposed from outside, communities often have not lost the practice of communal discipline nor experienced the high rates of suicide, alcoholism, and delinquency of their North American counterparts. Despite the resort to homicide in these Indian communities, especially for political reasons, local hostilities have been slower to accumulate in ways that weaken community bonds, although in one Tzotzil community in southern Mexico the growing number of homicides seems to be closely related to a breakdown in the traditional system of social control.

WILLIAM B. TAYLOR

* * *

# D

**DANCE** can be said to mark the entire trail of life, from cradle to grave, of the Indians of the Americas. A number of anthropologists in recent years have remarked that they now realize a more thorough study of the dances in earlier times would have been most helpful toward an understanding of the various cultures because they were so involved in the overall pattern on Indian life.

To many people Indian dancing means a group of contorted, bent-over figures, feet moving awkwardly up and down, a silly whooping punctuated by tapping the mouth with the hand, accompanied by weird and monotonous chanting undeserving of the title of music.

Indians have usually been presented to the public as a type of side-show attraction. The effort has been to make them savage or romantic, and the presentations have usually been cheap and gaudy. It started before the Revolutionary War and has been continued to the present day.

"Real Indian" showmen have sometimes been the worst offenders in giving a bad portrayal of their people. They have done either what they were told to do by some non-Indian producer or have played up to the popular notions in an effort to please their audiences. Sometimes they have been handicapped by a personal lack of knowledge of the former life and customs of their people.

The average American places Indian dancing in one of three categories: he takes it for granted, as something still going on just as it always has been and which he can see at any time he chooses to visit and Indian reservation; or he considers it a little boy interest, now outgrown; or he thinks of it as Wild West or Hollywood hoopla dreamed up for motion picture and television shows. In any case, he cannot believe that real, honest, figure of 8/100,000 per year to the extremely high figure of 120/100,000. On the average, modern Indian suicides are roughly one and one-half times the national age-adjusted rate and, like homicides, the rate has increased since 1967. Suicides are notoriously underreported, especially automobile "accidents" that are really suicides, and these comparative figures may be exaggerated. Suicides occurred before European contact but apparently were rare and usually associated with the shame of a wife's adultery. In the 1920s, after the establishment of many reservations, the rate of Indian suicide in North America was 10.2/100,000, roughly comparable to the national figure. While hard figures are lacking for Indian groups in Latin America, the contrast to North America seems substantial. Very few Indian suicides are recorded for Latin American groups; this is especially true of the areas of former highland civilizations such as Mexico, Guatemala, and Peru.

The important characteristics of North American Indian suicides, in addition to their apparently high incidence, are: 1) in general, and for most reservations that have been studied individually, far more males than females commit suicide (83% of the Indian suicides from 1959-66 compared to 74% for the general population); 2) there is a fairly strong pattern of teenagers and young adult men who have problems with alcohol committing suicide; 3) many of the suicides occurred in jail or at home shortly after release from jail for drunkenness; 4) hangings and self-inflicted gunshot wounds were the usual means of death, although in the 1960s there was a growing pattern of self-immolation; 5) suicide attempts seem to occur in clusters within extended families and high-risk groups such as boarding school students; and 6) suicides seem to be completed more often by Indians who moved to cities compared to members of the same tribe living on reservations.

With delinquency, also, North American Indians seem to have relatively high and rising rates in recent years compared to the general population, although the difference is exaggerated by the small groups of reservation Indians who have been studied. For the Wind River Reservation in Wyoming, the official delinquency rate has been 12 court appearances per 100 youth per year compared to 2.5 for the general population. Like the figures for Indian crime in general, the delinquency mostly involves minor offenses such as curfew violations, malicious mischief, disturbing the peace, minor in possession of alcohol, and drunkenness; and many of the charges have been for alcohol-related offenses. Indian girls perhaps have been more involved than their Anglo counterparts in running away from home and offenses against school property.

Explanations for these apparently higher rates of homicide, suicide, alcohol-related crimes, and delinquency among North American Indian men often center on the Indian as a "marginal man" who is caught in a cross-cultural conflict—not totally committed to or accepted by his tribesmen or the world outside the tribe. Conditions of poverty, poor education, unemployment and family disruption have led to feelings of aimlessness, frustration, and alienation not unlike the situation that produced the aggressive and often self-destructive Pachuco Gangs of East Los Angeles after World War II.

While these conditions and behavior seem to be common to lower-class life in general—part of a reaction of dominated peoples against the process of domination—Indian history has seen the play of some peculiar factors—particularly the reservation system—which account for some variation in the patterns of Indian crime compared to other groups. Not all of Indian crime can be directly attributed to white domination and culture contact. Some types of crime mentioned here occurred in pre-reservation times as well as afterwards, such as homicide and suicide, and some patterns of crime such as the prevalence of crimes against the person over crimes against property are consistent with aboriginal values. However, the semi-nomadic life of most North American groups in aboriginal times made the reservation a particularly disruptive change which has affected social behavior in important ways, and there seems to be good reason to authentic Indian dancing is of itself worthy of consideration as an art.

Dancing played a very important role in the lives of the Indians of most tribes. The Indians themselves probably never thought of it as art for they knew nothing of art as a subject in itself. It was, however, an important part of their lives and dancing was art in the truest sense for it was interwoven in their daily lives, part of almost everything that they did. In some ways the dance was the highest expression of all their artistic endeavors for it combined all other art forms—it embodied not only music and motion, but color, line, form, pattern, legend, poetry, and ritual.

Dancing was such an integral part of Indian life that it is difficult for the average non-Indian to understand its significance. And yet, perhaps many people in positions of power and influence did realize something of the importance of dance in Indian society, for government representatives and missionaries did everything possible to suppresss it as being the epitome of savagery, hence to be arbitrarily destroyed in order to "civilize" the Indians. Indian dancing was frowned upon from earliest reservation days and much of it completely prohibited. Bans were issued against the Sun Dance in the 1880s which were enforced at the point of arms. In 1904 the *Regulations of the Indian Office* established a Court of Indian Offenses which included bans on all dances as well as on almost all Indian customs and practices. These bans remained official until 1934 and unofficial on many reservations until the 1950s. Although removed by the Indian Office in Washington many of them were still enforced by employees in the field who had no understanding of Indian people or their rights and were intent on making white men out of Indians.

During the period of enforcement permission was granted to Indians over forty years of age to participate in Wild West and other type of shows—also to dance at home on such holidays as Fourth of July (Independence Day), Flag Day, Labor Day, Christmas, New Year, and so on. Anyone over forty years of age was considered hopeless as a candidate for civilization.

Once the enforced bans were removed and dances once more could be held at any time, small boys sometimes turned out to learn from the few old-timers but when school was in session the teachers scolded them and sometimes even punished them for daring to attend a dance. It took another twenty years for Indians to become interested enough in theor own culture to turn out in any great numbers for a dance and to bring the so-called "powwow dancing" to its present popularity. Much of this change of attitude was due to the rebellion of the blacks against their position of inequality and servitude and a similar movement quickly developed among young Indians.

Now there are "powwow" circuits throughout the Indian country and dancers from various tribes follow these circuits in the hope of winning prizes for "fancy" and "traditional" dancing. So far the dancing is mainly of the "war dance" type and little effort has been made to revive other dances which might be even more important from an artistic or aesthetic standpoint. However, there has been quite a revival of the Sun Dance among western tribes but this is a religious ceremony and not a secular dance. Nevertheless, even secular dancing has an importance to Indians that would hardly be ascribed to it by non-Indians. Indians do not go to a dance entirely for a good time. Even though most dancing today is of a social nature and much of the old significance has been lost, a dance is still an opportunity for a social, political, and religious meeting all in one. The dance often opens with a prayer by some old man or woman, and during intermissions there are usually speeches on matters of tribal importance.

In their hearts Indians remained Indians. It was impossible to entirely destroy their inherent love of beauty and their desire to express themselves in some artistic way. Interest in dancing seems to be growing all the time and even this social dancing is outstanding—often brilliant and expressive. There are certain "Indianisms" noticeable even in this modern dancing which go back directly to old days and which show definite age-old tradition that could not be destroyed, even though many young Indians today know little of the traditions involved.

Although there is no such person as a typical Indian, there were certain customs and characteristics common to most of the Indians of North America and even to some extent in South America. Consequently there are phases of Indian dancing that can be described in general terms. From observations among Indians of Woodlands and Plains, as well as some in the Southwest, it can be said that all these have a similar way of handling their bodies and feet in dancing. In other words, all have a similar manner of execution. The characteristic position is with knees slightly bent and backs straight, quite different from anything to be found in either classical or ballroom dancing. There is a great freedom of movement, almost a loose-jointedness, and except in a few dances, or for accent, the dancers seems to be relaxed.

In most dances the arms are used little or not at all. Formerly in many dances the hands were placed on the hips, fingers extended, making a straight line from fingertips to elbows— not palms on the hips and wrists bent, as we sometimes see today. Or one might hold a fan or other article in one hand and place the other on the hip. Hands often hang at the sides or are held with belt elbows, but they never appear to be dangling or "flopping" and are not thrown wildly about, as in American black or African dancing. In fact, even the most active dancing is generally dignified and controlled. There may have been some exceptions to this, as among tribes of the Northwest Coast, and in some medicine men's performances, but by and large these statements hold. This may sound as if the dancing is stilted, and we know that many early observers felt it to be, but actually a good Indian dancer uses every muscle of his body. When imitating birds and animals he shakes his head and shoulders, moves his back muscles, and sometimes brings his arms, hands, and fingers into play.

The Indian has a duplicate or a substitute for almost every known dance step. The very simplicity with which some of these steps seem to be executed is a compliment to the grace and skill of the performers. The Indian, wearing a flat-soled moccasin and walking on the natural surface of the ground, often used a toe-first motion of the foot. One of the fundamental steps, from which many more complicated ones evolved, is merely an exaggeration of the Indian's walk, combined with the bent knee feature. Most steps were double-beat steps, done to two beats on the drum.

There is a subtlety of motion that is usually completely lost to the casual observer but is one of the most interesting aspects of Indian dancing. Even when it is noted it is difficult to acquire. But it makes the difference between a genuine and a false interpretation.

Sudden but subtle shifts in weight and rhythms add to the difficulties of trying to imitate Indian dancing. For these reasons many observers, especially show producers, tend to discount authentic Indian dance as show material. They want exaggerated movement, spectacular leaps and jumps, great masses of performers, uniformity, and girls with little on but their figures. Indian dancing is generally the opposite of these demands.

Many people think of Indian dancers as being always in a crouched position. The only continuous "crouch," if it may be called that, would be the slightly bent knees. On occasion dancers get down into such a squat as to be nearly resting on their heels, but this cannot be considered a typical position. It is used mainly in contests, to test endurance and agility. In the old days the squat position was also used in part of the Scalp, or Victory dances and in the Eagle Dance. Even in such a position, the back is straight and the head up. The back is seldom hunched, unless in imitation of buffalo or in order to aid in telling the story. Occasionally we do see young Indians today who let their shoulders sag and their heads hang as they dance but this is not an old-time Indian dance attitude.

The well-known anthropologist, Clark Wissler, spent much time with Indians in the early 1900s. He remarked that he used to enjoy watching the important old men walk, for it would put the slouching gait of the white man to shame. But even then the young men were taking on the awkwardness of the whites. The beautiful posture of the old-time Indians made an impression on most people who saw them, whether standing erect, walking as if their moccasins barely touched the earth, or dancing with head and shoulders up and backs straight.

In some dances only men took part, others were danced only by women, while in social dances, men, women, and children all danced together. Men and women did not dance arm in arm, as white people do, in the old dances. As in the animal kingdom the male is outstanding in appearance, so among Indians the men wore the most striking costumes and did most of the dancing.

An Indian child learned to dance almost before it could walk. A baby, unable to stand alone, might be held erect, supported by his father's hands, and his little feet taught to stamp in rhythm to the drums and chants. He early imitated the steps of his father in the ceremonial dances.

One might almost say that every step and every motion had a meaning and practically every article of finery and decoration worn was symbolic and told its particular story. A dancer could not wear a costume just because he liked its appearance. He had to have the right to wear it.

Religious dances, of course, were ritualistic and sometimes had their own peculiar steps, used for no other dance. Often there was little that non-Indians would call dancing in these rituals. There was movement, to be sure, but sometimes only a swaying of the body, or flexing of the knees, or raising on the heels, but Indians often called these rituals "dances," which shows the importance given to dancing.

Indian dances ran the gamut of emotional experience and covered practically every phase of life: birth dances, children's dances, puberty dances, dances to celebrate weddings, medicine dances of magic and healing, dances for games and for pleasure, honorous dances, dances to welcome strangers, to cement alliances, of mourning, and to honor the dead; dances to assure good hunting and to celebrate the resulting success. There were dances of planting and harvesting, of preparation for war, and of victory and peace. When a chief was "raised" there were dances to honor him. There were dances of sacrifice, of appeal for future blessings, of thanksgiving, dances to portray dream experiences.

Women did not dance the active, vivacious dances of the men. Specially privileged women, who had been to war and distinguished themselves as warriors did, could dance with the men in men's dances. In recent years, coinciding with the women's "liberation" movements everywhere, there has been a movement among Indian women to dress in men's costumes and dance like men. Old Sioux Indians, and perhaps oldsters of other tribes, were horrified at this change in traditional women's roles and were sure that some great calamity would be the result.

Originally most men's dances were done with a minimum of clothing, breechclout and moccasins being the most important articles, along with proper personal headdress, face and body paint. Every limb was free to respond to the dancer's moods and emotions. But beginning in the late 1800s and continuing until recently, government authorities and missionaries demands that such nudity be curtailed and Indian dancers, when permitted to dance at all, were no longer able to paint their bodies and dance in the old way. So they wore suits of long, dyed underwear—red, blue, yellow, green, black, or even one half one color, the other half a contrasting color. For a time, fine dance ornaments, such as bustles, arm wheels, porcupine hair broaches, and beautiful war bonnets nearly disappeared among the Sioux, Cheyenne, and Arapaho, who were perhaps the most persecuted of any Indians because of their outstanding record of defiance toward the troops sent against them, and of government regulations, once they were settled on the reservations.

In some areas, notably Oklahoma, almost the opposite effect took place. "Show Indians" produced gaudier and more spectacular costumes, with great circles of feathers for bustles and neck ornaments and huge feather crests, sometimes referred to by more conservative Indians as "Zulu hats." Fortunately, at the time of this writing, both extremes are now moderating. There is a strong movement toward "old-time" and "traditional" costumes and some interesting developments are the result.

During the period while dancing was so restricted a new type of social dance developed which in many cases was encouraged by white officials, or at least not prohibited, because it was copied directly from white styles of dancing. Such dances as the Rabbit Dance, which for a time became popular among tribes as far away as the Seneca in New York State, were influenced by the Fox Trot and the Waltz. To the present time other such dances are still popular on many reservations, such as Indian Two Step, or the Arapaho Slug Dance. In these dances men and women do dance arm in arm, or holding hands with arms around each other's waists. The songs used are usually funny, or silly, but the dancers are not supposed to laugh during the dance he or she is pummeled, in fun, by the other dancer.

A little later on, real white dances became quite popular among the young people. Indians were encouraged to go to these white dances in another effort to get them to give up everything Indian. In actuality, the Indian dances were much more dignified and decorous than the white dances, where drinking usually took place and fighting sometimes broke out.

The white man's dances were usually done in "white man's" clothes although Rabbit Dance and another later dance, the Forty-Niner (nothing to do with the Gold Rush of 1849) were often done at Indian dances and those in "War Dance" costume also took part.

In former times even social dances were involved with religious beliefs and since religion played such an important role in Indian life it is logical to realize that all dances had religious significance at one time. The dancing of people here on earth portrayed the actions of spirits in the after-world. When the spirits were unconcerned for man's welfare the people danced to revive their interest.

Early observers claimed that the Plains Indians were

the finest dancers, with the Sioux at the head of them all. But Plains Indian culture was dependent mainly upon the buffalo hunt and with the disappearance of that great animal much of the culture disappeared with him. the Indian saw no further use for most of his dances and ceremonies in those empty days. Only a few aged warriors remembered, and so today, the younger Indians, who are now interested in reviving their own customs and dances, are working under a great handicap. The fact that they are interested at all, after the many years of persecution and opposition, is remarkable.

Different culture groups had different methods and manners of dancing. The Plains people were hunters and warriors. Many of their dances were naturally quite different in spirit and in character from those of their more settled agricultural neighbors to the east and southwest or from those of other tribes whose ways of life were different. War exploits and experiences played an important part in their dances but "the War Dance," especially as related to Plains Indians and to Indian dancing today, is largely an invention of the white man. Indians of the woodlands did have a real war dance, a dance of preparation for war, but with the Plains tribes there was no honor in going to war. It was expected of every young man. The celebration came with a successful homecoming—bringing horses, honors, scalps, without the loss of a man. Then the Victory, or Scalp dances were held and these have often been called "War Dance" by the whites. Scalp dances were usually performed by the women, who sometimes wore their husbands' war clothes and bonnets as a special honor to them and insult to the enemy. On the Plains these Scalp dances usually led in a circle to the right, whereas most of their other dances move to the left, in a Sun Circle.

The typical Plains tribes, of course, had no planting or harvest dances except for some tobacco ceremonies. But in addition to their most important religious ceremony, the Sun Dance (also known as Medicine Dance, Medicine Lodge, Thirsting Dance, Sacrifice Dance, New Life Dance) they had other minor religious ceremonies, buffalo and hunting dances, bird and animal dances, warrior society dances, dances of various women's societies, elaborate adoption ceremonies, puberty dances and ceremonies, dances known as beggars' dances which solicited aid for "the poor," dances belonging to various cults, such as Bear, Wolf, F[illegible], Thunder Dreamers, and so on. The Sioux alone had a list of thirty-five different dances and other Plains tribes probably had as many, but few of these are given today.

The most popular dance today all throughout the Indian country is the so-called War Dance, which ought rather to be called Warriors' Dance. It is the social part of the old Grass or Omaha Society Dance. Originally, only warriors with good records could take part but it has become a dance for everyone, and as mentioned earlier, even some women take part, as "warriors," nowadays. The Fancy War dancers use all the fancy steps they can think of and each contestant tries to outdo the others. It has become largely a contest dance.

There is good evidence that the Grass Dance originated among the Pawnee but the Sioux learned it from the Omaha, added to it, developed it, and passed it to other tribes, so that it has become known as Omaha Dance because the Sioux credited the Omaha for it. The Omaha wore braided grass tails on their belts, signifying scalps taken in battle. The Sioux did not understand this symbolism, so called it Grass Dance also, and so these names are still popular among many tribes, although most now speak of it as War Dance, following the misinterpretation of the whites. It is performed in variations of Fast, Slow, and Fancy War Dance.

Originally, there were only two wearers of the feather dance bustles, men especially chosen for outstanding bravery. Gradually other dancers were permitted to wear them and today almost every dancer considers a bustle as part of his necessary costume. The bustles have changed considerably over the years, the modern "swing bustles" and "neck bustles," being far larger and more elaborate than the simpler and more dignified original types.

At first, a "bustle dancer" wore, in addition to clout and moccasins, only the porcupine hair and deer-tail crest, or roach, which originated in the east and eventually made its way to the prairie tribes. Gradually other ornaments were added, such as bone bead or otter fur breastplates, quilled or beaded armbands and garters, fur anklets and strings of sleight bells. The bells became popular about the time of the Civil War and are still an essential part of the dancer's outfit, although originally each bell was worn to symbolize a wound. Before the bells, rattles of hoofs and turtle shells were worn around ankles and knees.

In some districts an older form of dance, called Straight Dance, has once more become popular. The dancers wear "traditional" costumes, which imply shirts, leggings, clouts, and moccasins, with long hair and often fur turbans, with very dignified danging— no fancy footwork. The Sioux call such dancing Straight-Up and it was performed by chiefs and other dignitaries, many wearing full eagle feather war bonnets. The true war bonnet was found only on the Plains but its origin may trace back to Mexico, or even to Central America, for representations of similar headdresses are found on ancient carvings and paintings of those regions. Some woodland tribes had headdresses of eagle or of turkey feathers but they did not have the elegance of the war bonnet, which came into its full development with the arrival of the horse. The eastern headdresses were usually "straight-up" bonnets without the grace, charm, or spread of their western counterparts.

During the late 1950s there was also a revival among the Kiowa of Oklahoma, of a former warrior society dance known as the Gourd Clan Dance. Many Indians, when speaking English, use the term "clan" to mean society or club. The dancers wear full costume, which includes a blanket, and carry rattles which they shake in time to the songs and jump hard on both feet, as in most of the old warrior society dances. This dance spread all over Oklahoma and then to many reservations in other states and is still very popular at this writing.

*"Shield Dance"* by Spencer Asah (Kiowa), date unknown.

A number of representative Plains tribes moved out onto the prairies from the woodlands within the past 200 years. The Village tribes, like Mandan, Arikara, Hidatsa, Pawnee, and a few others, did have planting and harvest dances but the nomadic tribes, depending almost entirely upon the buffalo, gave them up. Nevertheless, there are still many similarities between some Plains and Woodland dances. Calumet, or Pipe dances, were known to both areas and in some tribes Eagle dances, which were related in purpose and also in execution, were also given. Both dances were used to great strangers, to create ceremonial friendships and relationships, to bring success in hunting and war, to bring good luck or overcome back luck and to make peace between warring tribes.

The Calumet Dance was performed with two feather decorated wands, or pipestems, but motions of the eagle were incorporated in the movements. Eagle dances of these two areas was highly conventionalized, and although using eagle movements, little or no effort was made to portray eagles realistically through costuming. The Iroquois still have such an Eagle Dance, each dancer using a feathered fan in one hand and rattle in the other. In early times the dance was used as stated above, but today it celebrates existing friendships and is used to cure disease, to bring rain, to hearten the unhappy and depressed, for thanksgiving, and has until recently been given to obtain success in hunting. One of the old Iroquois war dances is also used today to bring rain, showing how the original function of a dance can be changed to meet existing conditions. It is remarkable that, after more than 400 years of contact with non-Indians, the Iroquois still hold many of their old dances and ceremonies.

Tribes of the Southwestern Pueblos and also of the Northwest Coast did have naturalistic eagle dances and yet there is strong evidence that the Southwestern eagle dances originated on the Plains, or at least were greatly influenced by them. But today it is the other way around and some plains tribes, notably in Oklahoma, are now doing eagle dances very similar to those of the Pueblos. There is so much visiting back and forth by Indians of various tribes today that a number of dances have become Pan-Indian rather than strictly tribal.

Scalp and Victory dances were common to tribes, not only across the United States and Canada but also to some tribes of Mexico and South America.

At present-day Indian shows and gatherings one of the most popular dances is the Hoop Dance. Good dancers of many tribes now perform it. Its present popularity began with Indians of Taos, perhaps fifty years ago. The dance probably originated among Indians around the Great Lakes, for a dance with one hoop was known to Menomini, Chippewa, and Ottawa, and the latter had a dance with two hoops. From this region the dance could easily have been picked up by Eastern Plains tribes. The Taos Indians have long been associated with southern Plains tribes and so, in some such fashion, they obtained the dance and called it to the attention of the tourists. At first the Taos dancers used only two hoops, but gradually more hoops were added. For a time four hoops were considered more or less standard and four is a sacred number to most Indians. Then they used six, still a sacred number, but today some dancers use a dozen or more. The Lake Indians used very small hoops, which of course increased the difficulties of the dance. The Ottawa permitted hoops in size only from the ground to the dancer's knees, but today the hoops used by most dancers are much larger. A hoop, being a circle, carried the symbolism of the circle—tribal unity, complete and perfect life, the return of the seasons, and so on. Some of the old symbolism remains and dancing in and out of the hoops symbolizes the difficulties encountered in life. With all the additional hoops the dance has become mainly a showpiece and contest dance, however. It remains a solo dance and each dancer has his own routine and series of tricks he performs, so no two hoop dances are ever alike.

Each area of the country had dances typical of the culture and activities of the region. As we travel across North America we find that at one time practically every activity of life was represented in dance. In the east there were special strawberry festivals when the wild strawberries were ripe. In the north there were dances portraying the excursions by canoe during seasons of open weather and snowshoe dances celebrated the arrival of winter and its enveloping blanket of white. In the south there were alligator dances. On the Plains there were many buffalo dances and horse dances. In the thick, dark forests of the northwest where a gloomy religion full of powrful, often dreaded spirits had developed, there was even an echo dance, intended to confuse malevolent spirits and keep them away from the villages. In the southwest almost every dance had the bringing of rain as its primary purpose.

The Indian, wherever he was found, was a product of his environment and his culture was built around it. Indians of all the heavily wooded regions had religions was gloomy concepts. The people of the open plains and prairies seem to have been happier. but, regardless of tribe or cultural development, all seemed to be content with their lot. Each tribe believed itself to be "the People," and the only personal desire was to be worthy and recognized among one's own. (Enemy tribes were usually designated as "snakes," or "adders."

The Indian culture of the Southwest remains strong but factions have recently developed between the "conservatives" and the "progressives," the latter intent upon following the white man's road. The culture of the Plains, Woodlands, California, and the Northwest Coast have suffered greatly through their contacts with modern civilization. The culture of the Woodlands was built upon war, farming, and hunting; that of the Plains on war, the horse, and the buffalo. The village tribes of the Plains, also being farmers, suggests that in this area there was an overlapping of Woodland and Plains features. With the exception of planting and harvest dances, however, we find both Woodlands and Plains can be roughly grouped together for dance styles, although Plains dances ordinarily move to the left, or clockwise, "following the sun," whereas Woodland people, both north and south, usually moved to the right, "with their hearts toward the fire." Both areas featured many solo dances but footwork seems to have been more elaborate on the Plains.

It is interesting to note that most Pueblo dances also move to the right, or counter clockwise. Does the fact that they are also farming people have anything to do with it? But Navajo also farm, and among them we find dances moving in clockwise circles again, with some dances in opposing lines. To add to the confusion, we now occasionally find Plains Indians dancing to the right.

Perhaps the most popular ceremony for the tourists in the southwest is the Hopi Snake Dance. Each Hopi village gives the Snake Dance every other year, alternating with the Flute Ceremony, also given to bring rain. So a Snake Dance is given every year but in different villages. The Snake Dance doubtless traces back to the snake cults of Mexico and Central America and it is certain that other Pueblo tribes had similar dances at one time.

The Hopi are also famous for their Kachina dances, which portray the activities of the gods, or spirits, of the Spirit World, but the most famous of the Pueblo dances of this type is the Shalako of the Zuñi. Many of the Pueblo have dances of lesser importance, such as Braiding of the Belt, eagle dances, buffalo or animal dances, in addition to planting and harvest dances, all of which involve a great deal of symbolism and have religious aspects.

The Navajo also had quite a variety of dances, some of which are still given today, but few of them have been seen by outsiders. The ones we most often hear about are the Squaw Dance, a white man's term for part of a ritual known as the Enemy Way, which today is given to cure sickness, the "enemy" being the disease; the Mountain Chant, and the Yeibichai, or Night Chant. Navajo are among the few Indians who designate a gathering as a "sing," or "chant," rather than as a dance, but in their original forms there was a great deal of dancing in these rituals.

Not too much has been reported for the desert tribes of southern Arizona and California but even in these regions there were some dances, held to assure a supply of food and also for recreation.

On the Northwest Coast and among the Eskimo, the dances are largely solo, but with much audience participation. there is also what we might call a cult of frenzy, with much exaggerated movements, not too much footwork, but swinging of arms, jerking of the head, spasmodic moving of the muscles, and a preoccupation with the fantastic and horrible. They used some of the most elaborate and spectacular masks found anywhere in the world.

In California we find dancing in lines again, with beautiful and detailed accoutrements, some jumping and leaping, but not the virtuosic footwork we find on the plains.

Indian dancing has sometimes been criticized because it lacks great jumps and leaps, but accounts by early observers give considerable prominence to jumping and leaping and the present writers witnessed surprising leaps by a Cheyenne dancer some years ago. The leaps he made were definitely Indian, showing no outside influence whatever.

Regardless of area, we always find some circle dancing for it is the most logical formation for group dancing. With the exception of something like the Sioux Elk Mystery, which progressed literally for miles, dancing is generally limited to a small space, either surrounded by an audience or with an audience on one to three sides. A dancer must dance in place, move in a circle left or right, or dance forward and backward. The same applies to a group, with the additional features of forming lines that move forward or backward, face each other, or sashay through each other. Or a group can also move in a spiral, which we find in stomp dances of the Southwest.

In some regions costumes have changed as much, or more, than the dances. From the beginning of white contact Indians admired the goods the strangers brought to trade. Cloth was early substituted for buckskin, commercial dyes for native colors, beads for porcupine knives for flint. Ribbons and mirrors, ostrich and peacock feathers, were added to personal adornment. The overall change was gradual and of the Indian's own choosing and Indian costume was often enhanced by the addition and substitution of new things. For awhile there was a trend to go too far but now there is much interest in going back to "traditional" costume.

No Indian would evern think of dancing without the proper song to accompany him. It would be impossible to separate song from dance and it would be difficult to answer the old question as to which came first, music or dance. Even today Indians are continually composing new songs for dances established long ago.

Singing is one Indian art that is not dying out, although on the Plains some of the old manner of singing is gone, as are many of the old songs. In some of the former ceremonies, such as the Cherokee Green Corn Dance (or Busk), at least one new song was required for each annual presentation. Plains and some Woodlands singers sing in a high, sometimes falsetto voice, with a quaver, or tremolo which white people think is bad but which the Indian likes and strives to cultivate. These people think it almost sacreligious to sing in a normal speaking voice, for all songs have a certain religious aspect and the high, quavering voice is used to approach the mysterious world of the spirit. Navajo, too, have songs in their Yeibichai that are unbelievably high in pitch. On the other hand, Iroquois, Pueblo and some desert tribes, as well as California and Northwest Coast people, generally sing in a more natural voice.

Older Indians often sang in a manner that sounded off-key to whites and this way of singing is no longer heard, but that it was deliberate and according to certain standards of earlier days cannot be doubted for the songs were repeated by different singers the same way each time.

Most Indian songs are short and repeated as many times as necessary for the occasion. Most have few, or no words, the tune being the important thing, meaningless vocables being used. There were special types of songs for differing dances and ceremonies. Indians did not need words to tell them what kind of a song was being sung for they could tell by its structure and its melodic progressions. When words were used, however, they were often very important, one word sometimes symbolizing a thought which would require an entire sentence in English for its translation.

Drums of various kinds were the usual accompaniment to the songs and dances, although there were some tribes which used no drums. The drum governed the bodily movements of the dancers; the song voiced the emotion, the appeal of the dance itself. Life was a great dance; dancing was life. All drums were regarded as having sacred, mysterious power so not just anyone could own or even play a drum. The sound of the drum represented all of the life forces and its rhythm was symbolic of the rhythm of the entire universe: the heartthrob of all creation.

There were some dances accompanied only by songs and rattles. Rattles were not children's toys but had great ceremonial value, being able to drive away evil, and sometimes to bring rain. There were many kinds and types of rattles, just as there were drums.

A foot drum was known to California, basket drums were used on the desert, water drums were common in the east, and some tribes, such as the Ute in their Bear Dance, used a morache, or raspidor—the notched stick. Hopi, Havajo, Apache, and perhaps a few other tribes use the bull-roarer, or buzzer, in some ceremonies, which has an association with the thunder.

From early Spanish records it is almost certain that dancing played as important a role in the lives of the Indians of Meso and South America. Very little of the original Indian dancing of Mexico and Central America has come down to us today because of the persecution of the conquistadores and the missionaries. There are remnants of ancient Mexican dances to be found in the highlands and other isolated areas of Mexico, and groups of Aztec dancers have been taking part in the Indian ceremonials held in Gallup, New Mexico, in recent years. Their striking headdresses are patterned after those of quetzal and rhea feathers shown in the old records. The Ballet Folklorico has won international acclaim for its outstanding performances but it presents little of the original Indian dancing. The late Miguel Covarrubias, noted artist and Director of the Museo Nacional of Mexico, who helped organize the Ballet Folklorico, stated to these writers following their portrayal of early Indian dances at the American Museum of Natural History in New York that there is much more indigenous material left in the United States than anywhere in Mexico. Nearly everything in the way of native material to be found in Mexico today shows a great deal of Spanish influence. The same might be said for the countries of Central America, where there is very little original dance material to be found, although the people are predominantly Indian by blood.

People are amazed to learn that there are still approximately two hundred different Indian languages and dialects spoken north of Mexico. But when we realize that before the Spanish Conquest there were about 1800 languages spoken in Meso and South America, representing literally hundreds of tribes, we know it would be practically impossible to have reports on all the dances. Today there are about half of these tribes still in existence, which is still a formidable number. In isolated regions of South America it would probably be possible to find some aboriginal dancing. Recent, as well as historical reports indicate that in many tribes there were dances for all of the most important occasions of life and the yearly tribal activities, just as there were for North America. At the southern tip of the continent, however, the dances seem to have been entirely of a social nature and no war or hunting dances have been reported.

In the Chaco area, on the contrary, there were Scalp dances similar to those of North America, with the women taking the lead, but with more running than actual dancing. A few tribes actually took scalps but others used heads or skulls as battle trophies. Such trophies were hung on a post in the center of the dance ground and one account states that an old woman began the dance in front of these trophies. Warriors had a triumphal victory call of tapping the mouth with the hand, as was also done by many North American tribes, but only in the heat of battle or following a victory.

The people of the Chaco had recreational dances during seasons of abundant food and favorable weather. They also had many dances of a ceremonial nature; dances to ripen fruit, to ward off jaguar attacks, for girls coming of age, to bring quantities of fish, to ward off and to cure diseases. Their drum was like some water drums of North America—a cooking pot containing water and covered with a rawhide head, struck with a single stick.

The Araucanians of middle Chile on the west coast were said to dance to a rather slow tempo, the dancers' feet hardly being lifted from the ground. In modern dancing there is considerable clowning and also use of masks.

Arawakan people north of the Chaco also used masks in some ceremonies. Masked men impersonated spirits and terrified the women, levying tributes of food and drink, but sometimes the women resisted the attack, apparently as part of the pantomime. One man, painted in red and black, with feathers on his head, entered the dance arena and amused the audience with his antics.

In one ceremony the men built a temporary house which was taboo to the women, then disguised with paint and feathers, danced for hours around it. In the case of an initiation ceremony some men ran around a central tree while others danced and shouted for joy. The wild running was carried out for three or four successive nights, then was followed by a feast of armadillo.

The Mochica of northern Peru had masquerades representing animals and strange beings. Some were dances, others dramatic scenes, more sophisticated than the performances of the most primitive tribes.

Before the Conquest the Inca had many dances with elaborate costumes, masks, animal skins, and special garments cut like everyday clothing. Costumes and dances varied widely from province to province. The dancers were principally men, and in some dances there was a great deal of jumping. A Warrior's Dance was performed only on solemn occasions, both men and women taking part, the men dressed for war. It was done in a circle, holding hands. The Emperor's family had a special dance, accompanied by a great drum which was carried on the back of a person of low birth and beat by a woman. Men and women again joined hands, this time forming long lines, sometimes with sexes mxed, at other times the men in one line, women in another. Two hundred to three hundred people took part. The dance was slow and dignified, with one step back and two forward, progressing across the Great Square to the place where the Emperor sat.

In another Inca dance, which seemed to please the Spanish priest who reported it, a man with a noble lady by each hand, twisted and untwisted without letting go. The priest probably liked this dance because it was similar to European dances with which he was familiar. At the same time, some masked dancers took the part of buffoons. The steps were very simple. The dancers were accompanied by drummers, sometimes using a single drum stick. In some dances each dancer carried his own drum, like the tambourine, or hand drum of North America. Dancers wore copper or silver bells and sometimes rattles of snail shells around their ankles.

Drums were scarce or non-existent in Brazil. In the eastern part they used bamboo trumpets, rattles, whistled, and a stamping tube made of bamboo about forty inches long. Dancing was so important that a new village site was chosen with relation to a good dance ground. During the dry season men and women danced three times a day, but many dances, including masquerades, were entirely recreational. It was usual for a singer with a rattle to stand in the center while the women circled about him and the men formed another circle outside of the women. Some male dancers also carried rattles.

In the Brazilian interior there were also periods when dances were performed three times a day, the first one as early as 3:00 or 4:00 in the morning, another a little before sunset, and an evening performance began about 7:00 p.m., lasting two hours or longer.

Boys and girls, as well as adults, took part. The women lined up, a young woman, serving as their leader, took her place in the center of the line. The women never left their positions but bent their knees and swung their bent arms back and forth while the Dance Leader shook his rattle and danced in front of them. He pointed his rattle at some girl, stamped his feet, belt low, then jumped as high as possible with legs outstretched, apparently to make an impression on the girl. The young men, usually armed with some weapon or a staff, gathered in a body and began dancing on the second or third song. A few blew bamboo trumpets and all stretched their legs apart while rocking their knees as they advanced on the women's line, the Dance Leader in front. When he turned to make a semi-circle they turned and leaped back to the place where they first gathered. Similar dances were given to promote the growth of crops and to bring success in hunting.

The Indians of coastal Brazil had dances in two straight lines, the men in front with bows and arrows, the women behind. In yet another tribe of this region there were circle dances to dramatize hunting, while others were done in a line to represent a "road to the sky."

Indians of the Pampas took to the horse as readily as did our own Plains Indians but did not develop a new culture of their own, as the Plains Indians did. Instead they copied the Spaniards in every way—riding techniques, and gear—except for the use of the bolas, which was their own and carried on to this day. Although Indian blood is still in evidence, the Indians of this region, as a people, are extinct. The Mexicans also adopted Spanish riding but used the lariat instead of the bolas.

Indians in the Amazonian forests made marvelous headdresses, necklaces, and many decorations of macaw, parrot, and other exotic feathers of tropical birds.

The Kamarakoto, living in the northern forest, had a Great Serpent Dance to cure snake bites and ulcers and also dances to aid in taking game and fish, as well as dances to prevent illness and trouble which they say were revealed to them in the very spirits which could cause them.

The Aymara, formerly a very warlike tribe living in Bolivia, now have dances they present for church fiestas, weddings, funerals, to dedicate a new house, for harvesting, phases of sheep raising, but all show Spanish influence and all are recreational except those for a fertility ceremonial following the harvest and to bring rain. Dancers sometimes had small, spherical copper rattles sewn to their costumes. They were accompanied by panpipes, a snare drum with laced heads, sometimes a cane raspidor, but singing for the dances here seems to have been unimportant.

Costumes today also show Spanish or mestizo influence and the masks used are of Spanish origin. Some are said to represent spirits but women and children are now allowed to look at them, which they formerly were not permitted to do. Parrot feathers, obtained from the jungle, are used but seem to have no ritual significance. Dance groups, which formerly had specific functions, such as war, hunting, and rain making, no longer have them. In one dance, held by unmarried people, the girls ask the boys to dance, which is also a custom among some Plains Indians.

There were many types of dances, some for men only, who trotted slowly in a circle, swaying their shoulders and playing panpipes. In a fertility ceremony, said by some to imitate mountain spirits, (which is the case with the Apache), a line of women do a posture dance, the men circling around them playing end-flutes.

In another dance, representing jungle Indians, men and women form lines and dance in unison, wearing feather headdresses and carrying bows and arrows. Circle dances of Spanish origin are performed by both sexes. Dance groups progress around the plaza, halting at each corner and occasionally at each side to perform. Some dancers imitate birds, other burlesque the Spaniards. There was also a dance in which the Inca Emperor was impersonated and a mock battle with slings took place.

Musical instruments are played only by men, usually

in troupes, or what we might call orchestras, but a women's chorus sings songs of hunting, important to the fertility ceremony, and both men and women sing together in rain making ceremonies.

In Colombia, also, dancing was once very important in making war, in religious ceremonies, for weddings, and initiations.

In summary we might say that in North, Meso, and South America dancing is still very important in some areas. Whether on a reservation or in the Indian communities of large cities in the United States dancing is the one sure way of getting Indians together. Some of the old intertribal jealousies and animosities persist, but Indian from diverse tribes will show up for a dance and these dances are now tending to ameliorate the old feelings and bring about understanding. Indians are beginning to recognize themselves as an entity, rather than as small reservation or tribal groups. On the reservations, however, the dancing is instrumental in retaining both tribal identity and cultural preservation.

The repertoire at present-day "powwow" (a misnomer, as the word really means a shaman, or medicine man), in addition to the ever popular Fast and Slow War dances, usually includes the following:

*Round Dance*, an old-time social dance, executed in a circle moving to the left.
*Indian Two Step*, a modern social dance of couples.
*Forty-niner*, a north modern circle dance, with fast limp step.
*Contest Dances*, known variously as Ruffle, Get Down, Braided Tail dances. Also Humming Bird and Hoop dances.
*Buffalo Dance*, known sometimes as Grass Buffalo because of its association with the Grass (War) Dance. This is not one of the old Buffalo dances. No buffalo costume or headdress is used. It is done in "War Dance" costume.
*Shield and Spear Dance*, by two young men.
*Eagle Dance*, usually a duet, by two male dancers.
*Mountain Spirit Dance*, Apache, associated with young woman's puberty ceremonies, occasionally

given, but seldom in the day time.

*Gourd Clan Dance*, now popular in the Plains area.

*Straight Dance*, called by Sioux Straight-Up Dance, a dignified full costume dance, formerly by chiefs and dignitaries.

Until recently a "giveaway" was an important part of almost every Indian gathering across North America, although no reference was made to it in reports of South American Indian dances. In former times bravery and generosity were practically synonymous and persons, groups, or societies "proved" their bravery by publicly giving away various presents: blankets, horses, beadwork; more recently: blankets, quilts, groceries, money, to tribal members and visitors. Although the custom is still carried on in many communities, it is no longer as prevalent as it formerly was and in some regions seems to have been discontinued.

With interest in Indian cultures now growing among non-Indians the time may come when the public at large recognizes Indian dance as a significant art form, part of the heritage of all Americans. The Indians may yet make great contributions to the world of dance, as they have in so many other fields.

REGINALD AND GLADYS LAUBIN

**DIGGING STICKS** were used primarily by agricultural tribes for cultivation operations such as clearing land, loosening soil, planting, weeding, irrigation, and building up the soil around growing corn and other crops.

The simplest tool consisted of a hardwood staff with a flattened and edged end and was used in the northeastern United States, southeastern Canada, and parts of the Southwest. In the northeastern regions implements of this type were provided with a footrest on one side.

Hoes and spades, digging tools with a flat-edged blade, were used commonly throughout the Eastern Woodlands, Southeast, Prairies, and to some extent in parts of the Southwest. The blades frequently were made from bone, particularly the shoulder blade of buffalo or deer. Some blades were of wood, especially where large shoulder blades were scarce. Stone, shell, and fishbone blades were also used.

Numerous chipped flint and some ground stone blades have been found in the Mississippi and Ohio valleys. These are roughly elliptical-, fan-, or rectangular-shaped, and the tops of many are stemmed, notched, or provided with side points for attaching the handle. The larger blades, some as long as one foot, are often classified as spades and the smaller or notched blades, as hoes. Most, however, could have been helved in either way.

**DISCOIDAL STONES** are circular-shaped objects whose great variety has made it especially difficult to pinpoint their use.

Their shape can vary greatly. Their perimeter is circular, the diameter can vary from 1 to 8 inches, and their thickness can vary from ¼ to 6 inches. Some are convex on only one side and flat on the other, while concave stones are concave on both sides. They can have the slope of a double convex or double concave lens. The latter often have a depression in the center, which sometimes is so large that the stone is a ring.

The first name given to these stones was chunky stones, from the name of a game played with them by Indians in the Southwest. Three types have been image of themselves. Something of the persistent sense of personal equality in Indian tribal law left its imprint in the laws meant to define and govern a great nation. Whatever is unique in the collective Amerian personality and way of life owes much to diffusion from the forerunners, the earliest pioneers, the First Americans.

Olivia Vlahos

**DOG**. Since human beings entered the Western Hemisphere via the Bering Strait from Siberia some 25-30,000 years ago, the domestic dog (*Canis familiaris*) has played an important role in the lives of the native peoples of the Americas.

Due to the extreme difficulty of determining the

domestic status of canids on the basis of skeletal remains, few specific details are known of the early relationship between dogs and humans in the Western Hemisphere. We can assume that in the case of the earliest examples, such as the dog recovered from Jaguar Cave in the Birch Creek Valley of Idaho, the animal may have served as a companion in the hunt, or possibly as an item of consumption itself. Dating to approximately 8,400 BC, the Jaguar Cave dog is the earliest clearly documented domestic dog recovered to date in the Western Hemisphere.

As most of the original domestic dogs in North America are probably derived from the northern wolf (*Canis lupus*), it is not surprising that a number of early sites in the Arctic and Subarctic have produced remains of canids provisionally assigned domestic status.

From an overview of the data, it seems apparent no evidence exists for the use of domestic dogs as traction animals for hauling sleds until comparatively recent times. While this lack of evidence may be a function of poor preservation in the archaeological record, it is apparent that once established, the tradition became a very widespread phenomenon.

**Table 1: Early Domestic Dogs from the Arctic and Subarctic Regions of North America**

| SITE/REGION. | PHASE OR CULTURAL AFFILIATION | TIME RANGE | PROBABLE USE |
|---|---|---|---|
| Namu, British Columbia | Paleoarctic Tradition | 7000-6000 BC | Aid in Hunting |
| Glenrose Cannery, British Columbia | Paleo-plateau Tradition | Aid in c. 5000 BC | Hunting |
| Iglulik Region, N. Canada | Pre-Dorset Culture | 2000-1000 BC | Aid in Hunting |
| Belcher Islands, Hudson Bay | Dorset Culture | 1000 BC-AD 500 | Aid in Hunting |
| Numerous Alaskan Sites | Thule Tradition | AD 100-1800 | Hunting and beasts of burden |

The southwestern portion of the United States has produced not only the largest quantity of early domestic dog remains in the Western Hemisphere, but has also generated the greatest amount of research on the subject. An environment favorable to the preservation of organic remains has been largely responsible for this abundance. Research has yielded evidence for a variety of breeds of domestic dogs in the American Southwest by at least the beginning of the Christian Era, and probably much earlier.

Possibly the earliest domestic dog in the Southwest was recovered in levels 7 and 8 of the Upper Member at Ventana Cave, Arizona. Dating perhaps as early as 2500 BC this domestic dog has been designated as such on the basis of firm osteometric evidence.

There remains considerable doubt as to the domestic status of these canids.

Two well-preserved mummies from White Dog Cave, near Kayenta, Arizona, are among the earliest examples of vastly different breeds of dogs in the Western Hemisphere. Dating between AD 1 and AD 450, these Basketmaker II culture dogs may have been kept as pets in addition to serving as aids in hunting game.

Archaeological sites associated with later cultures often produce remains of numerous domestic canids.

By Pueblo times (beginning about AD 700) the American Southwest was undoubtedly characterized by diverse breeds of dogs that fulfilled a variety of functions ranging from hunting companion to beast of burden (sleds and travios) to domestic pet.

Early domestic dogs are known from the eastern United States as well. Domestic dog remains were recovered from post-glacial deposits in Coles County, Illinois (see Table 2). Found in questionable association with the skeleton of an American Mastodon (*Mammut americanum*), these finds, if proven to be those of a *domestic* animal, may represent one of the oldest domestic dogs in North America (perhaps 10-12,000 years old).

A 7500 year-old domestic dog has been recovered from the Archaic Rodgers Shelter in Benton Couunty,

**Table 2: Selected Early Domestic Dogs from the Western United States**

| SITE/REGION | PHASE OR CULTURAL AFFILIATION | TIME RANGE | PROBABLE USE |
|---|---|---|---|
| Jaguar Cave, Idaho | Paleo-Indian | c. 8400 BC | Aid in hunting |
| Ventana Cave, Arizona | Cochise Culture | c. 2500 BC | Aid in hunting |
| White Dog Cave, Arizona | Basketmaker II Culture | AD 1-450 | pet and aid in hunting |
| Mancos Canyon, Colorado | Pueblo I to Pueblo III Cultures | AD 800 1150 | pet and aid in hunting |
| Black Mesa, Arizona | Pueblo II to Pueblo III Cultures | AD 1000-1200 | pet and aid in hunting |
| Pueblo Bonito, New Mexico | Pueblo II Culture | c. AD 1050 | pet and aid in hunting |
| Grasshopper Pueblo, Arizona | Late Mogollon Culture | c. AD 1275-1400 | pet and aid in hunting |
| *Awatovi, Arizona | Historic Hopi Culture | AD 1629-1701 | pet and aid in hunting |

*Represents an early introduction of European (Spanish) domestic dogs into the traditional Amerindian lifeway.

Missouri, and at the famous Middle Archaic Koster Site in Greene County, Illinois, remains of a domestic dog 7,000 years old have been uncovered. The Koster dog was subjected to ritual interment—an interesting occurrence if it is true, for by 5000 BC, the practice of ritual dog burials had been established in the Midwest.

On the Eastern Seaboard, the recovery of domestic dogs has been made from New York state and from Martha's Vineyard. During the Frontenac Phase (*c.* 2500-1800 BC) of the Late Archaic in New York, dogs were commonly buried with people attesting to their symbolic significance. During the Frontenac Phase dogs were placed in male burials.

**Table 3: Selected Early Domestic Dogs from the Eastern United States**

| SITE/REGION | PHASE OR CULTURAL AFFILIATION | TIME RANGE | PROBABLE USE |
|---|---|---|---|
| Polecat Creek, Illinois | Paleo-Indian | c. 12,000-10,000 BC | aid in hunting? |
| Rodgers Shelter, Missouri | Early Archaic Culture | c. 5500 BC | ceremonial, hunting aid |
| Koster Site, Illinois | Middle Archaic Culture | c. 5000 BC | ceremonial, hunting aid, pet |
| Various New York Sites | Late Archaic, Frontenac Phase | c. 2500-1800 BC | ceremonial, hunting aid, pet |
| White's Mound, Georgia | Deptford Culture | c. 500 BC | ceremonial, hunting aid, pet |
| Various Ohio Sites | Hopewell Culture | c. AD 1-200 | ceremonial, hunting aid, pet |

The presence of domestic dogs in nearly all U.S. sites that are Archaic or later in age attests to the importance of these animals in the variety of Amerindian cultures manifest by that time.

Early domestic canids from the southeastern United States are fewer in number although specimens exist from Kentucky and Alabama as well as from Georgia.

**Early domestic dogs from Mexico and Central America**

As in the case of South America, to be discussed below, very little is known of canid domestication in Mexico and Central America prior to about 3500 BC.

The earliest domestic canids in Mesoamerica, at present, are associated with the Abejas Phase (3500-2300 BC) of the Tehuácan Valley sequence from southeastern Puebla, Mexico. Not much can be said about these dogs other than they were probably consumed regularly.

Some of the earliest unquestionable domestic dogs

from Mexico have been recovered from sites of the Olmec culture, such as the one at San Lorenzo, Veracruz (1500-700 BC). The discovery of juvenile dog remains at San Lorenzo that are unquestionably the refuse of consumption has been reported. Here, at San Lorenzo, we have definite proof that the dog was being bred as a source of protein as early as 1500 BC—a tradition in Mexico carried on by later peoples, such as the Aztec to be discussed below.

About 8000 BC, during the Middle Formative Period of Mexican prehistory, dogs are represented in collections of ceramic figurines recovered from the archaeological context. Among other subjects, these artifacts depict dogs being carried affectionately by women, clearly indicative of their role as a domestic pet. Undoubtedly, dogs were also consumed during the Middle Formative Period.

With the rise of the Aztec or Mexica civilization about AD 1200, the region of central Mexico witnessed a great cultural fluorescence.

Sites associated with this period, termed the Late Postclassic (AD 1200-1520) have produced remains of a wide variety of domestic dogs including a hairless breed known as *xoloizcuintle* by the Aztecs. The xoloizcuintle, whose name means in Nahuatl, "he who snatches his food with teeth as sharp as obsidian and who represents the god Xolotl," was a very important animal to the Aztecs for economic as well as ceremonial reasons. In addition to being eaten, the hairless breed was valued as a living hot-water bottle for the treatment of arthritis, and a xoloizcuintle was usually placed with a corpse upon burial to serve as a guardian on the trip to a place of eternal rest.

With the arrival of the Spanish in the early 16th century AD, new forms of European dogs, previously unknown to the Amerindians, were introduced. Accustomed to much smaller breeds, a typical Aztec description of a Spanish canine is, "And their dogs were very large. They have fiery eyes—blazing eyes; they had yellow eyes—fiery yellow eyes. They were very tall." Many early Spanish accounts describe the use of large dogs in Mexico and Florida to subdue the indigenous populations of these regions.

In southern Mexico and Central America, the presence of the dog is not well documented before the Middle Preclassic (900-300 BC). The recovery of domestic dogs from a Maya site at Siebal in Guatemala has been reported. Here, by about 600 BC, at least two beeds of dogs were known, strongly suggesting a much earlier ancestry for domestic dogs in the area.

Dogs are also depicted in the written records of the Mixtec, Aztec, and Maya, where they often conveyed negative connotations such as "worthless rains" or a skin infection. Thus, we may see that the domestic pervaded many aspects of life in Mexico and Mesoamerica and served a variety of purposes in so doing.

## Domestic canid remains recovered in South America

Less is known of the history and dynamics of canid domestication in South America than in regions to the north.

The evidence for what may represent the earliest domestic canid in South America suggests the Falkland Island Wolf (*Dusicyon australis*). Historic records exist that indicate members of the genus *Dusicyon* were tamed if not domesticated for use as hunting companions by the Amerindian inhabitants of the Falkland Islands (Islas Malvinas), off the southern coast of Argentina. Although there is no archaeological evidence as yet to support such a position the possibility exists that South America may be viewed as a separate hearth of dog domestication utilizing *Dusicyon* as a basal ancestral stock in contrast to the wolf (*Canis lupus*) of Central and North America.

What may be the earliest domestic from the South American continent has been recovered from early Holocene Paleo-Indian sites such as Chobshi Cave, Ecuador; Hacienda los Toldos, Patagonia, Argentina; and Tagua-Tagua, Chile. These remains have yet to be established as domestic animals, however. Their early date (around 10,000 BC) however, and the fact they are associated with human material culture and remains of animals frequently hunted with dogs today, makes these finds especially interesting.

There exists a substantial hiatus in our knowledge of South American dog domestication between the appearance of dogs in Paleo-Indian contexts at the close of the Pleistocene (*c.* 12,000 years ago) and late prehistoric times (*c.* 2,000 years ago) when the record becomes more complete.

Perhaps the earliest examples of domestic dogs in South America are found in Peru in sites of the Cupisnique or Chavin culture dating to about 1400-700 BC. One such site, excavated at Supe, produced the mummified remains of a small brown dog which may

**Representations of the domestic dog in Mixtec and Maya codices dating prior to the Spanish Conquest in the 16th century AD. A. Dog from Codex Nuttall (Mixtec, pre-Conquest). B. Dog from Codex Tro-Cortesianus (Maya, pre-Conquest). C. Dog from Codex Tro-Cortesianus (Maya, pre-Conquest). D. Dog from Codex Dresden (Maya, pre-Conquest).**

**Table 4: Selected Early Domestic Dogs from Mexico, Central, and South America**

| SITE/REGION | PHASE OR CULTURAL AFFILIATION | TIME RANGE | PROBABLE USE |
|---|---|---|---|
| Tehuacán Valley, Puebla, Mexico | Abejas Phase | 3500-2300 BC | food and hunting companion |
| San Lorenzo, Vera Cruz, Mexico | Olmec Culture | 1500-700 BC | food and hunting companion, pet |
| Tlatilco, Valley of Mexico | Middle Formative Period | food and c. 800 BC | hunting companion, pet |
| Chupicuaro, Guanajuato, Mexico | Preclassic Period | 400 BC-AD 1 | ceremonial |
| Various Aztec Sites, Mexico | Mexica Culture | AD 1200-1521 | ceremonial, food, pet |
| Seibal, Guatemala | Middle Preclassic Maya Culture | 600-300 BC | ceremonial, food, pet |
| Lighthouse Site, Puerto de Supe, Peru | Cupisnique (Chavin) Culture | c. 1400-700 BC | ceremonial, food, pet |
| Ancon, Peru | Chancay Culture | AD 900-700 BC | ceremonial, food, pet |
| Macchu Picchu, Peru | Inca Culture | c. AD 1500 | ceremonial, pet |

indicate ceremonial interment. Domestic dogs have been reported from sites in the region of Ancon that date to c. AD 900-1476. These mummified remains have been recovered from extensive cemeteries indicating they may have been placed there as a result of ritual activities.

Among the oldest clearly domestic dogs from Peru are those associated with sites of the Salinar Culture dating to c. 300 BC-AD 200). Human burials located in Salinar cemeteries are often accompanied by a dog burial placed at the feet, again attesting to a significance greater than merely that of hunting companion.

From these finds, it is evident that domestic canines were well established in South America by 1500 BC and probably a great deal earlier. Dogs appear to have had ceremonial significance from a very early date in South America by 1500 BC and probably a great deal earlier. Dogs appear to have had ceremonial significance from a very early date in South America, and this trend is further reinforced in later examples. The Inca Empire (AD 1438-1532) was characterized by a dependence upon a small number of domestic animals. In spite of this reliance on so few domesticates, the dog appears to have been kept only as a pet and was never consumed. Inca utilization of the dog in ritual sacrifices is also well established and many fine examples of Inca dogs have been recovered from Late Horizon sites. For example, finds have reported at the Inca city of Macchu Picchu, near Cuzco in Peru. All evidence from these late sites indicates that the peoples of Late Horizon Peru were familiar with many varieties of dogs, including "hairless" and "toy" breeds.

The history of the domestication of canids in South America is as yet not fully understood, owing in large part to a lack of intensive archaeological investigation in many crucial areas (such as the Amazon Basin). It is hoped that as such archaeological studies are initiated, we may begin to fill in the gaps in our knowledge and learn to what extent South America may be viewed as a separate hearth for the domestication of canids.

In conclusion, it is probable the domestic dog accompanied the first inhabitants of the Western Hemisphere across the Bering Strait from Siberia perhaps 25-30,000 years ago. An important question yet to be answered is whether or not areas of the New World (South America in particular) should be considered independent centers of dog domestication. Archaeological evidence indicates the dog has served the Amerindian as a beast of burden, a hunting companion, and item of consumption as well as an inspiration for myriad folktales and mythology.

Many works exist on the relationship of living Native Americans and domestic dogs, but all serve to illustrate the continuity between the archaeological and contemporary examples. The domestic dog plays as vital a role in the Amerindian lifeway today as it has throughout most of the history of human occupation in the Western Hemisphere.

JOHN W. OLSEN

**DOLLS** and other miniature figures of human beings have been produced by American Indians throughout their history. They have been as varied as the cultures they represent, and the materials from which they were made were as diverse as the regions from which they sprang. Those figures produced as children's toys or as collector's items are *dolls*. Non-toys such as *effigies* are representations of specific beings. *Figurines* are carved or molded statuettes. *Religious miniatures* have supernatural connotations. Some figures may be classified as all four. Sometimes making the distinction between toy dolls and other figures is difficult or impossible, especially concerning archaeological finds where there may be no historical documentation concerning the use of the object.

Dolls, sometimes looking like miniature members of the family, were often used as toys by American Indian children. They were made of a variety of materials including stone, animal hair, animal hide, wood, shell, seaweed, grass, cornhusk, ivory, bone, clay, trade goods, and other substances.

Little girls mimiced their mothers' child-caring activities by playing with dolls. They learned household skills that they would need as adults. Boys were less likely to play with "baby" dolls and more often played games with dolls such as "going hunting," and "going to war," in imitation of their fathers. In these ways, playing with dolls helped to enculturate Indian children.

The costumes of American Indian dolls reflect cultural affiliation, climate, hair and clothing styles, as well as other aspects of culture such as art, war, social class, religion, and wealth. The materials from which the dolls were constructed also indicate the availability of naturally occurring materials and trade goods.

American Indian dolls have been sold as souvenirs

since white contact. Some of those dolls were used as toys; others joined collections as new exotic specimens; and others were sent home to show how the Indians dressed. Doll collecting was in full swing as a hobby by 1900, which greatly increased the demand for Indian dolls made by craft workers. Many of those dolls are preserved in museum and private collections. Buying Indian dolls is still a popular activity among tourists, and many tribes make and offer dolls for sale. The best are usually found in remote areas.

Miniature figures of human beings have played a role in the religions of American Indians for centuries. They were often the embodiment of the spirit of a person, place, or thing which was dealt with by a shaman or priest. Religious figurines were treated with great respect and were often feared for their power. Whereas toy dolls were most often dressed with attached clothing, religious figures were more often carved or molded.

**North America**

Eskimo toy dolls were often made of animal skins stuffed with reindeer hair or fur. Others were made of bone, ivory, wood, or mammoth teeth. They were often dressed in a parka and mukluks. Eskimos occasionally hung carved bone figures of human beings in their kayaks to protect them from capsizing. Ivory shaman figures have been recorded as early as 1850. As early as 1900 the Salish Indians of the Pacific Northwest Coast made carved cedar baby dolls in cradles covered with cotton quilt swaddling and lacing. The Tlingit Indians used carved wooden shaman figures which have been found in gravehouses.

Many of the Plains and peripheral Plains tribes, including the Blackfoot, Cheyenne, Dakota, Apache, Crow, Winnebego, and others, produced buckskin dolls stuffed with wool, vegetable fibers, clay, or animal hair. Their traditional clothing was decorated with seedbeads or porcupine quills. European clothing became popular after about 1870, but buckskin shirts and dresses were still in vogue. A rawhide cutout of a man was traditionally used in the religious Sun Dance of the Dakota. The eastern Dakota used a little carved wooden human figure, a "tree dweller," in a hollow log housing, in an eastern variant of the Grand Medicine Lodge Ceremony at least prior to 1908. The Ojibwa also used a little carved wooden human figure in the rites of the Grand Medicine Society. In about 1860 the Menomini Indians used wooden figures with cotton cloth costumes decorated with shells and beads. By 1919 they still used carved wooden figures to perform magic tricks.

The most popular religious miniatures in the Southwest are the Katchinas of the Hopi, Zuñi, and Pomo tribes. They are representations, in human form, of spirits of persons, animals, places, or things. Katchinas are made of carved cottonwood or cactus root, painted and decorated with bits of feathers, cloth, shell, and other materials. They are given to children at annual ceremonies, but they are not toys. They are religious objects for children to study. Among the Navajo Indians, simplistic carved wooden sacrificial figurines in human form are made by medicine men and placed near ruins to atone for violated taboos. Modern Navajo make and sell tourist dolls which are sometimes weaving rugs, that skill for which the Navajo are so famous. Stone fetishes in the human shape may be found among the Indians at Zia Pueblo. The Keres Indians of Laguna use stick figures of human beings in offerings during religious ceremonies. The Mohave Indians of Arizona made tattooed terra-cotta dolls. Some were infants; others were standing or sitting figures, sometimes on platforms. They were dressed in real skirts or breechcloths, beaded collars and earrings.

Cornhusk toy dolls, dressed in traditional clothing of cloth and buckskin with feathers and beads, were made by the Seneca in New York in the late 1800s. By about 1850 the Deleware still used spirit figures which protected them in return for a dance held in their honor and a new set of clothing each year. Those figures were often dressed in cotton cloth wrappings, leather moccasins, and many seedbead necklaces, silver discs, shells, and beads. The Iroquois made little wood carvings of snake dancers as late as 1935.

**Mesoamerica**

Effigies, figurines, and religious miniatures in the form of human beings are often found among Aztec and Maya ruins. They are sometimes found in grave sites and are usually considered religious in function. One cannot be certain that any of them were used as toy dolls. Some were household idols that may later have been used as dolls. Figures in the form of ball players, weapon-bearing warriors, female fertility forms, shamen, dancers, acrobats, and others have been found. They are made of terra-cotta or pottery (either hand-formed or mold-produced), jade, serpentine, and other stone. The figures depicted indi-

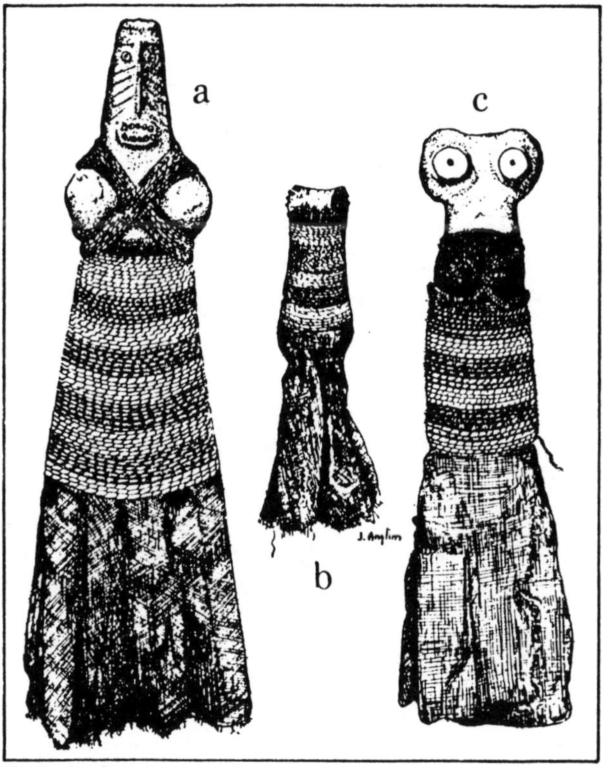


*Handbook of South American Indians.*

(A, C) Mataco and Pilagá clay dolls; (B) Pilagá doll made from a cow knuckle.

cate a preoccupation with war, fertility, and religion. Some are stiff and stylized. Others are ironic caricatures. Some are complicated and elaborate, while others are simple suggestions of the human form. They may be serene or active in appearance. Much is known about Aztec and Maya dress from their effigies, figurines, and religious miniatures.

The Seri Indians of Sonora in northwest Mexico, recently, make simple little carved wooden dolls barely suggesting the human shape, wrapped in cloth and bound with yarn.

**South America**

The most famous figurines from South America are those produced by the Incas. They are not as abundant as Mesoamerican figurines. Beautiful figurines of solid gold casting and of pottery have been recovered. A solid gold casting molded figurine from Columbia has been found which is at least 500 years old. It is a mace-carrying figure with rounded contours, shining surface, and false filigree in some parts.

Knitted dolls made of wool are still produced in Peru among the Quechua Indians, descendants of the Incas. They also produce dolls of clay, wood, and gourd. Modern dolls include masked dancers dressed in traditional clothing.

The Araucanian Indians of Chile produce dolls made of animal hide dressed in cotton clothing. Some are mounted on toy horses with loads of wool blankets. Dolls from Chile and Brazil are sometimes little cork- or wooden-headed figures with bodies of yarn-wrapped wire.

**DOMESTICATED PLANTS AND ANIMALS.** Little wonder that plants and religion were intricately linked by primitive man, for most of his food, shelter, narcotics, stimulants and medicine were derived from plants. Moreover, early man believed that the plants were inhabited by spirits and that it was necessary to propitiate these spirits. Thus among the agricultural Indians there were almost always special rituals connected with planting and harvesting, as well as sacrifices to the rain gods whose help was essential in producing good plant growth. In many groups of people plants are prominent in their creation myths.

Until nearly 7000 years ago all of the peoples of the Americas were hunters and gatherers, and they made use of an extensive number of plant species in their daily lives. Virtually all of the plants that could furnish edible roots, stems, leaves, fruits or seeds were discovered by trial and error, as were also those plants that could serve other purposes. In some regions a particular plant resource became a staple, such as the oak in the western United States. Twenty-seven different species of North American oaks provided acorns that could be used for food. In order to make the acorns suitable for human consumption it was necessary in most cases to remove the tannins by leaching with water. In many regions grasses became the wild food staple: for example, wild rice in the western Great Lakes region. Other wild food staples included camass in the northwestern United States, pinon in the Great Basin, mesquite in the Southwest and Mexico, potatoes in the Andes, and many palm fruits in tropical America.

Although many groups of Indians still had a hunting-gathering economy at the time of the Spanish conquest, probably the majority were farmers. This farming is perhaps best designated as horticulture, for true agriculture involves the use of draft animals which were not available until introduced by the Spanish. More than 100 species of plants were domesticated in the Americas, and the great majority, as might be expected, were food plants.

**Cereals.** Maize was domesticated in Middle America some 6000 years ago, and no plant was more important to the Indians. It was grown almost everywhere that horticuture was practiced, from sea level to over 11,000 feet in the Andes, extending from southern Canada to the Island of Chiloe. Swamps were drained, woodlands were cleared, deserts were irrigated, and terraces were built in mountain sides in order that the plant could be grown. In art, religion and everyday life most of man's activities were centered around this plant. For food it was prepared in a great variety of ways: popping and parching were probably the most primitive ways; hominy and meal were made from it; and by chewing or germinating the grain an alcoholic beverage could be prepared. In Mexico and some other areas the traditional method of preparing the grain for food was to soak the grain in alkali-water made from lime, wood ashes, lye or shells. Maize is now one of man's most nutritious foods, and recently it has been shown that the alkali cooking technique actually enhances its nutritive value.

**Legumes.** Only slightly less important to the Indians than maize, and frequently grown with it, were a number of different kinds of beans (*Phaseolus*). Maize and beans together supply a fairly adequate diet for man, for the protein content of beans is quite high and their amino acid composition largely complements that of maize. Beans appear at the earliest levels of horticulture in both Peru and Mexico. Domesticated forms of both the common bean (*P. Vulgaris*) and the lima bean (*P. lunatus*) have been found in deposits in highland Peru over 7000 years old, and the common bean appeared in Mexico more than 6000 years ago. The lima bean was to become known in Mexico at a much later date. The tepary bean and the scarlet runner bean appear fairly early in Mexico and were both to become important food plants.

The peanut (*Arachis hypogaea*), which apparently was domesticated in Bolivia, is found in coastal Peruvian deposits in the second millenium BC and is reported from Tehuacan, Mexico at the beginning of the Christian era. Different species of jack bean (*Canavalia*) were also grown in Mexico and Peru, and the chocho (*Lupinus mutabilis*) was cultivated in the Andes for its seeds.

**Cucurbits.** All the squashes and pumpkins had their origins in the Americas; five different species were domesticated. *Cucurbita pepo, C. mixta,* and *C. moschata* were domesticated in Middle America, and *C. maxima* in South America. Where the fifth species, *C. ficifolia,* a squash adapted to highland conditions, was domesticated is still uncertain. It has been suggested that these cucurbits may have been first grown for their edible seeds and that the thick flesh of the fruit, for which they are largely cultivated today, was a later development.

Other members of the cucurbit family were also cultivated for their fruits, including the chayote (*Sechium edule*) in Middle America and achocha (*Cyclanthera pedata*) in the Andean region. The bottle gourd (see below) may also have served for food at times.

**Roots and tubers.** The underground parts of a number of plants are important sources of carbohydrates. A far greater number of these plants became domesticated in tropical South America and in the Andes than in other parts of the Americas. Three of these plants, manioc, the Irish or white potato, and the sweet potato became important staples.

Manioc (*Manihot esculenta*), also known as cassava and yuca, was widely cultivated in tropical areas, and in some parts, particularly the Amazon region, was more important than maize. Manioc comprises both sweet and bitter varieties; the bitter varieties, which require special preparation to remove the poisonous cyanogenetic glucosides to make them safe to eat, were apparently more widely grown than the sweet kinds. The implements presumably used in their preparation are rather common in the archaeological record but the actual remains of the plant are seldom encountered. There is some disagreement as to whether the original type was bitter or sweet, but most authorities think that the sweet forms arose from the bitter.

Wild potatoes are common in the Andes, and in time one or more of them, probably in the area of Lake Titicaca, became domesticated. The Irish potato (*Solanum tuberosum*) is a highland crop and grows well at 15,000 feet, which is beyond the range of maize and most other cultivated plants. In the high Andes special methods of dehydrating the potato by repeated freezing and stamping on the thawing tubers produced a food, known as chuno, that could be stored for long periods of time. The Irish potato was unknown in Middle and North America until post-Conquest times.

The sweet potato (*Ipomaea batatas*) was cultivated in

Middle America, the West Indies, and northern South America in prehistoric times. The exact place of origin is as yet unknown, but some evidence suggests northern South America. There is fairly general agreement that the sweet potato had also reached some of the islands of the Pacific in pre-Columbian times. Although it seems probable that its introduction there was by the agency of man, a natural means of dispersal cannot yet be entirely ruled out.

Among other underground crops are oca (*Oxalis tuberosa*), ulluco (*Ullucus tuberosus*), and anu (*Tropaeolum tuberosum*), all confined to the high Andes. At lower elevations, species of yam (*Dioscorea*), yautia (*Xanthosoma*), and achira (*Canna edulis*) were cultivated in various parts. The yam bean (*Pachyrrhizus erosus*) was one of the few root crops, in addition to manioc and the sweet potato, known for Middle America; a related species (*Pachyrrhizus tuberosa*) was utilized in Peru.

**Fruits.** The term "fruit" botanically refers to the ripened ovary or ovaries of a flower, and thus both grains and pumpkins are fruits. The tomato, the husk-tomato, and the avocado are among the important fruits utilized as vegetables. Whether the origin of the cultivated tomato (*Lycopersicon esculentum*) was in Mexico, or in Western South America where its wild relatives occur, is still uncertain, but it seems clear that the fruit was more important in Mexico than in South America in pre-contact times. A husk tomato (*Physalis philadelphica*) was an important vegetable in Mexico, and may have been domesticated earlier than the tomato. The tree tomato (*Cyphomandra crassifolia*), another member of the nightshade family, was cultivated for its fruits in western South America. The avocado, a food rich in oils, was fairly widely grown. It apparently was domesticated independently in Middle America, the West Indies, and Peru.

Fruits that appealed to man because of their sweetness were rather numerous, and both Middle America and South America contributed many kinds. A large number of species of *Anona* — ilama, cherimoya, guanabanana, sweetsop, soursop, and anona — were domesticated. Other important cultivated fruits were pineapple (*Ananas comosus*), a cherry (*Prunus serotina*), the papaya (*Carica papuya*), sapodilla (*Achras zapota*), the guava (*Psidium guajava*), the hog plum (*Spondias mombin*), sapote (*Calocarpum viride* and other genera), cactus or prickly pear (*Opuntia*) and many more. The cashew (*Anacardium occidentale*) was valued more as a fruit than as a nut.

The coconut (*Cocos nucifera*), another fruit that eventually became an important food source in the Americas, apparently had an exceedingly limited distribution in Middle America at the time of the conquest. The coconut was at one time considered to be a native to the Americas, but it is now known to be indigenous to southeastern Asia. Whether its arrival in America was by floating or through the agency of man is still somewhat controversial.

**Condiments and flavorings.** The major condiment in the Americas was chili or red pepper of the genus *Capsicum*. Wild species, which are found from the southern United States to southern South America, are used in many present day dishes. Four species became domesticated: the chili (*C. annum*) in Middle America, two kinds of ajis (*C. baccatum* and *C. frutescens*) and the rocoto (*C. pubescens*) in South America. The last named species was adapted to the high Andes. The pepper became almost indispensable in the diet of the Indians and received almost the same reverence as did the staple crops. Red peppers are, of course, food as well as condiment, and supply both vitamins and minerals.

The vanilla orchid (*Vanilla planifolia*) became a cultivated plant in Mexico and was used by the Aztecs as a flavoring.

**Alcoholic beverages and stimulants.** Apparently primitive man discovered that beers or wines could be made from a large number of plants. In the Americas a chicha or beer made from maize had a very wide distribution. Manioc was also frequently employed for the manufacture of a beer. The root was chewed and then spat into containers. The mastication changed the starch into sugar, thus producing a suitable substrate for microorganisms that would convert some of the sugar into alcohol. Among other basic food plants, both quinoa and sweet potatoes were sometimes used to make beers. A large number of fruits were used to make wines, and since they naturally contained sugar no special processing was necessary to initiate fermentation. Among the cultivated plants, pineapples were often used, and among wild plants, palms and algarroba (*Prosopis chilensis*) were particularly important in South America. Several kinds of maguey (*Agave*) were used for making pulque in Middle America. In the eastern United States wild persimmons were used to make a beer.

The two most important caffeine-containing plants were cacao or the chocolate bean and various kinds of *Ilex*. Wild cacao (*Theobroma cacao*) had a wide distribution from Mexico to central South America, but only in Middle America did it become a domesticated plant, prized both as a food and drink. In time the beans or seeds became used as currency. Leaves of varius species of *Ilex* were used in South America to prepare a stimulating beverage, and one, *Ilex paraguariensis,* eventually became domesticated, and today is the course of yerba mate or Paraquayan tea. Apparently its use was rather local until the arrival of the Spanish, who were responsible for much of the improvement in the plant and its wider distribution. *Ilex vomitoria* was used for the "black drink" of the Indians of eastern North America.

Leaves of coca (*Erthroxylum coca*), the source of cocaine, usually with the addition of lime, were chewed in the Andean region and in a few other places. It served to allay thirst and hunger and to enable one to carry out physical exertion for prolonged periods of time.

**Narcotics and hallucinogens.** In no other part of the world did plants become more widely used as narcotics and hallucinogens than in tropical America. Like many of the food plants, and perhaps even earlier, they often became a direct object of worship. They were most often taken by shamans for magic, divination and the curing of disease but were also employed in boy's initiation ceremonies and in other ways. Although the Spanish tried to stamp out these "heathen" practices, they were only partially successful, and the use of many of these plants flourishes to this day. The majority of the plants used for these purposes have various alkaloids as their active ingredients.

Of these plants, tobacco had the widest distribution in the Americas and was the only one eventually to become widely used throughout the world. Tobacco was chewed, snuffed, smoked, licked or drunk, and its use was mostly religious or ceremonial in contrast to a secular use which largely came after the Conquest. Two species, both South American in origin, were domesticated — *Nicotiana tabacum* became the chief tobacco of South America and the West Indies (and eventually the rest of the world) whereas *N. rustica,* the stronger of the two species, was the tobacco of Mexico and eastern North America. Various wild species of tobacco, sometimes apparently deliberately cultivated, were utilized in western North America.

Mushrooms and flowering plants from several different families furnished the hallucinogens, most widely used in Middle America and western South America. In Mexico and Guatemala, teonanacatl, or the "flesh of the gods," (*Psilocybe mexicana*), as well as several other kinds of mushroom were of great significance. The genus *Datura* of the nightshade family furnished the greatest number of species used as hallucinogens. In eastern North America, the jimson weed, *D. stramonium,* was employed, in southwestern North America and Mexico, the angel's trumpet, *D. inoxia,* was used, and in northwestern South America, the tree Daturas, particularly *D. sanguinea* in the highlands and *D. suaveolens* in the lowlands, was prominent. Peyote, from the cactus, *Lophophora williamsii,* became the basis of a cult in Mexico in prehistoric times. Its use spread to the United States in the eighteenth century where it is now incorporated in the ceremonies of the Native American Church. A few other kinds of cactus were also found to have hallucinogenic properties. Ololiuqui, long a source of confusion as to its identity, has been determined to be seeds of morning glories (*Ipomoea violacea* and *Rivea corymbosa*). Several legumes have been used, particularly yopo snuff from *Anadenathera peregrina* of northern South America and the West Indies, and the mescal or red bean, *Sophora secundiflora* of the American Southwest and Mexico. Among the other important hallucinogens are caapi or ahuahuaso from *Banisteriopsis caapi,* a tree of northern South America and a snuff prepared from various species of *Virola* used in the north western Amazon and only recently known to science. Much of the information on the nature and uses of these plants derives from the studies of the Harvard botanist, Richard E. Shultes.

**Fibers.** Two species of cotton, distinct from the species of the Old World, were domesticated in the Americas. The archaeological record reveals that *Gossypium hirsutum* was the species of ancient Mexico whereas the textiles found in Peruvian graves were made from *G. barbadense.* Both of the American species of cotton are polyploids that arose from hybridization of two species followed by chromosome doubling. At one time it was postulated that one of the ancestral species had been carried to the New World from the Old by man, but more recent investigations do not substantiate this view.

The other important domesticated fiber plants include various members of the family Agavaceae. Henequen, maguey and sisal belong to various species of *Agave* and were cultivated in Middle America, while various kinds of cabuya, species of *Fucraea,* were grown in South America.

A number of wild plants, particularly palms and bromeliads, also furnished fibers used by the Indians, and bark cloth was made from some trees.

**Gourds.** Two plants produced fruits that were widely employed for vessels as well as in a number of other ways. Before the invention of pottery these plants must have been particularly valuable to man, and their use continued after the arrival of pottery, as it does today in many parts of the Americas. The fruits of both plants have been called both gourds and calabashes and sometimes the distinction between them is not made. However, the plants producing them are very different. One, usually called the bottle gourd, comes from a cucurbit (*Lagenaria siceraria*) whereas the other, the tree gourd, comes from a bignoniaceous plant (*Crescentia cujete*). The latter is a small tree, widespread in the American tropics, whereas the former is a large vine, also widespread in the tropics but whose cultivation extended into the temperate zone as well. It is generally agreed that the bottle gourd is native to Africa, but it is found in Mexico at 7000 BC and nearly as early in Peru. Thus it appears to be one of the oldest domesticated plants in the Americas, and how it arrived here has been the subject of much discussion. Some have held that it must have been carried by man, whereas others believe that the fruits must have floated across the Atlantic. Since the fruit has been shown to float for long periods in salt water without losing seed viability, the latter view is quite plausible.

**Other plant uses.** Among the plants used for dyes, two with wide distributions in tropical America merit special notice. Achiote, a red pigment, which was obtained from *Bixa orellana*, was used as a body or hair paint in South America as well as in other ways. Indigo or anil was obtained from *Indigofera suffruticosa*. Plants such as the cochineal cactus were cultivated as hosts for cochineal insects, which were used for a dye.

A large number of plant species were employed in medicine. Many of these were wild plants, but some plants cultivated primarily for other purposes, as, for example, the sunflower, also had medicinal use. Some of the drug plants, such as ipecac, have found their way into modern medicine. Rather surprisingly perhaps, the bark of the *Cinchona* tree, which yields quinine, was apparently not utilized by the Indians.

An extremely large number of plants were also employed as fish poisons. Over 100 different species have been reported with such use in South America. The legumes, barbasco (*Tephrosia*) and cube (*Lonchocarpus*) were particularly prominent in this regard. Although most of the plants used were wild, some apparently were intentionally cultivated for use as pesticides. The usual method of using them was to mascerate the stem or leaves in the water which caused the fish to be stupified so that they could be easily collected. The fish could then be eaten with no harm to man.

Arrow poisons, including curare, were also made from several plants. Latex from several plants was used to make rubber, the primary purpose of which seems to have been to make balls. Some plants furnished material for shampoos or soaps. A number of plants were deliberately grown as living fences, and other plants, such as marigolds and dahlias, were cultivated for their beauty as ornamentals, particularly in Mexico.

There was an early practice of horticulture in both Mexico and Peru. At present it is impossible to say where it was earlier and whether the developments were entirely separate or whether there was the diffusion of the idea of planting from one region to the other. The common bean is found quite early in both centers, and although the possibility exists that it may have been carried from one area to the other, it is also quite possible that it had independent origins as a domesticated plant in the two centers. Several other plants, such as chili pepper and squash, were also early known in both Mexico and Peru, but they usually involve different species of a genus, which appear to have been domesticated from species native to the respective areas. Thus there was not necessarily any early transfer by man of plants from one area to the other. The appearance of maize in South America, however, almost certainly involves an introduction by man from Middle America. According to our present knowledge, however, maize appeared in South America after horticulture was already established.

While a large number of species were domesticated in both Middle and South America, very few cultivated plants were developed in North America. The four most important horticultural plants in North America, maize, beans, squash, and tobacco, all apparently came by way of Mexico. The sunflower (*Helianthus annus*), however, is one plant that seems clearly to have been domesticated north of Mexico, and it is still not clear whether its domestication occurred before or after the North American Indians had acquired these other plants from Mexico. The Jerusalem artichoke (*Helianthus tuberosus*) also became at least a semi-domesticated plant in eastern North America. The marsh-elder or sump weed (*Iva annua*) appears to have been domesticated in central North America, although it had become extinct as a cultivated plant before the arrival of the Europeans.

Columbus introduced some of the Old World domesticated plants and animals to the Americas in his later voyages and in the 16th century a large number of Old World plants appeared in the Americas. The new plants had great impact on the Indian's diet in some areas and little or none in other areas. To this day, for example, in parts of the Amazon the Indians are still cultivating their traditional plants. Some of the newly introduced plants, for example, bananas and plantains, were so eagerly adopted that they became widespread in a short space of time and were sometimes regarded as indigenous to the Americas by the later Spanish.

At the same time that the Americas were receiving many plants from the Old World, they were furnishing many to the Old World, such as maize, potatoes, and peanuts, which were to become widely appreciated. The Indians' tobacco also soon spread around the world. It was perhaps, as someone has said, the Indians' revenge for their conquest by the European.

## ANIMALS

Animal domestication is a phenomenon which is difficult to explain or define accurately. Rather than limit the definition to any single condition, it seems best to consider several conditions and several classes or degrees of domestication.

A distinction must be made between "domesticated" and tamed "wild" animals. The latter generally are isolated individuals which are caught wild (usually when young) and tamed as pets. All tamed wild animals are utilized, at least as pets in an esthetic sense, so the fact of utilization should not enter into the definition of either a domesticated or a tamed animal — all animals taken purposely by man into his company are utilized in some way.

Domestication should apply to an animal species which meets the following conditions: That it (1) is integrated into human culture; (2) is kept forcibly under human control for a purpose; (3) is dependent upon man, either voluntarily or involuntarily, for survival under this prior condition; (4) generally breeds under the artificial conditions of human control; and (5) generally is modified into breeds (or strains) through selective breeding by man.

This definition gives several degrees of domestication: (1) ordinary, or highly domesticated animals — those which answer all conditions (generally widespread geographically, also); (2) semidomesticated animals — those which answer at least the first three conditions. Some semidomesticated animals, e.g., pearl oysters, silkworms, honey bees, etc., have been called "cultivated."

The reasons that some animals have been domesticated to any degree whatsoever are also difficult to state. However, they certainly involve cultural as well as zoological factors, and some of the following may be important: (1) cultural stimulus (either religious, economic, or esthetic), which gives and sustains a purpose and value to the act and the animals, and which in most cases probably originates in concentrated settled populations of peoples who have already had the knowledge and background of cultivated plants; (2) calm and docile disposition of the animal, which results in easy adaptation to confinement and generally involves no difficulty in breeding; (3) play instinct well developed (in mammals); (4) chance (meeting of the animal and the culture); (5) perhaps a symbiotic tendency of behavior in the animal, which manifests itself (a) in some sort of stratified social organization in nature and docile subjection to man in captivity, and/or (b) in some degree of attraction to other organisms, especially under stresses of nature, (famine, drought, cold, flood, extinction, etc.), because, generally, physically subnormal or exhausted animals are more easily tamed than robust healthy ones, and/or (c) in some "domestic" attachment to man which later turns into a domesticated symbiotic relationship.

It would seem that there exist many wild animals which are potentially domesticable, and perhaps chance has so far prevented their domestication; but, on the other hand, nearly all truly domesticated animals have an ancient history, and few new ones have been added recently. Hence, there may exist very good zoological reasons, or lack of certain factors, zoological as well as cultural, which have prevented and will prevent domestication of such forms. A study of seemingly domesticable animals, from the cultural and biological viewpoint, may clarify the positive factors favorable or necessary for domestication of others.

Fear is a strong factor in the behavior (and in the domesticability) of an animal. Young animals of these species are easier to tame than older members. However, some animals can be tamed in the adult as well as in the immature states (falcon, otter, etc.). There is obviously much to be learned about domestication, but also enough variability to preclude facile generalizations.

The establishment of special breeds of domesticated animals is an interesting phenomenon. The general idea of the mechanics of reproduction, and of heredity, must have been known to Indians, especially to those with cultivated plants and domesticated animals, but it seems that the conscious establishment of a breed is generally a function of a culture which gives a special stimulus to the production and preservation of the breed. Without some cultural stimulus, the perpetuation of domesticated stock appears to proceed haphazardly as far as selective breeding is concerned. However, with a stimulus from religious (producing breeds of black llamas, white llamas, white alpacas, and perhaps 5-toed llamas), or from economic pressure, or from war, hunting, or sheer amusement, special breeds will be perpetuated and perhaps consciously developed by merely isolating and breeding desired like-with-like and segregating the results. Special craftmanship, secret or public, with special hereditary groups of animal husbandrists, will subsequently develop, and this will accelerate the process of breed development and improvement. In addition, breeds or strains can be developed naturally and unconsciously by natural selection, when the domesticated animal in question is continually forced to live in more extreme conditions of climate or to perform more arduous conditions of work. In these cases, only those individuals with the inherent ability to survive and breed can perpetuate the species, with a consequent fixation of the naturally selected combinations of characters in the newly developing breed.

The Indians of the Americas learned a great deal from, and were helped by animals in their wild state. The period of domestication began when he held them in captivity for the gratification of his desires or they became attached to him for mutual benefit. In this process there are the following gradations:

1. "Commensalism" begins when food is left for serviceable animals to devour, so that these may give notice of danger or advantage. The coyote is said to reveal the presence of the mountain lion. Small animals are tolerated for their skins and flesh. Plants would be sown to attract such creatures as bees, and tame animals would be regularly fed at later stages.

2. Confinement is represented by such activities as keeping fish and other aquatic animals in ponds; caging birds and carrying off their young, gallinaceous fowl last; tying up dogs or muzzling them; corralling ruminants, and bobbling or tethering wild horses so as to have them near, keep them away from their enemies, or fatten them for eating. The Indians had no difficulty in breeding some animals in confinement, but few wild birds will thus propogate, and the Indians could obtain those to tame only by robbing nests.

3. Keeping animals for their service or produce, as dogs for retrieving game or catching fish, hawks for killing birds; various creatures for their fleece, hides, feathers, flesh, milk, etc., and taming them for amusement and for ceremonial or other purposes, were a later development.

4. Actually breaking them to work, training dogs, horses, and cattle for packing, sledding, hauling travois, and, later, for riding, constitutes complete domestication.

In pre-Columbian times the dog was the most perfectly subdued animal of North America, as much so as the llama in South America. But other species of mammals, as well as birds, were in different degrees rendered tractable. After the coming of the whites, the methods of domesticating animals were perfected, and their uses multiplied. Moreover, horses, sheep, cattle, donkeys, hogs, and poultry were added to the list, and these profoundly modified the manners and customs of many Indian tribes.

Domestication of animals increased the food supply, furnished pets for old and young, helped him to go about, multiplied his wants, furnished a standard of property and a medium of exchange, took the load from the back of women, and provided more abundant material for economic, artistic, and ceremonial purposes.

Domestication had a different development in each culture area. In the Arctic region the dog was preeminent; it was reared with unremitting care, and all its life it was trained to the sled. As the dogs were never perfectly tamed, it was no easy task to drive a team of them; yet by the aid of dogs and sleds, in combination with umiaks, the whole polar area of America was exploited by the Inuit, who found these an excellent means of rapid transit from Asia to the Atlantic. The Mackenzie-Yukon area is a canoe country, and domestication of the dog was not vigorously prosecuted until the Hudson's Bay Company gave the stimulus. But southward, among the Algonquian and Siouan tribes of the Great Lakes and the Plains, this animal attained its best as a hunter and a beast of burden and traction. It was also reared for food and for ceremonial purposes. Not more than 50 pounds could be borne by one dog, but twice that amount could be moved on a travois. The coming of the horse (*q.v.*) to the Great Plains was a boon to the Indian tribes, all of which at once adopted the new instrument of travel and transportation. The horse was apotheosized; it became a standard of value: and fostered a greater diversity of occupations. But the more primitive methods of domestication were still practiced throughout the middle region. In the north Pacific area dogs were trained to hunt; but here and elsewhere this use of the dog was doubtless learned.

In the California-Oregon area birds of gray plumage were caged, plucked, and then set free. On Santa Catalina island, birds called large crows by the Spaniards were kept and worshipped. In the Southwest, the desert area, the whole development of domestication is seen. The coyote was allowed to feed about the camps. The Querecho (Vaquero Apache) of Coronado in 1541 had a great number of large dogs which they obliged to carry their baggage when they moved from place to place. Some of the Pueblo tribes practiced also the caging of eagles, the rearing of turkeys, and, since the coming of the Spaniards, the herding of sheep, goats, burros and horses.

**Middle and South America.** South America, Central America, and the Antilles are noted for rich fauna, composed of a great number of unique or endemic forms, and invaders (some now distinct) from North America since earliest times.

At present there are many diverse species, but time has seen the extinction of many others, particularly large forms. Man perhaps hastened the extinction of some. This extinction, for one reason or another, reduced the Plains faunas particularly, though less so in the southern temperate areas than in the central and northern tropical parts.

Middle and South America are divisible into four subregions: (1) Guyana-Brazilia, (2) Central America, (3) Antilles, and (4) Patagonia-Chile. The first three constitute at least 75 percent of the whole region, and are tropical. The rich ethnozoology of these tropical subregions may be separated further into continental-tropical, and Antillea tropical on the basis of the different faunas. Patagonia-Chile is south temperate, and is characterized by the very large number of its primary endemic forms, which include the guanaco-llama-alpaca-vicuna fauna of the plains and mountains. This fauna, with and without domestication, was thoroughly utilized in many special ways by Indians.

The domesticated llama probably was derived from similar wild guanacos. The alpaca probably was domesticated from a now extinct wild ancestor. Domestication of the llama and alpaca undoubtedly was accomplished in Peru, Bolivia, Chile, or Argentina.

The other domesticated mammal of South America is the cavy (guinea pig); it probably was domesticated in the Central Andean region also, from the wild stock which exists there today.

The remaining domesticated animal, a bird, the Muscovy duck, was domesticated, in the Central Andean region.

## SOUTH AMERICA

**Domesticated animals.** Llama (*Lama glama glama,* or *L. glama*): Transport of burdens; meat, wool, hide, medicine, ceremony, sinew, pets.

Alpaca (*Lama pacos*): Wool, meat, ceremony, medicine, hide, sinew, pets.

Cavy, or guinea pig (*Cavia porcellus,* or *C. p. porcellus*): Meat, ceremony, medicine, pets.

Muscovy duck (*Cairina moschata*): Meat (with eggs), pets.

(The dog, *Canis familiaris,* and the turkey, *Meleagris gallopavo,* were not endemic, though they were found in South America in aboriginal times as cultural elements diffused from North America.)

**Semidomesticated animals.** Hunting huron (*Galictis furax*): Pets, hunting chinchillas.

Otter (*Lutra* sp.): Pets, fishing.

Extinct abrocoma (*Abrocoma oblativa*): Ceremony, food (?).

Extinct paca (*Cuniculus thomasi*): Ceremony, food (?).

Rhea (*Rhea americana* and *Pterocnemia pennata*): Food, feathers, pets.

Tree ducks (*Dendrocygna viduata* and *D. bicolor*): Food, pets.

Steamer duck (*Tachyeres pteneres*): Food, pets.

Trumpeter (*Psophia*): Pets, sentinels.

Chachalacas (*Penelope, Ortalis*): Food, pets.

Curassows (family Cracidae, several genera): Food, sentinels, pets.

Stone-plover (*Oedicnemus dominicensis*): Pets, sentinels.

Parrots (family Psittacidae, especially genus *Amazonia*): Pets, feathers.

Suckerfish (*Echeneis naucrates*): Capture of turtles, manatee, and fish.

**DRAMA.** Native American ritual was carried out because of the power possessed by the music and dances to heal illness, to win battles, to grow crops. The drama inherent in the rites was to some extent the manifestation of that power. Awe-inspiring occurrences that crossed and re-crossed the lines between real and unreal, physical and metaphysical were tangible expressions of the supernatural, enabled and taught by the spirits themselves. Drama as a conscious, independent form was not present. Still, it was invariably present in the ceremonies as historical events were portrayed, as clowns poked fun at themselves and everyone else, and as shamans became supernatural spirits.

**Animals influence on music and dance**

Dances, songs, and instrumental music were seldom created or used for entertainment, though some evolved into this as the magical symbolism and need faded. An example of this evolution can be seen in Cherokee dances that portray animals and their hunters. Since the turn of the century, these have served as informal entertainment, imitating the actions of animals and people. But earlier, when animals were crucial to the society, the same dances had been used in an attempt to control the mutual behavior of persons and beasts.

**Rain ceremonies**

In ceremonies seeking certain blessings, the thing sought was often acted out or symbolized. The Anasazi of about AD 700, ancestors of the southwestern Pueblo people, turned nearly all their religious power toward bringing rain. They used fringe on ceremonial garments, gourd rattles, and spruce boughs to imitate the streaming rain, its sound, and its fertile result. Lines of many dancers in modern Pueblo rites are another dramatic portrayal of flowing, falling rain.

The whole Pueblo community became involved when the Kachinas arrived from their homes in the mountains to spend six months living and dancing among the people. "Kachina" has three meanings: a spirit or natural force; a dancer in whom the spirit temporarily resides; and a Kachina doll, carefully carved by cult members for Pueblo children. The Kachina dancers wore elaborate costumes of many kinds — some with animal heads covered with fur, others carved and painted in geometric designs. Feathers, brilliant paint, hides and cloth decorated their bodies. On certain days, the Kachinas danced in the village streets, distributing food to each house and dolls to the children. Kachina ogres threaten to steal bad children, who were ransomed by their mothers. The night dances took place inside the kiva, a sacred house partly underground. Women, children, and elders were gathered when loud footsteps on the roof told them the Kachinas were there. The Kachinas came down the ladder, one after another, into the room filled with firelight, drumbeats, and sacred music. The dancers were the spirits of ancestors — not only to the uninitiated children, but also to the priests themselves whose bodies had been taken over for this time and purpose.

Clowns were present at some dances, and, like European court jesters, they often were able to speak more freely about serious things than ordinary people bound by ordinary etiquette. A Tewa Pueblo clown, the *kossa*, had special power to protect the Pueblo and increase fertility. When their pantomime and jokes became obscene, which was often, they pretended to be invisible. The Yaqui tribe of Arizona (U.S.) and Sonora (Mexico) had a one-man-band clown who played a flute and drum at the same time.

Another dance that masked serious, even frightening, reality with obscene hilarity was the Booger Dance of the Cherokee in the southeastern U.S. In this dance, several men took the parts of Europeans (the Boogers) who had come to visit the tribe. The picture thus presented of the white man is telling, for he was acted out as a wild, uncouth, noisy, pushy creature who only wanted to steal women or fight. When they finally agreed to dance, it became a mockery and exploitation of the Cherokee women (who remained serene), and, hence, the whole tribe. The name, "Booger" or "Ghost," (boogey-man) referred to any horrifying thing. This ceremonial impersonation of the invaders was believed by the Cherokee to have been given them by spirits before the arrival of whites as a protection against the coming foreigners.

A *potlatch* was a great feast and dance given by northwest coast families. The central action was extravagant gift-giving by the host. Each gift was preceded by a speech of praise for the donor. A potlatch was occasioned by a birth, marriage, or inheritance, and validated the status and hereditary rights of the participants, especially the host. If two people claimed the same inheritance, they gave opposing potlatches until the guests declared one supreme or until one gave away all he had and had to stop, thus being the loser.

Eskimo men frequently carried out a dramatic resolution of conflict. Instead of physically fighting, they had a duel in song, each ridiculing the other in excess with the audience sitting as judge and jury.

Eskimo shamans, like Siberian shamans, were possessed by spirits that could transport them to the living-places of the gods or to far-away regions to bring back animals to hunt. During such a "spirit-flight," the people would sit in a totally dark room with drum pounding. The shaman, usually bound and behind a curtain, would cry out, telling the people where he was, what he was seeing, and what supernatural beings he was encountering. At other ceremonies, the shaman danced around the fire in the great dance house while his personal song was sung and a drum pounded. He imitated animals and birds. Finally he shrieked — the signal that a spirit had entered his body and he would prophesy. More informal Eskimo dances included improvised pantomime.

Aztec ceremonials in ancient Mexico involved orchestras, choirs, and thousands of dancers in costumes of gold, feathers, and flowers.

This Indian tradition that includes comedy and tragedy acted out with pantomime, narrative, dance, and song with careful costuming and staging, had in the early 1970s manifested itself in a modern drama company, the Native American Theater Ensemble.

Based in New York and having roots deep in Indian country. The players are all Indian and from many different tribes. They have created and produced works from and about their past, such as *Na Haaz Zan,* Navajo creation myth, as well as stark presentations of frustrating, disintegrating, contemporary Indian life. These dramatists viewed traditional Indian ritual as pure and functional drama. They have taken a 20th century mode to capture and increase it, trying to engender and continue a shared cultural experience for Native Americans.

**DREAMS AND VISIONS** were sought at specific times by most tribes across the Americas under various circumstances and through strenuous effort, usually for the purpose of gaining the aid of a supernatural being. Dreams came unbidden but visions usually were sought through the performance of rites involving personal deprivation. Few tribes believed that the dream sought the individual, coming to him before and after birth and during mature life. Visions occurred usually during the time of fasting and among the hunter-gatherers. Parents prepared their children for vision seeking by making them go without food for a day or two. Algonquins and Salish believed that girls and boys were both eligible for these preparatory visions as a sign of favor from the spirits, but at puberty girls usually stopped the vision quest. A youth or man who desired a vision must stay away from women, since male and female powers were considered incompatible. The vision was commonly a major part of the puberty rites, and though a spirit might appear beforehand in a dream it was a chance occurrence,and a boy had to think constantly of the sort of power needed if he was to be sure of a spirit coming with aid and the promise of ability in hunting, war, gambling, or as a medicine man. Occasionally a vision brought an undesirable spirit such as a Water Monster, and the youth was advised to refuse the offered power.

The puberty vision followed a standard form usually for which a youth was prepared in advance. An animal disguised as a human would appear and take him to the forest, the sea, or other secluded spot and give instruction that might consist of a song to bring power and the giving of a fetish. If a reported vision did not take the proper form the older men of the group would say that it was a false spirit who had come and the vision should be tried again. Throughout the Great Lakes area, in the Mississippi Valley, and in other scattered groups the vision was a necessary part of a youth's growing up. If the quest for a vision was not successful a boy might cut off a finger to induce the Supernatural to take pity on him.

West of the Rocky Mountains the vision quest was not as important, and often only medicine men and shamans sought visions to gain help in curing disease, exorcising evil spirits, bringing rain, et cetera. Where visions were not an integral part of the Indians' life they were scarcely distinguishable from dreams. In certain areas such as in southern California a vision was made a certainty through the giving of a narcotic drink. In British Columbia and on the Plateau the visionary would plunge himself into a pool, rub himself with thorny branches until he bled, fast, and refrain from sexual intercourse with his wife until a vision came. Among the Kwakiutl, spirits would only come in visions to rich chiefs and when their sons were psychologically unsuited to the vision experience they would be secretly coached to simulate a vision experience.

Dreams or visions often were used as a means of relieving frustration, such as among the Eskimo when confined to cramped quarters because of bad weather. Visions then were interpreted as soul flights. This explains somewhat the vision of the shaman too. When called upon to predict or control weather, to supply game animals, to cure disease, to bring fertility to barren women the shaman was under pressure to get results through his visions. The subjective experiences of the hallucination were interpreted as real and the spirit that came might be a human being, a common ghost, a *Tornait*, or an animal spirit. Supernatural sanction through visions of the shaman often were necessary before major undertakings in various tribes. In the Prairies and the east the smallest raid would not be carried out until the shaman had told of the spirits' recommendations through his vision.

Many of the ceremonies observed by tribes were believed to have been established around visions. Actual performances of rites followed to the detail the prefiguration of a vision. Shrines and sacred objects were seen in visions or dreams first. The time of the performance of certain rites often was dictated by visions or dreams. Most Indians believed that the images seen in visions were not fanciful projections but the real glimpsing of the unseen world. Anything that was to take place in the world was already determined and prefigured and was available in a vision.

The Iroquois had a yearly feast called the Dream Feast when the problems and troubles of the year were expressed in dreams and purged by the telling of the dream to another person. If a man dreamed he was caught by enemies and burned alive he would tell his dream and villagers would enact a mock execution of burning him alive to purge the dream. Among the Osage, warriors were directed to try for visions and spirits came in the visions such as Canoe People, Property Woman, and War Spirit. The vision seeker usually was taken ill with an undiagnosed disease and mumbled a song taught in the vision. Then the medicine man and helpers would continue the song and address questions to the spirit regarding the visionary. Among the Blackfoot it was believed that the songs were cherished property and could be sold if the transfer were made physical through sexual intercourse. On the Prairie, the peace journey or *Hako* was an occasion in which visions did not come to individuals through their own efforts but were brought to everyone through way of a communal ceremony and the bidding of the *Tirawa.* In the Native American Church visions were common and expected through the eating of peyote. In these visions spirits or departed loved ones would appear, aid would be given in the solving of personal problems, and warnings would be made to abandon evil thoughts or deeds.

Visions were regarded most highly in areas that lacked organized religions such as the Plateau and Plains. An Indian's success in life seldom was due to his own efforts, but through the sanction of the supernatural through dreams, visions, or hallucinations.

Dreams came naturally during sleep and visions through strenuous ecstasy, and both served as the vehicles for spiritual guidance in all areas of Indian life.

**DRUM,** a percussion instrument, played an integral part in ceremonies and religious rites in many parts of the Americas. Drums were almost always played with dancing and singing. The drum beat often differed from the rhythm of the song, with the dancers' steps following the drum. The beat varied from steady pulsation to elaborate rhythmic compositions.

Drums were decorated with carving, feathers, fur, or paint. Often the decorations were symbolic or expressed the ceremonial purpose of the instrument, as a picture painted on a drumhead of the thunderbird breaking through the sky, releasing rain.

Hide drums were usually like a tambourine with skin stretched over only one side of a hoop; these were present in the Arctic, the Plains, and eastern U.S., and spread to other areas in the 19th century. Double-headed drums are probably modern. Foot-drums were planks over a hole in the ground or floor; slit-drums were a hollowed-out log or a canoe turned upside down. Baskets, boxes, and folded rawhide were beaten and scraped. On the Northwest Coast, men reached up with long poles and beat on the ceilings of the wooden dance houses, turning the whole building into a drum. In the 20th century, the pottery kettledrum, half-filled with water and covered with animal skin, spread from the southwest with the Peyote religion (now Native American Church).

Eskimo shamans used a drum like the Siberian shamans, a large, thin tambourine, perhaps four feet across and six inches wide. It was held upright and swung in a revolving motion back and forth so that first one side, then the other hit a thick drumstick held stationary in the other hand. Helping spirits came to the shaman through his drum.

During the Sun Dance of the Northern Arapaho (Wyoming), each singer brought his drumstick down on a big drum with terrific unison beats. When recruiting volunteers for war, the eight war captains of the Osage (Prairies) danced around the village twice daily, stopping to drum and sing.

The Aztec of Mexico had a wooden slit-drum called a *teponaztli* with separate tongues, each tuned to a different pitch. Elaborate melodic compositions were performed when these drums were played together.

**DWELLINGS.** The Western stereotype of the Indian, still featured in movies, is that the original Americans lived only in tipis, wore Sioux war bonnets, and spoke one "Indian language." In point of fact there were and are many Indian tribes differing from each other in regard to their ways of life, and their physical environment.

Their dwellings (just like the food, arts, crafts and clothing of each tribe) depended on the available materials, climates, topography, and flora and fauna. (It is interesting that none of the aboriginal tribes had any domestic animals — except the dog, and of domestic fowls, turkeys were raised only by the Pueblos). In building their homes, the Indians used many different materials and designs: the stone and plaster pueblos of the southwest; the cedar houses of the far northwest with skillful carpentry and elaborate carvings; the earth-covered, log hogans of the Navajos, the skin tipis of the Plains; the bark and pole houses of the Iroquois. Among the highly developed peoples of Middle America and Peru, buildings went much further; stone was used to build spacious and beautiful temples and palaces richly ornamented with carvings.

Most of the region east of the Mississippi was heavily forested. There the Indians lived in villages and settlements of substantial houses near streams and rivers, made with a framework of poles covered with mats or bark or plastered with mud mixed with straw. They protected their villages by palisades of closely set poles driven into the ground. Having no metal axes to cut down the trees, they peeled off the bark and used it. In the far north the Indians built a pointed tent of poles and covered it with a wrapping of birch bark. Farther south, they constructed a dome-shaped wigwam, like a frame of bent branches, covered with strips of tough elm bark. In the area which is now New

York, they built gabled long frame community houses, covered with strips of bark; they accommodated from 5 to 20 families. In the far north of this area they made a pointed tent of poles and covered it with a wrapping of birch bark. In the extreme southern regions, they constructed shelps covered with neatly woven mats of cane or branches. The Creek settlement typified the economic and social life of the southwestern tribes. At its center were the public buildings, set on terraces in the most important settlements. The "square" consisted of 4 shed-like structures enclosing an open space of hard-packed earth with the sacred communal fire in the center. This public center was surrounded by individual dwellings, composed usually of from one to 4 separate buildings.

While the religious and ceremonial life of the Woodland Indians (from Maine to Florida, from the Atlantic Ocean to the Great Lakes and the Mississippi Valley, and on through most of eastern Canada) was based on the corn, that of the Plains tribes centered around the buffalo and the worship of the sun. The latter tribes hunted buffalo and gathered roots and berries. Needing a movable dwelling, they invented the famous tipi, a cone-shaped tent, usually of dressed skins, mounted on poles meeting near the top. These portable dwelling were usually assembled and erected by the women as the Plains tribes went from place to place following the buffalo. A group of tipis often were placed in a large circle, perhaps around a central council tipi. The existence of the buffalo was here of utmost importance, since the long leaning poles of the tipi were covered with 12 or more buffalo hides sewed together.

In fact, in the Plains, the preparation of the buffalo hides was a whole industry in itself. On the ground near the tipi the women stretched out a large skin of the slaughtered buffalo, pegging it to the earth with wooden stakes. Bent almost double over the hide, they raked the flesh, scraping the skin down to an even thinness. They rubbed oily fat and brains into the surface of the hide with firm, massaging strokes. When the whole skin was covered with the fatty mass, they took a smooth stone, rubbing it slowly up and down until the fat was thoroughly worked in and then hung it in the sun to dry. The tipi provided more than a shelter and a place to sleep. The conception that the abode served the bare essentials of usage still remains. In 1886 the last great herd of buffalo was exterminated. Thereafter, most Indian families had to live in small one room log houses with single (or no) windows and dirt floors.

The basic furnishings were one or two castiron stoves, shifted during the seasons between the house, tent or outdoors, and several beds on which a number of individuals slept closely huddled together; others slept around the sides of the tent. Many families lived permanently in tents.

For the Fox tribe of Iowa life had two distinct phases, a sedentary agricultural aspect in the spring and summer and a nomadic hunting existence in the fall and winter. From April to August, the people lived in permanent villages. Here they had long-rectangular houses covered with elm bark, 50 or 60 feet long. There were openings at either end of the house, and 2 sleeping benches about 3 feet high and 4 feet wide, ran along the side walls. From September to April, these Indians used the small, mat-covered *wickiup,* a grass hut shaped like a beehive, a round or oval dome structure, which was easy to heat and simple to transport. The mat coverings, made of cat-tails, were rolled up and taken to deck the new frame when the family reached the camping site.

Most picturesque of all Indian dwellings were the multistoried houses of stone or adobe in the southwest Pueblos, built by the native Indians of New Mexico and Arizona and of a narrow strip of southern Colorado and Utah, a small portion of southeastern California, and considerable territory of northern Mexico. The word *pueblo* means a village. Southwest, it was once thought to be the work of an extinct people, but it is known now that the buildings perched on mesas and on lodges of canyon walls were built by the ancestors of the Pueblo Indians as defenses against nomadic tribes. Pueblo lands are rich in abnormalities and wonders, and the homes on them are difficult to approach, for they are built on far up the perpendicular walls which have to be climbed, although they are constructed in the vicinity of streams or waterholes. These buildings are erected in nooks and corners of the cliffs. With rough stone implements, the Indians hacked niches for footholes into the faces of the cliffs and climbed up with their loads of adobe earth; for the chief well-making material, they went to the beds of streams and gathered fragments of rock of various shapes and size or broke pieces from the adjoining cliffs and worked them into convenient form; or, from the soft sandstone or the brittle volcanic rock, they fashioned rectangular blocks. If no suitable stones were available, and adobe clay could be easily secured, they made bricks, dried them in the sun, and then carried them up to the shelvy rocks on which the houses were to perch.

In some localities excavations were made into the sides of the cliffs. They hacked into the sandstone or volcanic rock and scooped out their rude cells. Entrances were made from the faces of the cliffs, and were purposely difficult to approach. Beneath the doorways, along the sides of the cliffs, usually ran narrow, irregular, and often times dangerous paths, connecting one cave house with another. Into the rock, directly above the doorways on the outside, deep, narrow, holes were often made, for supporting poles, over the projecting ends of which skins could be thrown for awnings.

The water problem was somewhat solved by building rude cisterns (reservoirs) to catch the snow and rain. In some localities, towers, built of stone and adobe clay, were placed out on projecting rocks, from which an approaching enemy might be detected. Groups of the terraced, many-storied stone and adobe apartments were arranged around a plaza where religious ceremonies were held. The many-roomed houses (of the contemporary apartment houses type), sometimes 4 or 5 stories high, were the types completely different from any other Indian shelter in the Americas. Their style of agriculture was symbolic of their coordinate, orderly, cooperative society, fully integrated into its environment. The object of life for all members was to live harmoniously with each other and with the universe. Only if order and peace prevailed and the spirits of the dead were content would the rain fall, the harvest would be good, and people and animals would be healthy and fertile. The inhabitants of the pueblos tried to assure the harmony of the universe by a cycle of religious ceremonies observed throughout the year, and secret religious societies were responsible for the round of observances. The priests of the societies, who formed the town council, saw to it that the religious ceremonies took place on time; members of the council also decided town policy and sat in judgment on anyone accused of a crime. A warrior society carried out the orders of the council and provided for defense.

In the Southwest the Pueblo people lived in multistoried houses of stone or adobe, remaining in the same location for centuries and growing their crops by irrigation. They obtained their meat by hunting, but raised cotton for their clothing and excelled in pottery. Their ceremonials and artistic decorations stressed — and still stress — the importance of rain. The Indians farther south in this area lived until recently in bog domed-shaped houses made of poles and brush, covered with earth.

A dry and empty land across the southern Rocky Mountains (Utah, Nevada, southern California) was tramped over by the Indian tribes on a regular route each year, living on ripened seeds (acorns, sweet nuts from small pine trees, seeds from wild plants). They built a frame of poles, usually in a round or beehive shape, and tied on bunches of grass or desert bushes. In winter they heaped earth over the house.

The Indians of the Great Basin and the California desert utilized all the resources of their countryside. They wandered over it in small family groups, gathering seeds and nuts, digging roots, and snaring rabbits and other small animals. They made their clothing from the desert plants, weaving strings of sagebrush or desert willow into a sort of mat to serve as a scanty garment and weaving a winter wrap from strips of rabbit fur. Their dwellings were temporary, made of branches covered with bunches of grass or desert bushes; in winter they covered the whole with earth.

In aboriginal times the Puyallup of Washington (the Pacific coast) commanded the water entrance to the southern Sound. Their villages were located either on small streams which tumbled down to the Sound from the highlands of the Kitsap Peninsula, or along the river system which drained the west slope of Mt. Ranier and the country lying between the mountain and Commencement Bay. These streams pointed toward a hub at the mouth of the Puyallup River (today's Tacoma). This was a region with a heavy rainfall, a temperate land of swamps, extensive tide flats, damp, overgrown gullies and sudden floods. It was a land offering food for the taking, fish (salmon), clams, seal and porpoise, and elk and bear. Each village was located at the mouth of a stream above the tide flats. The houses were built of split cedar planks, the ridge pole of the rather high gable roofs following the length of the building. Doorways were located at each end on a line with the roof peak and one door facing upstream toward a narrowing vista of water and clear bank and the other facing the wider expanse where two waters met. The typical "village" suggested a cluster of small houses; it consisted of a single large communal dwelling, occupied by most of its inhabitants over most of the year and seldom left completely alone. The small stream provided the village with salmon, wood was found along its upper reaches and carried back or floated to the back of the house site, while hunting followed the course of the stream. The house was divided into 4 or 6 sections, each serving as the living quarters of a single family group. The house sections were at either side, one in each corner and, in larger houses, 2 facing each other in the center of the bed platform which ran around the walls of the house, of the storage platforms above, and of the drying racks which extended as high as the roof peak. Each family did its own cooking on fires built on stones let down into the dirt floor or directly on the hardened dirt. They were located along the center passageway in pairs. The central passage was used by all and the area of common recreations (story-telling, the playing of organized children's games). The sense of family privacy was, however, strong and centered around the cooking activities of each fire.

Along the Pacific Coast (from northern California to southern Alaska), the land of trees, the western red cedar was commonly used by the Indians for building material. They burned through the trunks to fell the trees, then split them into planks with wedges of horn or wood. The cross planks were tied with vines to the upright planks; this structure had no chimneys or windows. Some of the houses were more than 500 feet long, holding 8 to 10 families, and divided into compartments by hanging mats.

JOSEPH S. ROUCEK

# E

**EARTH LODGE** is an Indian dwelling partly underground, circular in form, from 30 ft. to 60 ft. in diameter, with walls about 6 ft. high, on which rested a dome-shaped roof with an opening in the center. The entrance was a projecting passage-way from 6 to 14 ft. long.

The earth lodge was used by the Pawnee, Arikara, Omaha, Ponca, Osage, and other tribes. Similar abodes were used in the Aleutian islands, and in southwest Alaska. There were habitations among some of the California tribes that had features in common with the earth lodge.

The method of construction of an earth lodge was first to draw a circle on the ground and excavate the earth within it from 2 to 4 ft. deep. About 1. ft. within the circle were set crotched posts some 8 or 10 ft. apart, on which were laid beams. Outside these posts were set others, one end of them braced against the bottom of the bank of earth at the periphery of the circle, and the other end leaning against the beams, forming a closed stockade. Midway between the center of the excavation and the stockade were planted 4, 6, or 8 tall crotched posts, forming an inner circle. In the crotches were laid heavy beams to support the roof of long, slender, tapering tree trunks, stripped of bark. The wall and roof were afterward carefully tamped with earth and made waterproof. The long entrance way was built in the same manner as the lodge, and thatched and sodded at the same time. The grass of the sod continued to grow, and wild flowers brightened the walls and roof of the dwelling. Within, the floor was made hard by a series of tampings, in which both water and fire were used. The fireplace was circular in shape and slightly excavated. A curtain of skin hung at the opening from the passageway into the lodge. The outer door was covered with a skin that was stiffened by sticks at the top and bottom, and which was turned to one side to give entrance to the passageway.

More than one family sometimes occupied a lodge. The back part, opposite the entrance, was reserved for the keeping of sacred objects and the reception of guests. In the winter curtains of skin were hung from the beams of the inner circle of posts, making a smaller room about the fireplace. The shields and weapons of the men were suspended from these inner posts, giving color to the interior of the dwelling, which was always picturesque, whether seen at night, when the fire leaped up and flinted on the polished blackened roof and when at times the lodge was filled with men and women in their gala dress at some social meeting or religious ceremony; or during the day when sunlight fell through the central opening over the fireplace, bringing into relief some bit of aboriginal life and leaving the rest of the lodge in shadow. Few large and well-built earth lodges exist today. Even with care a lodge could be made to last only a generation or two.

Ceremonies attended the erection of an earth lodge. Both men and women took part in these rites and shared in the labor of building. To cut, haul, and set the heavy posts and beams was the men's task; the binding, thatching, and sodding that of the women.

The Pawnee had the most elaborate ceremonies and traditions pertaining to the earth lodge. This tribe abandoned the grass house and learned to construct the earth lodge. According to their ceremonies and legends, not only the animals were concerned with its construction — the badger digging the holes, the beaver sawing the logs, the bears carrying them, and all obeying the directions of the whale — but the stars also exercised authority. The star cult of the people is recognized in the significance attached to the four central posts. Each stood for a star — the Morning and Evening stars, symbols of the male and female cosmic forces, and the North and South stars, the direction of chiefs and the abode of perpetual life. The posts were painted in the symbolic colors of these stars — red, white, black, yellow. During certain ceremonies corn of one of these colors was offered at the foot of the post of that color. In the rituals of the Pawnee, the earth lodge was made typical of man's abode on the earth; the floor is the plain; the wall the distant horizon; the dome the arching sky; the central opening the zenith, dwelling place of *Tirawa,* the invisible Power which gives life to all created beings.

**EARRING** is an ear ornament inserted through a hole pierced in the lobe or rim of the ear.

In mounds built in the Hopewell era (*c.* 200 BC-AD 400, Ohio), many ear-discs and earrings were found. In later Mississippian mounds (*c.* AD 700-1500, southeastern U.S.), large, polished shell discs with pictorial carvings like Mississippian gorgets are believed to be pendants. In 16th century Mexico, Indians wore gold earrings imbedded with colored stones. From the earlier Mexican Toltec culture (*c.* AD 900-1100) came a gold dangle-type earring with a stylized animal figure, probably a butterfly, and three tiny bells suspended beneath it. Modern southwestern Zuni works in silver have a similar style, with abstract designs and long dangling beads and other suspended forms. The first Navajo silver earrings (*c.* 1870) were large hoops of silver, each made from one silver dollar. In the early days when Navajos were learning from Mexican smiths, one pair of earrings was paid for with one sheep.

Stone and pottery ear plugs shaped like spools have been found in California and Arizona; similar ones of shell plated with copper came from Ohio. Long, slender, engraved bird bones to be stuck through pierced ear lobes, like sticks have come from California mounds.

An earring sometimes showed high status or wealth and was given to honor a person. In such cases, the ear-piercing was given to honor a person. The ear-piercing was often accompanied by ceremony, and each procedure cost the donor — usually a parent or relative — a standard price. An ear ornament probably of this origin was the Seminole (Florida) Pendant hanging from a loop inserted in the ear lobe, accompanied by perforations all around the rim of the ear with smaller loops inserted in them.

**EDUCATION** of the American Indians began with the first mission school founded by the Jesuits for Florida Indians in 1568. The first 300 years of formal education for Indians was dominated by the church, with the goal of "Christianizing" and "civilizing the heathen," especially by missionaries.

While it was not certain that the English would maintain their hold as planters in Virginia, Sir Edwin Sandys, Treasurer of the Bay Company, proposed in 1619 to found a college in the colony for English and Indian youth in common, and received an anonymous gift of L500 for the education of Indian youth in English and in the Christian religion. Other gifts were added. By advice of the King and the Bishops L1,500 were collected in England. The Company appropriated for the purpose 10,000 acres of land at Henrice (near Richmond). But the massacre of the whites by the Indians in 1622 effectively nullified all these plans.

Evidence of early interest in the matter of Indian education was found in Harvard's charter of 1650, which dedicated the college to "the education of English and Indian youth . . . in knowledge and goodliness." The second building at Harvard, erected in 1654, was called "the Indian College" and contained the college press on which John Eliot's Indian Bible and various grammars, tracts, catechisms, etc. were printed. It was built by funds collected in England. Its design was to furnish rooms for 20 Indian youths who,

Indian children in a typical classroom setting

on a level with the English, might pursue a complete academic course, for which they should have been prepared by a "Dame's school," and by "Master Corlet's Grammar School." But the results were wholly unsatisfactory. There were some Indian undergraduates at Harvard in those days but only one seems to have been granted the B.A. degree: Caleb Cheeshateaumuch, in 1665.

Dartmouth College was the outgrowth of Wheelock's Indian school at Lebanon (Connecticut). Dartmouth royal charter of 1769 provided that "there would be a college erected in our Province of New Hampshire by the name of Dartmough College, for the education and instruction of youth of the Indian Tribes of this land, in reading, writing and all parts of learning which shall appear necessary and expedient for civilizing and Christianizing children of pagans, as well as in all Liberal Arts and Sciences, and also of English youth and any other." (Dartmouth College started as "Moors' Charity School for Indians," for the education of their youth and of missionaries to them). The motto on the college seal is *Vox clamantis in Deserto.* (A list of subscriptions made in its behalf from 200 places in Great Britain is still preserved, chiefly collected by the preaching there by an ordained Indian Christian minister, Sampson Occum). But the missionaries sent forth from the college were not successful and the whites soon monopolized the advantages of the institution.

There sprung up several other schools in New England. But the success of these various religious efforts was questionable, to say the least. For instance, the general attitude of the Puritans toward the Indian was revealed by an incident in 1637 when the Pequot tribe resisted the migration of settlers into the Connecticut Valley; a Pequot village was burned to the ground and some 500 Indians were burned to death or shot. The surviving Pequots were sold into slavery. The Puritans gave thanks unto the Lord that they had lost only two men and Cotton Mather was grateful to the Lord that "On this day we have sent 600 heathen souls to hell."

Just as the Puritans had ideological difficulties in

handling the Indians, so did a Founding Father, Thomas Jefferson, who was so concerned with the concept of liberty that he once raised the question whether the condition of the American Indians, without any government at all, was not the most desirable. On the other hand, quite interestingly, the Declaration of Independence of July 4, 1776, referred to the American Indian as: " . . . the present King of Great Britain . . . has excited domestic insurrections amongst us, and has endeavoured to bring on the Inhabitants of our Frontiers, the merciless Indian Savages, whose known Rule of Warfare, is an indistinguished Destruction of all Ages, Sex and Conditions."

Beginning with President Washington, the stated policy of the federal government was to replace the Indian's culture with that of the white man. This was considered "advisable" as the cheapest and safest way of subduing the Indians, of providing a safe habitat for the country's white inhabitants, of helping the whites acquire a desirable land, and changing the Indian's economy so that he could be content with less land. Education was a weapon by which these goals were to be accomplished. The Indian's lack of "civilization" was the ideological justification used for taking his land, and education was clearly to play a very secondary role to the use of force.

From September 17, 1778, when the first treaty between the United States and an Indian tribe was signed with the Delawares, until 1871, treaties established the main legal bases for the federal policies with respect to Indian education. The earliest treaty containing a specific provision with respect to education was the treaty with the Oneida, Tuscarora, and Stockbridge Indians of December 2, 1794. Through treaties and agreements, the Indian tribes ceded to the U.S. almost a billion acres. Although treaty provisions varied, in general, the Indians retained lands for their own use which were to be inalienable and tax exempt; the government in turn agreed to provide public services such as education, medical care, technical and agricultural training; specific provisions for education were, in fact, included in a substantial number of treaties.

The first gesture establishing congressional responsibility for Indian education was a statutory provision of March 30, 1802, appropriations not to exceed $15,000 annually to "promote civilization among the aborigines." At the request of President Monroe, the Congress passed an act on March 3, 1819, the organic legal bases for most of the educational work of the Indian Service, aiming to "civilize" Indians by converting them from hunters to articulturists. The funds were apportioned among the societies and individuals — usually missionary organizations — prominent in an effort to "civilize" the Indians; the annual appropriation, known as the "civilization" fund, lasted until 1873.

The Office of Commissioner of Indian Affairs was created by Congress as a part of the act on July 9, 1832, although the Bureau itself had been established in 1824. The office was under the direction of the Secretary of War and subject to the regulations prescribed by the President. But in 1849 it was moved to the newly established Department of the Interior, although army officers continued to be employed as agents.

The attitudes of the early Commissioners of Indian Affairs shaped the policies of Indian education for the century that followed; the annual reports of the Commissioners were clear indicators of these attitudes.

As early as 1838, the educational policy of "civilizing" Indians through manual training in agriculture and the mechanical arts became established practice. During the later part of the treaty period, greater concern was expressed over the reluctance of Indian children to attend the white man's schools, and treaty provisions regarding compulsory attendance were developed.

In 1871, the treaty period was ended when Congress decreed that "No Indian nation tribe within the United States shall be acknowledged or recognized as an independent nation, tribe, or power;" but this did not rescind the obligations of the federal government under the nearly 400 established treaties.

In the last three decades of the 19th century, the

slaughter of the buffalo herds, the principal source of food for the Indians, reduced the Indians to the point of starvation in the Plains; many Indian tribes were also decimated by epidemics of smallpox, cholera, and other infectious diseases introduced by the U.S. Army and white settlers. A new policy, "The Peace Policy," was introduced by President Grant; reservations were distributed among the major religious denominations, delegating most power to church bodies and giving the right to nominate new agents and direct educational and other activities of the reservations. The missionary dictatorship tried to crush Indian culture and institutions, and the military was frequently called in to reinforce the missionaries' orders. Several severe rebellions were crushed. The completion of the white man's conquest of the Indian was reached in 1890 by the murder of the Sitting Bull and the massacre of a Sioux band at Wounded Knee, South Dakota.

The basic approach of subsidizing various religious groups to operate schools for Indians ended only in 1897. However, the Bureau of Indian Affairs had started building its own educational system in the 1870s, based on the model created by Gen. R.H. Pratt who founded the Carlisle Indian School in Pennsylvania in 1879 in abandoned army barracks, run in a rigid military fashion, and with heavy stress on rustic vocational education. The approach was to provide a maximum rapid coercive assimilation into white society. The Carlisle School set a pattern that was to dominate the federal government's approach to Indian education for half a century — until it came under devastating attack in the Meriam Report of 1928. (The school had been closed in 1918).

The act of Congress in 1882 helped the development of the federal school system by authorizing the use of abandoned Army posts or barracks.

The counterpart of the educational policy whose objective was to "dissolve" the social organization of Indian life on the reservations was the Dawes Severalty Act of 1887, designed to "dissolve" the Indian land base. This legislation ushered in the "Allotment Period" in the history of Indian affairs, and was carried out with a missionary zeal — halted only by the reform legislation of the New Deal; it had diminished the Indian tribal economic base from 140 million acres to approximately 50 million acres of the least desirable land. The interrelationship between the educational policy and the land policy of this period was obvious — coercive assimilation. (Under the Dawes Act of February 8, 1887, purchase money to be paid by the federal government for surplus lands not allotted to individual Indians were to be held in trust in the Treasury of the United States, and was to "at all times be subject to appropriation by Congress for the education and civilization of such tribe or tribes of Indians or the members thereof." Thus the money was to pay the costs of taking Indian children from their homes and placing them in federal boarding schools. Since many Indian families refused to send their children to school, in 1893 Congress legalized the technique of starvation to enfoce compulsory attendance.

The investigation of the Navajo school situation in 1919 by both the Congress and the Board of Indian Commissioners showed that of an estimated 9,613 Navajo children eligible for schools, only 2,089 were actually attending schools. This started a campaign in 1920 to educate Indian children in the now overcrowded schools and the transportation of all Navajo children in and above the 4th grade to other nonreservation boarding schools throughout the West and Southwest, since each agent on the reservation received a quota which he had to fill.

During the 1920s, corruption, exploitation, mismanagement, and the general failure of the Indian programs stimulated a prolonged Senate Indian Affairs Committee's debate (published in the Meriam report in 1928). The call for sweeping changes produced the Indian Reorganization Act of 1934, and President Roosevelt appointed John Collier as Commissionery of Indian Affairs to shape a "New Deal" for American Indians. But the intellectual and financial support of Collier's program lost momentum or had been undermined before the end of World War II. At any rate, the tribal councils had been given more powers for self-government and many more day schools on reservations had been introduced and expected to replace boarding schools. But in the 1950s a reaction in Congress against economic help to Indian tribes resulted in the termination of several reservations, a policy aimed to "get the government out of the Indian business." The division of tribal property among the individual members of the tribe was to encourage Indians to merge into the broader society. But most Indians wanted self determination, as tribes, and did not want to terminate the rights and privileges in their tax-exempt reservation land.

Since the 1960s a "New Policy" emerged. Two major federal government laws put money behind this policy — The Indian Education Act (1972) and Indian Self-Determination and Educational Assistance Act (1975). This led to a policy of local self-determination for Indian tribes and Indian communities, and to a greater responsibility of Indians as teachers and administrators. There has been a rapid expansion of the number of Indian students in colleges, most of them aided by government scholarship funds, a rise of schools on reservations operated by local native school boards with government funds. Basically, the education of the Indians since 1965 has been especially influenced by the acceptance of the broad policy, known as "cultural pluralism," which propounds that minority groups are to be integrated into the economic, political, and social spheres of the society, but could retain their cultural differences without discrimination or deprivation.

In 1978 there were about 275,000 Indians aged 6-17, inclusive, and about 90% of them were enrolled in schools in 4 categories or types of schools: (1) schools with practically all-Indian enrollment; the Bureau of Indian Affairs operated boarding and day schools, Indian-controlled School Boards, contracted mission or other private schools and public schools operating on or contiguous to reservations; (2) public schools, contiguous to Indian reservations or in native communities, with 50 to 90% enrollment; (3) public schools with 10 to 50% Indian enrollment (mainly in large cities); and (4) public schools with 1 to 10% Indian enrollment (mainly in large cities). The proportion of Indians graduating from school was approximately the same as the proportions of other ethnic groups having a similar socioeconomic or income background. On standard tests of school achievement, Indian pupils fell below national averages, as a group. But the relatively low academic achievement is not because Indian children are less intelligent than white children. In fact, several studies based on intelligence tests which did not require reading ability showed Indian children to be at or slightly above the level of white children. The difficulty was that the Indian children had lived in a community or neighborhood characterized by poverty.

Since the majority of Indian pupils attend public schools with white children and are taught with white children, both groups have the same teachers. But the schools operated by the Bureau of Indian Affairs (BIA) had about 1,800 teachers who had passed a federal civil service examination and had been assigned to BIA schools. In 1968, there were 1,772 teachers (61% women) and 15% Indians. Salaries ranged from $6,176 to $15,119. (Employment in Alaska was accompanied by a 25% cost of living supplement). Indian teachers have tended to stay longer in service than non-Indians. Of school administrators in BIA schools, 28% were Indian.

Before about 1960, the number who completed high school had been small and most did not go on to college, a substantial number going into a 1- to 2-year vocational training program, such as that of the Haskell Institute maintained by BIA at Lawrence, Kansas, offering secretarial and trade training. In general, there has been, however, a very rapid increase in the number of Indian youth entering a university and finishing a 4-year course.

There is only one Indian college: the Navajo Community College in Arizona (Corsicana), founded in 1968 by the Navajo tribe and supported by the federal government in recent years; it holds that uniquely Indian values, skills, and insights are highly functional in the modern world today and it is possible for Navajos to direct and control their own institutions — and that this is the only way they will ever be able to assume total responsibility and self-support, at least as a group. The institution is ruled by a Board of Regents consisting of 10 Navajos, one from each of the 5 administrative areas of the reservation, 2 members elected at large and appointed by the Tribal Chairman, and 3 ex-officio members: the chairman of the tribe, the chairman of the Navajo Education Committee, and the President of the college student body. The Indian faculty members have organized a Curriculum Committee searching for and formulating a Navajo philosophy of education in which the present and future are rooted in the values of the traditional past.

A further impetus to higher education for Indians came in 1976, when $500,000 was provided for 50 fellowship Indian students accepted for professional study by universities; this grant came from the Indian Education Act, allocating money for the academic year 1976-1977 to cover tuition costs and subsistence for students in engineering, law, medicine, business, forestry, and fields related to one of these areas.

Early in the 1970s, the federal government provided funds to assist Native Americans to reform and direct their educational systems. The Indian Education Act of 1972 and its successor, the Indian Self-Determination and Educational Assistance Act of 1975 provided funds and required Indian direction and Indian responsibility for the design programs. The Bilingual Education Act, part of the Elementary and Secondary Education since 1967, provided funds for the employment of teaching staff speaking the local home language of Indian and Eskimo communities.

The report of the American Indian Policy Review Commission, created in 1975, recommended that all government-aided Indian programs should be brought together under a federal Indian department, or an independent agency reporting to the office of the President; that Congress should enact legislation that would aid tribal governments and Indian communities to take responsibility for control of education according to their desires. Among other objectives was that of recruiting and training Indians to serve as teachers in practically all schools with a predominantly Indian enrollment.

In 1977 initiative was taken by several hundred Indian organizations seeking and receiving money from the federal government for educational programs. (For instance, under the Indian Education Act and for fiscal year 1976, approximately $18 million was granted to school and tribal educational projects in the form of 210 separate grants, aimed to supplement existing education programs and to train Indian personnel for work in the schools). This amplified the program started in the late 1960s, whereby the BIA contracted with a local Indian school board on a reservation to give the money to pay expenses of a BIA-operated school to the Indian Board taking responsibility for the school. By 1975, there were 15 of these Indian-contracted school boards; these have banded into a Coalition of Indian Controlled School Boards.

The Bilingual Education Act has a major application in Indian education, stressing the use of the child's home language in his learning to read. For Indian children speaking English at home, the tribal language is treated as a second language to be learned after the pupil has been using English in the school; the basic aim is to teach respect and familiarity with the native customs, culture and traditions. In fact, nearly all specialists working in the field of Indian education favor the study of Indian history and culture in the elementary school and include them in junior and high school curricula.

With respect to the 70% of Indian youth in communities where Indians are the largest cultural group, Indians have been gaining greater control over educational programs and policies. They will have to decide how far the schools should go in pushing Indian youth toward assimilation into the white man's dominant culture, how the native language should be treated in the schools, and how much time should be given to the history of culture of the Indians as well as of the local tribe.

## CANADA

As early as August 1635 the ambitious Jesuits were teaching the catechism and the first elements of letters in the Quebec area; on Champlain's death, they opened a seminary at Quebec to prepare young Indians for holy orders. These missionary efforts failed to succeed. In 1670, during the reign of Charles II, instructions were given to the governors of the British colonies that Indians desiring to place themselves under British protection should be protected. Later it was found necessary to form an office devoted solely to the administration of Indian affairs. In 1755 Sir William Johnson was appointed Indian Superintendent, with headquarters in the Mohawk Valley (in which is now the State of New York). The establishment of that office was the genesis of future Indian administrative organization in North America; following the American Revolution, this office was removed to Canada. By a special provision in the British North America Act of 1867, the administration of Indian affairs came under the jurisdiction of the government of Canada. Indian affairs were made the responsibility of the Department of the Secretary of State. In 1873, they became the responsibility of a branch of the Department of the Interior. In 1880, a separate Department of Indian Affairs was formed; in 1936 Indian Affairs were assigned to the Department of Mines and Resources. From January, 1950, Indian Affairs was a branch of the Department of Citizenship and Immigration; in January 1966, it became a part of the Department of Indian Affairs and Northern Development. Its function is to assist the Indians to participate fully in the social and economic life of Canada; a broad range of programs in the fields of education, economic development, social welfare and community development, was inaugurated, including child and adult education.

Historically, the educational record has been, until recently, rather poor. With the first Indian Act of 1876, the Indian became irrelevant and transformed into an ethnic group, encouraged or coerced into continuing social and ideological change — and appeared to be dying out. The administration, among other things, saw the Indian as another ethnic minority to be assimilated, or at least made to adjust to the dominant white society, although in comparison with the U.S., the Canadians kept their hands clean of the cruel oppression; and there were no major Indian wars in Canada. A series of treaties completed between 1871-1877, signing over the Indian rights in the Prairies in return for small "reservations" (reserves), food rations, and agricultural training and equipment, made Canada's Indians wards of the state without rights of their own. The paternalistic policy of the government saved the Indian from famine and from the exploitation of the American whiskey-runners, but did not save him from the white men's diseases.

Between 1920 and 1930, parallel with the failure to promote the political and economic welfare for the Indians went negligence in providing them with educational facilities. At the close of World War I, in the late 1940s and 1950s, there was a sharp upturn of the Indian population, greater organizational activity, and the rise of some leaders sufficiently Western-educated, talking of Indian personality, independence, Indian culture, and even Indian nationalism, and asking for the control of the management and shaping of the direction of Indian communities, proclaiming that they, as Canadian citizens, still suffer standards of living and education far below the general Canadian level. Indians may vote at federal elections but with regard to provincial elections, they are governed by the electoral laws of the various provinces. Education is generally under the jurisdiction of the individual provinces, but the provision of educational service to Indians is the responsibility of the federal government.

The "in-school" education program from pre-school to secondary grades is carried out through the operation of federal schools, or by agreements with provincial schools (in which case the tuition costs are paid by the federal government). The schools follow provincial curricula, but are encouraged to offer special instructional materials and programs related to Indian heritage and culture. Student residence, boarding homes and counselling services are provided for students who are prevented from attending schools in their home areas.

The federal government also provides a program of financial assistance and counselling services in the post-school areas, including vocational, occupational and post-secondary training in provincial institutions and universities. Adult education courses are also available offering basic education, educational upgrading and social education. An employment and relocation program offers on-the-job and in-service training services; relocation grants; counselling and follow-up services and mobility assistance.

It is difficult to secure qualified teachers. Indian children are encouraged, through financial assistance, to enter the teaching profession to serve their own people. When engaged in the Indian day-schools in isolated areas, most teachers receive furnished and heated quarters for which "a moderate pay deduction" is made.

In general, 63% of Indian children no longer attend segregated reservation or residential schools; most recently a significantly higher proportion attend high schools, and Indian students are becoming less of a rarity on university campuses. At any rate, the limitation of educational opportunities or educational financing have resulted in greater inequality of opportunity among Canadians than exist among Americans; this also applies to the Canadian Indians.

## MIDDLE AND SOUTH AMERICA

The region is extremely diverse in the size, population, and technology of its various nations, despite their common inheritance in philosophy, religion, language, and education. The density of population is relatively low, since the area is primarily agricultural and is just beginning to enter upon a large-scale industrialization, chiefly in certain coastal areas. The political history has been characterized by a great deal of instability and a tendency to use revolution as a means of election or change of government. Immigration from Europe, Africa and Asia, has been very important, especially from Europe. All of these historical determinants have influenced the development of education. In general the tradition has been that of an elite, or "two-track" education, although the process of change toward a universal, or "one-track" system of education has been under way from the beginning of the 20th century, especially in Mexico, Uruguay, and Brazil.

Before the coming of Europeans, the New World

was neither wholly a wilderness nor a cultural vacuum. Indigenous Indians have been on this hemisphere for more than 10,000 years, and through the centuries have developed ways of life of their own — cultures that, before 1492, were deeply rooted and solidly established. Those cultures have been carried over, in varying degrees, to the present time. Before the conquest there were millions of Indians in Mexico and Central America; other millions were in South America. These peoples were not exterminated by the Conquest; they have persisted to the present time — many as Indians, many more as mestizos (descendants of Spanish or Portuguese and Indians) or otherwise "assimilated." These Indian and Indo-European peoples constitute the great mass of the Latin American population, and they have conditioned, in highly significant ways, the growth and development of educational institutions.

Although the Indian people are not evenly distributed over Latin America, who can deny that all of South America partakes in some measure of the Indian cultural influences — or, at the very least, of the carry-over of colonial policies that responded to the fact that there were millions of indigenous peoples in the New World? Tangible evidence is found in language, in customs and foods, in arts and crafts, etc. Much more subtle, but no less real, are the effects produced by Indian cultures on current socio-psychological patterns, on schemes of values, on social and economic institutions. Cultural developments in such countries as Mexico and Ecuador, which have felt a particularly strong impact of Indian cultures, reflect vividly the indigenous contribution — both in what has been accomplished and in what has been left undone. The establishment of social institutions has been handicapped by (1) the relative paucity of resources (schools and other institutions constituting an "overhead" cost that, in these countries could not be borne without a fatal impairment of vital functions); and (2) the slowness of the process of incorporating into European patterns an Indian population that outnumbered their European fellow citizens. On the other hand, the evolved cultural patterns mirrored the effects of acculturation — the Indian, while being modified by European patterns, in turn modified the imported culture.

Educational thought in Mexico (and to an increasing degree in Peru, Guatemala, and other Indo-Hispanic countries) has been modified through interaction with the Indian peoples. Literacy programs, for instance, must be adjusted to the Indian and his languages. The European concept of literacy had to be changed in the face of non-European schemes of values, of a radically different cultural experience. Then, because of large non-Christian populations, greater than normal emphasis was placed on the missionary and religious aspects of education — an emphasis which explains many of the achievements and deficiencies of colonial and 19th century education.

Among the very first steps taken after the Conquest was the founding of numerous schools; in many instances these schools were especially concerned with the native mestizo population; most of these schools were exclusively for Europeans. In some areas the schools were primarily for the training of members of the clergy, but also for "community education," and with the teaching of simple trades and skills. But these institutions could not accomplish the impossible — the complete Europeanization of millions of culturally diverse Indians scattered over millions of square miles of territory. Furthermore, it must be noted that "public education" is not understood in Latin America as it is in the United States. In colonial Latin America, the close association of church and state placed an entirely different connotation on that concept. There, the church was the principal avenue through which the state expressed its interest in education; the state made grants-in-aid to the church schools and most of the state's support of education was channeled through the agencies of the church, and that interest embraced all the people. "Religious education" under those circumstances was — and is — "public" education, not "private."

A large portion of educational endeavor in Latin America was concerned with the Indian's conversion and incorporation into the new society. The educational work of the colonial period was carried on principally by religious orders — notably the Franciscans, Domincans, Augustians, and Jesuits; the influence of the Jesuits was particularly strong and lasting. (The order was suppressed in the late 18th century).

But all the educational efforts on behalf of the Indian were nearly nullified by the socio-economic conditions confronting him.

Spaniards who arrived in America in the 16th century looked for conquests, not settlements, quick returns not steady development, and for resident populations which would do the work for which they were unsuited, disciplined to engage in manual labor or commerce. They found several sedentary, agricultural peoples unprepared for long wars and used to steady and prolonged manual labor. The invaders were militaristic, energetic, and fanatically religious seekers after gold and glory. The outcome of this confrontation was tragic.

The misadministration by the colonial administration resulted in Indian revolts and frequently of Creole native descendants of Spanish conquistadores.

Throughout its period of domination in the Americas the Spanish monarchy was harassed by a difficult juxtaposition of the real and the ideal. The mercantilistic theory propounded that the colony existed primarily for the use and benefit of the mother country; simply, it was supposed to show a profit. As the Spanish crown's financial difficulties and obligations multiplied, the importance of this profit increased. In order to show a profit, the mines, pearl fisheries, and farms had to be worked. While imported Negro slaves partially solved the problem in the hot coastal areas, in the highland mines such as Potosi, Huancavelica, Guanajuato, and Zacatecas, the Indians had to be forced to work; the same was true in all the farming areas of temperate climate. Madrid was caught in a dilemma between its humanistic concern for the welfare of the Indians and its urgent need for the gold and silver. The religious orders, especially the Franciscans, working hard to convert the Indians, saw much of their work frustrated; the Creole entrepreneurs and landowners, who needed the reluctant labor of the Indians, played on the Crown's dire financial straits and the royal administrators. Evolution of the colonial labor system mirrored the twists and turns of these policies. The Crown, under strong religious pressures, abolished widespread enslavement of the Indians; but it also admitted their lack of Catholic religion. The result was the *encomienda* system whereby Indians were "entrusted" to supposed Spaniards for indoctrination and physical care; in return the *encomenderos* were allowed to exact work from them.

Although the system worked efficiently in some areas, it also became soon obvious that many clerics and some administrators were dissatisfied that all exploitation of the Indians had ceased. The famous "News Laws" (1542) called for a gradual but definite abolition of the *encomienda* system and the substitution of wage labor. (These laws caused open rebellion in some cases). A new system emerged. Known variously as the *mita* and *repartimiento,* it provided for forced, paid, Indian labor on a selective service basis. In many cases a certain number of Indians from selected villages were collected in the public square of the principal town on a fixed day of the week or month, and there *repartides* were divided among the local Spanish employers.

The system was abolished only before the end of the colonial period. Many Indians eventually found their way into a free market situation where their exploitation continued on a cultural rather than a formalized basis. Others, especially those in the isolated agricultural areas, soon fell under the labor system known as "debt peonage," whereby, through various devices, they and their children became so hopelessly indebted to the owners or administrators of the *hacienda* or workshop that their departure was impossible. Many also became sharecroppers, which, given their lack of education and their conditioning to a life of servility, tied them effectively to one employer. (These two labor systems exist and coexist in many parts of Highland Latin America to this day).

By the middle of the 17th century, the Indian population continued to decline; this meant that formerly prosperous industries and agricultural areas were abandoned.

This century saw also the first formative era in the colony. A large *mestizo* class was coming into being. Spaniards were being born who had never seen Spain and who thought of themselves as Creoles and Americans. These young, disgruntled, upperclass Creoles, influenced by the European Enlightenment philosophy, supported the wars of independence.. But the turmoil brought few changes. For instance, the Andean Indian certainly did not profit by the wars; in fact his status and level of living actually deteriorated after independence. After all the Creole was his exploiter and traditional enemy. What little protection he had ever obtained had been from the Crown; after the wars the Crown was gone and the exploiters controlled the new societies. (Peru even witnessed a brief Indian revolt which wanted the return of Ferdinand VII of Spain). The new rulers of Peru and Bolivia quickly restored the Indian tribute payments which had been abolished by the Spaniards.

The wars of independence, to the chagrin of Simon Bolivar, hardly transformed Latin American society with regard to the Indian.

From the time of their independence in the 19th century, the policies of the various states south of the border has been strikingly similar: the Indians are viewed as a hindrance or dead weight to racial amalgamation. Any policy of ethnic pluralism makes the ruling classes uneasy, and they want to liquidate all the symptoms that might consider their societies as being "backward." For, after all, 40% to 50% of the continental population are illiterate (and literacy ranges from 30% in Bolivia to 87% in Argentine (as pointed out by UNESCO). When a majority of the population is illiterate and lives in semi-slavery because of caste and language, it is difficult to speak of the enlightened self-interest of the individual. Thus in the school training programs there are evidences of cultural deprivation. The environment and class status appear to be a dominant factor in the people's welfare and the attendance in schools. Often classes are conducted in an alien tongue in which the Indian knows only a smattering. Thus a pupil from the poor and racially different group is discriminated against because of the drawbacks of his environment and social inferiority. This prevents national unification and the spread of democratic institutions. The spirit of national education does not exist. The state refers to the Indians but does not refer to them as Peruvians, for instance, equal to the rest, since they are considered an inferior race. The ruling cliques feel that the entire process of Westernization (whether it is known as assimilation, incorporation, or integration) is good for the Indians, that the Indian problem can be solved only by the Indians forgetting that they are Indians; that they must stop forming component parts of the belts of misery surrounding the great cities, and no longer form a part of the great mass of unemployed migrants, moving about all the time searching for work.

In the various regions within each country, the whites — whether they call themselves *ladinos* (of Spanish descent), *gente de razon* ("civilized people"), or *mestizo* (mixed) — differ only in observing the local guidelines dominating inter-ethnic relations. In the regional metropolises those who exploit the Indians consider themselves a privileged elite (or as they are called in Yucatan, the "divine castes"); together with the local oligarchies, which include departmental and provincial officials, and the wealthy bourgeoisie they sponsor what is called "the national consciousness," by aiming to do away with the Indian cultures. The result is that the Indian is "alienated" — a feeling of noninvolvement in and estrangement from the dominant society and culture; he feels that his own cultural background is without value and thus is oppressed, defensive and isolated. And he is right, since the legal equality which is granted by law in each Latin American country, is a monopoly of the whites, the Creole (whites born in the Americas) and the mestizos (those of mixed white and Indian ancestry). The Indian thus has withdrawn into his communal and ethnocentric survival isolationism.

Only if the Indian learns Spanish and accepts Western clothes and mentality, can he achieve any recognition — as did the 19th century Mexican President Benito Juarez (1806-1872). But then such a successful Indian is no longer viewed as an Indian.

In their efforts to cope with the Indian problem, Latin American nations have run the gamut of sociological approaches. Mexico, formally committed to complete integration of its Indians since the 1910 revolution, has freed them from peonage and settled perhaps 70% of them in agricultural communities where land is held collectively. To ease them into the mainstream of Mexican life, the National Indian Institute (Instituto Nacional Indigenista — INI), under the Ministry of Public Education, which coordinates all Indian agencies, was founded in 1948. It has founded 12 "Coordinating Centers" staffed with men equipped to teach their charges everything from Spanish to how to grow taller corn. The central purpose is, of course, to nationalize the Indian: that the Indians become aware of belonging to the Mexican state. This has continued to be the most important source of directed social change, concentrating on the improvement of realistic educational facilities, health programs, agriculture, and communications, while making no direct effort to manipulate the symbolic and belief structure or social system of the Indians. (The INI has been frequently aided by the UNESCO and the Organization of American States through pilot or training programs).

There have been other general forces encouraging the Indian to acculturate, the favored position of mestizo culture as opposed to the disadvantaged one of the Indian and the incentives offered by the national government. This carrot-and-stick situation has brought increasing numbers of Indians into the national society. Movement is accompanied by "passing" or acquiring some prestigious cultural traits and by separating oneself from close ties with the Indian group. "Passing" is easier for the wealthier Indian with extensive mestizo contacts already formed. He may change to a Spanish surname, adopt Western dress, and marry a mestizo woman. In all cases, "passing" requires speaking Spanish and adopting a mestizo outlook. But, even so, the man himself may not be fully accepted as mestizo, although his children most likely will be.

Government incentives, in addition to the distribution of land — the *ejido* program — have improved educational opportunities in Mexico and have also done something to increase political participation. In 1936, under President Lazaro Cardenas, 1934-1940, the Autonomous Department of Indian Affairs was founded, followed the next year by the Department of Indian Education. Despite opposition, the former group was able to redistribute an additional 45 million acres to the Indians by 1940. In 1942, the government established Indian brigades to instruct communitities in modern agricultural methods to help Indians make full use of their land; the brigades offered instruction in crop diversification, animal husbandry, pest and disease control, and the use of modern agricultural machinery, and helped to organize producer and consumer cooperatives, repair old roads and build new ones and install better telecommunications networks.

Formal education is officially recognized as an important means to integration; it signifies, to a great extent, the transmission and adoption of mestizo culture and values.

Until about 1940 the new educational program of Mexico gave first priority to bringing literacy and primary schooling to the countryside, particularly to the physically-isolated Indian villages where Spanish was to many an unfamiliar language, for the self-contained traditional communities had their own cultures to which schools were extrinsic and the goals of the revolution were irrelevant. (At that stage in cultural orientation, the schoolhouse often replaced the church as the center of village life). Yet, in the early 1970s, there were still rural communities with no school or in which the school was still an extrinsic element. And the extension of the primary system in rural areas is still severely handicapped by a shortage of trained and willing teachers. The regular staffs were supplemented by a system of cultural missions, teams of dedicated specialists travelling around villages, teaching, instructing the poorly trained teachers and assisting in community activities. They are still active in the countryside and helped with social brigades of university students on vacation.

At the other end of the spectrum stands Brazil, whose tiny Indian minority is made up of primitive jungle tribes, some 150,000 at the very least. The Brazilian Indian is a descendent of pre-Columbia civilizations who, preserving the beliefs and customs of his tribes, possesses specific socio-cultural characteristics that are quite distinct from those of the rest of society. Even when he is not a pure Indian and lives like any other member of the Brazilian population, he retains a kind of loyalty to his ethnic identity. Since there is no realistic prospect of integrating these "savages" in the foreseeable future, Brazil's Indian Protection Service concentrates on protecting them from the larcenous — or murderous — forays of Brazilian whites.

The lot of Mexican and Brazilian Indians is idyllic when compared with that of the Indians of the Andes. When Francisco Pizarro and his conquistadors destroyed the Inca Empire, they pushed the Indians out of the fertile valleys up into the inhospitable highlands. Ever since, the descendants have led a life so bleak that they ease their misery by dulling their senses with *chicha* (corn beer) and *coca* (cocaine).

The Indians living along the shores of Peru's Lake Titicaca delight tourists with their picturesqueness — but they nearly all are illiterate, tuberculosis-ridden and extremely backward. Although Peru abolished serfdom several decades ago, and Ecuador followed suit in 1964, serfdom is still prevalent.

Bolivia was the first of the Andean nations trying to improve the conditions of its Indians; its government, soon after the country's 1952 revolution, outlawed the very word *indigena* (native) and allotted its Indian peasants both land and the vote. A good step was the policy of Bolivia's army drafting brigades of young Indians and setting them to work clearing the lowlands of the mountains. After a year's service, the recruits were offered free land, a grubstake, and transportation for their families. Some accepted immediately and others trickled back later. Some other experiments in resettling Bolivia's Indians in the lowlands have been less successful. By in 1963 Bolivia exported rice and sugar for the first time.

More recently, Peru also launched a drive to bring the country's Indians down from the Andes to the rich eastern slopes and integrate them into Peruvian society. As part of this effort, Peru's first agrarian reform program adopted and, through a kind of domestic peace corps, is striving to modernize Indian farming methods.

Of importance is the contemporary Indian movement *Indigenismo,* aiming to elevate the precarious standard of living of the Indian in Latin America and to incorporate him materially and spiritually into the ordinary civic life of the country in which he resides — while preserving his own culture and without diminishing his specific psychological personality. Today *indigenismo* is considered a policy of change, to be carried out by the state and other institutions, while respecting the human dignity of the Indian, his communities and his traditional culture regardless of its level of development. Its most widely accepted goal is the integration of the Indian into national life while at the same time according his peculiar cultural traits the consideration to which they are entitled. The movement rejects the paternalistic methods of dealing with the Indians; when this approach is used, the Indians merely take what is offered; their spirit of enterprise is undermined, and they are encouraged to become dependent on the handouts confered by public charity. Contemporary *Indigenismo* favors an active methodology that encourages Indian groups to express their needs and desires and to participate in the planning and execution of programs affecting them. The movement recognizes the importance of programs in the fields of health, agriculture, housing, and so on, but it maintains that they must be well coordinated and integrated. In such an integrated endeavor, economic and educational programs will play a key role, education being considered in the broadest sense of the word to embrace efforts to create new habits and change attitudes. In the economic

**WHERE THE INDIANS ARE**

| Country | Percentage |
|---|---|
| Bolivia | 63 |
| Guatemala | 53.6 |
| Peru | 45.9 |
| Ecuador | 39 |
| Mexico | 30 |
| El Salvador | 20 |
| Panama | 20 |
| Honduras | 6.7 |
| Nicaragua | 5 |
| Colombia | 2 |
| Venezuela | 2 |
| Chile | 2 |
| Paraguay | 2 |
| Argentina | .4 |
| Costa Rica | .3 |
| Brazil | .2 |
| Uruguay | 0 |

sphere, agrarian reform constitutes one of the most effective means of improving the life of the Indian population, since most of them depend upon agriculture.

Contemporary *Indigenismo* faces many serious problems. Indians continue to be discriminated against in many ways, as is shown by their poverty, by the inadequate services they receive, by their nonparticipation in civic life, and at times by paternalistic legislation and programs that treat them as if they were children. Programs, especially in the educational and economic fields, have been badly focused and inadequately financed; nor have they been available to train the skilled and dedicated technical personnel to carry on this work. Meanwhile, the sectors that exploit the Indian population and benefit from its present plight have offered much resistance, both openly and subtly. In general the non-Indian population has shown no positive attitude towards the integration of the Indian, nor has it acknowledged his values and rights. Political and ideological position have arisen that frequently disorient action or serve as instruments helpful to forces interested in avoiding substantive changes. The experiences with past programs have not changed much the negative attitudes of the Indians, although all the South American nations show the will to improve the living conditions of their Indians, estimated at between 15 and 30 million.

JOSEPH S. ROUCEK

**EMBROIDERY** was done by Indians who characteristically decorated the articles they used in everyday life. The materials with which they embroidered were animal hair, porcupine and bird quills, beads, and wool. When European glass beads were received in trade by Indians in the early 19th century they supplanted quills for the most part. Some tribes believed in a myth which held that the teacher of embroidery was the spider who sent embroidery designs to women in their dreams.

It is among the Plains Indians that embroidery techniques on hides, chiefly buffalo, were widespread. Plains tribes decorated their clothing, including robes and moccasins, tipi covers and linings, containers, drums, shields, and other utilitarian articles with paint and embroidery of dyed horsehair, porcupine quills, and trade beads. Each tribe embroidered distinctive designs sometimes related to pictographic painting, sometimes abstract or geometric.

In the Great Lakes area dyed moose hair and porcupine quills were embroidered with fine stitching onto a base of deerhide, birchbark, or cloth to make clothing and pouches. Early geometric designs were replaced by curvilinear floral patterns which Huron girls learned in French Canadian convents in the 18th and 19th centuries. Some of this type of embroidery is still being produced today using silk embroidery thread instead of porcupine quills. Floral motifs in Woodland beadwork were also adapted from embroidery taught in convents and observed on clothing of French and English travelers.

Some Eskimo embroidery combined split quills of bird feathers with moose hair. The Tlingit and Tsimshian tribes of the Northwest Coast embroidered on hide with porcupine quills and beadwork in floral designs.

In the Southwest weavings were frequently decorated with embroidery in geometric designs. Today only the Hopi continue this tradition. Among the Hopi, only men embroider with wool on cotton kilts, sashes, shirts, shawls, and ceremonial dresses. The cotton, raised by Hopis until the beginning of the 20th century, is now obtained from commercial sources. Hopi women still wear plain weave white cotton wedding dresses which are embroidered later for other ceremonial uses with bright colored wool yarn. Formerly wool yarn for embroidery was ravelings from bayeta; today commercial yarn is used. In the mid 19th century Indians of the Rio Grande pueblos developed embroidery on clothing to a high degree including black or white kilts and shawls of cotton or wool embroidered in bright colors. At Acoma, unlike most pueblos, embroidery was done by women who produced richly embroidered shawls, shirts, and dresses first made of cotton, later of finely woven wool.

Related to embroidery is quillwork, a distinctively North American Indian art form. It consists of embroidering or weaving porcupine, or sometimes bird, quills on animal hides in a great variety of articles such as tobacco and tinder pouches, knife cases, cradles, robes, shirts, leggings, belts, moccasins, and horsetrappings and on birchbark containers.

Skillful and patient technique produced smooth, even quillwork. Quills were gathered by men hunting porcupines and worked by women who kept the quills in cases made of buffalo or elk bladders. The quills were sorted, softened in water, then flattened by pulling between the teeth or using a shaped bone tool. Quills were used in their natural colors of white and brown and were dyed yellow, red, blue, green, or black with vegetable dyes. Later aniline dyes of brighter colors were used. Most tribes sewed quills with an awl. Quills are so short that each one made only a few stitches. Designs were usually stencilled, traced, or drawn on hide or birchbark with a brush, knife, or stick although some women worked out their designs as they embroidered. Early designs were geometric and angular. After European contact, designs became more naturalistic with human, animal, and floral forms.

Plains Indians, including the Sioux, Cheyenne, Arapaho, Arikara, and others, applied quills to buffalo and deer hides in elaborate decoration of costumes, pouches, moccasins, and horsetrappings. They decorated pipe stems with intricately braided quills. Among Indians of the Eastern Woodlands, such as the Seneca and Ottawa, quillwork was probably the most widely used decoration of costumes. An important art form among the Micmac Indians of Eastern Canada was quillwork in geometric designs on birchbark made into boxes. Indians of Western Canada, such as the Chipewyan, were technically unsurpassed in their finely split quillwork found in knife cases, pouches, and costumes of elkskin of the 18th and 19th centuries. On the Northwest Coast the Tlingit and Tsimshian tribes,

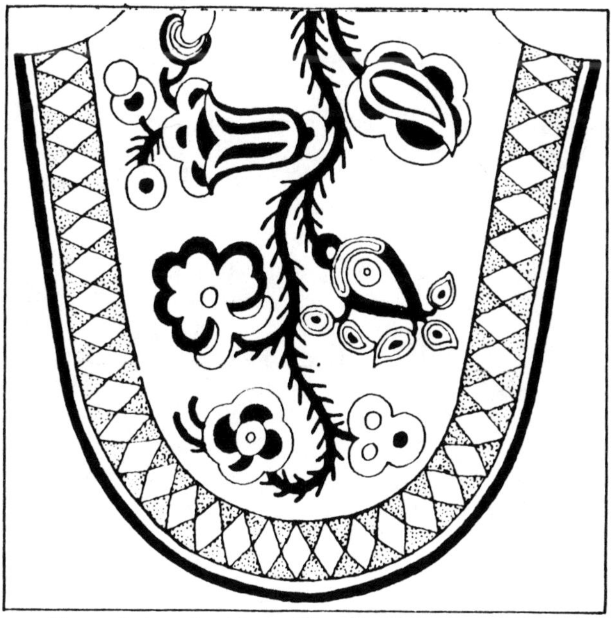

Moose hair embroidery with quillwork border, Kaska.

influenced by their inland neighbors, used porcupine quilling on their clothing made of hide. In the early 20th century Karok Indians of Northwest California made finely woven covered baskets in which they worked quills with maidenhair fern stems.

Quillwork, Blackfoot.

**ENGRAVING AND INCISING.** Among the Indians of the Americas, as no definite line can be drawn between the lower forms of relief sculpture and engraving, all ordinary petroglyphs may be classed as engravings, since the work is executed in shallow lines upon smooth, rock surfaces. Point work is common on wood, bone, horn, shell, bark, metal, clay and other surfaces. Each material has its own particular technique, and the designs run the entire gamut of style from graphic to purely conventional representations, and the full range of significance from purely symbolic through esthetic to simply trivial motives.

Perhaps the most artistic and technically perfect examples of engraving are those of the Northwest Coast tribes of North America, executed on slate utensils and on ornaments of metal, yet the graphic productions of the Inuit on ivory, bone, and antler have sometimes a considerable degree of merit. With both of these peoples the processes employed and the style of representation have undergone change because of contact with the white man.

The steel point is superior to the point of stone, and this alone would have a marked effect on the execution. The picture writings on bark of many of the northern tribes, executed with bone or other hard points, are good examples of the native engraver's art, although these are not designed either for simply pictorial or for decorative effect. The ancient mound builders were clever engravers, the technical excellence of their work being well illustrated by examples from the mounds and dwelling sites of Ross County, Ohio and by others from the Turner mounds in Hamilton County, Ohio.Shell also was a favorite material for the graver's point, as is illustrated by numerous ornaments recovered from mounds in the middle Mississippi valley.

In decorating their earthenware, the native people often used the styles with excellent effect. The yielding clay afforded a tempting surface, and in some cases considerable skill was shown especially by the ancient potters of the lower Gulf States, who executed elaborate scroll designs with great precision. The point was used for incising, trailing, and indenting, and among ancient Pueblo potters was sometimes used upon dark-painted surfaces to develop delicate figures in the light color of the underlying paste.

## SOUTH AMERICA

Engraving of metal was occasionally used in Peru, but was much less common than embossing. Some of the early sheet gold cut-outs from the Titicaca region (Early Tiahuanaco?) have details added by means of incised lines, but they are poorly done. They are the earliest examples of engraving (about AD 700). Later cups from Cuzco and the Chimu region are carefully engraved in complex designs.

* * *

# F

**FAMILY.** The biological family, that is, parents and children, constituted the household for most Indians of the Americas. The household was very nearly a self-sufficient economic unit and as such an independent social and political unit. With the exception of large game, all foods belonged exclusively to the households of the persons acquiring them. Food-gathering activities were conducted largely by independent households under the leadership of the household head.

But, though the household was the most stable social and economic unit, some factors tended to disrupt it and others to enlarge it or to extend obligations beyond it. The main disruptive factors were divorce, which occurred easily and frequently, and wife abduction. These, however, merely realined households.

The household was often enlarged by the inclusion of relatives, especially grand parents, who had no households of their own. It was also temporarily enlarged by the addition of the spouse of one or more of its children. Up to a year of matrilocal residence as bride service was common and, in any event, a young married couple usually remained with one family or the other until they had children or their own house. A household might also be augmented by polygyny or polyandry. These forms of marriage were probably not produced in some area by economic factors, but unusual individual wealth was a condition upon which they rested. A man could not hold one wife, to say nothing of several, unless he were a diligent hunter and brought home many buckskins. Polyandry was usually an extension of hospitality and sex privileges to the husband's brother, who would eventually acquire a wife of his own. But it meant that one woman had to provide an increased amount of seeds. The average household was about 6 persons, according to census data, but additions might bring it up to 10.

These additions to the household, however, were not permitted to threaten the welfare of the biological family. Those who were able-bodied shared the tasks of food seeking. Old or infirm persons, especially grandparents, cared for the children. But when starvation was imminent or the exertion of long treks for food excessive, infirm persons were abandoned to perish. Necessity thus strictly limited expansion of the household.

There were also responsibilities if there were not strict obligations to persons outside the household. Whether a village were large or small, several related families usually lived in the proximity of one another. These were usually the households of parents, their married children, brothers and sisters and their spouses, and other close relatives who, in some localities, were further related through cross-cousin and pseudo cross-cousin marriage. These related family traveled together and camped near one another. Though not obligatory, food was freely shared with them. The male members of these households assisted one another in abducting a wife or in defending a wife against abduction and rendered mutual assistance in other ways.

The nature and extent of the manifold duties and obligations between kinfolk is a rich field for extended inquiry. In order that obligations to a relative shall have significance, there must be assurance that one will see him sufficiently often and under sufficiently well-defined circumstances. Lack of consistency in post-marital residence and frequent change of residence for practical reasons brought certain relatives into close association at some times and widely separated them at other times. There was, for example, no assurance that the maternal or paternal grandparent would be present to care for children, that a sister's son or a brother would be on hand to help build and require a dole of seeds, or that any particular relatives would be able to defend one's wife against abduction.

The more stable social conditions were more favorable to the development of readily definable patterns of bahavior between kin. A person knew when and under what conditions he would see his different relatives. Thus, a man knew that he would see his different relatives. Thus, a man knew that he would be in frequent contact with his father's sister, so that it was possible for him to help support her, to marry her step-daughter, and to have her sons as his closest companions. A man would live near his father's sister so that he could help support her and associate with her son only if the father and his sister had decided to remain in the same locality.

### Mesoamerica

The most important social institution among agricultural Indian groups is the family. Marriages are often arranged by the parents of both paties through an intermediary or friend. Mutual consent of the partners, their parents, and important relatives is necessary; if any one of the interested parties resists, the marriage cannot take place. Marriage serves as a means of establishing kinship relationships among families within the group, a device for improving one's social status through marriage into a higher-status family, an arrangement for an economic division of labor, and a means of having children born and reared.

Within the context of the larger group, it is the household (usually made up of husband, wife, and their children) which is accorded social, economic, and political recognition. Unmarried people are not regarded as full-fledged members of the community, and they cannot participate in group decisions. If one's marriage is terminated through divorce or death of one of the partners, the group will not accord original social status to the surviving partner until he remarries. But marriage alone is sufficient to establish the social standing of the couple: they must have children to completely validate their position in the group.

Indian families do not practice primogeniture. At the death of the parents, their assets, including land are divided equally among the surviving children. In order to prevent these assets from falling into the hands of members of other groups there are rigorous rules against marriage outside the particular Indian group itself. The continual division and subdivision of assets produces a communal ownership pattern with the Indian group.

Within the Indian village, much importance is attached to the participation of each household in both private and public religious rituals. The highest religious prestige is accorded to those very old households whose moral ascendancy is great by virtue of years of experience, contribution to the community, and ritual performance. On the private or family level, precolonial Indian rituals and beliefs continue. Publicly, Roman Catholic ceremonies are scrupulously observed.

Within the Indian community, group interests dominate over those of the individual. The community emphasizes adjustment of individual differences in the name of group solidarity. Although the individual is responsible for supporting himself and his immediate household, his goals are expected to be pleasing the gods and contributing to the community rather than accumulating individual wealth.

**South America**

A state organization on a modern pattern can be ascribed to the higher Andean civilizations, where it was associated with the ayllu system still found in the region. However, stratification occurs on simpler levels. Apart from distinctively political groupings, we must take cognizance of the family, the extended family. The patrilineal house community; the patrilineal band; patrilineal or matrilineal moieties and clans.

The individual family is universal and in some instances figures as the only significant economic and social unit. The *Yahgan* exhibit a much weaker sense of kinship for the larger local group bearing a topographical name and only an attenuated sentiment for fellow members of the same dialectic division. Their far more land-minded *Ona* neighbors attach importance to their 39 territorial groups, which approximate Steward's concept of a patrilineal band. Since they are emphatically exogamous, they might be classed with the autonomous landowning "clans" of the *Southern Diegueño* (California) were it not for a doubt as to the inflexibility of the unilateral reckoning. It appears that even married women did not lose all contact with their native group and that the overwhelming majority of males had a lifelong connection with the hereditary hunting grounds. Nevertheless, men were not precluded from settling in an alien district with the owner's permission; and the precise nature of a female's tie with her native territory is not certain. Hence, the *Ona* system, though hardly definable as "loose," does not quite attain the rigidity of a unilateral organization and may be taken as a borderline case.

The *Witoto* house community, on the other hand, strictly defines the status of its members. Marriage is patrilocal and exogamous, and all those born within the settlement bear the same surname. Here, then, males and females are brought together exactly as in a typical patrilineal clan. The *Yagua* in the same area have similar "clan" malocas.

Definitely unilateral types of aggregation, such as moieties and clans, have a fairly wide but far from preponderant distribution. They are conspicuously lacking in the Chaco and regions southward. In a great many populations of intermediate cultural status, such as the tropical forest areas and coastal Brazil, the extended family prevails—a residential unit comprising the native blood-kindred of a settlement plus the affinities who dwlel with them. Since it does not fix the alinement of members once and for all, it falls under the head of "loose" organizations.

Loose systems, however, may have a distinct bias toward either rule of descent; indeed, without such trends it is impossible to conceive the origin of full-fledged clans. Hence, one should not be surprised to find characteristics of unilateral systems among loosely organized peoples. However, one must be careful not to ascribe a matrilineal or a patrilineal pattern on the basis of such elements: such classification must rest on explicit statements that children are reckoned kin with their mother or their father. To illustrate the danger of not observing this precaution, many tribes of the

Amazon-Orinoco area practice atrilocal residence, a frequent concomitant of and hypothetical condition for matrilineal clans. But it is not an adequate cause of such clans, since the avuncular marriage reported in the same region excludes the possiblity of such a system. Inheritance or succession in either line is a safer index: the nepotic rule of the *Chibcha* certainly makes it plausible that they once had matrilineal clans. Yet there, as well as elsewhere in the world, property and rank of different types have been known to descend according to diverse principles.

The bilateral or conjugal family, consisting merely of father, mother (or mothers), and children, underlies all sociopolitical types. Among the *Guató, Mura,* and *Nambicuara*, it was the only permanent sociopolitical unit, and, though several families might associate with one another seasonally for special activities, they lacked permanent cohesion and had no leader or chief.

The problem of dealing with crime and other offenses was very often the family's responsibility. Indians very frequently considered crimes to be personal matters, and accordingly left judgment, retaliation, or other settlement in the hands of the persons and family involved. Among the Hidatsa, for example, gangs of youth of about twelve years of age frequently harassed the young girls of the tribe. Rape was a common occurrence. In the case of a rape, the boy might be whipped by the girl's brothers, or the boy's sisters might try to restore good relations by expressing regrets or presenting the girl's family with gifts. In any case, the young man lost face, as it ws considered cowardly to force a woman into sexual relations.

One criminal distinction not found in contemporary societies was universally present among the Indians—namely, the distinction between good and bad magic. It was permissible to use witchcraft to harm a recognized criminal, but should witchcraft be used against an innocent person it was considered a crime of unprovoked aggression.

Throughout their history, the Indians had their own methods for dealing with crimes in their communities. Toward the end of the nineteenth century, however, a feud between two Sioux chiefs resulted in the murder of one by the other. The Indians reached their own settlement according to traditional means, but a federal trial was nevertheless held. Public interest was much aroused by the trial, which resulted in a sentence of death for the defendent. But the Supreme Court ruled that, in the absence of related legislation, the federal courts has no jurisdiction in the case. The outraged reaction to this decision led to passage of the Major Crimes Act of 1885. This act, along with later acts of Congress, empowered the federal government to try cases involving Indians that were related to the so-called ten major crimes—including murder, rape, arson, burglary, and incest. Civil matters, however, remained in the hands of tribal courts, except in a few cases where tribal authority has been limited by federal legislation.

**FIRE MAKING**. Nearly all Indians of the Americas knew how to make fire. The two chief aboriginal methods of fire making are those of rotary friction and of percussion.

The rotary friction method, with use of a plain hand drill, is by far the more common of the two methods, occurring as it does throughout North America, the southern Middle American and Antillean regions, and almost the whole continental South American region down to the Strait of Magellan.

There are two main methods of fire drilling were the one without, and the other with, complete piercing through the hearth.

Fire making by percussion, or "strike a light" method, was found less so throughout the Americas.

As a general rule, fires once lit were not allowed to die, but were carefully conserved and kept going day and night. Within or near the dwelling, when not in use, they were fed roots, rotten wood or other slow-burning material or may be banked under ashes. The arrangement of the fire logs in star-shaped fashion with the burning ends toward the center was reported and is probably fairly widespread, and easily lends itself to conservation of the fire; as the fire dies down the logs are pushed inward. On journeys by land, fire was commonly carried along—as fire sticks or firebrands, in clay pots or in sections of bamboo, on sherds, and so forth; on journeys by water, through similar means or on an earthen or shell hearth aboard the watercraft.

Torches of many kinds were used: bundles of dry grass stalks, plain bark, resin-rich woods, bark or other plant material dipped in or impregnated with wax, oil, resin, or gum; bark tubes filled with copal resin; and so forth. Candles of various types were recorded, usually among tribes who had a good deal of contact with whites.

**FISHHOOK** is one of the many devices used by American aborigines for catching fish for food. Though generally not as efficient as the net, weir, and fish spear, it was commonly made in a variety of forms. It was used throughout almost all of the Arctic, Subarctic, Great Lakes region, Northwest Coast, Plateau, and northeastern United States, and in parts of the Great Basin, Plains, California, Southwest, and Southeast in the United States.

The Indians used two basic types of fishhooks, the gorge and the more familiar design incorporating one or more hooked points. The gorge was a straight or slightly curved sliver of wood, bone, stone, shell, or copper with both ends pointed and the line attached in the middle. It was designed to be swallowed with bait and to turn sideways when the line was tightened, lodging in the stomach or throat of the fish. The familiar "J"-shaped type of fishhook was made in several ways. Some were carved or ground from a single piece of bone, ivory, or shell or hammered from naturally occurring copper. In northern areas this type was commonly made from a point of bone, thorn, ivory, or copper lashed to or imbedded in a straight or curved shank of wood, stone, or ivory at an acute angle. The resulting composite hooks were normally a rough "V" shape with the line usually attached at or near the end of the shank. Some were multipointed, and a few had barbed points. Some Eskimo composite hooks had shanks carved in a manner allowing them to be used as lures or jugs rather than as baithooks. In historic times steel fishhooks rapidly replaced the older types.

**FISHING**. Indians were skillful in fishing, and employed a great variety of methods. Only the Indians of the Prairies, where lakes were absent and the muddy rivers were poorly stocked with fish—and those of inferior quality only—paid little attention to fishing, and instead sought game and wild fruits. Elsewhere the fishhook and the fishspear, the net, trap, and weir, were as indispensable as the bow and arrow; and dried

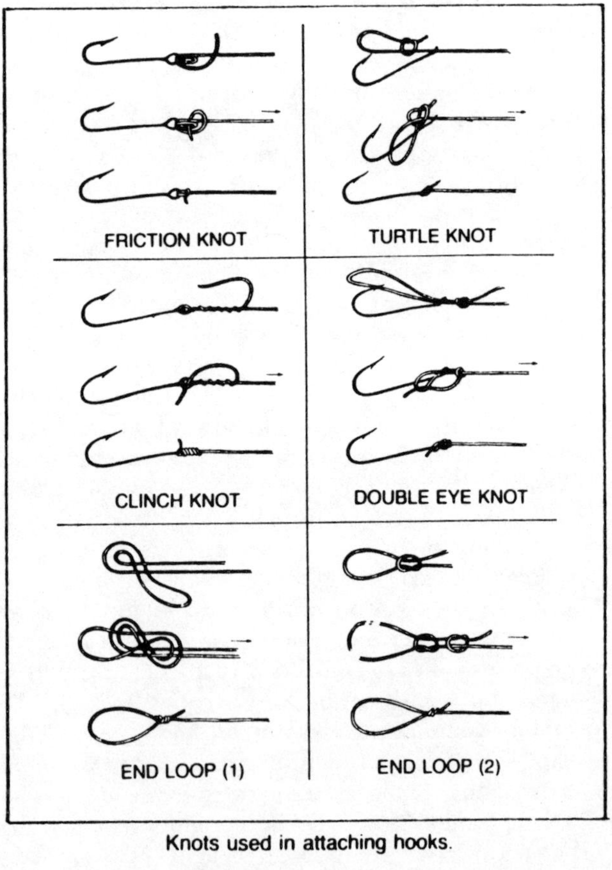


Knots used in attaching hooks.

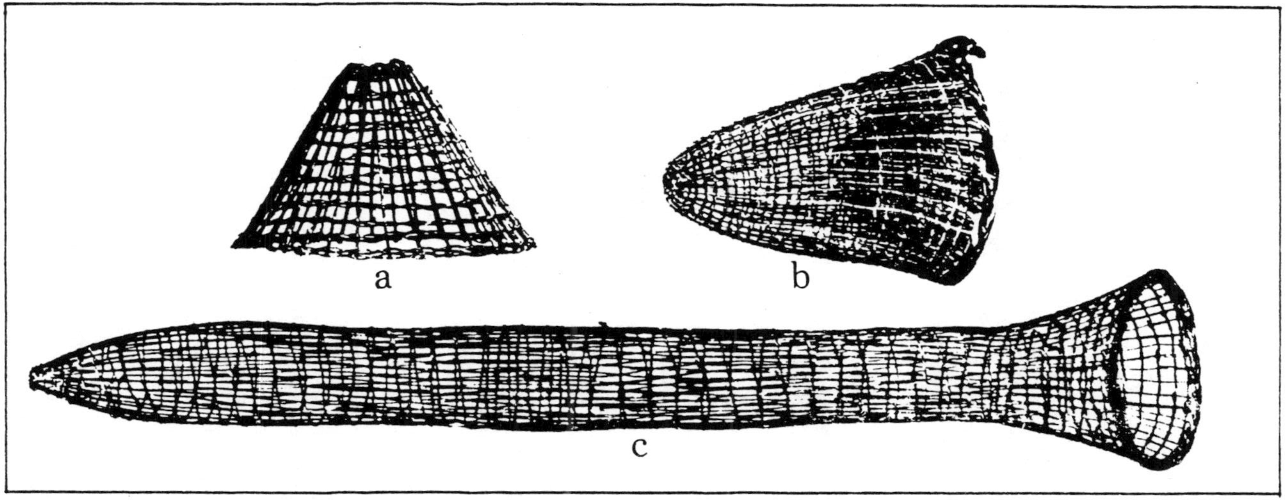


Pomo fish traps: (a) open on top, plunged over small fish; (b) funnel pot, for small fish; (c) a narrow trap which is laid in a current, thus preventing a fish from backing out and too narrow for them to turn

fish was a staple food in nearly every community during the first two months of winter.

The Indians were well acquainted with the barb, which they used on spears and harpoons; but they generally avoided it on fishhooks. Their bait was either some part of a fish—the eye, or the skin from the belly—or else a piece of bright bone, ivory, or even stone. Among the Eskimo and Kutchin it was carved to imitate a fish. The Indians of the Atlantic and Pacific shores fished from canoes in the bays and gulfs, catching mainly cod, halibut, and salmon; the northern Indians and the Eskimo used their canoes for trolling, and fished through the ice of the lakes for whitefish, trout, and salmon trout. For set lines the natives used a gorge—a short pencil of bone or hardened wood sharpened at both ends and inserted inside a piece of meat or fish, with the line attached to the middle. The Eastern Indians captured large numbers of sturgeon, salmon, and eels with torches and spears. Two men would go together in a canoe at night; one sits in the stern and paddles and the other stands with a spear over a flambeau (of birch bark) placed in the head of the canoe. The fish, attracted by the light, come in numbers and the spearman then takes the opportunity of striking them. Some tribes in British Columbia similarly speared (or clubbed) by night the salmon that were migrating up the rivers. By day they often adopted a method common among the Indians and Eskimo of North America: they set lures, such as a bear's tooth at holes in the ice and speared the fish that approached the bait.

Several tribes employed pronged and gaff for hooking salmon. A modification of the instrument—a pole generally about ten feet long armed with a row of bone spikes for two feet from one end—served the Nootka for both herring and oolakan; drawn through a shoal of herring it nearly always impaled three or four fish. Special tools of this kind were not uncommon, for the Indians were quick to conceive or borrow new ideas that related to fishing (and hunting).

Despite their variety, all these methods yielded a small amount of fish compared with the number caught with nets, traps, and weirs. It is curious that the Eskimo, who employed a kind of square seine for capturing seals, never adopted the same method for fish until about the time of the discovery of America, when it was introduced from Siberian tribes into Alaska and spread eastward as far as the Mackenzie Delta in Canada. The Northern, Eastern, and West Coast Indians all used the seine, setting it under the ice during the winter. The Eastern Indians also had bag-nets and dip-nets, which they usually employed in conjunction with weirs. The material of these nets varied considerably: the Pacific Coast Indians generally used nettle, their inland neighbor's hemp, the Eastern Indians nettle or hemp, Northern natives willow-root or caribou thongs, and the Eskimo willow-root.

The Indians turned weirs to full advantage. Certain rocky canyons left only a few narrow openings for the passage of the migrating salmon; there the Indians planted their basket-traps, and plied their nets and spears in the swirling water below them. On the seacoast, again, the receding tide often left a few fish stranded in pools among the rocks. These natural weirs probably suggested the construction of artificial ones in suitable places. Some Indians built dams of stones in the shape of large horseshoes along the banks of tidal rivers to impound the salmon when the tide went out, and in the Arctic the Eskimo laid straight stone dams across streams that the salmon trout ascended, leaving small openings in the lower rows, but completely closing the uppermost. The Indians of eastern and western Canada had fences of piles and brush, many of them so elaborate and extensive that their construction required the entire community. These log weirs provided many tribes with two-thirds of the yearly food supply, so that their destruction by floods or enemies was a terrible disaster.

The community weir, like the buffalo or caribou pound, was a powerful factor in welding the different families of Indians into a single, social unit. Every man contributed his labor to the building and maintenance of the weir or pound, and every man was entitled to his share of the booty. At the weirs each man retained whatever fish he caught, but allowed no family to remain hungry. The Indians realized that every man had his days of ill-luck when fish seemed to elude his weapons; that accidents and sickness attacked the strongest and ablest hunter, making him dependent for a time on his fellow-men; and they insisted on an equitable division of food, permitting no one to hoard it while his companions starved.

The fishing of the sea-mammals required not only ingenuity but courage. However uncertain the weather the Indians fearlessly went to sea in their dugout canoes (during the months of April and May), to attack the whale. The whaling equipment of the West Coast tribes closely resembled that of the Eskimo, which was adopted by whites until the whaling-gun. One observer described it: "The harpoons which they use to strike the whale or any other sea-animal, except the otter, are contrived with no common skill. The shaft is from eighteen to twenty-eight feet in length; at the end whereof is fixed a large piece of bone, cut in notches, which being spliced to the shaft, serves as a secure hold for the harpoon, which is fastened to it with thongs. The harpoon is of an oval form, and rendered extremely sharp at the sides as well as the point—it is made out of a large muscle-shell, and is fixed into another piece of bone, about three inches long, and to which a line is fastened made of the sinews of certain beasts, of several fathoms in length; this is again attached to the shaft; so that when the fish is pierced, the shaft floats on the water by means of seal-skins filled with wind, or the ventilated bladders of fish, which are securely attached to it. The chief himself is the principal harpooner, and is the first that strikes the whale. He is attended by several canoes of the same size as his own, filled with people armed with harpoons, to be employed as occasion may require. When the huge fish feels the smart of the first weapon, he instantly dives, and carries the shaft with all its bladders along with him. The boats immediately follow his wake, and as he rises, continue to fix their weapons in him, till he finds it impossible for him to sink, from the number of floating buoys which are now attached to his body. The whale then drowns, and is towed to shore with great noise and rejoicings."

Almost as strenuous as whaling was the sea-otter fishing of the Pacific Coast Indians. For this, equipped with light harpoons and with bows and arrows, Indians set out in two very light canoes. If they found an otter sleeping on the surface of the water, the harpooned it and dragged it to one of the boats, where it fought with its claws and teeth. Usually it sighted their approach and dived. The two canoes then followed in its course, separating in order that one or the other might be within bow-shot when it rose for breath; but the otter was swift: the pursuit often lasted several hours before it was killed.

The same Indians lured seals within range of their arrows by wearing wooden masks, covering their bodies with branches and imitating the actions of a seal basking among the rocks. Sea-lions, which were less timid and more frequently came ashore, were attacked with clubs; the Haida Indians killed large numbers of these animals during their spring excursions to the west coast of the Queen Charlotte islands. But the most skillful fishing Indians of sea-mammals were the Eskimo. Like the Pacific Coast Indians they harpooned the whale, the seal, and also the walrus from their boats during the summer months.

**FOOD AND DRINK.** Many of the most widely used and important foods known in the Americas today are of Indian origin. They are sold, enjoyed every day, and often even prepared as the Indians did. Such classic dishes as barbecue, steamed lobster, succotash, spoon bread, cranberry sauce, and mincemeat pie, are inherited from Indians. Until the discovery of America, the rest of the world knew nothing of such foods as avocados, sweet or Irish potatoes, pineapples, tomatoes, peppers, pumpkins or squashes, maple sugar, and, of course, corn. Without corn, which most Indians regarded as a gift from the gods to be treasured and surrounded with ceremony, and which was cooked in numberless ways, the colonization of America might have faltered. The wild rice of the Great Lakes region, which is now considered a gourmet delicacy, was often used, and is still harvested by the Ojibua.

To a considerable extent, religious customs and beliefs determined both what foods were eaten and how they were prepared. For example, tribes of the Northwest, after eating salmon, would arrange every bone of the fish in a certain way to assure that the fish would return to life to be caught and eaten again. Many tribes had taboos against certain foods. Salt was tabooed by the Onondagas, for instance, and neither the Apaches nor the Navajos would eat fish or the flesh of bears or beavers.

Most Indians preferred cooked food to raw, and they had many methods of cooking and seasoning their food. Among the methods used were stoneboiling (putting hot stones into a basket or pot of water); drying; freezing; and smoking. The various cooking methods obviously affected pottery and basketry types. Flavoring was accomplished by the use of seeds, roots, flowers, and grasses. The north Pacific tribes used the tender inner bark of hemlock and spruce. In the southwest, mesquite beans, cactus and yucca fruits, and the agave were important.

Five distinct areas provided the Indian foods and recipes we use today. In the Southwest, the Pueblo tribes, the Papagos ("Bean People"), and Hopis grew peppers and beans which were made into savory chili, soups, guacamole and barbecue sauces. Along the Northwest Coast, seafood was the staple, and here women of the Tlingit, Kwakiutl, Salish, and other tribes steamed and broiled salmon and dozens of other fish and seafood from the Pacific and the western rivers. On the vast Plains, nomadic tribes such as the Sioux and Cheyenne roasted buffalo over campfires. In the South, Cherokees and other tribes had long enjoyed an impressive list of fragrant soups and rich stews, and they baked the same assortment of corn breads known today. Two particular American favorites, the clambake and Boston baked beans, were also staple favorites of the Narragansetts, Penobscots and Powhatans, who, like the Iroquois and other timber people of the East, steamed their dinners in earthen pits.

Their method, still in use today, is now called "fireless cooking."

From all these regions, American Indians have bequeathed varied, imaginative and indispensable dishes. American Indian cuisine may rightly be considered continental cooking, indigenous and unique.

**Securing and preparing**

Among the Iroquois the women did the gardening; the men were the hunters. In the early days the Iroquois made much use of both fresh and dried fish and meat. The many lakes and streams of the Iroquois country yielded an abundant supply of fish during the spring fishing season. During the season of the fall hunt, long and toilsome expeditions to secure game were undertaken by the men. When times of scarcity occurred the Iroquois found it necessary to supplement the larger game by adding the meat of many of the smaller animals to the diet. In the old village site bones have been found of bison, deer, elk, black bear, porcupine, raccoon, martin, otter, woodchuck, muskrat, beaver, skunk, weasel and dog. Domestic pigs, geese, ducks, and chickens became sources of food after their introduction into Quebec about 1620.

After the formation of the League, when the Iroquois became settled in more permanent villages, their food supply shifted more and more to an agricultural basis, and agricultural products came to form the major portion of their diet.

The entire process of planting, cultivating, harvesting, and preparing food for the family was in the hands of the women. A chief matron was elected to direct the communal fields, each woman caring for a designated portion. Certain fields were reserved to provide food for the councils and national feasts. Ceremonies were observed and special songs were sung at the time of planting and harvesting. Sacrifices of tobacco and wampum were made to the food spirits.

Through a mutual aid society, in later years known as a "bee," the women assisted one another in their individual fields when planting, hoeing, and harvesting.

They laughed and sang while they worked. Each woman brought her own hoe, pail, and spoon. When the work was over a feast was provided by the owner of the field, and everyone went home with a supply of food, usually corn soup and hominy.

Corn (maize) has always been the principal food of the Iroquois. Corn pits have been found at old village sites. Even before the formation of the League, corn, beans and squash were cultivated. Because they were grown together they were sometimes called "the three sisters." The Iroquois spoke of them as "our life" or "our supporters." Considerable mythology and many ceremonies centered about them.

Ears of mature corn were neatly braided and hung to dry in long festoons within and without the Iroquois homes. Large quantities of corn were dried in a corn crib, built of unpainted planks in open slat construction, through which the air circulated freely. The corn crib is a characteristic feature of the small farm on the Iroquois reservations. Its use was adopted from the Indians by the early settlers.

The corn used by the Iroquois was of two common types, white dent and white flint, with occasional red ears. The white dent corn, called Tuscarora or squaw corn, was hulled or eaten on the cob, a custom adopted by the white settlers and still followed throughout the country. Flint corn was used in making hominy.

Both the green and the mature corn were used in the preparation of many popular dishes that continue in use today. Green corn was boiled on the cob, roasted on the cob in the husk, scraped and baked, scraped and fried in cakes, combined with green beans and stewed with fat meat as succotash, made in a soup when green or dried, or scraped when green and baked in a loaf.

Coarsely ground meal was made from mature corn either hulled or unhulled, pounded in a stone or wooden mortar. It was used as plain mush, combined with meat, dressed with oil, or baked as unleavened bread.

Hominy was made from the flint corn. It was prepared by soaking shelled corn in lye until the hulls could be removed. The plain hominy, hominy or hulled-corn soup in which the hulled-corn was combined with beans and pork or beef, and boiled corn bread in which the hulled corn was usually combined with beans, were popular dishes made of mature corn.

Charred corn was used the year around. Corn to be charred was selected when well along in the milky stage. The ears were set on end in a row before a long fire. Roasting proceeded until the moisture was dried from the kernels. Then the corn was shelled and further dried in the sun. The charred corn was so reduced in bulk and weight that it could be easily stored or transported. If to be kept for some time, it was cached in earthen pits. It could be preserved for several years and was used both uncooked and cooked or pounded fine and mixed with maple sugar. In the old days it was made up into cakes for the use of the hunter or warrior. In later years the charred corn has been used chiefly at ceremonial functions.

Many of the Iroquois food preparations, such as succotash and hominy, have grown popular on the American table and the names by which the Indians knew them have been added to the American vocabulary.

The cultivation and use of the several varieties of corn by the Iroquois gave rise to a need for special implements and utensils for handling the corn products. In every Iroquois home was to be found the mortar and pestle, the hulling basket, a hominy sieve basket, a netted scoop for removing ground corn from the mortar and for sifting out the coarser grains, a corn scraper, ladles, trays of bark and wood, and a long paddle for stirring corn soup and for removing the loaves from boiling water. The Mohawk used a soft hulling bag or basket in which the corn was twirled to remove the hulls after it had been boiled in lye.

Ten or more varieties of beans, varying in size, shape, and color, were cultivated by the Iroquois. Since the Iroquois did not use milk and cheese, beans were their only nitrogenous food when meat failed. The beans used were commonly known as bush beans, wampum, purple and white kidney beans, marrow-fat beans, string, cornstalk, cranberry, chestnut, lima, hummingbird, white (small), wild peas, bean vines, and pole beans.

Beans were used alone to some extent but seem to have been more often combined with corn or squash when prepared for eating.

Squashes and pumpkins, both fresh and when dried for winter use, have always been favorite foods of the Iroquois. Crook neck, hubbard, scalloped and winter squashes and hard pumpkins, artichokes and leeks, as well as corn and beans, have been cultivated by the Iroquois. Wild cucumber, turnips, and edible fungi were also used as food. Sunflower oil was used in the preparation of many dishes.

Blackberries, blueberries, checkerberries, choke cherries, wild red cherries, cranberries, currants, dewberries, elderberries, gooseberries, hackberries, hawthorns, huckleberries, June or service berries, red mulberries, small black plums, red and black raspberries, strawberries and thimble berries were all used by the Iroquois, though there is no evidence that they were cultivated. Acorns, beechnuts, butternuts, chestnuts, hazelnuts and hickory nuts were eaten. By 1779 apples, peaches, pears and cherries had been introduced from Europe. Muskmelons and watermelons were much used in later years. Fresh wild strawberries, dried blackberries, blueberries, and elderberries or huckleberries were combined with hominy and corn bread to give added color and flavor.

Maple sugar was an important article of the diet and was used almost as much as salt is today. Maple sap was used as a beverage, both fresh and fermented. Salt was little used. The sunflower was grown in quantities and its seed used for medicinal purposes.

Gourds and tobacco were cultivated by the Iroquois. The gourds were made to serve many useful purposes, as cups, dippers, spoons, and bowls in the home, and as rattles in the ceremonies and dances. Tobacco (Nicotiana rustica) was raised for both secular and sacred purposes. The Iroquois believed that tobacco was given them as a means of communication with the spiritual world. By burning it they could send up their petitions. Special tobaccos were used in ceremonies.

Tobacco was cast on the waters, especially on falls and rapids, to propitate the spirits within and was put in small bags attached to masks to make them more effective. The men and some of the women smoked tobacco mixed with suma leaves and red willow bark.

## Cooking

In the old days, fire for cooking was usually built in a sunken pit. Foods were grilled in the flames, boiled in pots of clay supported over the fire by stones or branches, or baked in hot ashes raked aside from the fire. Strips of inner bark, the ends which were folded together and tied around with a splint, formed a primitive emergency kettle. The bark kettle was suspended between two sticks over a fire and filled with water, into which the meat was dropped. By the time the bark had been burned through the meat was cooked.

The making of clay pots for use in cooking must have occupied much of the time of the primitive women. The characteristic extension rim on these early Iroquois pots provided a ridge where a bark cord could be tied around the neck without slipping, so that the pot could be hung from the crotches of branches set, tripod fashion, over the fire. The rounded base made it possible for the pot to maintain an upright position when set in the fire or soft earth. With the coming of the colonists, kettles of copper, brass, and iron replaced the baked clay pots. Cook stoves have been in use on the reservations for many generations.

## Obtaining fire for cooking

Fire was made to serve many purposes in primitive life. The Iroquois used fire to hollow canoes and mortars out of logs, to fell large trees that were to be used for buildings, and to provide heat for cooking and for other domestic uses.

In pre-colonial days fire was started by friction, and the Indians had many devices by which a spark could be secured. The device characteristically used was a bow and shaft or pump drill. It consisted of a weighted upright stick or spindle of resinous wood about one inch thick and 1½ to 4 feet in length, to the top of which was secured a leather thong or string, the ends of which were attached to the ends of a bow that was 3 feet in length. A small wheel was set upon the lower part of the shaft to give it momentum. The base of the spindle was inserted in a notch in a piece of very dry wood, near which a piece of frayed rope (tow) or decayed wood (punk) was placed. When ready to use, the string was first coiled around the shaft by turning it with the hand. The bow was then pulled down quickly, uncoiling the string and imparting a spinning motion to the shaft, revolving it to the left. By the momentum thus given to the wheel the string was coiled up in a reverse manner and the bow was again drawn up. The bow was then pulled downward again and the revolution of the shaft reversed, uncoiling the string, and recoiling it in reverse as before. This alternate revolution of the shaft was continued until the rapid twirling of the spindle created a friction which, as it increased, ignited the powdered wood upon which it rested. The piece of tow that was placed near the point where the spindle rested on the board, took fire and quickly lighted kindling that had been placed nearby.

**Preservation and storage of food**

The Iroquois built shelters for their farm and garden equipment and well ventilated corn cribs of unpainted planks in which corn could be dried and kept, and they dug underground pits or caches (root cellars) for the storage of corn and other foods. The pit was dug in the dry season, and the bottom and sides lined with bark. A watertight bark roof was constructed over it, and the whole thing covered with earth.

Corn, beans, berries and other fruits were dried for winter use. Braided bunches of corn were hung beside long spirals of dried squash and pumpkin, outside the log cabin or from the rafters within the cabin. Charred and dried shelled corn was kept in bark barrels which were buried in pits. Pits of well preserved charred corn have been found near ancient village sites. The bark barrels were of all sizes, with a capacity ranging from one peck to three bushels. They were made of black ash bark with the grain running around the barrel, and were stitched up the side and provided with a well-fitting bottom and lid. In addition to storing corn, the barrels were also used to store beans, dried fruits, venison and other meats, and articles of clothing and personal adornment.

Surplus meat and fish were dried, smoked, or frozen for later use. For storing the dried meat bark barrels were lined with deer skin.

# G

**GOLD AND GOLDSMITHING** were almost unknown by the Indians of North America. A few gold objects resembling Mexican work found in mounds of the Ohio valley probably indicate that these mound builders had contact with Mexicans. The most interesting gold ornaments made by Indians were a few found in mounds in Florida. They include flat pendants and discs of thin sheet gold. Most gold seen in Florida by early Spanish explorers was probably recovered by Indians from Spanish vessels wrecked on their way home from gold producing areas of Mexico and Central America.

In the Southwest today gold is set with turquoise in jewelry made by a few of the best Hopi and Navajo silversmiths.

In pre-Conquest days the Indians practiced placer mining, and were in possession of large quantities of gold. The Spanish were fascinated by the prospect of reaping huge riches from the gathering of gold in the Western Hemisphere, and mining began soon after the Conquest. It started first on the island of Hispaniola (Santo Domingo (1492-1515), and was continued in Cuba and Puerto Rico (1515-1530).

### Peru

In Peru, the center of the Inca empire, Inca gold was used almost entirely for luxury articles and ceremonial objects. Bangles and sequins to be sewn onto clothing, tupu (Topo) pins for fastening women's garments, plates to be hung around the neck, and figurines representing men, women, llamas, and alpacas were found at the *Inca* shrine of Titicaca on the island of that name. Cups shaped like the wooden ones (Qiro), earplugs, larger statues, and a variety of ornaments for litters and costume are mentioned by the chroniclers. Certain walls of the Temple of the Sun in Cuzco had gold bands across them. Lists of gold objects taken by the Spaniards at the time of the Conquest give an excellent idea of the variety of objects made and the ingenuity of the *Inca* craftsmen.

### Colombia

The main producer of gold during the colonial period was Colombia, where the gold produced until the end of the 16th century has been estimated to have reached approximately 4,000,000 ounces.

The first scientific studies of indigenous goldwork were made only a century ago by the Colombian philologist Ezequiel Uricoechea. His *Memorias sobre las Antiguedades Neogranadinas* (Reminiscences of New Grenadine Antiquities), published in Berlin, contained the first descriptions, as well as drawings and chemical analysis of Chibcha objects.

Nearly 30 years later a number of pieces were found in the Department of Antioquia. One, in the form of a raft bearing a chief and seven retainers, appeared to depict the investiture ceremony that gave rise to the legend of El Dorado. Liborio Zerda wrote a series of articles describing and illustrating the objects that were published in book form in 1883.

In 1892 the government commissioned Vicente Restrepo and his son, Ernesto Restrepo Tirado, to prepare archaeological contributions for the Madrid and Chicago international expositions. They assembled, classified, and photographed hundreds of gold objects from all over the country for the Madrid Exposi-

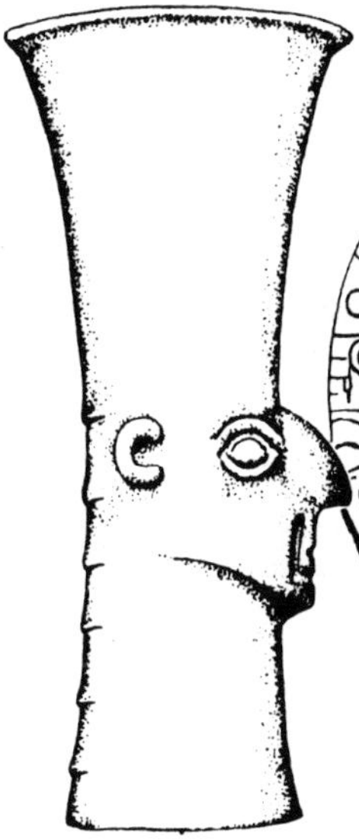

GOBLET

BREASTPLATE

BREASTPLATE

PERUVIAN GOLD AND SILVER

BREASTPLATE

tion catalog. Each also published basic works on Colombian archaeology. It was about this time that individuals began building collections by buying from the *buaqueros,* diggers who made a business of robbing prehistoric tombs.

In 1936 the government restricted the export of archaeological material and organized official archaeological services under the Ministry of Education. Three years later the Bank of the Republic decided to buy up indigenous goldwork, not as a form of capital investment, but to establish the Gold Museum for the enlightenment and enjoyment of the people.

During the next 15 years the bank acquired 6,276 pieces — over four times the total number of goldwork in collections throughout the world. In 1969 the Gold Museum was housed in modern quarters in the bank in Bogota. The bank's cultural center also includes a library of books printed before and during the colonial period and contemporary works on philosophy, history, science, and technical subjects.

The largest and most significant part of the bank's gold collection, from the standpoint of art and archaeology, came from burial grounds uncovered since 1939 in the upper valley of the Calima River in the Department of Valle del Cauca. These pieces of the so-called Calima style include complete sets of body adornments from a single burial and are related stylistically to the famous stone statues of San Augustin on the upper Magdalena River. They are considered older than either the Chibcha or Quimbaya pieces.

The Calima pieces also reveal stylistic similarities to the coastal cultures of Peru and Central America. Since the Calima goldwork is highly developed as a craft and is apparently contemporary with the beginnings of the Chavin Period in Peru about AD 300, archaeologists believe that the earlier, primitive stages of prehistoric goldwork antedated the Christian era by several centuries. No Colombian objects have yet been found, however, that use the primitive method of simple hammering alone; all reveal more advanced techniques.

The Indians melted gold in stone or baked-clay crucibles, using wooden or clay blowpipes to fan the flames. The gold was poured into single open molds or closed two-piece molds. The more complex cire-perdue, or lost wax, method was also used. The lost wax method consisted of modeling a core of clay and powdered charcoal with a bone or wood instrument, coating the core with wax, then adding an outer shell of the clay and charcoal mixture pierced by entrance and outlet openings. After drying, the entire piece was heated, causing the melted wax to run out. Molten metal was then poured in to replace the wax. When the mold cooled, the outer shell was broken and the cast polished.

Sometimes metal, wood, stone, or shell objects were sheathed with gold foil. Metallic plating was achieved by dipping pieces in molten gold, by sheathing them with a veneer of fine gold leaf, or by surface oxidation of the copper present in gold alloy. Soldering was very common, so that sometimes a single object could be made up of three different types of gold alloys. The decoration includes both engravings pressed into the surface and designs standing above the surface in relief. Decorative bangles and precious stone inlay work are also found.

In Brazil the first gold mine was opened at the end of the 17th century in Minas Gerais, and Brazilian economy, then lagging, was stimulated as the rate of the population increase of the country was greatly

Gold artifacts from Coclé, Panama.

stepped up. Soon after the discovery in Minas Gerais there were big strikes in Matto Grosso, 1721, and Goiaz, 1726. The economic development of Goiaz was helped greatly by the mining.

* * *